H. C. BANKOLE-BRIGHT AND POLITICS IN COLONIAL
SIERRA LEONE, 1919–1958

AFRICAN STUDIES SERIES 64

GENERAL EDITOR
J. M. Lonsdale, *Lecturer in History and Fellow of Trinity College, Cambridge*

ADVISORY EDITORS
J. D. Y. Peel, *Professor of Anthropology and Sociology, with special reference to Africa, School of Oriental and African Studies, University of London*
John Sender, *Faculty of Economics and Fellow of Wolfson College, Cambridge*

Published in collaboration with
THE AFRICAN STUDIES CENTRE, CAMBRIDGE

AFRICAN STUDIES SERIES

A list of books in the series will be found at the end of the volume

H. C. BANKOLE-BRIGHT AND POLITICS IN COLONIAL SIERRA LEONE, 1919–1958

AKINTOLA J. G. WYSE

Assoc. Professor of History Fourah Bay College
University of Sierra Leone

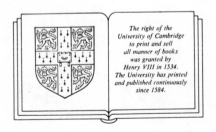

The right of the
University of Cambridge
to print and sell
all manner of books
was granted by
Henry VIII in 1534.
The University has printed
and published continuously
since 1584.

CAMBRIDGE UNIVERSITY PRESS

CAMBRIDGE
NEW YORK   PORT CHESTER
MELBOURNE   SYDNEY

Published by the Press Syndicate of the University of Cambridge
The Pitt Building, Trumpington Street, Cambridge CB2 1RP
40 West 20th Street, New York, NY 10011, USA
10 Stamford Road, Oakleigh, Melbourne 3166, Australia

First published 1990

Printed in Great Britain at the University Press, Cambridge

British Library cataloguing in publication data

Wyse, Akintola
    H. C. Bankole-Bright and politics in colonial Sierra
    Leone, 1919-1958 (African studies series; 64).
    1. Sierra Leone. Bankole-Bright, H. C., 1958
    I. Title. II. Series
    966'.403'0924

Library of Congress cataloguing in publication data

Wyse, Akintola J. G.
    Bankole-Bright and politics in colonial Sierra Leone: the passing
    of the Krio era 1919–1958/Akintola J. G. Wyse.
    p. cm.–(African studies series: 64)
    Includes bibliographical references.
    ISBN 0-521-36515-5
    1. Sierra Leone–Politics and government–1896–1961. 2. Bankole
    -Bright. H. C., d. 1958. I. Title. II. Series.
    DT516.7.W97 1990
    966.4'03--dc20   89-25427
                                                                 CIP

ISBN 0 521 36515 5

This work is dedicated to my parents, and family
(Fredrica, Ayodele, Adeyinka, Akintola and Abiola)
and to the Memory of
Lerina Bright-Taylor

Contents

		page
	Preface	ix
	Abbreviations	xii
	Introduction	1
1.	Growing up: background to his family and early life	3
2.	Background to politics in the twentieth century	16
3.	Politics in earnest: the setting up of the N.C.B.W.A., 1919–1924	32
4.	In the Legislative Council, 1924–1939: the drama of confrontation	59
5.	In the Legislative Council, 1924–1939: constructive opposition	87
6.	At the crossroads: the flickering flames of Congress and the challenge of W.A.Y.L., 1936–1939	108
7.	In the political wilderness: the turbulent years, 1939–1951	133
8.	Second innings in Parliament: the twilight years, 1951–1957	164
9.	Bankole-Bright and colonial politics: an assessment	179
	Notes	192
	Bibliography	251
	Index	263

Preface

This book owes much to the promise I made to Dr Bankole-Bright's sister, Lerina, in 1974 to tell the truth about her brother. My interest in the study was also sustained by the conviction that something ought to be done about Bankie, to repair the neglect with which history has treated this 'ardent nationalist'. Further, the picture literature has portrayed of the Krios of Sierra Leone, as a loyal, conservative, elite conscious, privileged, and preferred segment, in the colonial society of Sierra Leone, needs a radical revision. This study challenges views which perceive the Krios as co-regents of the British colonial government and 'maximum participants' in the colonial system. Bright, too, is seen in a more positive light than that of an exclusive ultraconservative particularist opposed to the peoples of the then Protectorate of Sierra Leone. He was neither a man who was wholly obsessed with a determination to maintain the elitist structure in the Colony, nor was he indifferent to the sufferings and interests of ordinary folk. New interpretations are therefore offered on old themes.

In putting across my thesis, I have used the methodology suggested by Professor Hargreaves in the opening pages of *Aberdeenshire to Africa* (Aberdeen, 1981): 'The political history of European relations with Africa – of imperialism...must be approached through capital cities.' The approach is also apt for the study of colonial politics and the activities of the early nationalists through biographies. In this case, the life history and career of Bankole-Bright is a leitmotiv for an investigation into the realities of politics in colonial Sierra Leone, 1919–58.

I was first attracted to the subject of Bright by the near obscurity of the man in the literature in spite of his considerable contributions to such pan West African organisations as the National Congress of British West Africa and W.A.S.U. What little was said about him was presented in negative terms. History did not appear to have given him the credit he merited; and for me this neglect made him an intriguing subject for research.

I briefly looked at some records while I was in London in 1973, but actual research on the subject began in 1976. In that year, I visited the Public Records Office (P.R.O.) in London and studied the CO267 Series (Sierra Leone). These and other major documents indicated in the bibliography form the bulk of official sources. They are supplemented by oral evidence and newspaper reports.

Preface

Bankie was not an easy subject to study because of strong prejudices connected with his name. Also he did not leave any private papers. Consequently, I had to depend on oral evidence to provide the background, the human angle, not obtainable from official records. Here, again, one encountered the problem of getting information from people who worked with him, fought with him, or knew him. Many appointments ended with frustrating results.

However, I was extremely lucky in getting the enthusiastic and empathic support of Bright's sister, Lerina (deceased), who supplied much of the information on her brother's family background. His niece, Hannah Neal, was no less supportive. Her critical support and help in procuring old pictures of her uncle, and her mother's encouragement are gratefully acknowledged. I was also able to get a fairly representative group of informants who were contemporaries and opponents of Bright. They are identified in the list in the bibliography. Their co-operation was most appreciated.

Without the financial support of some academic bodies the study would not have been started. To this end, my sincere gratitude goes to the Commonwealth Scholarship Commission, Association of Commonwealth Universities, and to Dr Arthur Porter, then Vice-Chancellor of the University of Sierra Leone, who nominated me for the award of a Commonwealth Academic Staff Fellowship, 1976/7. This enabled me to do archival work in Britain for nine months. While there I was attached to S.O.A.S. London University, where I had the benefit of the research experience of some of its staff in the History Department: Dr Humphrey Fisher, the late D. H. Jones, and Professor Richard Gray. I acknowledge their individual help and the courtesy extended to me by the Head, Professor Roland Oliver, in allowing me to make use of the facilities of the school and take part in his famous seminar series at the Commonwealth Institute, London.

In Nigeria, the University of Calabar Senate Research Grants Committee generously awarded me a grant to visit archives at Enugu and Ibadan, in which latter place I consulted the Herbert Macaulay Papers. My sincere thanks go to them as well as all archival and library personnel in Britain, Sierra Leone and Nigeria, who helped in numerous ways to supply me with the required information.

I am greatly indebted to many people for their help and support in various ways: Ms Wurdle, who helped me find material on Bright's medical student days; Professor G. Shepperson and Christopher Fyfe of the University of Edinburgh; Professor J. D. Hargreaves of Aberdeen University; Professor John D. Y. Peel of Liverpool University; Dr Paul Richards of London University; Professors Eldred Jones, A. D. Williams, C. P. Foray and other colleagues at Fourah Bay College, University of Sierra Leone.

Professors Okon E. Uya and G. N. Uzoigwe of the Department of History, University of Calabar, were both helpful and supportive. David Johnson of the same department and Emmanuel Quansah of the Law

Department were kind enough to read my scripts and to offer useful criticisms. To all of them, and others whose names I cannot list here, I give my sincere thanks.

My warmest appreciation and thanks go to my dear wife, Fredrica, and my children for putting up with my changing moods and for constantly reminding me of the benefits of family life.

Finally, I acknowledge with gratitude the efforts of a conscientious band of ladies who typed drafts of the manuscript and Mrs K. Yilla of the Department of English, Fourah Bay College who did the final version.

Akintola J. G. Wyse

Abbreviations

A.P.C.	All People's Congress
A.R.B.	*Africana Research Bulletin*
C.O.	Colonial Office
C.P.R.	*Colonial and Provincial Reporter*
D.G.	*Daily Guardian*
D.M.	*Daily Mail*
E.B.I.M.	Election Before Independence Movement
F.C.B.P.	Fabian Colonial Bureau Papers
J.A.H.	*Journal of African History*
J.H.S.N.	*Journal of the Historical Society of Nigeria*
J.H.S.S.L.	*Journal of the Historical Society of Sierra Leone*
J.M.A.S.	*Journal of Modern African Studies*
M.S.S.	Manuscripts
N.C.B.W.A.	National Congress of British West Africa
N.C.S.L.	National Council of Sierra Leone
P.E.P.U.	Protectorate Educational Progressive Union
P.N.P.	Peoples National Party
S.D.U.	Settlers' Descendants Union
S.L.A.S.	Sierra Leone Aborigines Society
S.L.G.F.M.	*Sierra Leone Guardian and Foreign Mails*
S.L.I.M.	Sierra Leone Independence Movement
S.L.P.P.	Sierra Leone People's Party
S.L.S.	*Sierra Leone Studies*
S.L.W.N.	*Sierra Leone Weekly News*
S.O.S.	Sierra Leone Organisation Society
U.P.P.	United Progressive Party
W.A.Y.L.	West African Youth League
W.J.	Wallace-Johnson

Introduction

When Bankole-Bright died after a long illness on 12 December 1958, 'friends' and political foes alike praised him as a nationalist. Sir Milton Margai, the Prime Minister, observed in his tribute that:

> the death of Honourable Dr H. C. Bankole-Bright can best be described as the end of an epoch. For the grand old gentleman of politics was a stalwart pioneer in a field which held very little rewards. But as God would have it, he achieved in his life time some of the things for which he worked very hard. His contributions to West African journalism, to the political consciousness and activity of Sierra Leone, to the general cause of freedom and justice are too numerous to mention. We will remember him for all these and for his part in helping Sierra Leone gain its present constitution.
>
> I have many memories of the late Dr H. C. Bankole-Bright but I remember him most of all for his wit, his lively debates and his ability to put his point across very effectively during his leadership of the official opposition of the last government ... death will not easily silence the achievement of a man who did so much for his country and people. History and those who write history, will make spacious room to record the life and achievements of the late Honourable Dr H. C. Bankole-Bright.[1]

Sir Milton's speech is an appropriate reference point to put Bankole-Bright in the perspective of Sierra Leone history. But perhaps Bright's biography may not have much meaning by itself, the impact and relevance appropriate to the intriguing historiography of Sierra Leone, if it is not studied in conjunction with an analysis of politics between 1919 and 1958, especially with regard to the position and performance of his people, the Krios, under the colonial regime. In short, the life and times of Bankole-Bright cannot be divorced from the politics of Sierra Leone in the period under review. The structure and content of the chapters reflect this approach – hence the title of this work.

Furthermore, the study brings to mind Miles F. Shore's prescriptions for a

> biography which recognizes that every human being, however ordinary or extraordinary, has certain basic needs for love and self-esteem from others,

1

must struggle with hatred and self-centredness which interfere with essential relationships, has had parents of a certain type and a life story marked by good and bad luck, by painful and rewarding experiences, and has unconscious residues from psychological development which influence behaviour.[2]

The basic points indicated here were reflected in Bright's life history.

1

Growing up: background to his family and early life

Sierra Leoneans were to be found in almost every African country on the West Coast in the nineteenth century.[1] Variously called Saros, Black Englishmen (*Oyinbo Oji*, as in Igbo country), Liberated Africans, or Creoles (Krios), they were the descendants of Black Returnees from Britain and the New World for whom the Sierra Leone colony had been founded in 1787, and Liberated Africans from various parts of Africa. They appeared in many roles as 'bearers of civilisation', 'cultural frontiersmen', minor functionaries in the European establishments that dotted the coasts, or as substantial merchants, and itinerant petty traders. The chief motivation for many in this peripatetic group, who had had to leave their homeland for a number of reasons, but especially because of the limited opportunities it offered them, was the pursuit of commerce.[2] On the other hand, quite a large number of them were able to successfully combine, in the best tradition of the three Cs – Christianity, Commerce and Civilization – their pursuit of material gains and the fulfilment of the role fashioned out for them by late eighteenth-century and early nineteenth-century British philanthropists, as 'beacons of light' for the civilisation of 'Darkest Africa'.[3]

Among this legion of Saro immigrants was Jacob (Galba) Bright. He was a 'diplomatic agent' in Sir George Taubman Goldie's commercial empire, i.e., he was a member of that ill-used band of African traders and adventurers who were employed by Goldie to secure treaty rights for his companies. It was during this time that Mr and Mrs Bright had their second son, Herbert Christian Bankole, on 23 August 1883, at Okrika, on the edge of Igbo country, thirty miles north of Bonny, in the then Oil Rivers (in what is now Rivers State of Nigeria).[4] Little did the parents know it, but by having young Bankie in Nigeria they had performed the first symbolic act of making a politician with a pan West-African outlook. More important, their son was destined to be, half a century later, the subject of intense debate; one which was to arouse the strongest passions either for or against.

Jacob Bright, like many of his compatriots, had his ancestral home outside Sierra Leone. Certainly, in the case of the Brights, it was Yorubaland, but his natal home was the village of Wellington on a low-lying plain of grass land and marsh, seven miles east of Freetown. There the first Bright, John, had come from a recaptured slave ship as an infant in his mother's arms in 1823. Dumped among fellow recaptives from different ethnic backgrounds, and for whose rehabilitation Wellington had been founded in 1819, Bright and his mother were baptised and received into the Anglican faith. He may have got the name John Bright then. Though it was unlikely that he was named after the famous English Liberal, it was not uncommon for the names of eminent nineteenth-century public figures to be chosen by English pastors for their wards. John was educated in Church schools, but, at a later date, *c.* 1836, for 'want of a resident Missionary in Wellington', he and his mother were 'obliged to become Wesleyans', though at heart John remained 'a Churchman'.[5]

As other studies on the Liberated Africans have shown *ad nauseam*, the rosy picture of a self-sufficient agricultural community, which philanthropists had dreamed up for the motley collection of settlers and recaptives in the Sierra Leone colony, failed to come up to expectations. Poor planning, bad organisation, lack of incentive and a poor and infertile soil made this dream unrealisable. And although writers have generally accused the early settlers of an unwillingness to pursue agriculture, it is clear from the evidence of extensive farming by the Nova Scotians on the slopes of Tower Hill, then a more verdant area known as Wansey Hill before 1806, that other reasons besides apathy should be found for this failed arcadian promise. To be sure, these early colonists, especially the Liberated Africans, resilient, enterprising, inventive, adaptable and resourceful, soon learned to divert their energies to something much more rewarding – trade.[6] The most outstanding feature of Sierra Leone history in the nineteenth century is, therefore, the phenomenal transformation of a group of people, some of whom were, less than twenty years previously, rescued from slavery, to a vigorous and pioneering trading community. People from this society pioneered trading networks into the hinterland and, using old and salvaged slave ships auctioned by the Admiralty Court, they plied the coast selling sundry goods in Yorubaland and Igbo country, among others.[7]

In Freetown there was a burgeoning community of merchants. The exploits of some Liberated African commercial mandarins like the Ezzdios and the Isaac Pratts are better known than others, though little is known about the way some of them raised their capital. William Lewis, for example, the father of Sir Samuel Lewis, began trading with half a dollar.[8] We do not know why John Bright left Wellington, except, of course, that it could be hazarded that he wanted to broaden his horizons. Neither do we know how he acquired his capital. He may have got it by thrift and industry, or through savings from garden produce, an important economic activity of the rural Krio of Freetown. However, by the middle of the nineteenth century, he was fairly well established as a 'rich recaptive Aku Spirit Merchant'[9] in East Street – 'one of the leading merchants of Freetown, whose name was associated with every movement of importance or in the interest of the country'.[10] As an established name in Freetown high society he was also a very conscientious churchman, and a liberal Church benefactor. Indeed, letters from Reverend James Quaker, the first African Principal of the

4

C.M.S. Grammar School, to the C.M.S. Headquarters in London, tell of John Bright's generous donations to the Anglican Church, even though he was a Wesleyan Methodist. To avoid embarrassing queries from his own sect, Bright devised a way of giving money 'in memory of some event or other in his life'.[11] He established a tradition as a Church benefactor and a concerned citizen – and his family has maintained that tradition with some consistency.

First-generation Liberated Africans, mindful of the short-comings of their own formal education, wanted their children to acquire a better education and follow the professions.[12] And the fact that the British administration needed a cadre of literate Africans whose body chemistry made them better able to work as minor functionaries, or perform in key professions like Medicine and Law, in a climate that was still hostile to the white man, also created among the Krios a powerful incentive towards a white-collar orientation. Law and Medicine were therefore two professions which attracted scions from rich merchant houses. And although the first qualified Krio doctors, Africanus Beale Horton and Broughton Davies, two medical students sponsored by the War Office in London in 1855, were not sons of merchants, the list of qualified doctors and lawyers in the second half of the nineteenth century represents a roll call of many sons of merchant families.[13]

Jacob, born on 24 October 1843, the son of John, opted for medicine. After he had gone through his primary and post-primary education, he went to England in 1865 to train as a doctor. Fate proved unkind to him; six months later his father, whose health had never been robust, died and he had to return home. Denied the opportunity of following a medical career, Jacob turned to commerce.[14] Forty years later, his son, Bankole, was to gratify his father by studying medicine.

When Jacob assumed control of his father's business at East Street he found it much impoverished.[15] Undaunted, he stuck to commerce. However, perhaps finding that opportunities for expansion were limited in Freetown, he followed the examples of his compatriots and decided to seek his fortune in the Niger. The abolition of the Slave Trade in 1807 and the vigorous campaign to replace it with legitimate commerce, an objective reinforced by the need for raw materials to sustain the industrial expansion of Britain, made the creeks and riverain states along the Niger River the centre of militant commerce in the nineteenth century. The turnover from the palm oil trade and its allied concerns was such that for many, the Niger River was El Dorado.[16] Saros from Sierra Leone were found in large numbers in the Niger Delta. A good number of these immigrants went to the Delta as missionaries, but the majority of them were traders.

Jacob joined this group with his wife in the 1870s. His wife, Letitia, was the daughter of another well-known Freetown merchant, R. B. Williams. Young Jacob subscribed to the local tradition of one merchant family marrying into another merchant family, thus creating an almost caste-like exclusive society, when he secured the hand of Letitia in 1877.[17] It was not long after this that they went to the Niger, where he became a diplomatic agent in Goldie s company. Shortly after the birth of Bankie, he returned to Freetown with his family and a mute nurse who looked after the baby.[18]

His stay in the Niger Delta was obviously a remunerative and successful one, because when he returned to Freetown he started his own business from the ruins of his father's at Sawpit, in Little East Street. He dealt in cotton materials, which were made to his own design and specification, and a number of sundry goods, including galver articles made of toughened plastic. According to one informant, the name Galba was later added to his given name as an indication of his popularity among his customers.[19] Such a gesture was not uncommon in nineteenth-century Freetown. Many merchant families were given sobriquets after the products which were mostly identified with their dealerships, or because of some affectation. So we had 'Cutlass' Metzger, 'Cocoa' Nicol, 'Tabacca' George, 'Iron Pot' Coker or 'Head Head' Thomas (Malamah Thomas), and Singer Betts who used to sell Singer sewing machines. Since Jacob sold a lot of galver articles, such as bangles, his illiterate customers soon called him 'Galaba' Bright, a corruption of galver. Bright made it neat with the form 'Galba'.[20]

Jacob Bright established a flourishing commercial concern in the 1880s comparable to the other leading merchant families like the Malamah Thomases, the Colenso Bishops and the Booksellers – the Shorunkeh Sawyerrs.[21] He was also a founder member of the Sierra Leone Chamber of Commerce, established in June 1892, to protect the interests of the commercial firms in Freetown.[22] And by the turn of the century Jacob Bright had salvaged the fortunes of the first Bright and had become a fully re-established member of the local aristocracy. But Bright was a shy man, of retiring nature. He shunned all publicity,· and he never showed any indications that he aspired to membership of the City Council, the traditional training ground for aspiring politicians, or the Legislative Council, though he had all the recommendations for such a position. In fact, he was once considered for nomination to Council. He did not accept the offer because of a 'failing health', recalled his son in 1931, but he participated fully in the affairs of the colony, subscribing to various donations for worthy causes. His advice, often sage and practical, was frequently sought by his peers and younger men. More important, he continued the role of his late father as a Church benefactor. A regular and conscientious churchgoer, he often subsidised the 'church funds to meet the monthly and quarterly expenditure of the Circuit'. And, not surprisingly, he was rewarded for such public services by being appointed Senior Circuit Steward and a Trustee of the family church – the Gibraltar Methodist Church at Kissy Street. He held the post of Steward for twelve years.[23]

The Brights, father and son, had something else in common – they both married twice. John Bright's second wife, Mary Ann Bright, died thirty-seven years after her husband, aged eighty-seven years. She was a woman of considerable influence in her day.[24] Jacob's second wife was a widow, Mrs Hannah Selina Shepherd, daughter of Adam Martyn, a former Master of the Supreme Court of the Colony.[25] Bankie, the grandson, did not marry a second time, despite his estrangement from his wife later in their lives.

Jacob's family was quite large, though its size and composition was not unusual for that period.[26] Selina's three children, Odulami, Adjai (boys) and Lerina were added to his first wife's children – a girl (long deceased) and three boys – John, Bankole and Jacob, to make seven.[27] He may have had other children outside the marital home; certainly Bankole had a half brother – Ibrahim Bright, about whom more shall be said later. Bright's family was large, but then, during this period, the cost of living was not too high; for example, palm oil cost between 9s. 0d. and 9s. 6d. per kerosene tin (4 gallons); foofoo – a staple diet of most Krio – was between 2s. 0d. and 2s. 6d. per basket; meat sold for 8d.–9d. per pound, while the prices of rice ranged between 2s. 0d. and 2s. 3d. to 6s. 6d. and 8s. 0d. per bushel, depending on its quality and state; the catalogue prices for shirts and suits ranged between 2s. 11d. and 8s. 11d. and 24s. 6d. and 54s. 6d. respectively.[28] Besides, Bright was wealthy enough to afford such a family size, and traditional enough to accept many children as gifts from God. And, unlike their present descendants, fathers made it an obligation to care for their children, however diverse their origins. They did not have any moral hang-ups about having extra-marital relations, despite their strict Victorian upbringing. On the contrary, this lifestyle emphasised an African background that was polygamous. Over a century of Christianity had not weaned the Krios from this basic African lore, though they would keep the forms and appearances of a monogamous life laid down by 'civilised' and polite society.

Jacob sent all the children by his first wife to study abroad. Those of the second marriage cannot be documented. But Bankie, twenty-eight years older than Lerina, was responsible for the education of his sister, the last child of the second marriage, through elementary to college level.[29] The Brights were a closely knit family.

The up-bringing of Bankie was typical, reflecting the constituents of Krio society which finely balanced Western values with African lores and customs. Wealthy middle-class families of Freetown – the 'aristos', as they were called – were imbued with a high religious fervour, a strict code of discipline, a mid-Victorian infatuation with personal industriousness and moral conscience, and a rigorous adherence to the tenets of the Church, virtues which recall their Victorian ethos.[30] Parents scrupulously instilled these values into their children. They were taught to go to church regularly. In many homes, children could not go visiting on Sundays if they did not attend the morning service. They were encouraged to go to school and exhorted to follow a strict moral code; the African virtue of respect for one's elders and one's traditions was also drummed into their heads. Bankie, averred his niece, was a great devotee of Krio lores, rituals and customs. Hard work was valued. In some homes, for example that of A. E. Tuboku-Metzger, the children were taught to do household chores and to work in the garden.[31] Bankie and the other Bright children went through this crucible.

On the other hand, this background of high moral tone and religious scruple sometimes injected into its adherents an intolerance towards the weak-willed and the unsuccessful; others affected arrogance or over-assertiveness, especially when this kind of background was married to affluence. Bankie later acquired the reputation of a positive and over-confidently assertive individual who did not suffer fools, black or white, gladly. His outspoken bluntness, in many ways admirable, was unrelieved by his overbearing manner and conceit. He made much of his elitist background. 'He believed in aristocracy however decadent and out of date',[32] charged his arch-political opponent, the socialist I. T. A. Wallace-Johnson.

Herbert Christian Bankole-Bright began his schooling at Mrs Rice's (née Dove) Private School at Dove-Cut, in the east end of Freetown. He then went on to attend the Methodist Boys' High School together with his brothers.[33] This school and the C.M.S. Grammar School were both founded by missionaries in 1874, and 1845 respectively. For a long time they remained the premier boys' schools in the colony, turning out the first generation of educated men throughout Anglophone West Africa who used European methods and civilisation to challenge colonial rule in their respective countries. In Sierra Leone, children of the leading families in Freetown, or even from the hinterland (later to be proclaimed the Protectorate of Sierra Leone),[34] went to either of these two schools, according to their denominational preferences and religious associations; and they sometimes became students at Fourah Bay College. The Brights did not, however, attend the latter institution.

When Bankie entered the Boys' High School in 1898[35] the Principal was the remarkable Reverend J. C. May, F.R.G.S., a stern disciplinarian, and 'an erudite and passionate teacher'. He and his father contributed greatly to the founding of the Boys' High School in 1874. The name of the Mays was therefore synonymous with the institution. J. C. May was the first Principal of the school, and so he was able to see the school through its infancy and to shape it according to the high standards of scholarship, moral code, and discipline he set for himself.[36] He was assisted by such luminaries of the teaching profession as S. T. Peacock, W. G. Nicol, B.A., T. A. Faux, J. T. Roberts, who later became a Principal, E. J. Dauphin, and T. C. Parker. To these and four junior masters were entrusted the duty of moulding the youths into responsible and literate citizens. The curriculum was, of course, heavily weighted towards classical studies: Latin, Greek, French, Ancient Histories, English and 'its usual branches'; but there was some attempt at including practical disciplines: Arithmetic, Algebra, Geometry, Trigonometry, Mensuration, Book Keeping, Phonography and Physical Science.[37]

This classical-oriented education, however, did not make them book-quoting dilettantes despite the sneering comments of some scholars. On the

8

contrary, such exercises as poetry and drama, the study of works of Homer and other ancient writers, were of direct relevance to people who were to later articulate the aspirations of their compatriots.[38] They inculcated into them an ordered mind, a logical thinking, and the art of public speaking. In latter days High School boys were well known for their command of the English language. Some were more successful than others in utilising this training. A good example of these is Bankole-Bright.

From an early age he ingeniously combined a brilliant eloquence and a respectable scholastic ability. Records on the latter are not available, but he certainly impressed his schoolmates to a sufficient degree to receive the accolade of 'Dux'.[39] On his elocutary expertise there is much information, agreed upon by all, including his most hostile critics, that in his halcyon days Bankole-Bright was the 'best platform man' in Freetown, 'a brilliant speaker', 'a verbal gymnast', an orator who could 'charm a bird from his perch'.[40] But this was a later development of a boy who, endowed with a sharp and enquiring mind, had shown more than a passing interest in debates and impromptu discussions in his school days. Indeed, he was once chosen among others to give a public speech during the anniversary celebration of the Wesleyan Methodist Boys' High School Juvenile Missionary Association in 1899.[41] Bankie had a fascination for public speaking. This, and his irrepressibly flamboyant nature, which revealed itself as he grew older, were two of the formative influences which led him into politics. Another was his deep concern for the underdog, the defenceless, and the oppressed.

For the moment, however, making a vocation out of politics had to wait until he had acquired the necessary qualifications for a much more materially rewarding career. The frustrated effort of Bankie's father to study medicine was assuaged when he encouraged his son to pursue that profession. When young Bankie left school *c.* 1904, he was apprenticed for a short time to the surgery of Dr W. Awunor Renner, M.R.C.S. (Eng.) 1880, L.K.Q.P. and L.M. (Ireland) 1881, one-time Acting Principal Medical Officer in the West African Medical Service, and one of Freetown's leading doctors.[42] In 1905 he left Freetown and registered in May of that year as a student in the Royal College of Surgeons, Edinburgh. The College offered a five-year professional degree course leading to the L.R.C.P. & S. (Edinburgh) and L.R.F.P. & S. (Glasgow). The curriculum included courses in Therapeutics, Surgery, Surgical Anatomy, Midwifery, Medical Jurisprudence and Anaesthetics. Although it was a completely autonomous institution, carrying on a friendly rivalry with the University of Edinburgh, its students had to take certain courses in the University.[43] Some months were also spent attending courses in other institutions, for instance, the Royal Infirmary in Edinburgh, and London Hospital. And for six months Bankie was apprenticed to a Dr Campbell. From his rooms at Lauriston Gardens, Edinburgh, he commuted to all these places in the extreme Scottish weather.[44] Happily, neither the weather nor the fact that he was an obvious minority in a European country had any ill effect on his studies. On the contrary, his academic record shows

9

that his scholastic career at Edinburgh was not undistinguished.[45] Furthermore, he combined a successful academic career with full participation in students' affairs. Debates were an outstanding feature of these activities. In fact, it is recorded in the *Student*, the magazine of the students at Edinburgh University, that Bright seconded a motion for debate in a meeting jointly organised by the Afro–West Indian Association and the Indian Association at the Non-Associated Societies Hall in 1908. The motion proposed by George Joseph 'with his usual eloquence' read thus: 'That the success of a cause depends more on its organisation than on its inherent justice.' Bright 'ably supported' the motion which was carried by nineteen votes to sixteen.[46]

This piece of information is significant, for it shows that Bright was maturing, that he was revealing positive signs of political awareness and articulateness. Whether he gained anything from the content of the debate is doubtful, considering his efforts in the 1950s. What is important, however, is that a young man of twenty-five was beginning to react to the colonial situation, to be critical of the way African peoples were being ruled. His horizons had begun to widen to cover issues affecting other colonies in the British Empire. This is evidenced by a letter he wrote to Keir Hardie, the founder of the Labour Party, apparently condemning British actions in various parts of Africa. Hardie replied in 1906 thus:[47]

> My Dear Sir,
>
> I am obliged by your approval of anything I have been able to do to assist your race and I regret that I cannot do more. The terrible event which happened in the Sudan the other day, with its attendant brutalities, reduces the administration of that country under British rule to the level of that of the Congo Free State, while the wholesale massacre of natives which is now going on in South Africa, under the pretext of suppressing a rebellion which does not exist, fills one with shame and horror. I hope the day will speedily come when your race will be able to defend itself against the barbarities being perpetrated against it by hypocritical whites, who regard the blackman as having been created in order that they might exploit him for their own advantages. The press and politicians for the most part keep the people in this country in ignorance of the real treatment meted out to the natives, and not until they, the natives, are in a position to hold their own can they expect to be treated as human beings..
>
> Yours sincerely,
>
> J. Keir Hardie

Records on African students in Edinburgh are hard to come by, especially so in the case of Bright who was not registered as a student in the University, though he attended courses there and obviously met with students from other parts of Africa and elsewhere. We do not know who all his African contemporaries were or how he related with them.[48] Certainly he was the contemporary of Ishmael Charles Pratt, another Sierra Leonean, who registered in May 1904, and graduated about the same time as Bankie. It is also possible that he knew Akiwande Savage, a student from Nigeria with

Sierra Leonean connection, who left Edinburgh in 1903. Another Nigerian who must have been a contemporary of Bright was Bandele Omoniyi. He was a student activist who could lay a modest claim to literary fame with his *A Defence of the Ethiopian Movement* (Edinburgh, 1908). Since Bright left no private papers when he died in 1958 we have no evidence to categorically state that he continued to associate with his Edinburgh African colleagues in later life.

In 1910 Bright qualified as a physician with an L.R.C.P. & S., L.R.C.S. (Edin.); and L.R.C.P. & S. (Glas.). He returned home the same year and set up private practice as a doctor at 15 Pultney Street, Freetown.[49] His two brothers of the first marriage followed different careers. John St Hawley Ekundayo, the eldest, followed the career of his father as a businessman. He studied commerce in Germany, and when his father died in 1910 he took over the family business, and eventually sold it and started his own.[50] John Bright and the Shorunkeh-Sawyerrs are two exceptions, fully documented, of the general tendency for children of the first-generation Krios to leave the world of commerce for white-collar careers.

Jacob Galba Iwuchuku Bright studied Law in England and returned home to practise. Shortly afterwards, in 1912, he emigrated to Nigeria.[51] Contemporaries used to say about the two brothers that considering Bankie's zest for politics and love for debate he should have been the lawyer and Jacob should have followed the medical profession. But interestingly enough, Jacob established an enviable reputation as a lawyer within the short span of life he enjoyed. His trenchant pleadings at the bar in Nigeria earned him the name of 'the Sierra Leone jigger'.[52] He was popular, well loved, and respected by a large circle of friends and admirers. But fate struck on 23 June 1920, when he died at a very young age of 34 years, leaving a widow, Evelyn Ayodele (née Reffell), who had shared her life with her husband for a little more than two years.[53]

Fate was also hard on Jacob, senior. His son, who had acquired the professional qualification denied him, had been back less than six months when the father expired on 10 October 1910, aged sixty-seven years. He did not live to enjoy the fruits of his labour, or to follow the career of a favourite son. Symbolically he died at Bankie's residence in Pultney Street,[54] though there are views about the dubious role Bankie played during the proceedings. The tragedy of his father's death did not, however, prevent Bankole from marrying his fiancée in January 1911. Out of respect for his father the wedding was quietly, but impressively celebrated. The leading citizens honoured the occasion with their presence at Wesley Church, where the wedding was solemnised on a Sunday morning. The officiating clergy included the Reverend J. C. Thomas and the Reverend W. G. Nicol, an old teacher of the bridegroom. At the organ was a local celebrity, the maestro himself, Professor E. J. Greywood. Another renowned musician was the composer, Professor J. S. T. Davies, the first African Assistant Post Master-General of the Post Office, who contributed a 'brilliant festal march by way of finale'. Distinguished guests who signed the register included B. R. Williams, the maternal grandfather of the bridegroom, Councillor F. A. Bishop, the bride's brother, Hon. J. J. Thomas, nominated member of the Legislative Council, and Dr W. Awunor Renner, the most senior African medical doctor at that time, and the man who introduced Bankie into the medical profession.[55]

We do not know how long the courtship had lasted before the nuptial knot was tied. The Society column of the *Sierra Leone Weekly News* reporting the return of Addah Maude Bishop to Sierra Leone in 1910, informed its readers that she had been away in England for many years.[56] She may have met her future husband while he was studying in Britain or, as was not uncommon, she may have been his childhood sweetheart. Whatever the case might be, Bankie could not have made a better choice. In an age when one's antecedents and the name one carried mattered, one's choice of partner must be judicious. Addah was an 'aristo' in her own right, having come from the Bishop family – a house as distinguished as the Brights, if not wealthier. She was the youngest daughter of Theophilus Colenso Bishop, a wealthy merchant (deceased), a one-time Mayor of Freetown (1898), a Justice of the Peace, and a nominated member of the Sierra Leone Chamber of Commerce.[57] The bride's brother was also a Justice of the Peace and a Councillor.

The combined dignity and wealth of the two families naturally boosted the prestige and standing of Bright in a status-conscious society. The marriage was blessed with four children: two boys and two girls. The wedded life of the Brights was, however, not one of uninterrupted domestic bliss. He and his wife had some difficulties even leading to a court case. The children also did not strictly follow their filial obligations. At the ages of eleven and nine the two sons were despatched to London for schooling – the eldest was to study Medicine and the other Law, but they followed their own inclinations. The daughters are now dead. The elder of the two died young, and the other, who did in fact study Law, died eight years after her father. The sons are now supposed to be in Britain.[58] They do not appear to have any more connection with their father's native land.

All this was in the future, but it is relevant to bring in this piece of information here to suggest that what people saw in the forties and fifties was not the brash young man of the twenties and thirties, full of confidence, his mordant wit putting white officials at extreme discomfort; it was rather the pale shadow of a man who had a zest for living but had been worn down by life's misfortunes. His domestic difficulties played some part in this. In the early years of his career, that is in 1911–34, however, he was in the prime of life, positive and demonstrably outspoken. He pursued a successful private practice, though there is more than one opinion about this. Some attest that Bankie was a good doctor, popular and useful; others did not think highly of his professional competence. Indeed, one writer has alleged that after setting up practice on his return home, he 'abandoned the profession altogether' several years later.[59] Another, a contemporary, in a 1956 publication, dismissed him with this comment: 'In private practice, but spends most of his time in journalism (he owns a paper) and politics. He is one of the best known politicians in West Africa, one of the original members of N.C.B.W.A. in 1920.'[60] The local British administration, hardly a disinterested observer, dubbed him an 'unsuccessful medical practitioner'.[61] Apparently, he was not interested in getting a job with the government. At least, there is no evidence that he even applied for a government post, though it is extremely unlikely, considering the government's opinion about local medical practitioners, that he would have been given an appointment if he had asked for one.[62] There is evidence, however, that Bankole-Bright unsuccessfully applied for the post of Medical Officer to the City Council in 1918. He competed with other doctors such as A. E. Easmon, I. C. Pratt, G. N. Metzger, and M. L. Jarrett. Easmon won the contract with seven votes. Bright polled three and Jarrett one.[63] Still, he did have retainers from a number of commercial firms; and he was able to educate his sister Lerina, and all his children. He did inherit some property, and his wife's wealth could also have been a useful supplement, but the greater part of his money came from his practice which, by 1925, had been expanded to a private nursing home, Daphne's Nursing Home, named after his daughter.[64] Besides, his life style indicated that he was wealthy enough to indulge in his fancies, even if the cost of living was not so high: his Churchillian cigars were a particular fixture of the man's personality; his regular champagne sessions, his elegant attire – a neat array of coats, top hats, Anthony Eden hats, tails and spats – did not depend on pin money either. He used to dress himself up in elegant African costumes on occasions also. The picture of Bright in traditional attire speaks for itself.

Physically, he was a huge man, very tall, with a tendency towards a slight stoop; he had an extraordinarily large head with protuberant eyes, and a deep reverberating voice to go with his size. His forbidding presence was, however, relieved by his sartorial extravagance and a warm heart, if one got near to him.[65] And if stories are to be believed the ladies were not unimpressed; nor for that matter were they unattracted. In short, Bright was an Edwardian dandy. His elegance and eloquence are two things on which there are no conflicting opinions. In his person Bright represented the exotic extravagance of an age which recalled the pace-setting life-style of the good Queen Victoria's son, the Prince of Wales, later Edward VII. Freetown had its own social circuit; its 'At Homes', its soirées and musical evenings.[66] Oddly enough, for one as bouncy and flamboyant as Bright, he hardly ever attended social events, but at one such occasion his wife 'entertained guests with a humorous musical recitation' and, at another, during the American pan-Africanist W. E. B. Du Bois's visit to Freetown in 1924, she sang a solo. At the reception her husband gave the vote of thanks 'with credit'.[67]

However, any suggestion that Bright's early years were taken up with his personal appearance would not only be unfair to him, but it would also ignore his positive involvement with politics from the onset. Indeed, according to his niece, when Bankie was in Scotland he was inducted as a member of the Masonic Lodge, the Scottish Constitution (Lodge No. 52), but on his return to Freetown he stopped attending Lodge meetings because he was too tied up with political affairs. His activities during his youth indicate that he was very much interested in current affairs, and so it was to be expected that he should take this hobby in earnest at a more mature age. Contemporaries say that he was more of an orator than a literary man. That may be so, but Bright apparently thought that he could more effectively put across his views, given the political situation at the time, through the newspaper, than from the platform.[68] Not that there were not other newspapers doing a good job. There was even an attempt in 1901 to launch a magazine, *The Creole Boy*, 'to fill the want among the younger members of the community'. It came out with some issues which impressed one reader to write congratulating the launchers. Unfortunately, the editor, D. O. Wilson, died the following year in 1902 at the age of 35 years. The paper died with him. However, the existing papers were continuing the tradition of a reading public which went back to the beginning of the nineteenth century when the first newspaper was published in 1801.[69] The newspaper, the *Aurora*, which Bankie founded and edited was a revolutionary paper with a different and refreshing approach. The language of this weekly tabloid was unrestrained, and its tone abrasive; and its attacking sting was acidic. A peculiar feature of the paper was to sensationalise the faults of the government and to harass European officers who appeared to have been let off lightly by an indulgent government from some misdemeanour perpetrated on an African. Although the *Weekly News* (founded in 1884), the best newspaper in the period under review, was as critical of the administration as any other paper, and always expressed its views unreservedly, it still managed to do this in restrained language. Managed by Cornelius May of the highly respected May family, the paper remained respectable.

As a government official once commented,

> The paper does not criticize government measures in much detail as a rule, and certainly does not habitually set itself against the measures adopted by the government. Thus it mentioned at various times with approval the government measures to meet the scarcity of rice last year, and to improve the protectorate roads etc. At the same time it devoted much space to rather high sounding verbiage about uplifting the natives, and it seizes upon any possible occasion for alleging and advertising miscarriages of justice, maltreatment of natives by government officials, etc.[70]

Other newspapers like the *Sierra Leone Guardian and Foreign Mails* and the *Colonial and Provincial Reporter* kept within this moderate circle. However, Bright's brashness and intemperate verbal assaults soon incurred the hostility of the administration and he was immediately categorised as a demagogic rabble-rouser. One official, F. J. McDonnell, the Solicitor-General, was so incensed by the tenacity with which Bright's paper pursued the case of Dudley Vergette, Curator of Intestate Estates, charged with misappropriation of funds, that he blurted out:

> I had no conception until my arrival here of the almost fanatical bitterness of the race feeling which exists amongst a section of the Creole community of Sierra Leone, a section which is probably not large but is very vocal and is ever on the watch for any error or weakness on the part of European officials whom it may pillory in the columns of its press.[71]

It was unfortunate that the colonial administration only saw the *Aurora* as a negative critic which gloried in the misfortune of white officials, but what was uppermost in Bankole's mind were the interests and concerns of his compatriots. And in this regard Omu has argued that newspaper editors saw themselves as 'guardians of the rights and liberties of the people as well as the interpreters of their ideals and aspirations'.[72] So, for that matter, Bright was outraged by the contemptuous attitude of the administration towards Sierra Leoneans. He did not believe that they were given chances enough to have a say in the running of their country. Rather the administration wanted them to remain a down-trodden and passive lot accepting what was doled out to them. Bright's exhortation was that people should fight for what was their due. More important, Bright's orientation was seen in a positive light by some people. Indeed, it was through his paper that he first met I. T. A. Wallace-Johnson, later to be his arch political opponent, who was to confess in 1958 that Bankie had inspired him to follow the profession of journalism. In 1912 when he first met Bankie, Wallace-Johnson was a pupil at the Collegiate School and, like most school boys of his days, he had taken to the *Aurora* because of its 'tantalizing excitement'. He had gone to submit an article for publication entitled 'The Labour Problems in Sierra Leone as seen by a School Boy', and Bright had impressed him as a 'master of the English language'. The editor had then told him: 'Boy, you will make a good journalist if you carry on in this way.' Wallace-Johnson was offered a fee of half a crown for his article, and he later became a regular contributor to the *Aurora*.[73]

Copies of the *Aurora* are not readily available,[74] and so we cannot evaluate the contributions Wallace-Johnson made to the paper, but this episode in the lives of these two is significant because in later years Bankie was to be unfavourably compared with Wallace-Johnson: the one was an arch conservative, the other a radical; Bright kept the hand of the clock back, Wallace-Johnson actively fought for independence; the former opposed integration with the then Protectorate peoples, the latter was the first Colony politician to bridge the gap between the two peoples;[75] and many more comparisons.[76] That such strait-jacket categorisations are never always accurate will be one of the major contentions of this study. The historical relevance of Bankie and his own contributions to the development of politics in his native land would therefore be of paramount importance in the discussion that follows.

2

Background to politics in the twentieth century

Sierra Leone, or more specifically, the Freetown of Bankie's lifetime, has had a long and enviable tradition of political awareness and constitutional legitimacy. From the very first days when the Nova Scotian immigrants, thwarted and disappointed by Britain over land rights and other promises, made some futile attempts to take over control of the colony, to the emotionally charged debate on the 1947 Constitution, Freetown has always been the central pivot of political turmoil. On the other hand, political realities during pre-independence days made it certain that the last word remained with the colonising power. Even so, Freetown's record of successful representation, within certain limits, is not undistinguished.

At the same time it is equally relevant and germane to this work to state that there is a continuous theme in Sierra Leone history of a register of disappointments for the aspirations of the early settlers and their Krio descendants.[1] The unfulfilled promises of the pre-Crown Colony era, initial favour and then disownment by Britain, and the discrimination experienced by their educated professionals in the hands of a prejudiced administration, are just a few of these disappointments. The Krios had the belief which, in retrospect, seems unrealistic, but perhaps at that time was consciously nurtured by Britain, that they would be the political heirs of the British. They were rudely disillusioned by developments in the 1940s. The dramatic flashpoint of this disillusionment was the introduction of the 1947 Constitution which made it crystal clear that in a democracy of one man one vote the Krio could not expect to exercise political power. It put a stop to any chimerical hopes entertained by the Krio people that they would ever achieve this in Sierra Leone. Some never forgave the British for what they considered a betrayal.[2]

Notwithstanding all this, the curiously astonishing fact is that the Krio remained attached to the British. The profoundness of this phenomenon is well illustrated by the example of Bankie, who, though he was regarded by the British administration as a demagogue and rabble-rouser, could still talk with irritating consistency about his 'organic connection with the British Crown'. Another Krio, C. D. Hotobah-During, a lawyer and political activist, also proclaimed that his 'four years in England were never to be forgotten being the most glorious days of my life amidst surroundings no better to be found in any other parts of the world I travelled and which

16

moulded me for the remaining years of my life in this sinful world'.[3] Unfeigned loyalty to the Imperial power was exhibited in the 1887 Jubilee celebration of the reign of Queen Victoria, as on many other occasions, when Sam Barlatt, spokesman for the Creoles (Krios), though not agreeing with everything the British had done for them, exclaimed:

> I cannot, however, endorse the spiteful animadversions of hasty foreign observers. In their criticisms there is always evident, not only a deficiency of imaginative insight and sympathy, but a lack of humility and an utter want of charity. But I can say that I am proud of one thing, and grateful for it, and that is, that the instruction I have received has in many respects helped me on the path of real progress; I have been lifted to a higher plane than that occupied by my fathers.[4]

This 'British mentality' was strong among the Krios, and it could not be exorcised easily.

But this, their 'Englishness', has called forth disparaging remarks about 'Black Englishmen', more often than not despised by 'puritanic' Englishmen for copying the English badly.[5] The ludicrity of referring to England as 'home' has of course been the subject of many sneering comments in a number of works.[6] Viewed objectively, the Englishness of the Krio was not merely aping the English but rather a reflection of the period during which their society was formed. It must be seen in perspective. As recent works have argued, the Krio still retained their Africanness and other individual ethnic characteristics, but their training and long association with the whiteman had enabled them to adopt the institutions and mores of the British, to establish a society that was on the one hand stratified and, on the other, opened ended. In other words, for one to be recognised in society one must go through a process of induction, a rites of passage. One such means long identified with the Krio was education. It was the key to social acceptability. And so, therefore, 'throughout the nineteenth century the Creole inhabitants of Sierra Leone regarded the pursuit of education as a particularly useful method of raising their financial and social status'.[7] Like all developing communities these people were not without social ambitions; and the making of their society went through an evolutionary process. For instance, the Nova Scotians had come into contact with western civilisation in the New World, and when they came to Freetown they already had some education. They came as Christians with their own churches. They breathed a free spirit. They were very possessive of their freedom, and they were very conscious of their rights. Some of them even looked down with contempt upon Europeans.[8] When the other immigrants, such as the Maroons and Liberated Africans, came, they were at first kept out of the social ambit of the Nova Scotians. In time these barriers were broken down, each group influencing and being influenced by the other, until a fairly identifiable society emerged inheriting in part some Nova Scotian attributes: their individuality, their passion for free speech and self rule, their cultural arrogance and their inordinate capacity to fragmentate. Some of these features helped to create

17

an elite-conscious society. Furthermore, given the role Britain played in the establishment of their community, the Krio believed that they owed an obligation to the British to be grateful; hence their Britishness. To be sure, it can be argued that the initiative taken by the Saints (a group of eighteenth-century philanthropists and evangelicals in London who provided the intellectual climate out of which the agitation for the ending of the slave trade emerged), in suggesting the founding of a colony for freed slaves as one practical solution of the slave-trade question, made it possible for a Krio ethnicity to evolve eventually.[9]

This statement made by J. C. O. Crowther underlines the attachment of the Krios to England. 'Everyone of us' he said, 'ought to be proud of our British connection.' 'Being a Creole or Sierra Leonean', said another elderly Krio lady, '[is] not a nationality, it is an act of grace.'[10] There is a double meaning here. The statement can be interpreted as an appreciation to God for his mercies, or it can be a statement of pride of achievement. In any case, this veiled smugness, sometimes unwittingly exposed, is one characteristic of the Krio which infuriates outsiders.

At the same time while recognising Britain as their patron they equally consider that having been emancipated, 'civilised' and educated, they were as good as their benefactors, and they therefore demanded equal treatment in jobs, politics and society.[11] Attesting to the successful acculturation of the Krio, Elizabeth Isichei has noted:[12]

> The way in which these Sierra Leoneans [*sic*] not only survived their traumatic experiences, but in a single generation mastered the language and skills of Europe so successfully that they became a prosperous professional and merchant elite, is a major triumph of the human spirit.

However, the growing racism of the nineteenth century, and the disastrous fall of a few prominent Krio men, made the British unwilling to accept the Krio as equals. In fact, they considered them superficial. Commenting on the political maturity of the Krio in 1898, Governor Frederic Cardew pontificated,

> it is dangerous to allow a people, a large number of whom are quite uneducated and have but recently emerged from barbarism and the remainder of whom with some few exceptions are only half educated and civilized (the worst), to be imbued with the idea (of democracy). And from my experience of over four years in this colony I do not think the people are sufficiently advanced for local or representative government; they cannot appreciate its benefits, as is evidenced by their attempt to work a municipality.[13]

Admittedly, this broad side from Cardew must be seen in the context of his disenchantment with the Krio, whom he believed had fomented the Hut Tax War of that year. But he was merely subscribing to similar views which had been expressed thirty years previously by, for example, the influential traveller/writer Richard F. Burton.[14] The Krio, then, were not given political

18

and social recognition. At best where these were conceded by the British it was done grudgingly.

Thus, the government operating in the British Crown Colony of Sierra Leone in the nineteenth century was a far cry from Granville Sharpe's optimistic hope for a self-governing black community.[15] First, the experiment of partnership in company rule gave way to Crown Colony government in 1808. The Order-in-Council provided for a Governor and an Advisory Council consisting of the Colonial Secretary and Chief Justice, and one unofficial member chosen by the governor, 'from the most considerable of the Protestant inhabitants of the colony' (Royal Instructions of 1811). Despite certain restraining constitutional provisions, the Governor exercised extensive political power. In contrast to the pre-Crown Colony era when, at least up to 1799, faint-hearted, even if sometimes well-meaning, attempts were made to conciliate African opinion by appointing them to junior magistracies and allowing some sort of 'representative assembly', Crown Colony government made no such concessions to African political aspirations; that is, if we overlook the sole exception of Charles Heddle, a mulatto who was appointed an unofficial member to the governor's Council in 1846–71. The Council doubled as an executive and legislative body, and it was this type of administration which governed Sierra Leone until 1863.[16]

The modern constitutional history of Sierra Leone began in 1863 when the British Parliament inaugurated a new constitution for the colony. It expanded the Governor's Council to become a Legislative Council comprising his four advisers and three or four unofficials nominated by the Governor, cognisance being taken when appointing 'not only those who are most likely to support the government but those who will be taken to represent and will really inform you of the wishes of the more intelligent portion of the community'.[17] Whether or not London was responding to pressures from nascent activists, or the constitution was one of those timely concessions that sometimes give the impression of a far-seeing ruling authority, the significance of the 1863 development is that it gave an opportunity to men, well qualified, who would not have been elected since there was no provision for this, to participate in the legislative exercise of their country. Thirty years later a Municipal Corporation was also conceded to the citizens.[18]

The second half of the nineteenth century was the apogee of Krio affluence and articulateness. How wide a degree of political influence they had is doubtful.[19] Certainly, some members of the elite had friends in the local administration; probably, and sometimes, their advice was listened to.[20] But with their vocal press, their wealth, status and education, a reasonable number of Africans could pass all the tests of an accomplished middle class: the Ezzidios, the I. B. Pratts, the Malamah Thomases, the Sawyerrs, the Betts, the Brights, the Grants and Lewises – names of Africans who had secured remarkable achievements for themselves, read like a roll of honour.

And so there was no wanting of candidates for nomination into the Legislative Council. Indeed, Africans did collaborate with their white counterparts at the time when Black/White relations were still reasonably good, to form a Mercantile Association in 1851, to defend their interests. It was this Association which elected the first African member, John Ezzidio, a wealthy merchant, to sit in the Legislative Council. But this demonstration of incipient political maturity did not go down well with Whitehall, partly because the political philosophy at the time was strongly hostile towards democratic tendencies, and partly because the administration was afraid that a member elected by a mercantile class would only seek the interests of that class to the disadvantage of other sections of the society. Therefore, the action was not to be seen as a constitutional precedent to be followed. However, Ezzidio's successor, William 'Independent' Grant, was also associated with the merchants, and he could therefore be said to be their representative.[21]

The 1863 constitution remained unchanged for the next sixty-one years. Still, it gave an opportunity to Africans to have a forum to express their views on policies, to challenge some administrative decisions, to check an abuse of power in 'disregard of all local opinion', and to make suggestions.[22] On the whole between 1863 and 1924 not less than fifteen Africans were nominated as unofficial members of the Legislative Council. Some, like Samuel Lewis, held the seat for as long as twenty-one years. After Ezzidio, the other Africans honoured with the distinction of nominated members were William 'Independent' Grant (1870–8); W. Lumpkin (1870–7); Syble Boyle (1870–9); I. B. Pratt (1880–1); T. J. Sawyerr (1882–94); Sir Samuel Lewis (1882–1903); T. Colenzo Bishop (1894–8); A. S. Hebron (1899–1906); J. J. Thomas (1901–16); C. E. Wright (1903–11); J. H. (Malamah) Thomas (1907–12); A. J. Sawyerr (1911–24); E. H. Cummings (1912–24); and C. May (1921–4).[23]

M. Wight has explained that a Legislative Council in a Crown Colony like Sierra Leone was not a sovereign legislature, but that it was 'sovereign within its power'. In other words, it could only legislate for what was allowed it by the Imperial Parliament. Since policies were determined at Downing Street, the local administration merely implemented these, though of course a margin of initiative was conceded to them to suit local requirements. With his built-in official majority of government officers, augmented by unofficial nominated members who were expected 'to support government in general policy and not oppose it on any important question without strong and substantial reasons', the governor could virtually carry through any measure in the Legislative Council. To put it baldly, the 'capacity of the unofficial members is really advisory. The main function of the Council is the ventilation of grievances'. Fyfe also noted a subtle but far-reaching change in 1896, after the appointment of an Attorney-General:

> It became the practice for government bills to be discussed and approved in the Executive Council before he introduced them into the Legislative. Thus debates

20

became a formal adjustment of measures already decided, rather than legislative deliberations, the senior official members, their assent already given, tending to resent criticisms as a slight on their abilities, the unofficial made to feel they were opponents not partners.[24]

Professor Tamuno's study of the Legislative Council confirms the analysis of Wight. But he even goes further to argue that granted that there were these constraints on effective parliamentary manoeuvre, 'unofficial members, particularly the African members, made half hearted attempts to impress upon the government the need for economy. These attempts, we emphasize, were neither impressive nor effective on a large scale.'[25]

Tamuno no doubt came to such a conclusion after considered judgement based on research; but, even so, such a general statement is hardly true of the early Legislative Council Representatives in Sierra Leone. Some did take their jobs seriously and, though they believed, like Ezzidio, Lewis, and Grant, that their role was to help the government, where they could, yet they were stout defenders of the interests of their people. Hargreaves' study of Sir Samuel Lewis, the first Black African to be knighted by a British monarch, underlines this point.[26] Lewis, for example, believed that nominated members did not 'study to oppose any and every measure proposed by government but rather to give it frank support whenever they can honestly do so'.[27] They could also be very critical of government policies as was demonstrated during the Hut Tax War of 1898. Not only that, but inside and outside the Legislative Council, Grant, Ezzidio and, more important, Lewis, inspired and identified themselves with great issues of the day such as agriculture, affairs of the hinterland and, in the case of Lewis, the Freetown Municipality question.[28] Officialdom did not always listen to their advice and suggestions, but sometimes their contributions were appreciated. And when they left the Legislative Council, they bequeathed a creditable record of legislative competence to their successors which these tried to emulate. If less success crowned their efforts, one must remember that by the turn of the century anti-Krio sentiments in the establishment had crystallised considerably. Whatever the Krio did would not impress the administration.[29]

Besides, to really effect changes in policy, apart from ensuring a parliamentary majority, one had to have an organised force to exert pressure on the government. In the nineteenth century there were no such things as political parties. Though the people of Freetown were politically conscious and vociferously articulate, they had not yet, in the nineteenth century, attained that level of political sophistication that would make for mass involvement or political mobilisation. But when they made the effort it is a moot point whether, because of their hostile attitude to nascent political mobilisation, the British authorities helped, if they did not hamper, the political education of their protégés. As Fyfe has observed:

In Sierra Leone, as elsewhere in the colonies, the government in London neglected the chance of training up a people in friendly partnership with their

21

Administrators, shutting their eyes to Burke's picture of the state as a partnership in all science; a partnership in all art; a partnership in every virtue, and in all perfection.[30]

Nevertheless, active citizens, in and out of the Legislative Council, endeavoured to articulate their grievances through *ad hoc* committees and associations, the Church (for instance, the Native Pastorate Crisis of the middle of the nineteenth century),[31] mass petitions, memorials, memoranda, delegations to London, private visits of individuals to London to lobby friends and acquaintances to champion the colony's interests and, of course, most important, the newspaper. Attempts were also made at organised pressure. Sometimes they took the form of cultural movements, for example, the Dress Reform Society (1887) which not only extolled the African's pride in his race and culture, but also produced some notable activists. The line dividing the Society's kind of activity and political protest was very thin indeed.[32] More examples of positive public efforts can be given: the Sierra Leone Mercantile Association, a middle-class organisation set up in 1851 as a collaborative effort of black and white merchants, had its wrists slapped when it aspired to play a constitutional role in electing the first African to sit in the Legislative Council as a nominated member in 1863.[33] It became moribund until June 1892 when it was inaugurated as the Sierra Leone Chamber of Commerce, with a large African membership. The leading African merchants, incipient activists, and fathers of future political agitators, were all members of this organisation.[34] The Sierra Leone Bar Association had been in existence – along with other professional bodies – before 1899, but really came alive in 1919 'to further the interests of the practising Bar and to strengthen the profession in the discharge of the duties it owes to the community'.[35] More grass-roots level organisation was represented by the Carpenters' Defensive Union (1885). S. H. A. Case's modest Trade Union effort, the Mechanics Alliance (1884), with a newspaper of its own, *The Artisan*, had a brief life.[36] The West End Limba and Limited Creole Society (1916) was a much later development in the early part of this century. In fact it was in this era that organised groups with political/professional/economic and cultural orientations began to emerge.[37] Martin Kilson dates this phenomenon from 1909, though in 1908 the Sierra Leone Native Defence Force had been founded to initiate and promote 'the thought and actions of the people'.[38] The following surfaced during this period: the Civil Servants' Association (1907–9); Abayomi-Cole's Sierra Leone Farmers' Association (1904–9); the Rate Payers' Association (1909); the West End Benevolent Society (1917); the African Progress Union (1919); the Emergency Fund Committee in 1918, and the proposed Sierra Leone Inter-tribal Association (of Colony and Protectorate peoples) set up to fight the Criminal Code introduced in that year;[39] the Sierra Leone Agricultural Society (1922: resuscitated in 1924 with a membership open to Colony and Protectorate citizens); the Sierra Leone Aborigines' Society (1924); the Young People's Progressive Union (1929); and the National Congress of

British West Africa (1920). In the Protectorate, the Committee of Educated Aborigines (C.E.A.) was founded by educated citizens in the Northern Province in 1922, while P.E.P.U., founded in 1929 by Southern Province inhabitants, had a brief existence. It was reconstituted in 1946.

These organisations were undoubtedly relevant to the causes they championed and they may have had, in varying degrees, some success at representation. Certainly, the Rate Payers Association set up to organise the election of candidates into the Municipal Council, established in 1893, was successful in this limited objective and more. And the agricultural pressure groups did come out with some useful suggestions for an agricultural policy. The loud protests made by organised groups against the Criminal Code in 1918–20 also did succeed in getting the government to put off its implementation. But there was one big flaw in early twentieth-century mobilisation efforts – they had no sustaining character. In this regard, newspapers consistently bewailed the jerky and intermittent existence of organisations to no avail.[40] Organisations appeared to burn brightly in the heat of the moment and then flicker and die a natural death due to disuse and lack of sustained leadership.[41] In fact, none of the examples given above, notwithstanding some evidence of occasional brilliance, matched the endurance and impact of the Congress, whose moment was yet to come in the inter-war years.

However, in the nineteenth century, and in the first half of the present century, the newspaper was the most powerful and effective weapon of pressure, of articulation. Fred I. Omu, a historian of the press in West Africa, makes this remark about newspaper owners in colonial Africa: 'Those who conducted them reasoned that, in the absence of a democratically elected government, the press was the most effective constitutional weapon for ventilating grievances and influencing the trend of events.'[42] The nineteenth-century activists used the press to advantage: Blyden, Horton, William Rainy, William 'Independent' Grant, J. C. May, Sir Samuel Lewis, and T. J. Sawyerr were the most outstanding publicists of their era.[43] Their sons and kinsmen continued the tradition in the succeeding century, for instance, Cornelius May, brother of the founder of the *Sierra Leone Weekly News* (J. C. May, 1884), who went on to be Mayor of Freetown and nominated member of the Legislative Council.[44] Others, if not newspaper barons themselves, used the press extensively, such as E. S. Beoko-Betts, A. E. Tuboku-Metzger, D. T. Arkeboh Betts, a local historian, Orishatukeh Faduma, and Professor Abayomi Cole. Indeed, as already noted, Freetown held an enviable record of a good and effective press dating as far back as 1801 when the government first issued its *Royal Gazette*. By the second half of the nineteenth century over half the existing newspapers were owned or run by Africans. And, according to Martin Kilson, by 1900 Sierra Leone's educated population had seen about thirty-four newspapers at different times. Some of these, owned by Africans, including Grant's *West African Reporter* (1874–84); T. J. Sawyerr's *The Negro and the Sierra Leone Weekly*

Advertiser (1861); the Afro-West Indian, William Rainy's *The Sierra Leone Observer and Commercial Advocate*; J. C. May's *The Sierra Leone Weekly News* (1884–1951); H. A. Case's *The Artisan* (1884–8); and *The Sierra Leone Times* (1890–1912), edited by J. A. Fitzjohn and financed by J. H. Malamah Thomas.[45] To these were added by the turn of the century, *The Sierra Leone Guardian and Foreign Mails* (1900), edited by J. S. Labor; T. J. Thompson's *The Colonial and Provincial Reporter* and *The West African Mail and Trade Gazette*; a monthly magazine, *The Creole Boy*; and Bright's *Aurora*.

Some of these newspapers were short-lived. One, for instance, *The Sierra Leone Ram* (1886) only came out once.[46] But there was one outstanding characteristic about the Freetown press: it managed to maintain a high quality of reportage. Its literary output was very high, and its prose elegant. The production, presentation, and content of Freetown newspapers in the nineteenth and early twentieth centuries were decidedly more superior technically and intellectually than more recent efforts. As if compensating for the absence of elected representation, the press made an invaluable contribution to the development of politics in Sierra Leone by creating a forum through which the grievances of the people could be aired. No subject was beyond the competence of its contributors. Abayomi Cole's articles on metaphysics, for instance, 'the Philosophy of Paganism', on culture and religion, which discussed topics like polygamy and African esoterica, A. E. Tuboku-Metzger's informed treatises on government policies and institutions in the Colony and Protectorate, J. C. Shorunkeh-Sawyerr's satirical exposés on government policies, and for light-hearted trivia, an advert in the *Weekly News* (22 September 1894) warning shopkeepers and others that John Macauley, alias *Taka Wuroh*, a great swindler and notorious burgler, was on the loose, reflected the variety, depth and embracing nature of newspaper reportage. In contrast to the insipid and obsequious banalities that seem to fill more contemporary papers, newspapers in our period of review carried well-thought-out articles on every facet of government, written by leading citizens and ordinary folk. The double standards of colonial rule and discrimination received maximum exposure. Suggestions were also made for the conception and implementation of an agriculture policy, and other economic endeavours.[47] Perhaps as an example of nascent tourism and visual history, a reader, J. B. Chinsman, even suggested that the City Council should buy Bunce Island from the colonial government so that its caves and tombstones could be preserved as historical monuments of the slave trade. Such vivid reminders could help to enlighten the people on the horrors of the nefarious traffic in humanity as no book could. Chinsman also recommended the setting up of a farm on the island.[48] Useful suggestions such as Chinsman's were quite common in the papers at this time; and, of course, this dismisses the charges of indifference sometimes levelled against colony inhabitants.

Papers like the May family newspaper, the *Weekly News*, managed to maintain a high level of respectability and restraint. Its criticism of government policy, when it deemed it wrong, was no less fierce, for all that. And because of its more balanced editorial and presentation of views, it even received a left-handed compliment from the colonial government.[49] By the 1920s it had secured for itself the distinct title of the 'best newspaper in West Africa'.[50]

On the other hand, newspaper criticisms could be vitriolic, so extreme as to border on the scurrilous. And colonial authorities were not noted for their sufferance of criticism. The Sierra Leone government was no exception to this general rule. Indeed, the incessant harassing by the press became so uncomfortable that one governor referred to the Freetown press as 'a very unruly member' of the community.[51] One paper, the irreverent *Aurora*, was particularly notorious for its acerbity, radicalism and waspish criticism of the establishment. This four-paged tabloid, founded and edited by Bankole-Bright, succeeded in surpassing its contemporaries in its criticisms of the government.[52] Strident in its demands, vituperative in its presentation of juicy titbits on official indiscretions, it soon assumed the dubious reputation of the worst rag sheet in Freetown. In official eyes, the *Aurora*'s main *raison d'être* was to watch out for any error or weakness on the part of the European official and then to criticise it in its columns. If the type of journalism favoured by the *Aurora*'s Editor/Proprietor angered and dismayed the government, it, however, made one lasting contribution to politics in Sierra Leone: it was a formative influence on the career of Bankie's political rival in the 30s, I. T. A. Wallace-Johnson.[53] This says much for the youthful vigour of the *Aurora* and its impact on the young.[54] Unfortunately, the *Aurora* did not survive for long. In 1925 Bankole-Bright handed over the editorship to E. T. E. Nelson-Williams.[55] It continued publication for a couple of years more, but it appears not to have gone beyond 1927.

On the whole, to be fair, the government did not make many overt attempts to muzzle the press, at least up to the time of Wallace-Johnson's irruption in the late 30s. However, it viewed the press with extreme distaste, and officials very much resented its criticism.[56] Generally, the colonial administration tended to ignore positive and wholesome suggestions from newspapers, and this contemptuous attitude and obvious lack of enlightened response was indeed unfortunate.[57] It made no small contribution to the worsening of Anglo–Krio relations on the one hand, and the under-development of the territory, on the other. Granted that it is the nature of newspapers to sensationalise issues, to exaggerate and overstate their cases, the fact is that by the turn of the century there were real burning issues of immediate relevance to the people that needed to be discussed and be resolved. Given the fact that there was no elected representation to put them through, newspapers sought to raise and articulate these questions.

On the question of elected representation articulate citizens argued that nominated representation was inadequate for their needs. Conceding that these nominees sometimes sought the interests of fellow citizens, they, at the same time, also pointed to the fact that as government nominees their first allegiance was to the administration. To this end, therefore, an elective legislature, part or whole, was long overdue. And, because of a pressing need to solve the questions of the day, aspirants demanded a greater say in the government of the country through elected representatives.[58] They argued that the limited concession of an elected Municipality with an African majority was a long way off in satisfying these demands. Besides, the competence of the City Council was limited by the very narrow areas of performance accorded it, and by the overriding authority of the central government.[59] The issue of elected representation was therefore very much a vocal topic in the Legislative Council and in the press in the early part of the twentieth century.

Political aspirations apart, the turn of the century introduced an unwelcome phenomenon – social distance between the white administrators and the Krio elite. Though, of course, there had been some incidents in previous years, Black/White relations had been generally wholesome in the nineteenth century. But during the second half of the last century the growth of racial bigotry and the onward march of the 'new imperialism' gave rise to a more discriminatory attitude by colonial rulers to educated Africans in their possessions. And in the Sierra Leone context this generally meant the Krio.[60] They were maligned and disparaged as 'B. A. Dunelms',[61] 'savvy niggers', 'The scourge of the coast', and 'descendants of slaves.'[62] The lapses of a few well-placed Krio elites were used as evidence to discredit the whole group.[63] Residential discrimination was added to contempt when, in 1904, on the ostensible grounds of combatting a health hazard, Europeans were evacuated from the city and rehabilitated in an exclusive residential area at Hill Station. This beautiful hill-top arcadia had a sweeping panoramic view of Freetown. And it was linked with the capital by a mountain railway, built at great cost, and run for the exclusive convenience of the white residents.[64] This shift of the European population obviously affected the financial position of the Krio house owners who could not now rent their houses to the government for their white employees. But, more important, this social segregation was regarded as an affront. E. M. Mereweather, for instance, was a governor who was notorious for his deep prejudices. He never liked the Krios; and he discontinued the practice of his predecessors, Leslie Probyn and G. B. Haddon-Smith, of inviting leading Krio citizens to 'At Homes' in Government House, because they 'had partaken freely of his drinks and cigars'. Such churlishness did not endear the Europeans to the Krio elites, who believed that with their education, wealth, and status, they were the equals of white administrators. Thus, when Governor R. J. Wilkinson arrived in Freetown to assume office in March 1916, he was greeted with the advice that he must not allow himself to be influenced 'for the worse' by others; and for that reason he should reside at Fort Thornton, not at Hill Station which 'is the compound provided for, and occupied by, European officials as if you are sent to be their governor not ours'. And then a long list of questions that he must look into followed, for example, the poor health

26

conditions in the city, the sorry plight of the Protectorate, and native industries. Finally, he was lectured by the writer thus: 'The People called Creoles [*sic*], are peculiar, and you have enough time to study and know them; therefore, treat them as you would your own people, and remember this; they are made by God to enjoy all the blessings of his life as any other God's hand made in any part of the globe.'[65] Wilkinson did not heed this advice.

Job discrimination was another sore point. Krio parents, at great cost to themselves, had sent their children to pursue professional courses, believing that there was a demand for their talent, only to find when they returned that the door was slammed in their faces. Largely because of prevalent racial theories and prejudices the West African Medical Staff was set up in 1902. It became a white preserve, and African doctors, however brilliant, were excluded from that service.[66] Even the eminent African doctor, a Sierra Leonean, Dr W. Awunor-Renner, who acted as P.M.O. (Gold Coast) was denied the respect he merited.[67] Only one African, a mulatto, E. J. Wright, born and bred in England, was appointed as a Medical Officer in W.A.M.S. and given terms normally enjoyed by European officers, because he was coloured, and because it would '*pro tanto* help to contradict the colour bar accusation'.[68]

Few African lawyers were given jobs in government services in Sierra Leone because it was 'undesirable to do so'.[69] The first permanent appointment to the bench was E. S. Beoku-Betts in 1937, though acting capacities were filled by Africans, for example, S. J. S. Barlatt. In order to eat, Sierra Leonean doctors and lawyers had to open private practices or emigrate to Nigeria and the Gold Coast where, for some strange reasons, not merely explained by the fact that they provided the educated personnel required for these jobs, they seemed to be able to assume more responsible positions. Examples are too many to list here, but L. E. V. MaCarthy, a barrister son of a former judge advocate in Sierra Leone, was appointed a Crown Counsel within two years of arriving at the Gold Coast;[70] W. Awunor-Renner, the doctor's son, had been refused appointment in Sierra Leone despite his persistent and spirited attempts to seek employment in the Legal Department, or as a District Officer. He got the job of Police Magistrate at Winneba, Gold Coast, in 1921, within a short time of going to that colony.[71] Lower down the scale, Ben T. During, First Class Senior Clerk, a Sierra Leonean who had worked continuously for eighteen and a half years, for fourteen of which he was chief clerk in Nigeria, could not get a comparable post in Sierra Leone when he expressed a wish to return home. He was told that 'vacancies in the higher grades of the Native Staff in the colony are of comparatively rare occurrence'.[72]

It was also government policy, after the experiment Governor Probyn initiated of appointing African Assistant District Commissioners had lapsed, following the retirement of the last incumbent, A. E. Tuboku-Metzger, in 1917, not to appoint Africans to the administrative cadre for the specious reason that they did not have sufficient character to be appointed as junior Administrative Officers. In any case, they, that is, Krio officers, would not command the respect of the native chiefs.[73] 'In my opinion', stated W. D. Ellis, an official in the Colonial Office, 'Freetown Creoles are worse than useless as Administrative Officers in the Sierra Leone Protectorate where they are both hated and despised.'[74] It was a policy that was consistently followed up to the attainment of Independence, even though in the other African colonies like the Gold Coast and Nigeria, Africans had been appointed to administrative posts in the forties. And, in Sierra Leone, the governor had also declared in 1945: 'Provided Africans possess the qualifications prescribed respectively for the administrative and other unified services, there is no bar to their appointment to these services.'[75]

It is not a justification, but the obvious reluctance of Government to appoint Krio aspirants to administer the Protectorate is better understood if one recalls that the territory was divided into two and administered under different laws and customs. After the Colony was established the British Government had been reluctant to extend its rule into the interior though urged to do so by eminent Krio personalities like Sir Samuel Lewis, not only to guarantee the economic survival of Freetown, but also to spread the ameliorating influence of European Civilisation. However, in 1896, Britain proclaimed a Protectorate over the hinterland of Sierra Leone, primarily to forestall French expansion in the backyard of the British possession, and because of a belated realisation that the latter's economic future depended on the annexation of the interior.[76] In the peninsula, the present western area, British institutions, British law, western concepts, religion, and civilisation, that overlay basic African traditional values, were the norm.[77] By 1853 the Colony inhabitants were acknowledged as British subjects. Juxtaposed with this largely literate and western-oriented society was a basically traditional society under one colonial administration. This situation of two peoples with different outlooks implied that there would be stresses and strains, prejudices and attitudes. There was definitely a cultural hiatus; the Krio were guilty of ethnic arrogance, derived mainly out of the belief that they possessed a superior culture civilisation to that of the interior peoples and that they were so many distances removed from their less fortunate brethren.[78] And, of course, when it suited them, the Church and the administration encouraged the Krio to hold on to such beliefs.[79] Furthermore, the cultural differential was compounded by the differences in laws and the complex and untidy administrative divisions which governed the two peoples: the Protectorate Ordinance (1901), the Protectorate Courts Jurisdiction Ordinance (1903),and the Protectorate Native Law Ordinance (1905), a set of codes and regulations, governed the Protectorate. Cognisance was given to some traditional laws and customs. Under this set of codes that operated in the interior, a Colony-born resident could have an uncomfortable stay in the Protectorate.[80] More important, the colonial administration was afraid of Krio influence in the Protectorate and it did all it could to discourage it by all sorts of ordinances, by disparaging the Krio to the Protectorate people, by designating the one 'non-native' or 'Colony born', and the other 'native' or 'aborigine'. The Bo School was founded specifically for Protectorate boys, where they were taught to eschew everything associated with the Colony inhabitants and to follow their tribal inclinations.[81] In other words, British policy deliberately fostered antagonism between the two peoples.

On the other hand, as it has been argued elsewhere, this did not stop the Krio from showing an interest in the Protectorate. There were personal relationships, even blood relations, between Colony and Protectorate inhabitants; matters relevant to the Protectorate were raised in the Legislative Council and discussed in the newspapers.[82] In fact, the papers in this period made a lot of noise about the needs of the Protectorate. For instance, they complained about the inadequate health facilities and the absence of a good educational infra-structure in the interior. Unfortunately, the Krio were predestined to play the role of hostages to history, and so their good intentions were sometimes misinterpreted.[83] A good example of this was the Hut Tax War of 1898 fought by the Protectorate against the advance of colonial rule. The Krios were roundly condemned by the government for inciting the Protectorate to rebel against British rule. Ironically, it was these very Krio, these trouble makers, who suffered the most when in that rebellion hundreds were massacred by the Mendes and Temnes, largely, it was believed, because they represented the onslaught of western culture and imperialism. The suspicion and hostility resulting from this incident had a lasting effect on Colony/Protectorate relations.[84] This may have disappeared with time, but the institutionalising of divisive policies, in law, status and administration, made people see themselves as being different and separate. And so the dichotomy of politics in Sierra Leone is a colonial inheritance.

Socially ostracised, their professionals suppressed and maligned, the Krios' pre-eminent economic position in the nineteenth century was grievously eroded by Lebanese (they were known locally as Syrians) competition at the turn of the century. The Lebanese came to Sierra Leone in the 1890s and they moved about the streets of Freetown as itinerant hawkers selling coral beads (hence they were known as 'Corals'). But, by the first quarter of this century, this bedraggled group of immigrants had, through thrift, co-operative effort, solidarity, business acumen, and perhaps questionable business tactics, supplanted the Krio commercial mandarins of the nineteenth century. No doubt they were helped by the favours they received from the Establishment and European commercial firms.[85] However, because of their success and their unfortunate arrogant disposition they incurred the wrath of the Krio. No question was more galling than the Syrian question in this period judging from the frequency of its appearance in the newspapers, and the dramatic confrontations this gave rise to – for instance, the Anti-Syrian riots of 1919.[86]

Commenting on these concerns, the note in newspapers was sombre, plaintive, querulous, often defiant, and sometimes plainly aggressive. But it was not all gripe. Positive suggestions were also made to bring about changes; for instance, that made by A. J. Shorunkeh-Sawyerr, to unify the two halves of the territory to give equal status and opportunity to the inhabitants;[87] also that suggesting a change of the legal system, especially the repeal of the Assessors Ordinance. Of great importance were the suggestions for agricultural reform. It was much discussed in the press, and the evidence does suggest that the Krio initiated a positive attitude to agricultural policy in Sierra Leone. Preoccupation with agricultural questions in this period recalled the pioneering days of Sir Samuel Lewis, 'Independent' Grant and A. Abayomi-Cole, all of them agricultural enthusiasts.

Popularly known as Jesus-passing-by because of his propagation of the holy gospel, Abayomi-Cole was a versatile intellectual, a jack of all trades. His boundless energy sustained an impressive list of literary essays. He published numerous treatises on agriculture and concocted recipes for making soap and brandy! He acted on a number of occasions as a government scout in search of suitable plantation sites and was made a correspondent of the Imperial Institute on the recommendation of Governor Probyn. Cole was also noted for his experiments on food to diversify and improve the diet of Sierra Leoneans and for his campaign against the mosquito. Professor Cole was the motivating force behind the movement to form agricultural organisations.[88]

Another enthusiast, a Krio merchant, reputedly the richest African of his day, was the eccentric recluse, S. B. Abuke Thomas of Wellington. He was convinced of the absolute need to improve agriculture, and when he died he left over £50,000 to found an Agricultural College at Mabang to teach Agricultural Science to Krio boys. Unfortunately, the dream of this far-seeing pioneer was not given the support it merited. The disused building of quaint architecture along the old Railway Line at Mabang is the only testimony to the memory of Abuke Thomas and his dreams.[89]

These problems filled the papers at the time, but they were not peculiar to Sierra Leone. They were common to all the British West African Colonies, with the possible exception of two which were more exclusive to colonial Sierra Leone: the Syrian question and the Colony/Protectorate rift. The common factor in the experiences of the four dependencies was buttressed by the fact that the first educated elites of West Africa shared the same background: they were missionary educated; they went to the same schools, the C.M.S. Grammar School (1845) and the M.B.H.S. (1874) until similar schools were founded in their respective colonies. They had familial links, for example, the Dove, Awunor-Renner, Easmon and Casely-Hayford families of the Gold Coast and Sierra Leone. Socially, they belonged to the bourgeoisie and they manifested this by a display of middle-class pretensions. Finally, they had a cosmopolitan outlook. They were West Africans. All these factors inspired leaders of the four colonies to organise a movement to articulate their grievances against the colonial administration, to act as a pressure group, to make demands that would reflect the interests of the

30

people, to agitate for the sharing of authority with the Imperial Power. This, then, was the background from which the first proto-nationalist pan-West-African Movement – The National Congress of British West Africa – emerged in 1920.

3

Politics in earnest: the setting up of the N.C.B.W.A., 1919–1924

The N.C.B.W.A.

It is one of the ironies of colonialism that at the time when the Imperial Power, Britain, was engaged in a titanic struggle with Wilhelmine Germany, her African subjects made no overt attempt to overthrow her rule. This is not to say that they did not have reasons enough to revolt; and certainly there were a few disaffected areas in the Gold Coast (Ghana) and Nigeria, where disaffection erupted into violent demonstrations;[1] there were also faint rumblings of political challenge. But to a large degree Britain's West African subjects loyally supported her war effort, convinced that she was fighting for the liberty of the free world of which they were a part. Dr J. K. Randle, a Sierra Leone immigrant practising medicine in Lagos, summed up the feelings of his articulate colleagues thus:

> The fact must however, not be disguised, even here, that in recent years the administration of the government of this colony has not given the people entire satisfaction. The people see that government is not carried in their interest. But, however painfully true this is, let us not forget the wider principle that we are citizens of the British Empire[2]

The note is querulous, but the statement also implied an undeclared truce.

In Sierra Leone, a strong emotional upsurge led to a public call for the formation of a Krio regiment – 'The King's Own Creole Boys', 'to fight, and if possible die, for our Gracious King and good old England'[3] A. J. Shorunkeh-Sawyerr, Nominated African Member of the Legislative Council, was jubilant over the demise of the German ship, *Professor Woermann*, when it was torpedoed by H.M.S. *Caenarvon* on 27 August 1914.[4] Dr M. C. F. Easmon, a Sierra Leone doctor, among others, saw active service with the troops in the Cameroons during the war. Sierra Leoneans believed that the Great War was their war.

This euphoria, however, soured at the end of the war when the hopes of educated Africans were rudely shattered by the indifference of the colonial powers to their demands and aspirations. Articulate Africans had supported Britain during the war hoping that in return for this loyalty some political concession would be given to them after its conclusion. They were soon disillusioned when it became clear that Britain was not ready to recognize the claims of her subjects to share power with her. For that matter, it appeared that Woodrow Wilson's demand for self-determination for subject peoples was limited to European peoples. It remained a platitude for Africans.[5] And when British and Commonwealth leaders patted each others' backs and lauded the unique imperial destiny of Britain, her system of government, the freedom and unity shared in her 'United Nations of the Empire', they were clearly referring to the white dominions. Scant regard was given to her African subjects.[6] Moreover, the war, primarily a European conflict, caused a great deal of dislocation and economic distress in the African colonies; and the immediate post-war years were a harrowing experience for Britain's African subjects, occasioned by strikes, riots and food shortages.

The trauma induced by this background of tragedy, economic and social distress, diminishing hopes and disillusion, was given a psychological lift by the new awareness and rising expectations demonstrated by Black Peoples all over the world. This phenomenon was epitomised by such pan-Africanist movements as those led by Du Bois and Marcus Garvey. The demythologising of the Whiteman's superiority in the experience of African combatants, and the consequent rise of African Nationalism, also provided the ingredients for an awareness that served as a positive inspiration and impetus to the educated African elites to found an organisation that would agitate and secure for them a share in the government of their territories.[7] In March 1920 delegates from the four British West African Colonies resolved to found a National Congress of British West Africa, *inter alia*, for 'the better and more effective representation of our people' in the affairs concerning them, and the promotion of unity among them.[8]

The idea of founding a Congress was first mooted in 1914 in a discussion between J. E. Casely-Hayford, a barrister from the Gold Coast, generally regarded as the founding-father of the Congress, Dr Akiwande Savage, a Nigerian doctor of Sierra Leone descent, and F. W. Dove, a Sierra Leonean barrister, while they were on a ship. There was no follow up because of the war.[9] In the meantime people had begun to question the African's place in the British Empire; there was a growing clamour for fuller citizenship for Africans in that polity.[10] On 29 September 1917, an open invitation was sent out by the *Gold Coast Leader* to the four British West African Colonies summoning delegates to a conference.[11] The response was positive, but the degree of enthusiasm for the Congress idea varied from colony to colony.[12]

Much has been written about the Congress. Kimble, Kilson, Eluwa, Ayodele Langley, and Olusanya have discussed it in its pan-West African context or regional form. All have stressed its elitism, its bourgeois orientation, its narrow outlook, and its apparent inability to establish a popular framework. The present work questions the rigidity of these views as they relate to Sierra Leone.[13]

Many people in Sierra Leone regretted that the initiative for the founding

33

of this pan-West African movement did not come from that country, being Britain's 'oldest colony', and whose Krio inhabitants, because of their long association with the West, and their lead in education and western civilisation, should have rightly assumed the leadership of this resurgence.[14] Critics suggested that 'indifference to public affairs' and selfishness were to blame for this omission.[15] These comments, as it has been argued elsewhere, should be accepted with reservation. But, on the other hand, certain basic and pertinent questions were raised about the efficacy of such a movement.[16] In the heady atmosphere of generated enthusiasm they seemed fractious, but in retrospect they were realistic, for they reflected the peculiar circumstances of the Sierra Leone colony which were nothing like those in the other territories. For instance, going into the heart of the matter, 'Rambler', a regular columnist in the *Weekly News*, insisted that before one talked about a West African Congress the first priority must be 'union between the classes and the masses, between the high and low; between the rich and poor, and mark well, *between the people of the Colony and the people of the Protectorate*, if Sierra Leone is to make any headway'.[17]

Rambler's grasp of realities and his prophetic reservations proved all too accurate, because it was essentially on this question of 'representativeness' that the Congress foundered. More materialistic objections were raised by 'Oakbrook', another *Weekly News* contributor, who compared the proposed Congress to the 1814 Congress of Vienna; it was too large and too grandiose. He doubted whether there would be enough hard cash to sustain it.[18] These reservations were well meaning, but at the time when 'negro resurgence' and African solidarity were gathering momentum in the face of the contempt shown to educated Africans by racist white administrators, these forebodings threatened to distract people from the greater need for mobilisation.[19] Consequently, these warnings were swept aside and several preliminary meetings were held and a steering committee was eventually appointed in Freetown. By the end of 1918, the Sierra Leone Committee 'was way ahead of the others in organising for the conference'.[20] Not only that; as it happened, it was also the only branch to survive beyond the 1930s after the others had languished.[21]

The meetings of 29 April, and 6 May 1918 are important.[22] The first was chaired by A. S. Hebron, a barrister, and the first President of a resuscitated Sierra Leone Bar Association. It unanimously passed a resolution moved by J. A. Fitzjohn, a journalist,

> that this meeting of Sierra Leoneans welcomes the proposal of a West African Conference in the belief that it will have the effect of bringing the peoples in the British West African Colonies into closer union, of stimulating interest in matters concerning their common welfare and of giving increased weight to public opinion in West Africa; and further pledges itself to do all in its power to promote such a conference at as early a date as circumstances will permit.

The second meeting, again with A. S. Hebron presiding, nominated thirty names, and twelve men of 'repute' were elected by a show of hands. The following were thus founding members of the new organisations: J. H. Malamah-Thomas, a nominated member of the Legislative Council, eight times Mayor of Freetown, and a prominent and wealthy Krio businessman, A. S. Hebron and Cornelius May, editor and proprietor of *S.L.W.N.* (these three had generated enough enthusiasm, and had exerted some effort, to get interested people together); L. E. V. M'Carthy, the barrister son of the Queen's Advocate in Sierra Leone in the 1880s, soon to be appointed to a senior post in the Gold Coast; Professor Orishatukeh Faduma (W. J. Davies), educationalist and cultural nationalist; S. J. Coker, R. C. P. Barlatt; S. J. S. Barlatt, a barrister (elected Mayor 1919); Dr G. N. Metzger; A. E. Tuboku-Metzger, retired African Assistant District Commissioner, and a solid nationalist; J. A. Songo-Davies, retired African Assistant District Commissioner and amateur agriculturist; J. A. Fitzjohn, a journalist; Ven. Archdeacon Wilson; Reverends F. H. Johnson, J. B. Nicols, H. M. Steady, of the A.M.E. Mission, A. T. Sumner, the Mende linguist and father of the future Minister of Education, Doyle Sumner; Councillors E. A. C. Davies, E. A. C. Noah, D. C. Parker, and J. Jenkins-Johnston; Dr J. Abayomi-Cole (popularly addressed as Professor), cleric, herbalist, political pundit, a dietician, and agriculture propagandist; E. S. Beoku-Betts, a personable and urbane young barrister; M. S. Brown; H. Deen, an Imam; W. P. Golley; S. T. Jones; J. F. Knox; J. S. Labor, agriculture propagandist; J. B. Luke; T. J. Reffell; J. T. Richards; H. C. Solomon; and S. D. Turner. The Executive consisted of J. H. Malamah-Thomas, President, L. E. V. M'Carthy, General Secretary, and J. A. Songo-Davies, Treasurer. Thus, by February 1919, the Sierra Leone section had been established.

The list suggests a heavy representation of the professions and a significant proportion of clergymen – a point which underlines Ayandele's contention that 'the church was the incubator of African nationalism'.[23] Apart from one medical doctor and a cleric/native doctor, there was a sprinkling of a few retired civil servants. All these men shared one thing in common: they came from the top drawers of society – they were the elite; and this, of course, proved to be a structural and organisational weakness. On the other hand, some important people were missing, including prominent citizens like the redoubtable brothers, A. J. and J. C. Shorunkeh-Sawyerr, and E. H. Cummings (a former Mayor who had attended the first meeting) who kept themselves aloof for various reasons, not least because of personal feuds and mutual animosities – the bane of Krio co-operation.[24] Even Bright was initially excluded from the founding members of the Congress.[25]

The Protectorate was at first represented solely by A. T. Sumner, whose recent literary effort had received enthusiastic acclaim from the press. How long he remained in the Committee was not clear. Why his name ceased to appear in the list still needs to be explained, unless, of course, he was precluded from active participation because he was a government employee.[26] That the committee made an effort to get to the Protectorate is evident from an admission by the Secretariat in July 1920, that 'the committee in its present propaganda work has unfortunately been unable to reach the Protectorate and some of the villages, owing to the present season; but nevertheless communications have been exchanged and the work in these districts has been going on quietly'.[27] We do not have the registers of the local branch nor any of its papers to determine the size of its Protectorate membership, but views expressed in the *S.L.W.N.*, which is a major source of information for this episode in Sierra Leone history, and the documented membership of another Mende intellectual, the Reverend Max Gorvie, as well as the participation in Congress activities by Protectorate residents in the Colony, suggest that some Protectorate people were attracted to the movement.

The question of Protectorate representation in the Congress must nonetheless be pursued further, because the absence of an identifiable Protectorate caucus is one of the major criticisms levelled against the Congress politicians. It is instructive to recall, however, that in the other colonies, Congress membership consisted mostly, if not entirely, of coast dwellers, inhabitants in the Colony areas – Accra, Lagos and Bathurst (Banjul). The case of Freetown was therefore not unique. But it has often been argued that in the other colonies Congress politicians had ethnic and consanguineal links with interior dwellers, while those in Sierra Leone had no such links between the Colony and Protectorate. To this contention the present writer has argued elsewhere, as he will do in this work, that these assertions are obvious features that blind us from seeing areas of commonalities, of contact, and the identification of common interests between the two peoples.

Bankie's incursion into politics

A fuller discussion of the Protectorate theme will be more appropriately done in another section. A look at what was happening in the local Branch between 1919 and 1920 is called for at this point. By the latter date, Sierra Leone had picked her delegates to the Accra Meeting: F. W. Dove, a barrister, and leader of the delegation, L. E. V. M'Carthy and Bankole-Bright, 'the youngest member of the Sierra Leone Committee'. The inclusion of Bright in this delegation must have surprised many people because he had not shown much positive interest in the Congress idea; if anything, he had appeared hostile to it.[28] But a man with Bright's undoubted talents as a fearless and articulate critic of government, a newspaper editor who exposed the government in his paper, and a keen debater, could not be left out of the leadership. He was of positive value to the organisation. And so, naturally, within a short time of becoming a member Bright had dominated the Councils of the Sierre Leone Committee, even receiving precedence over much older and experienced politicians.[29]

The inaugural conference which took place in Accra from 11 to 29 March 1920 made a wide sweep of the problems and issues of moment in the Colonies.[30] In the conference sessions delegates presented papers on specific topics. Two papers were of particular relevance to Sierra Leone: Bankole-Bright's paper on 'Sanitary and Medical Reforms (the Segregation of races and the position of African Medical Practitioners in Government Service)', and Frederick Dove's paper on 'Syrian Immigration'. Bright's oratorical brilliance was employed to advantage in relating the woes, the frustrations, the needs, the complaints and the hopes of his African compatriots. Complaining was not enough. He also made suggestions on how the government could improve the medical services in the colonies; and it is important to state here that Bright's interest in medical and sanitary questions was sustained with remarkable consistency throughout his career. Dove's discussion of the Syrian question touched a sore point, made all the more poignant because it evoked fresh memories of the crisis of the previous year – the Anti-Syrian Riots of 1919 – and the false accusation that the government had made against the Krio elites of having engineered the civil disturbance. Clearly, Sierra Leoneans believed that the colonial government was to blame for the continued presence of an alien minority that had acquired an unassailable economic position in the territory and had repaid this by showing contempt and arrogance towards the inhabitants.[31] It was not the first, and it would not be the last time, that their expulsion was called for. The Syrian question was to remain a cancerous irritant throughout the colonial period.

At the end of the discussion of the papers presented, the meeting resolved itself into the National Congress of British West Africa for 'the better and more effective representation of our people'.[32] Numerous resolutions were passed – eighty-three in all – covering 'pretty well the whole field of African administration'.[33] The most important and significant of these resolutions dealt with those concerns which aimed at protecting the elite's socio-economic interests and enhancing their opportunities in a colonial society, but which, looked at more broadly, articulated and concretised the needs and aspirations of a burgeoning literate mass.[34]

The Congress put forward demands for: (a) a partly elective Legislative Council in each of the Colonies; (b) the establishment of an elected Municipal Council; (c) the setting up of a British West African Court of Appeal as well as a West African University to serve the four dependencies 'on such lines as would preserve in the students a sense of African Nationality'; (d) a West African Press Union; (e) the repatriation of the Syrians; (f) the separation of the executive arms of the administration from judicial functions; (g) the cessation of discrimination against Africans in the Civil Service: and (h) the amendment of certain obnoxious ordinances (for example, the Assessors' Ordinance of 1895). All these may have pandered to the class interests of the elite, but the larger gainers in the long run were the masses.[35] Most certainly, suggestions for compulsory education throughout the British West African Colonies and the raising of the standard of education in the schools, went beyond the exclusive pale of the elite.

But it took some time before even some of the more modest of the demands by Congress could be met, and a high-powered deputation had to be sent to the British government in London to argue the case of the African people. A delegation was picked, partly financed by donations, and partly by the personal contribution of key personalities in the colonies like T. Hutton Mills and F. W. Dove.[36] It comprised Hutton Mills, Casely-Hayford and H. Van Hein (Gold Coast); Chief Oluwa and Egerton Shyngle (Nigeria); E. F. Small and H. M. Jones (The Gambia); and Bankole-Bright and F. W. Dove (Sierra Leone). Bright's youthful vigour and his charismatic appeal must have impressed his much older colleagues for them to appoint him as Secretary-General of the London delegation.[37]

The delegation was empowered to seek the aid of solicitors in London to advise them on reforms, such as elective representation, and 'to take such preliminary steps and undertake such propaganda work, and to do all acts necessary and expedient' to secure their objectives. It kept within this brief, and even went beyond it, in the personal lobbying efforts of the members. Arriving in London between September and October 1920, the deputation went through the rounds of institutions and organisations that would help their cause.[38] First, it transformed itself to the London Committee of N.C.B.W.A. and its Secretary, Bankole-Bright, met leaders of various organisations and established contacts with a number of personalities; and it is probably through these means that he was able to establish a link with young African activists in London which was to blossom into a concrete symbol of African solidarity – the West African Students Union (W.A.S.U.). Meanwhile, a number of organisations showed a great deal of interest in the cause of the West Africans: the A.P.U. (an Amalgamation of the Union of African Peoples and the Society of Peoples of African Origin) organised meetings to publicise the cause of the Congress; the Reverend J. H. Harris of the Anti-Slavery Society, a liberal commentator on African questions, extended a welcoming and helpful hand; members of the delegation were lionised in London society; distinguished politicians like Lloyd George, Asquith, and Churchill were approached; the League of Nations Union granted an interview and extended an invitation to the Committee to discuss industrial questions; a mysterious socialist even offered the unsolicited advice that unless the Congress collaborated with socialism they would never win their cause. In answer Bright gave this retort: 'We are not Bolsheviks. If we have to fight year after year, we shall fight constitutionally.'[39] The rebuff underlined the liberal western orientation of Congress.

But, despite all the sympathetic noises made by well-meaning personalities, in spite of the sympathy of papers like the *African World* and *West Africa*, the Congress had to run the gauntlet of the Colonial Office. After all, it was this office which was responsible for the Colonies. And it was its antagonism towards the pretensions of Congress which eventually destroyed the London Mission. The plan of the Congress was to work through the many contacts, referred to above, to present their petition and memoranda to the Colonial Office for onward transmission to His Majesty for his sympathetic consideration.[40] But that Office had, over time, become apathetic and intolerant of the pretensions of the educated elite, the purveyors of the 'vermin of African self-rule'.[41] Their stolid attitude to the demands of Congress was most discouraging, and this was further complicated by the backstabbing tactics of the colonial government. At the same time, at the local level, personal rifts, feuds, rivalries, and petty jealousies conspired to reduce the effectiveness of the Movement. What was more soul-destroying was the fact that the Colonial Office was convinced that this new wave of nationalism was 'an organised ramp for a small unrepresentative elite of westernized intellectuals', and, consequently, it was unwilling to countenance the Congress leaders. Nevertheless, it felt it necessary to get the views of the Colonial Administrators.[42] The opinions of these proconsuls have been recounted again and again and commented upon by authorities on the political history of West Africa, and we need not repeat them here in detail; but two examples are worth quoting if only to remind ourselves of the decisive impact of gubernatorial influence on issues affecting their administrations, and because of the dramatic way in which the London talks were torpedoed by the governors' denunciations.[43] Sir Frederick Guggisberg, the Gold Coast governor, was outraged because he had been bypassed by the Congress in going direct to London, and he warned the Colonial Office not to have anything to do with this unrepresentative group until he had had the opportunity of consulting with representatives from various communities in the territory. Aristocratic Sir Hugh Clifford of Nigeria let loose a barrage of sharp penetrating shots against the self-appointed body which represented nobody in Nigeria. What was even worse, he alleged, some of them were not even Nigerians! All the governors were convinced that representative government would be premature, and that it would undermine good government. And, given the local situation in the territories, the Governors had no difficulty in getting African traditional rulers to repudiate the Congress. All the governors stressed the unrepresentativeness of the delegates.[44] This last point was the whip handle used to demolish the claims of Congress, and writers have since made an issue of this weakness. Unrepresentative they decidedly were, but it could hardly have been otherwise. In a largely illiterate society, the educated, the elite, considered it their moral duty to assume responsibility for, and to speak on behalf of, their less fortunate compatriots. To this end, it is worth recalling that political development in Britain generally followed this evolutionary direction until a reformed parliament made it possible for democratic institutions to emerge which allowed some say to a greater number of people. And if the Congress politicians, very much nineteenth-century liberals in outlook, very much married to principles of constitutionalism, followed the example of their masters, they merely underlined their attachment to British political ideology and traditions. But then, in the colonial situation, the authorities never admitted this concept as valid. They believed that educated Africans copied Britain too closely, and this aping of British culture, asserted Ormsby-Gore, Parliamentary Under-Secretary of State for the Colonies, was resented by the Englishman.[45] Given this attitude, represented by an important Minister like Ormsby-Gore, it is not an exaggeration to suggest that the British government's resentment sprang not so much from the conviction that the Congress was unrepresentative, but from an unwillingness to play the game according to the rules laid down by Britain's own historic and political traditions. Many examples of this attitude abound in the colonial histories of African peoples.

On the other hand, individual governors believed that the pace of African development must not be hurried; they were convinced that they were the sole arbiters of the rate and pace of political evolution. More important, they were concerned about the effect an educated minority might have on African traditional government. And in this dilemma of preserving traditional forms of government on the one hand, and restraining the intemperate impulses of the western-educated elite on the other, colonial administrators gave an ironic twist to colonial policy, which in itself was a recognition of the realities of the situation. They used the very people they had denounced as unrepresentative, as the new leaders of their African subjects when a limited representative government was conceded. In this regard, the comment of Dr Obadiah Johnson is relevant here. Writing to the radical Africanophil, E. D. Morel, in 1912, he strongly deprecated the aspersions cast on educated Africans by the Europeans. To the sneering remark – 'these educated Africans, pshaw, they are all thieves and rogues', he retorted, 'but yet, none of them has been able to do without them!'[46] This irony is one of the intriguing features of colonial rule that elude satisfactory explanation.

However, in 1921, the weight of official opinion was overwhelmingly against countenancing the Congress, believing rather precipitately, that they were asking for self-government. Repeated assurances that they meant 'to maintain strictly and inviolate the connection of British Empire'[47] did not seem to have done much to change Whitehall's truculent disposition towards the Congress. J. E. W. Flood, one of the most prejudiced officials in Whitehall, considered that 'the people of West Africa are not ripe for representative institutions and it would be a very cruel unkindness to any West African colony to grant any such constitution'. Consequently, the Colonial Office advised His Majesty that the time had not yet come 'for the introduction into any of the West African Colonies and Protectorates of the Legislative and legal reforms prayed for by the Congress'.[48] Colonial Secretary, Lord Milner, was unable even to grant the London Committee an interview; and Winston Churchill, his successor, pleaded his inability to change the policy of his predecessor. The Congress Delegation therefore returned home in 1921 empty-handed. There was little positive achievement to show for the enormous cost the deputation had been to Congress.[49] Yet within four years of the London fiasco three of the Colonies were granted a partly elective and enlarged Legislative Council: Nigeria, 1923; Sierra Leone, 1924; Gold Coast, 1925; and the Gambia, much later, in 1946.

The reasons for this *volte-face* can be better appreciated when examined against the peculiar circumstances existing in individual Colonies, and such a survey covering a wide area is beyond the scope of this work.[50] Nevertheless, the analyses of political scientists and historians suggest that there were a few common factors and considerations that linked local peculiarities together to give a fair picture of consistency in colonial policy. It seems that the British government, on mature reflection, after its hasty dismissal of the claims of the Congress, came to realise that the Congress politicians were not the Jacobins they had suspected them to be, nor were they 'extremists of the Marcus Garvey type'; their demands, in retrospect, therefore appeared to be of limited dimensions, and so to win them from the temptations of extremism it was best that some concessions be given.[51] Added to this, the local men on the spot, governors like Guggisberg and Clifford, 'progressive' and 'enlightened', had set in motion certain constitutional reforms that would have been part response to the political demands of their subjects, and it therefore made sense to give a tidy picture by including the other Colonies in these reforms. Or, again, it may be that the governors' liberal attitude harmonised with Britain's plans for her African subjects.[52] Since imperial powers never admit succumbing to pressures from their subjects anyway, and they have attached to themselves a mystique of an omniscient, omnipotent, and benign deity that conveniently anticipates disaffection by timely concessions, it is difficult to assess the degree of influence Congress politicians were able to exert to bring this change. The Congress, for its part, believed that its agitation was responsible for the granting of these constitutions.[53] Given the realities of the colonial situation one must accept this claim with reservation. However, it is equally true that the local branches of Congress exerted as much pressure as they could summon to get the British government to respond to their demands.

The Sierra Leone section of the N.C.B.W.A.

When the Sierra Leone members of the London Committee reported to the Sierra Leone Committee about the mission, they received a rapturous welcome. At a meeting on 4 April 1921 in the Wilberforce Memorial Hall, Freetown's Hotel de Ville, Bankole-Bright 'kept his audience spell bound for the space of two hours' with his account of the mission. His paper, the *Aurora*, denounced Clifford's dismissal of Congress 'as vapid outpourings of a Hyde Park Orator'.[54] Reviewing the year 1921, the *Weekly News* editor stated that the significance of the Congress Movement was that it was established at all; this denoted a sign of the times. And it was comforting to observe also that there were indications of enlightened government under a

41

hard-working administrator like Wilkinson, 'the ablest, if not the very ablest of the governors of Sierra Leone for the past 25 years'. But the Editor wondered whether the sign would be allowed to grow or die.[55] In May 1922, the Congress called on the new governor, and in response to a toast raised by Attorney-General McDonnell, Bankole-Bright reiterated the position of Congress: 'it is because this West Africa pleads for a strong organic connection with the British Empire, because she stands for equal rights and opportunities, and yet more, because she holds out the flag that taxation must go with effective representation etc., that I rise with very great pleasure to respond'.[56]

Stripped of the excitement over Bankie's dramatic accounts of his lobbying efforts in London and the defiant assertions from Congress, the cold fact stared them in the face that if they wanted to be taken seriously they must organise themselves. This became urgent and imperative because the grievances that had given rise to the setting up of the Congress had remained largely unrepaired, and complaints of discrimination became more strident. Another ominous development was the Colonial Administration's policy of sowing discord between the Colony and Protectorate. The Administration took delight in putting up the people in the Protectorate against the Colony by innuendoes and covert devices. For instance, as early as in 1921, not only was the local administration convinced that the Congress was confined to Freetown alone, without any relevance to the people in the Protectorate, but also, when E. S. Beoku-Betts rather foolishly sent a petition to London, without the knowledge of the governor, asking for elective representation, Wilkinson was quick to paint the Congress in the worst possible colours. Noting that only one of the unofficial Krio members in the Legislative Council and a representative of the Protectorate, Alimami Fofana, the Madingo tribal headman in Freetown, had signed the petition, the governor, with the obvious intention of proving that the Congress was without popular support, dismissed the two signatories with these comments: the first, he said, was a novice whose appointment had not yet been confirmed; the Madingo chief was an alien without any chiefdom in the Protectorate. He did not have any political importance.[57] It was comments like these, unhistorical and tendentious, to show that there were no common interests between peoples in the Colony and the Protectorate, and that any effort on the part of articulate citizens in the Colony to identify with the Protectorate was suspect and fraudulent, which began to fill official despatches in this period.[58] The suffusion of this kind of reportage in the records has therefore given a negative evaluation to any integrationist effort by the Colony, whether self-interested or otherwise. But the Congress was not unresponsive to suggestions from the public. In the meetings of 14 and 18 April 1921, important seats were occupied by tribal and other community leaders, church dignitaries and other leaders of thought. But, far from satisfying the articulate public, this parade of dignitaries, intended to demonstrate co-operation, merely incensed one correspondent, 'Buyufu', to denounce the Congress in very strong terms.

He did not stop there – he also made concrete suggestions for the Branch to consider and implement:[59]

(1) the reconstitution of the present Committee to give grass roots foundation;
(2) insistence on the obligations of members to support the Congress more, morally and financially;
(3) the appointment of a General Secretary and three Under Secretaries whose specific duties should include the efficient execution of Congress policies in Freetown, the Rural Area, and the Protectorate;
(4) the setting up of cells that would propagate the aims and objectives of Congress – these were to be empowered to raise funds in their locale.

Below these Under-Secretaries, a chain of command was to be erected through local representatives in principal villages and in towns in the Protectorate, who would look after the day to day running of the Congress. Another opinion argued that the invitation to Protectorate men to 'occupy a prominent place in all our organisations' would be an added boon to strength and unity.

Undoubtedly, the identity of these correspondents would have strengthened the Congress's case here but, from whatever perspective one looks at the above suggestions, it is clear that they were blueprints for the organisational pruning of the Congress, to give a wider regional spread and to make it more populist. The fact that this was never realised, for reasons which we will suggest anon, hardly supports claims made by Langley and Spitzer that the Congress made 'scant effort to discover the opinion or get the support of non-Creole leaders', to attempt an outreach to the Protectorate, because it would have been out of character to do so.[60]

On the contrary, the passage suggests that articulate people in the Colony were concerned over the cleavage between the peoples of the two parts of the country, and these people, like Abayomi Cole, as individuals, were to use practical means of integration to establish closer rapport. Also, the response of the leadership to this popular reaction points to the fact that the elites were not insensitive to public opinion, or were oblivious to the shortcomings of their organisation. Thus, after the elections of 1921, the Executive was reconstituted to provide for a number of Secretaries. Bankole-Bright was elected as General and Organising Secretary; his assistants were R. C. P. Barlatt (Eastern District, i.e., those villages to the east of Freetown); the Reverend B. L. Thomas (Western District) and J. A. Songo-Davies, a man with wide experience in the Protectorate (the Provinces).[61]

These changes obviously did not have the desired impact because in 1922 a group of educated people in the northern part of the Protectorate levelled a very serious accusation against the Colony politicians: they claimed that they had neglected the interests of the Protectorate. Although this was vigorously denied by the Colony, the *démarche* does raise a number of questions.[62] Did the Congress make vigorous efforts to penetrate the Protectorate? If they did, why did the Protectorate people not respond? More important, given the structure of politics and the administrative set-up in colonial Sierra Leone, did integrationist moves have a fair chance of success?

Of course, answers to these questions have been suggested in general works on Sierra Leone history which generally blame the Krios for this state of affairs.[63] But, in fairness to the Colony people and the Congress, which in fact generally reflected the people's opinion during our period of reference, and for a better understanding of the nuances underlying this cleavage, and as an explanation of why co-operation between the two sides always appeared to be stillborn, we must recognise the following parameters: there was a cultural chasm between the two (though not to the point that personal relations were not established) and this was exacerbated by institutional and administrative discrimination erected by the colonial establishment; for instance, the two territories were governed differently and schools and institutions like the Government Bo School and the Njala Training College were set up in opposition to the Colony; also the differing level of education and economic and social progress, sometimes very pronounced, and the discriminatory designations of 'native' and 'non native', 'alien' and 'Colony born' made it psychologically almost impossible for people to feel that they belonged to the same polity.[64] The following passages will elucidate on these points.

In 1923 the Congress met in Freetown. The capital was taut with excitement in the months preceding the conference. Its programme was enthusiastically advertised in the local press, and an opportunity was seized to point out that if governors consulted each other when they wanted to introduce legislation then it was correct for African subjects to do the same.[65] Fervent hopes were expressed that the governors would now show more empathy to the Movement, which was not one that was hostile to, or opposed to, the authority of Britain. 'Co-operation' was the watchword, the printed media assured its audience. Noting the release of the names of the Committee for the New Constitution, the Editor of the *Weekly News* wondered if the Congress was so unrepresentative whether the British would have made the concession implicit in the Constitutional proposals.[66] This favourable response from government was claimed as a victory for Congress agitation in pre-conference meetings in Freetown among the Mohammedan Community. Bankole-Bright featured prominently in these meetings.[67]

The New Year opened with a flourish. The *Weekly News* gave an effusive welcome to the delegates from the other colonies attending the three-week conference (28 January–16February). The first days were used for the exchange of courtesies, church and mosque services and the remembrance of departed pioneers, before the conference entered into the serious business of reviewing the activities of the Congress, its impact, and its structure.[68]

In spite of the rhetoric which suffused the meetings, Congress politicians did show evidence of a strong awareness of the colonies' problems, and a determination to come to grips with them. The papers that were read at the conference forcefully advanced this view. On the second day of the second session of the Congress each branch presented a review of its activities. Sierra Leone, the host country, expressed its determination to go on with the fight, despite the aloofness of some people. The problems of finance and personnel were also elaborated upon. The Gold Coast Branch hoped that through patience and forebearance it would teach the people to recognise the necessity of a united front. Nigeria, because of its domestic problems, was unable to send a delegation, but the Secretary of the Congress, with the obvious suggestion that this came as a result of representation by Congress activities, was pleased to report that the flogging of women in that colony had now ended, and that prisoners would now be represented by Counsel. The report from the Gambia was sombre. It appeared that the Branch was going through a period of disintegration, though of course it showed remarkable recovery to be able to host the third session in Bathurst in 1925.[69]

Next, mention was made about the proposed constitutional changes in the West African Colonies. A draft constitution of Congress was introduced, and a resolution on the question of the repatriation of ex-King Prempeh of Asante, was considered and then adopted. Finally, the report of the Secretary of the first session of Congress was read and adopted with a vote of thanks. Plans for the continuing activities of the Congress were then discussed. The Congressmen convinced themselves that they had reasons to be confident of a brighter future. It must, however, be pointed out that stories contained in the reports of apathy, feuding among members, financial constraints, and the continuing discrimination by officialdom, did not augur well for the cohesion and strength of the movement. Nevertheless, in the papers presented, suggestions made by the readers gave encouraging signs that they had not lost hope. Between 31 January and 5 February, several papers were read by Sierra Leonean delegates: T. E. Nelson-Williams read an exhaustive treatise on 'Constitutional (including Municipal) Reforms'. With particular reference to the City Council he argued that that institution was greatly handicapped and that radical reforms were needed. Proof vindicating this warning was to be offered in 1926.[70]

E. S. Beoku-Betts, a past Secretary of the local branch, presented a paper on one of the most serious contemporary problems, entitled 'Judicial Reforms with particular reference to the Assessors' Ordinance and a West African Appeal Court'. A forceful and interesting dissertation, the paper condemned the racially motivated colonial policies of Britain. These included discrimination against African lawyers, and the 'catapulting of inexperienced men to high posts because they were white'; the summary conviction imposed on Africans without benefit of legal counsel; and the severity of the Assessors' Ordinance and its inherent injustice. Betts made a strong attack on these with all the legal ammunition he could muster.[71] The issue of the Assessors' Ordinance was of particular poignancy, because it was widely believed to be a political weapon, disguised in judicial clothing, used by the colonial authorities against their critics. It was a recurrent question during the colonial period.

Dr J. A. Williams' paper on 'Medical Reforms' was also a catalogue of complaints and accusations: the commercialisation of the profession; the expensiveness of drugs; the deplorable sanitation in the Colony; and a host of many other iniquities. However, he had a few suggestions to make. He asked that an expert be appointed in the W.A.M.S. to perform major surgical operations; also a resident African medical officer (unmarried) should be assigned to the Connaught Hospital. The rise in infant mortality, he argued, demanded a programme of public lectures on the registration of births and deaths, so that the people could be weaned away from their ignorance of medicine.

On the same day, to a large audience that included the Reverend Heisler, Principal of Fourah Bay College, and his Vice-Principal, T. J. Evans, the Reverend J. T. Roberts of the Methodist Boys' High School, C. A. E. Macauley and O. Wallace, Inspectors of Schools, Professor Orishatukeh Faduma, an American-trained Sierra Leonean educationalist, presented a long paper on education. First, he called for a conference of educationalists to discuss the problem of education; then he proposed a gradual plan of compulsory education, the training of teachers and the establishment of Anglo-vernacular schools, as well as Agricultural and Industrial schools. The Congress demand of 1920 for a West African university was reiterated, stressing that there must be a humanistic approach to education in the Colony. The points raised were of sufficient interest to generate a lively discussion.[72] Reverend F. S. Oldfield, another speaker, made some useful comments on the representation of West African views in London. And the Congress Vice-President, Casely-Hayford, introduced a paper by a Mr Duncan, on 'Commercial Enterprise, with special references to the Gold Coast'. Lack of co-ordination, it was argued in the paper, made it difficult for people to harness the wealth of the colony, but if trustworthy leaders, and business techniques, could be introduced much profit would result from this endeavour.[73]

Finally, Bankie presented a 'well-written, clear, and graphic account' of the London delegation of 1920. The report, with only slight alterations, was accepted by the meeting. The rest of the conference was taken up with festivities, such as a Children's Festival at Victoria Park, on 7 February, visits to places of interests, and a discussion of the financial affairs of the Congress. Before that, on 8 February, Cornelius May, Editor of the *Weekly News* and the only trained journalist in the West Coast, of thirty-seven years' standing, gave a paper on 'Press Development in British West Africa'. He enjoined his colleagues to make a complete study of the press laws.[74] A congratulatory telegram was received from the President of Liberia during the session; and, on the 13th, the Colonial Secretary acknowledged greetings from the Congress. 'By some oversight', the letter explained, 'it had not been presented earlier'.[75] A number of resolutions were passed during the succeeding days. For example, 28 March was declared as Congress Day in all four Colonies, and it was resolved that a West African Press Union be formed. On 15 February, the Congress unanimously elected as its President Hutton Mills, for a second time, and Casely-Hayford, Vice-President; Van Hein and Akiumi, Treasurers; Kitson Mills, Financial Secretary, assisted by Dr Nanka Bruce. S. R. Wood was made Secretary of Congress. On 16 February, the nineteenth day of Congress, the meeting was brought to a close. Farewell speeches were made by Faduma and Bankole-Bright. A hymn written by Casely-Hayford, and set to a tune composed by his son, Archie, was played by Professor Greywood of Sierra Leone. The next session was scheduled to take place in the Gambia in 1925.[76]

The *Weekly News* claimed the Congress a success. This was not exactly the case. And it is arguable whether Congress changed government policy. It did not succeed in eliciting a more favourable attitude from the local authorities either. However, this author does not subscribe to that school of writers who too often hastily dismiss the deliberations of the Congress as pandering to their own desires, needs, and aspirations.[77] Admittedly, being the educated ones, the elite, they stood to gain immediately from any concession given by the Imperial Power. Nevertheless, issues relating to legal reforms, medical facilities, and education, affected the lower classes as well. The latter were the greater and long-term gainers. And it is to the credit of thinkers like Faduma, that the types of education that were introduced much later in the colonial period had been anticipated long before, and suggested, by Africans themselves. However, the bald truth is that the colonial authority determined the rate of progress of its colonial subjects, and no amount of discussion, rhetorical or not, could sway it from its schedule.[78]

With particular reference to Sierra Leone, how much impact did Congress make on the government? Did it convince it that it was representative? More to the point, was it able to bring in Protectorate citizens to the movement? To answer these questions a discussion of the 1924 Constitution is in place.

The Constitution of 1924

Between 1923 and 1924, when the Constitution was introduced, a number of developments took place, and the chronology of the process is rather involved for us to accurately pinpoint the success of Congress. It is a fact that Congress continued to mount pressure on the British government through memoranda, visits to the Colonial Office in London, interviews with colonial officials, delegations and demands for the granting of the elective principle. At the same time it seems that government was contemplating constitutional reforms. And these came largely as a result of Slater's efforts. However, the mechanism chosen and the strategy adopted clearly did serious harm to the relationship between the two administrative parts of the territory.

Ransford Slater, a Cambridge Wrangler, had served with Sir Hugh Clifford in the Gold Coast before he was posted to Sierra Leone.[79] As Colonial Secretary he was no doubt involved with Clifford's constitutional reforms, and this might have inspired him to adopt a progressive attitude to the demands of his subjects,[80] for he appeared to have come determined to push through a programme of reforms. How much we should ascribe this to the brief he received from the Colonial Office, or how much this was due to his own personal inclinations is hard to say. It is certain from a letter he wrote to the Colonial Office that he was told to explore the situation, and to make recommendations. It is equally true that Slater was a determined and pushful man, and he seemed to have claimed credit for the granting of the 1924 Constitution.[81]

In 1922, like Rowe and Cardew before him, Slater began his administration with a meet-the-people tour of the Protectorate to acquaint himself with its problems. The intention was well meaning, but during his sojourn he managed to put across to the people of the Protectorate, through certain ill-advised statements, the belief that their lack of development had been caused by the selfishness and particularism of the Colony. Furthermore, it was unfair, so the argument went, that being the larger and wealthier part of the possession, making a much larger contribution to the economy, the Protectorate had no representative in the Legislative Council. He told Chiefs in the Southern Province that laws enacted in the Legislative Council were without the consent of the traditional rulers and their people.[82] It may be that Slater was being naive, blandly mischievous, or plain provocative, but what he succeeded in doing was to rekindle a number of sore points and to officially endorse a conviction that the Colony had been holding back the progress of the Protectorate. Yet with characteristic irony Slater did much to advance to more important positions in the Civil Service, these very Krio people that he had besmirched.[83] Even so, there is no denying that his anti-Colony pronouncements caused a great deal of havoc. Thirty years later a noted authority was to say the same thing when Lord Hailey commented, in 1956,

> Creoles with their advanced standards of education and their passion for adopting British political institutions have been largely responsible for Constitutional developments in the colony. At one time, Freetown and its affairs went far to monopolize the attention of the government. The Protectorate seemed to be only a secondary consideration.[84]

Statements like these, made by people of authority, rather than enlighten, have unfortunately given the impression that the Krio wielded a lot of influence in Sierra Leone during the colonial period. It is obvious that if they were so powerful that they could 'monopolize the attention' of H.M. government, they should have been able to get the British to grant them their desires! But the British were not so obliging. Slater's and Hailey's statements are the stuff from which myths are made!

As a matter of fact these were prejudiced views, which conveniently forgot that it was the colonial government that dictated the pace of economic and social development in a Dependency. But when expressed by the Chief Executive Officer in the Colony they encouraged a group of educated Protectorate inhabitants to form a 'political' movement – The Committee of

Educated Aborigines (C.E.A.) in 1922.[85] It was the first modern political movement in the Protectorate. The leaders, who presented a petition to the governor in the form of an address, included: H. Kabia-Williams, government dispenser, President, J. Karefa-Smart, Vice-President, S. E. Carew Kamara, Secretary, W. Caremba M. Caulker, Assistant Secretary, J. R. Kamara, T. Maila Williams, D. Lorbour Kanne, E. Bangura Hallowell, A. R. Koromah, D. B. Koroma-Hollowell, Bassi Kamara, Yambah Koromah, Bobboh Bangura, Momoh Sankoh, Sembu Kamara, E. Kareba Kamara, and Alpha Kamara. The petitioners all came from the Northern Province. In their memo, choosing to speak for the Protectorate as a whole, they complained that for long they had borne the backwardness of their conditions with stoic calmness, waiting on the government to do something. They had always felt that their interests had not been looked after by the Krio, who seemed to be enjoying all the benefits from the wealth of the country, two-thirds of which was produced by them, the deprived, the greater part of the country. What they demanded, as of right, was direct participation in the affairs of the country. They wanted representation in the Legislative Council and more development for the Protectorate. The C.E.A. maintained that they were particularly impressed by the governor's observation that he was much exercised by the 'anomaly of a somewhat glaring character' of the Legislative Council making laws for both the Colony and the Protectorate, when in fact the latter had no representation in the legislature.[86] But then the Krios could hardly be blamed for this state of affairs, given the nature of colonial rule. We have already noticed, for example, that scarcely two years previously when they asked for elective representation, they were refused and were told that they were unrepresentative. The colonial authorities told them that they were self-appointed, that they were not chosen to speak for the people and so they could not make demands on the peoples' behalf. Yet, with an inconsistency that one finds difficult to explain, Slater stood the argument of unrepresentativeness on its head when he warmly welcomed the memorandum of the C.E.A. They were not chosen by the people; they came from one area of the Protectorate but they spoke for the whole. Purblind, and full of his own conceit, Slater did not see the illogicality of his position on this issue. On the contrary, he observed that none of the addresses he had so far received satisfied him so much as that of the C.E.A., as it touched on various important points, and it furnished him with the necessary information which he required from the Protectorate. To him 'the most important topic in the aborigines' address [is] their request for direct representation in the Legislature', and, as the subject was close to his heart, he promised to 'recommend it in his despatch to the Secretary of State'.[87] The intention here is not to split hairs but to draw attention to the fact that Colonial Officials applied double standards when treating the Colony *vis-à-vis* the Protectorate. This kind of duality was cumulative, and it has largely contributed to the dichotomy in Sierra Leone political history.

As a pressure group the C.E.A. was short-lived. However, it succeeded in bringing into sharp focus and debate the differing levels of development in the two parts of the possession and the iniquitous situation of the greater part not having any representation in the legislature, but being expected to obey laws passed by that body. Nevertheless, in putting their claims, which documented evidence could not support in many instances, neither the C.E.A. nor Slater appeared to have taken into consideration the realities of the colonial situation. Studies on the colonial policies of Britain make one thing clear – that is, that colonial rule in a Crown Colony was a bureaucracy. No matter what representations were made, concessions were given according to some mystical schedule, which, apparently, only the colonial authorities were competent to programme. More important, the petitioners conveniently forgot those times when Colony politicians from Sir Samuel Lewis to A. J. Shorunkeh-Sawyerr and other individuals in the press had argued the case for government attention to be given to the Protectorate. For instance, when Wilkinson, the predecessor of Slater, arrived in 1916, he was advised to pay close attention to the Protectorate.[88] He responded by building roads and nothing much else.[89] Still, the accusations and perhaps unjustified criticisms levelled against the Krio politicians by the C.E.A. rankled. A. E. Tuboku-Metzger, Vice-President of the local Congress, a former African Assistant District Officer, and a man who had had some experience working in the Protectorate, gave an angry retort. He lectured the C.E.A. at length on their sins of omissions, but he observed that their aspiration to represent aboriginal interests in the Legislative Council was a legitimate one, and was 'in accord with the desire and the request of the Congress whose aim is not only to unify the interests of the Colony and Protectorate but also to create an organic unity of the peoples and tribes of the Colony and Protectorate'.[90] To this end, the Congress had suggested, a month previously, that three Africans be elected to represent the interests of the three Provinces of the Protectorate. The representatives should not necessarily be Paramount Chiefs or Sub-Chiefs, but literate people. Indeed, another politician, A. J. Shorunkeh-Sawyerr, had asked the governor in the Legislative Council in July why government had not implemented the provision under the Protectorate Native Laws Ordinance (1905) for an Assembly of Chiefs, which, presumably, was to train the chiefs in the art of debate and parliamentary procedure. He was told 'I do not think that many chiefs would understand the Bill, the legal provisions of which are rather complex.'[91] This point is germane to our study, because Congress and Colony politicians have always consistently argued and maintained their stand on these two issues: (1) opposition to the presence of uneducated chiefs in the legislature because they believed that these people, as representatives of their subjects, would not be free to express their views on important questions, since by virtue of their positions they were at the mercy of the District Commissioner; (2) insistence on literacy as a criterion for membership in the Legislative Council. The correctness or wisdom of this position aside, the point to be stressed is that later developments proved that the claims of the Colony politicians were not without basis. The deliberate decision of the British administration to dismiss these fears as mere humbug, and their refusal to treat them with the consideration they demanded, at this stage, contributed in no little way to the bitterness and misunderstanding of the forties and fifties. And so for that matter the invitation extended to the C.E.A. by the Congress must be seen as a positive gesture for the educated people in the Colony and Protectorate to work together. It was an offer of alliance and co-operation. Tuboku-Metzger told the C.E.A. that their claim for representation 'will be endorsed by Congress without a dissentient voice if the educated Aborigines will identify themselves with the Congress movement and explain its uplifting purpose to every chief and sub-chief'. This was followed up in 1923 with an invitation to tribal headmen in Freetown to be unofficial members in the Executive Committee of the N.C.B.W.A., Sierra Leone branch. Unfortunately one of the weaknesses of the Congress was that it was rather delinquent in advertising itself. For instance, it was not until 1922 that the branch was able to visit the rural areas to explain the aims of Congress. And it could have done better in 1923 than to admit that it had been unable to send any deputation into the interior. But it insisted that 'there have been communications passed and mutual goodwill exchanged. It is well known that the people of the hinterland have declared to stand along their confrères in the colony, and rely on their judgement. They have taken this position as a result of long and tried friendship.' The reality did not justify this effusive optimism.[92]

Indeed, neither the C.E.A. nor any Protectorate group responded to Tuboku-Metzger's invitation. On the other hand, an interesting development occurred two years later. What appeared to be a broad-based movement cutting across the division of the two units emerged at this time. It called itself the Sierra Leone Aborigines Society (S.L.A.S.). Founded on 11 December 1924, its membership was open to all Sierra Leoneans in the Protectorate as well as in the Colony. The Society's manifesto proclaimed its commitment to establish 'intercourse among all classes of Aborigines to further their interests, whether those interests be political, educational or social, and to promote the welfare of Aborigines'. The Executive comprised the following: H. T. Kabia-Williams, President, F. A. Miller, Vice-President, J. B. Liverpool, Treasurer, N. E. Ansumana Curtis, Honorary Secretary, T. A. Blake, Financial Secretary, J. L. Mammah, Assistant Secretary, and James Brown, Organising Secretary.[93]

The absence of papers is a serious handicap to any meaningful comment on this movement; least of all, we cannot say categorically that the society emerged as a response to the invitation put out by Tuboku-Metzger, though it is a possibility. However, there are some interesting features about the Society that give us a handle to use in arriving at a few conclusions. First, the names suggest that the membership was made up of people in the Colony and Protectorate, and this is a point of historical importance; for here we find evidence of the two peoples starting a single movement on an equal footing

51

for the first time in Sierra Leone's history. To be sure, there was an abortive Sierra Leone Inter-tribal Association of Colony and Protectorate elements in 1918–19, which was a development of the Emergency Fund Committee (1918) set up to fight the introduction of the Criminal Code in the Colony and the Protectorate.[94] It has a relevance to the theme of integration moves, but it is on a slightly different perspective, because the initiative was by a Krio leadership and, no doubt, the executive would have been dominated by Colony representatives. In the case of S.L.A.S., although the list shows a preponderance of Krio-sounding names, the fact is that the Executive Committee was headed by a Protectorate citizen, and there were other Protectorate people in that body. More important, H. T. Kabia-Williams was the President of the C.E.A., the body that had denounced the Congress; and we find him next to F. A. Miller, an Executive member of the Congress. Pa Miller, as he was known, appeared to have played a consistently interesting role of a binding force, in lending the prestige of his name and dignity to a number of new political movements in Sierra Leone. We do not know much about the other names in the S.L.A.S. Executive, but Miller's name and Kabia-Williams's indicate a link between Congress or at least, a section of the Congress, and the educated elite in the Protectorate. This conclusion is reasonable, because the movement lasted for one year only. The following year, a correspondent to the *Weekly News*, 'Scutator', querulously asked why it was necessary to form S.L.A.S. when there was already in existence Congress, which catered for Aborigines and Colony people alike. He saw this as an uncalled for duplication and he enjoined S.L.A.S. to transfer its allegiance to Congress.[95] We are at a loss to know what happened for, after this date, nothing more was heard about S.L.A.S. It seemed to have disappeared without a trace. And it can only be regretted that lack of information about this movement has denied us a chance to speculate on what the political history of Sierra Leone would have been if such an organisation had got off the ground.

But, on this elusive co-operation between the Colony and Protectorate, Kilson has argued that it was not in the interests of the Protectorate elite to align with their counterparts in the Colony.[96] That may be so but, in looking at this phenomenon further, a few points need to be stated. For instance, the restrictions placed by colonial authorities on the movement and association of chiefs outside their chiefdoms inhibited a free flow of ideas. As Thomas Decker's pamphlet on the chiefs of Sierra Leone has demonstrated, covert and subtle administrative practices, as well as the structure of authority in the Protectorate, made it imperative that for any meaningful intercourse between the Colony and Protectorate to succeed it must have the blessings of the chiefs, the acknowledged channels of communication. In this regard then, these restrictions may have hindered any rapprochement between the two sides. And this is assuming that the chiefs were willing to respond to these overtures from the Colony politicians where these were manifested. The possibility cannot be dismissed that traditional rulers were naturally suspicious of black 'foreign' influence and culture. They resented any competition with their own influence and power which they jealously guarded. Mutual recriminations between 'settlers' and chiefs were another dimension to this question.

Other views have suggested that the Protectorate feared the possibility, given the level of their development then, of being smothered by the sheer weight of the Colony's educational pre-eminence and other advantages. At the same time, the educated elite in the Protectorate, the natural allies of N.C.B.W.A., were few in number then, and most of them were government employees who, because of government regulations, even if they wanted to, could not, it would seem, publicly associate with a political movement. So it was a question of putting off overtures from the Colony until they felt reasonably equipped to compete with the Colony on an equal footing. Protectorate leaders who proclaimed loudly in the 40s and 50s that the future of Sierra Leone was in their hands, and that they meant to use their majority power to the advantage of Protectorate inhabitants lend some support to this reading of the situation. We shall refer to this question in a later chapter.[97] However, this much can be said here: the demise of S.L.A.S. meant a missed opportunity for the integration of the two parts. Consequently, the duality in colonial politics was perpetuated in Sierra Leone. Political organisation took place in one without reference to the other. And it suited the colonial government to keep it that way!

Indeed, when the Constitution was promulgated, it reflected a number of interesting pointers: nominated (not elected) Protectorate representation was granted – but only because government had been so inclined to balance traditional against educated elites, the Colony against the Protectorate. More to the point, it is indicative of the contradictions in colonial policies that none of the educated elite were named except Paramount Chiefs who, of course, were directly under the thumb of the government. It was a sham, a confidence trick. And it gave force to doubts expressed by Colony politicians about the government's sincerity. Even more perplexing, the very government that had denounced and disparaged Krio politicians conceded to them elective representation. This *volte face* must have astonished the *Weekly News* into asking in January 1923, if Congress was so unrepresentative would the government have proposed such concessions?[98]

But the paper was reading too much into government policy. They were not given these concessions because the government was convinced that Congress was mandated to speak for the people, but because it felt that the issue of constitutional reforms could not be delayed any longer, given developments in other West African Colonies, *inter alia*. Indeed, the evidence shows that the impetus for constitutional reforms arose out of a petition by the Freetown Chamber of Commerce (an exclusively European body, though it was not so previously) asking that an additional unofficial member be appointed to represent commercial interests in the Legislative Council. The government responded favourably to this representation because it was not against such an appointment in principle. Besides, it was then contemplating reforms to bring about constitutional development in Sierra Leone in line with other British West African territories (e.g., Nigeria). Thus the whole question of constitutional reforms was then brought to the fore.[99] Slater was instructed to work out a programme.

In a letter submitting his findings to the Secretary of State for the Colonies, the governor reviewed previous representations, going back to 1920, for an enlarged Legislative Council to take in Protectorate representatives and other unofficial members, including elected representatives and a nominated member to represent commercial interests. Over time, the governor explained, agitation for an enlarged Legislative Council with elected representation had increased, especially in the Colony and, though this was from a 'relatively small minority', it was a powerful one, capable of moulding 'the thought of the majority of tomorrow'. Therefore, it seemed to Slater, concession was 'ultimately inevitable'. The fact that this had already been granted in Nigeria and the West Indies made it advisable and wise to give it to Freetown which had a 'highly educated public'. On representation from the Protectorate the governor declared himself convinced about the justness of the inhabitants' demands for direct representation and he did not think that there would be legal problems in bringing into the Legislative Council a people who were not British subjects. Neither Slater nor the Colonial Office thought it wise to have chiefs elected by their peers, because they were much less 'educated and civilized and hardly ripe'. 'Representation by selection should precede representation by election', decided W. D. Ellis, the official handling affairs in the Colonial Office.[100] Equally so, Slater was adamant in his refusal to consider a suggestion by the Colonial Office for the inclusion of an Unofficial Member in the Executive Council to give advice on a subject while under deliberation, rather than to be a critic after policy had been decided. The Governor considered the suggestion premature for a number of reasons – for instance, delicate issues on race, or the suspension of an official, could not be usefully discussed in the presence of African members in the Executive Council![101]

It was finally decided to have an enlarged Legislative Council of twelve official members (ex-officio) and ten unofficial members: one European member to represent commercial interests, and another nominated by the governor; three Africans elected by qualified voters in the Colony, and two more nominated by the governor; and three Paramount Chiefs nominated by the governor to represent the interests of the Protectorate. The Executive Council remained the preserve of European officials.[102]

When the proposals were made public there was a reaction, especially from Krio politicians inside and outside the Legislative Council. A target of their complaints was the provision for Protectorate members in the Legislative Council. They objected to their Legislative Council being invaded by 'foreigners'. Writers have picked this furore as evidence of Krio particularism – an unwillingness to integrate[103] – but this interpretation cannot be that simple. Certainly, in a strictly legal sense, they had a point in objecting to what they called foreign elements sitting in the Legislative Council because that was what they were, essentially, by virtue of British designation. Indeed, the Colonial Office itself had raised some doubts about the legality of including non-British subjects in the Legislative Council, and had wondered whether they would be required to take the oath of allegiance.[104] Under the dualistic administration imposed by the British, there was no provision for the Krio to be part of the Provincial administration. And the protesters reasoned that in a situation where Colony settlers experienced all sorts of legal disabilities it was hardly right for the British administration to force upon them people who, for administrative purposes, were made different. For instance, under the 1924 Constitution, Protectorate inhabitants in the Colony could vote, if they fulfilled the requirements, for representatives in the Legislature. Krio inhabitants in the interior had no such voting rights. At best their legal status in the Protectorate was nebulous.[105] The rationale behind British policy was therefore deemed lopsided. On the other hand, legalism in politics could not be rigid, and it was advisable to be pragmatic and flexible; for, after all, though divided administratively and treated differently, the two peoples had had long contact with each other. And as the *Weekly News* pointed out in 1929, the Krio people had been in the Protectorate long before 1898 (*sic*) when the British established their rule in the hinterland.[106] They had established relationships, including familial connections; and there had been times when they had identified themselves with Protectorate causes. This being the case, argued the highly respected A. J. Shorunkeh-Sawyerr, Senior Nominated African Unofficial Member in the Legislative Council, if government wanted to regularise a situation that had been developing for some time (i.e., where the Legislative Council was *de facto* legislating for the Protectorate), then declare the Protectorate a British Colony; make the two parts one, so that all would be governed by the same laws, and have the same benefits under the British Crown. He told his audience, 'if Protectorate people are aliens, as learned authorities have asserted, and they are to be brought into the Legislative Council to join British subjects, then make them British subjects or annex their territory'.[107] The call was repeated in 1929 and 1948.[108] The government's response was curiously negative, just as it was when Shorunkeh-Sawyerr made this appeal in 1923. Then, Slater had lamely replied that it was not necessary to declare the Protectorate a British Colony. An Executive Council Meeting of 12 May 1924 decided not to accept Sawyerr's motion 'praying that inhabitants of the Protectorate should be declared British subjects'.[109]

Why the British authorities refused this amalgamation when in fact they merged larger territories of different ethnic groups having the same administrative confusion inherent in the duality of the Colony and Protectorate system (such as Northern and Southern Nigeria), between 1906 and 1914 still cannot be explained satisfactorily.[110] More to the point, it is pertinent to this work to reflect briefly on what could have been the political consequences if the two units had been integrated as early as 1924, instead of 1951. For Betts, the man who had raised this legal issue, making a positive effort at reconciliation, welcomed the chiefs in this vein:

> There can be no difference of opinion that the interests of the Colony and the Protectorate are one, and it will be in the interests of both communities if we realise to the full this identity of interests, mutual dependence upon one another, and kinship, and it is my sincere hope that this new Legislative Council, where representatives of the Colony and Protectorate sit together will be the means of cementing that friendship and fostering that comradeship which is desirable.[111]

The motion was seconded by P. C. Bai Kompa and carried unanimously. Earlier, Beoku Betts had moved a resolution thanking 'His Majesty who had been so good as to approve [the Constitution] and to record the conviction that the addition of elected representatives of the Urban and Rural Section of the Colony, as well as of the Representatives of Paramount Chiefs to the official and nominated elements of the Council cannot but be fraught with the greatest advantage to the administration of two loyal territories under His Majesty's sway which are indissoluble and mutually indispensable and are the natural complement of one or the other'.[112] Slater himself endorsed these sentiments when he confessed that he 'heartily agrees with the principle that the interests of the Colony and Protectorate are indissolubly connected' and he promised that 'there will be no desire during my administration to place those interests in antagonism to each other'.[113] The citizens of Freetown also held a public meeting in honour of the chiefs at the Wilberforce Memorial Hall where the hope was expressed that they would co-operate with the people of the Colony.[114]

The working of the Constitution did not follow the pious hopes of Betts. Neither did Slater's assurances prove to be anything except mere rhetoric. On the contrary, the evidence suggests that government policy was opposed to collaboration between the two peoples, while the contributions of the chiefs, the representatives of the Protectorate, were not so tangible as to allow us to make any useful assessment. But one thing the Constitution would have done, if the suggestions made by Colony citizens had been given the consideration they merited, would have been to make integration between the two sides much smoother and less tempestuous and agonising than it was in 1951.

However, the Constitution of 1924, with all its short-comings, was welcomed even in the Protectorate as a step forward, though power still remained firmly in the governor's hands. In the Colony, aspiring legislators made full use of the elective provision.[115] The electorate, based on a restricted franchise, was treated to an electioneering campaign for the first time on an extensive scale. Bankole-Bright advertised his candidature with *élan*. He told voters that he was not presenting any stereotyped manifesto of platitudes which in the end might not have any meaning, but he would campaign through meetings and he would answer questions from the people. As he saw it, voters were faced with two serious questions:

(1) Are they electing elusive phantoms that will not face issues, who would not dare, whose ambitions are wrapped with selfish motives, unreliable and spurious as gold?

(2) Are they prepared to use their representatives who are tried and proved true, and honest men whose patriotism are unsoiled, men experienced in political matters, given assurances that their interests are for the people's welfare, laboured disinterestedly to that end, not obsessed by an intense longing to acquire what may be termed the by-products of public service to the neglect of their main duty?

Signed Yours for Motherland, Bankole-Bright.[116]

The elections, which were held on 28 October 1924, were not conducted under a party system, but the candidates were known to have represented the local Congress: Betts polled 607 votes; Bankole-Bright 562 votes, and A. E. Tuboku-Metzger 173, thus becoming First and Second Urban Members and Rural Area Representative, respectively.[117] Slater was enthusiastic over the response of the Colony people. He told the Colonial Office that 90 per cent of the voters turned out, and there were only twelve spoilt votes. Analysing the voting and the interests represented, he noted that Betts was supported by A. J. Shorunkeh-Sawyerr, 'a distinguished member of the old Council'. Undoubtedly the two successful Urban candidates must be regarded as belonging to the 'more forward party'. Barlatt, an ex-Mayor of Freetown (373 votes), and Songo-Davies (199 votes), a former African Assistant District Commissioner, were supported by the conservative and Church elements. They were less energetic in wooing the electorate.[118] 'It is perhaps not without significance', confided the governor,

> that both Mr. Betts and Dr. Bankole-Bright are the Editors or Proprietors of Newspapers in Freetown. Dr. Bankole-Bright has the reputation of being rather violently anti-European, but Mr. Betts has not hitherto been regarded as an extremist in any way (for some obscure reason he described himself as the 'Labour' Candidate). Rural Area polling was heavy also. Tuboku-Metzger, a retired Native Assistant District Commissioner, takes an active part in public affairs. It may be expected that he will not infrequently oppose government, but he should prove a useful member.
>
> On the whole, I consider the elections have been a distinct success. They were conducted with good humour and no little vigour. It is true that the contests turned on personal considerations rather than on any political issues – there being at the moment apparently no such issues to divide the local community, and it is perhaps open to doubt whether the best candidates were elected. Nevertheless, the result was decisive, and we can be reasonably assured that we now have on the Council at least three members who will speak authoritatively for an element which unrepresented would always have been a source of some anxiety.[119]

This optimistic and complimentary report, exceptionally rare in colonial circles, was to give way to disparagement and wholesale condemnation two years later!

In the Protectorate, after consultations with the Provincial Commissioners, the governor chose the following chiefs to represent their areas in the Legislative Council. Slater's report ran thus:

> P. C. Bai Kumba of Mande Chiefdom, Upper Mendi (35 years old). He had been ruling since 1909, when he succeeded his father, Kabba Se. He attended various Mission Schools, and the Tabernacle School in Freetown. He spoke English quite well; P. C. Bai Kompa, Koya Temne (55–60 years) had been a chief since 1917, before that he was a regent in 1907 – a most intelligent chief; and P. C. Tucker of Nangoba Bullom Chiefdom, Bonthe District (58–60 years) – he had integrity, and had been a Paramount Chief since 1914. He spoke English well.

The governor assured London that he was satisfied that his choice would make useful members of Council 'as soon as they become accustomed to its procedure'.[120]

But the chiefs were little more than pawns, everyone agreed – even the government that nominated them.[121] As for the articulate members, the elected representatives, a study of the documents revealed the interesting fact that the system gave them little room to manoeuvre, and that their efforts to become good parliamentarians were often frustrated and negated by official truculence, apathy, contempt, and the overwhelming weight of the government's majority in the chamber. Nevertheless, within the narrow limits of the forum accorded them by the colonial regime, they made full use of the elective provision. They attempted to influence government policy and they vigorously advocated the interests of their constituents. For these efforts they gained minor concessions from the government.

That they did not have huge successes was because British policy was manifested in a carrot and stick procedure. Early activists, with suitable inducements, judiciously administered, were allowed to go only thus far and no farther. This being so, it is difficult to accept the argument advanced by some commentators that these early politicians should have done more. They could not have accelerated the rate of political emancipation in the Colony either. The colonial system did not operate that way.

4

In the Legislative Council, 1924–1939: the drama of confrontation

Politics in Sierra Leone in the inter-war years were dominated by two personalities: Dr Bankole-Bright and E. S. Beoku-Betts. These years were known as the era of the Double Bs. One was a doctor who should have been a lawyer, the other a lawyer, who had wanted to be a doctor.[1] Both shared the same political, social and economic background. They came from the elite – the cream of Freetown Society, locally referred to as the 'Aristos'.

Ernest Samuel Beoku-Betts was the son of C. W. Singer-Betts, a dealer in sewing machines (hence the Brand name, Singer). Betts' business premises were sited in the same locality as the Brights', East Street. Young Ernest attended the C.M.S. Grammar School and Fourah Bay College. After securing a B.A. in 1913 he proceeded to England the next year to study law. He appeared to have had an impressive scholastic career, for he returned home in 1917, after an absence of three years, with a Second Class Honours degree in Law (LL.B.) from London University and a B.C.L. from Durham University.[2] On his return he set up a private legal practice, and promptly threw himself into current affairs. He became a regular contributor to the *Weekly News*. He was one of the first public-spirited individuals to respond to the invitation put out by the originators of the Congress idea in 1918.[3] Stung by the escalating racism of the period, he demanded (though he had no chance of getting one) an official statement from H.M.G., making its position clear on the question of whether the colour of a man's skin should make any difference within the British Empire![4] His energy seemed boundless. Betts' name was soon associated with a large number of organisations, the most important being the resuscitated Sierra Leone Bar Association, in which he held the post of Secretary. He was a City Councillor between 1919 and 1926.[5] And when he was elected Mayor in 1926, he secured the ultimate accolade of civic honour and dignity. He got the dubious distinction of being the last elected indigenous Mayor for the next twenty-three years, during which time the City Council was controlled by the colonial government.[6] Betts bundled all this into a busy life which found time for active participation in sports. He represented Sierra Leone in international cricket and tennis matches between 1928 and 1932. Eventually, he became Chairman of the Board of Trustees of the Sierra Leone Cricket League.[7]

On 26 November 1919, Betts married Miss Janet Syble Boyle-Hebron, daughter of Mr and Mrs Abe S. Hebron. The father was the President of the

Bar Association and a distinguished pillar of society. The cream of Freetown society, of course, honoured one of their kind at this 'High Class Wedding'. Bankole-Bright proposed a toast on behalf of the medical profession, thus returning the compliment Betts had accorded to Bright's brother, J. Galba Iwuchuku Bright, when the latter got married the previous year, and Betts served as best man to the groom.[8] In short, Betts and Bankie were close friends – a friendship that must have begun in their childhood days when they were neighbours, but which matured in their adult years, lasting for over thirty years, though contemporaries claim that it did go through some rough passages. At least, up to 1937, when Betts took up a government post, the two appeared to have collaborated successfully enough for their names to be given to the epoch.

If personal looks were anything to go by, Betts had an edge over Bankie, who tended to have a brooding and forbidding countenance, not helped by his abnormally large head, protuberant eyes, and deep stentorian voice. Meeting Bright, contemporaries and relatives maintain, one got the feeling that one was before a presence. There were some who were in mortal terror of this powerfully built man.[9] Betts, on the other hand, had an appealing urbanity. He had a smiling countenance that exuded warmth and invited confidence, though O. G. R. Williams of the Colonial Office disliked him on sight: 'My personal impression for what it is worth is that he is the least attractive of the Africans whom I have so far met, not many, I admit. He had an air of covert insolence, or so I thought, which is rather irritating.'[10]

Not many would agree with Williams. Ambitious, Betts certainly was, and he seemed to bask in honours and laurels, but he was a brilliant jurist with a penetrating intellectual mind.[11] He also had a modest claim to literary competence.[12] Betts was an effective speaker but not as compelling and eloquent as his friend. He had polish, a suavity, which was contrasted by Bankie's haughty, abrasive, direct and challenging manner. Nevertheless, hitched together, they were a formidable combination. They certainly caused a great deal of discomfort to the administration. Consequently, the colonial authorities' assessment of these two legislators was negative: they were 'rabble-rousers', 'unsuccessful professionals', and 'extremists'. But then it was the practice of colonial officials to disparage their most unrepentant critics. In any case, were Betts and Bright nationalists/assailants, or, in Ayandele's trenchant words, collaborators and deluded hybrids? Is it possible to make distinctions that are not in absolutes?[13]

Bright and Betts, like their contemporaries among the elite, believed in the imperial mission of Britain to Africa. She was not without blame, of course; but she had done much for the Africans, for the Krio especially, and among colonial powers she was the best.[14] Thus she must be supported. Bankie often referred to his 'organic connection with the British Crown';[15] and this, his attachment to things British, made one critic say of him that 'always for him Sierra Leone was an extension of Britain'.[16] Yet no one in the inter-war years was as passionately committed to Sierra Leone as Bankole Bright; nor, for that matter, in an era which later radicals chose to refer to as conservative, was anyone as radical or violently critical of British colonial rule as Dr Bright. His nationalism, his stout defence of what he regarded as the interests of his compatriots are positively reflected in the issues he championed. Even the establishment acknowledged this, though grudgingly. Thus a confidential report on Bright supplied by the Sierra Leone government in 1931 noted that Bankie came into prominence 'ten to eleven years previously by means of fluency of speech (sometimes perhaps reaching the height of real oratory)'. His representations in the Legislative Council the report continued, were largely concerned with 'Natives and salary of individual Africans of [the] public service'.[17] 'In politics', enthused his pen artiste,

> Dr. Bright is not the sort who plays ducks and drakes nor does he believe in window dressing speeches, as some of his African colleagues do. He takes it seriously, even more than his Medical Profession, and since he was elected to the Legislative Council of Sierra Leone, he very often combated the arbitrary thunders of the European members by an artful display of forceful words.[18]

So went on the evaluation of contemporaries as widely different as the above examples. And the fact that Bankie was hardly the blue-eyed boy of the local administration, or the Colonial Office, for that matter, scarcely qualifies him as a collaborator. The point is that Bright admired British institutions and customs, but he demanded that he and his people be treated with courtesy and equality. Hence, while he could congratulate a governor for being knighted or even move a resolution supporting Britain's declaration of war against Germany, he could also, with equal facility, tell the governor to his face to come down from his high horse if he believed that his people's integrity had been insulted. Bright was a 'loyal subject', but not a pliant toady that 'would not offer any factious opposition' to the government 'when dealing with general legislative business'.[19]

The causes embraced by the Double Bs. could neither be classified as those that pandered to the socio-economic aspirations of the elite exclusively. They were much more complex than that. Issues, such as government and race discrimination, health facilities, the Assessors' Ordinance, unemployment, the Syrian (Lebanese) question, workers' compensation and women's franchise are not exclusive to the elite; they cut across social, economic, as well as ethnic lines – one way or another the ordinary man was affected. And, for that matter, questions relating to the Protectorate were also raised by Colony representatives in the Legislative Council. In short, their interests were wide ranging, they covered the whole dependency, though there were some of special importance to Bankie and Betts. The latter, for instance, was very much interested in labour and immigration questions. Bankie's were more political, but he was particularly interested in medical questions. On these he made some significant contributions in the form of criticisms of government policy and suggestions for reform.

In the Chamber of the Legislative Council, the very first question raised by

Bright concerned workers in the Printing Office, and another about the salary scale of a Miss Cole, Senior Health Visitor. Bright complained about the inequality between the technical clerical staff in the Printing Office where a second-class technical staff officer earning £54–£90 p.a. was not pensionable, while a fourth-grade clerk on £50–£96 p.a. was pensionable.[20] As regards Miss Cole he was of the opinion that the monetary rewards for her services were inadequate. He suggested that her scale be brought up to the level of First Class Dispenser. The response of the government was favourable, and, indeed, at the end of this first session of the Legislative Council sittings in 1924, the governor commended the new members 'whose vigilance was exceptional'. 'Almost without exception', Slater noted, 'they contributed to deliberations something by way of useful criticism, suggestion or information.'[21] The honeymoon did not last long.

Bright's sympathy with workers scored a point when he was invited to address the Sierra Leone Workmen's Union in August 1921 on the subject of the moral, social, and political aspirations of the working man.[22] It would not be the last time workers would ask him to speak to them. This point, and the following, are important to note, because too often Bright and his peers have been accused of neglecting workers and keeping themselves aloof from their problems. The other side of the picture needs focusing. Thus, Bright's aristocratic pretensions notwithstanding, he was very much interested in the welfare of the less privileged in society. And so, for example, he strongly opposed the government's proposal to increase Municipal Burial Fees in 1927 (in order to raise revenue and to site new cemeteries) on the grounds that it was a 'class legislation', since only the wealthy might be able to afford the higher fees. Eventually, alternative means were found to secure the objectives of the government. King Tom Cemetery was one result of these efforts.[23]

From questions about workers, Bright increasingly began to delve into the mysteries of government. He sought to influence government policies by sharp, penetrating, and often embarrassing questions, to publicise the inconsistencies and prejudices of government, with a view to inducing government to change its errant ways and to govern in the true interests of its subjects. He wanted to know, for example, how many Africans were employed in this department or that; why the Reverend A. T. Sumner who had recently been promoted with increased salary, had not had his allowance increased; the number of Europeans qualified to hold certain posts and whether there were no qualified Africans who could be appointed to this or that position?

As an illustration the following are selected from questions he asked the administration on 25 November 1925. He asked 'whether it is a fact that medical practitioners of this colony are debarred from issuing medical certificates to government officers and from placing them on the sick list? If so, why has this system come into operation under the present administration, considering that under past administrations medical practitioners were allowed to attend to and issue medical certificates to government officers consequent on instructions from a past Secretary of State in this matter?'

Of course, the Colonial Secretary, answering for the government, denied the accuracy of Bright's claims, and on this one question, which was regularly raised by Bankie, the government doggedly refused to give the questioner satisfaction. Undaunted, he would ask questions which sought information about how government treated its African staff, as, for example, when he asked about the emolument proposed 'to be attached to the office of Assistant Postmaster-General now that it is proposed to give the appointment to an African.[24]

In his meetings with Whitehall officials, for example, Ormsby-Gore, Parliamentary Under-Secretary of State for the Colonies, he made a number of demands ranging from allowing medical practitioners to issue certificates to civil servants, equal opportunity for all in the services, the appointment of an African dentist, Uel John (the first to so qualify) in government services, to a repeal of the Assessors' Ordinance. The Colonial Office thought that 'he asked too much'.[25] Soon an administration that was noted for its lack of enthusiasm for Africanising its services began to be annoyed by Bright's ferret-like persistence. When Bright and his elected colleagues called attention to the position of the Chief Clerk in the Governor's Office, pointing out that it should rank equally with those of the other Chief Clerks, Slater waspishly objected: 'As a matter of principle I deprecate the intervention of unofficial members of the Legislative Council in domestic details of this nature.'[26] The disapproval of the governor made no impression on the dauntless Bright. In fairness to Slater, however, we must acknowledge his efforts at advancing Africans to senior posts during his administration. It was, however, during the latter part of his tour that promotions for Africans entered a period of slump, mainly because of the administration's disenchantment with the Krio following the 1926 strike.

Bankie continued to harry the administration with incessant queries. Between 1925 and 1928 he had asked eighty-nine questions compared to Betts' eighty-two and Tuboku-Metzger's seven.[27] Indeed, looking at the accounts of the proceedings in the Legislative Council one may be forgiven for thinking that Bright and Betts were the only members in the Assembly. In time, an open breach occurred between Bright and the government over the Prince of Wales's visit to Sierra Leone in 1925.

The Prince of Wales affair

It was a simple enough matter. The people of Sierra Leone were enthusiastically expecting the visit in April of the Prince of Wales, the future Edward VIII, to their 'ancient and loyal' country. Just before he arrived, the government announced, contrary to protocol and custom, that the Legislative Council, instead of the City Council, would present an address to his Royal Highness. Bright objected strongly to what he considered an insult

63

Bankole-Bright and politics in colonial Sierra Leone

to the City Fathers. He alleged that government action was deliberately aimed at spiting the City, which normally did such honours to visiting personalities. Bright was not splitting hairs or being fractious. For him, a fundamental issue was involved, that of the dignity, respect and integrity of an institution that was wholly African 'controlled'. A constitutional principle was also involved here – freedom of speech, the right of the elected representative of the people to express disagreement over a line of action taken by the government if he felt it was wrong. His standpoint is better understood if it is recalled that barely four months back the Head of State of neighbouring Liberia, President C. D. B. King, a Sierra Leonean immigrant in that republic, had paid an official visit to his native land, and it was the City Council,[28] not the Legislative Council, which had given the Civic address. Outside the Legislative Council, another solid nationalist, J. C. Shorunkeh-Sawyerr, forcefully argued that it was unprecedented and irregular for the government to deny the City Council its accustomed honour.[29]

To this furore the government countered that since the Legislative Council now included Protectorate members (conveniently forgetting that the Protectorate representatives had existed during President King's visit), it was fitting that that body should do the honours to reflect the new composition of the Legislature. It was a fair enough argument, if that were true. But not one Protectorate member was included in the Select Committee appointed to draft the address, even as a token gesture.[30] And this, of course, makes the government's case a hollow one. The matter would have passed off quietly, but so strongly did Bright feel about what he considered an affront to his people's pride that he expressed the intention of bringing a motion of censure against the government in the Legislative Council. The government's reaction gives us an indication of how it muzzled opposition by veiled threats and subtle leverage.

The governor had not been present when Bankie gave notice of his motion, so at the earliest possible occasion he sternly warned that anybody who supported the motion would be regarded as a disloyal subject; not only that, he predicted that the motion was bound to fail.[31] As to the latter it was a foregone conclusion since the government was always assured of a guaranteed majority. But what was more amazing was that the 'authoritarian and deliberate Bright' refused to be felled by this gubernatorial stick.[32] He proceeded to move such a motion and, in spite of his undeniably well-argued speech (at one point Slater departed from parliamentary protocol and shouted 'Rubbish!'), he predictably lost it. It was not even seconded. His elected colleagues who could have supported him explained, at least Tuboku-Metzger did, that they had been dissuaded from supporting their countryman because of the fear of being cast in the role of disloyal subjects![33] Betts' friendship with Bright proved insufficient to repulse official displeasure in this instance. As for Bright, he refused to append his signature to the address.[34]

By this action, in sacrificing an opportunity to demonstrate his attachment

64

to British royalty because he felt strongly about a principle, Bright underlined his singleminded independence. He was to demonstrate this many times throughout his career. To him, it mattered not whether people supported him on an issue – if he felt strongly about it, rightly or wrongly, he would pursue that matter through, whatever the costs. This could not be said for most of his contemporaries. And though Betts' lack of support, without explanation, can be called to question in this instance, this episode did not seem to have affected their friendship. Friendships in Sierra Leone at that time had been known to break for less. Bright showed this same tenacity and perseverance, in another sparring session with the Administration.

The Stocks affair

In December 1925 it was reported that a European District Commissioner in Bonthe District, E. H. Stocks, had assaulted an African Customs Officer, J. E. Barber, for alleged insolence. Apparently, Barber had kept his hands in his pocket, lounging, when he saluted Stocks. The latter, irritated and annoyed by what he considered to be insolent behaviour by this African junior officer, struck Barber's cap from his head.[35] It could have been a minor affair and easily forgotten, but in the state of Anglo-Krio relations in the inter-war years, the opportunity to put a stop to what appeared to be racial arrogance, expressed in sundry physical attacks on African citizens by white officers, seemed too good to let go. The Stocks assault was the latest of a series of attacks on Africans by an officialdom that was increasingly becoming cynically complacent about the complaints of its subjects. In October 1918, a former Mayor of Freetown, E. H. Cummings, the father of six-times Mayor of Freetown, E. H. Taylor-Cummings, was publicly assaulted by a Lt. Gaumont.[36] In the court case which followed, Cummings' complaint was dismissed by E. A. Vergette, an Acting Police Magistrate.[37] Happily, the judgement was overturned on a decision by Chief Justice Parrodi in the Supreme Court. Gaumont was fined 10s. with costs of appeal.[38] The frequency of attacks was coming at such an alarming rate, especially during the incursion into Sierra Leone of white troops returning from the First World War, that Governor Wilkinson had to issue a public notice stating that 'no man, whatever branch of Her (*sic*) Majesty's Service he may belong to, can claim the right, much less enforce the right to be saluted by civilians whether they be natives or non-natives (Govt. Notice for Royal Gazette, March 2, 1919. Signed by W. B. Stanley, Acting Colonial Secretary)'.[39] That was six years before the Stocks affair. Since then there had been occasions of white officials violating Africans with impunity. A good example was a police officer, the overzealous Inspector Rabbit, who invaded the privacy of the homes of citizens and meted out rough justice to alleged breakers of the law.

The government made matters worse by appearing to condone the actions of its white officers. For example, answering to a question raised by Bankie

65

in the Legislative Council with reference to the assault on Barber, Slater contended that Stocks had been provoked. He believed that the District Commissioner, 'who was an officer particularly even tempered', was ordinarily on excellent terms with his African subordinates. No doubt, the governor maintained, Stocks' action was highly reprehensible but, on the other hand, junior officers should show respect through the conventional way.[40]

If the governor's statement was meant to assure his African subjects that the incident was not another demonstration of a wave of violent racism, the result was the opposite, because his standpoint looked suspiciously like a white-wash job. As the *Weekly News* put it, the paper was willing to let the incident by 'as an aberration of the sense of fitness of things to be allowed, as one of the freaks of the African climate on the mental and moral balance of Europeans, had it not been for the novel and strange point of view which the answers of government gave to the straight and pertinent questions put by Dr. Bankole-Bright'.[41] The affair became a *cause célèbre* and evoked a popular backlash. A public debate was carried on in the newspapers and, in the early months of 1926, when another dramatic crisis, the Railway Strike, occurred, the Stocks–Barber affair successfully competed with the Railway Strike for front-page reportage.[42]

Taking his cue from the *Weekly News*' observation that the government appeared to condone Stocks' action with a plausible but unconvincing argument, which in itself smacked too much of a desire to maintain official prestige, a correspondent, Olorungbemi, called on his compatriots to sink all petty differences and jealousies and unite. The government's reaction, he argued, struck at the root 'of our liberty' and it was a menace to the safety of every loyal citizen.[43] And Bankole-Bright, never one to avoid a fight, was way up front shaking his fists at the face of Slater's administration. Not satisfied with the governor's answer to his questions he gave notice on 24 March 1926 that he was going to move a motion condemning the government's complacent attitude.[44] When put on 30 March, the motion read 'Council regrets to notice a demonstration of colour prejudice underlying such action [Stocks' assault] and views with grave apprehension the condonation of such a policy.[45] Again, Bright lost the motion, supported this time only by his ally, Beoku-Betts. Tuboku-Metzger, the Rural Area member, who was the only leading politician to say a few complimentary things about Stocks, with whom he had worked when he was African Assistant District Commissioner in Bonthe, abstained from voting. Undeterred, Bright insisted, as he had every right to do, that the Secretary of State's attention be drawn to the incident and that records of the debate be sent to H.M.'s Minister for the Colonies.[46]

The consistent loss of his motions and the frustration of his representations by a truculent and implacable administration did not necessarily make Bright a Don Quixote futilely tilting at the windmill. On the contrary, he understood the realities of politics in a colonial dependency, and he was well aware that the room for manoeuvre was restricted and circumscribed. Consequently, what little option was left to the elected unofficial representative in the Legislative Council, he was ready, willing, and able to exploit. This is clear from a speech in December 1925 at a meeting of the Select Committee for the 1926 Estimates.[47] With slightly veiled insolence, he congratulated Governor Slater

> on the production of such an interesting volume [the Governor's Address to the Legislative Council] which is no little display of great mental activity, and I think Your Excellency should be congratulated further on being the proud possessor of a good pair of lungs as was evidenced by the physical energy displayed for two hours in reading your address. I am only apprehensive that he who will have to succeed you, whether he is something more than a senior wrangler, on searching the archives of this Council, will discover that he has a formidable task before him.

He then went on to a more serious note. He confessed that he was happy that Slater welcomed constructive criticisms provided they were not sectional. As for him and his elected colleagues they recognised the sacred trust reposed in them and they had no desire to foster sectional interest 'but to voice the public view thereby advocating public interest'. Now, if this principle was conceded by their 'official brothers', and they also remembered that the human being was not infallible, then unofficial members need not be regarded as interlopers. 'They have a right to make enquiries and searching enquiries too.' Finally, putting things in a nut shell, he observed, 'one quite appreciates the fact that Your Excellency, ensconced, as it were, amongst the gods, cannot come down to these small things ... Your Excellency is the Rock of Gibraltar, your power is almost infinite, it is for us therefore to bring to your notice the things deserving of attention.'[48] The second Urban Member then proceeded to enumerate the 'things deserving' of His Excellency's attention: improvement of the economic position of the people, not on paper alone but in a concrete form; raising of the status of the African Staff which was bearing the heat and burden of the day, and many other issues.

To be fair, sometimes the Administration grudgingly recognised the merits of the Unofficial Members' criticisms. This was true of the instance when H. C. Luke, the Colonial Secretary, replying to the points raised by Bright in the meeting referred to above, noted that there was evidence of 'a little ray of constructive criticism', and that was the members' observation that government had not provided for the training of Africans outside the Colony through scholarships![49] The Administration promised that this omission would be considered in the future. The Colonial Secretary's observation is important here because, for one thing, this was the first, if not the only, official admission by the government that Colony politicians advocated the interests of their Protectorate brethren. Secondly, scarcely six months later, Luke was to condemn the whole group of elected members with the most disparaging and contemptuous opinion imaginable, even surpassing Slater who had been impressed in 1924 with 'the care with which unofficial members draft[ed] legislation', 'the vigilance of the new members in this Council', which was exceptional, and their useful criticisms and suggestions.[50] Such was the worth of official assessment.

However, just as Bright was strongly determined to defend his fellow Africans, so was he relentless in attacking white officials guilty of over zealousness or plain bullying, such as was the case of Inspector Rabbit; or one of misappropriation of public funds, like the example of Dudley Vergette, Curator of Intestate Estates. Rabbit was seconded from the London Metropolitan Police to help reorganise the Sierra Leone Police Force after the 1919 strike and anti-Syrian riots. Apparently, Rabbit tended to be over enthusiastic in his job, and was not above bending the rules. In one case he was charged with trespass for arresting a stone thrower at No. 2 Savage Square on flimsy evidence. The judge called his action 'worse than crime, a blunder'.[49] While the government admitted the 'speculative offence' of Inspector Rabbit, it did not deem it as warranting a case for dismissal 'as it might erode respect for the Police'.[51] Nonetheless, a question was even asked in the House of Commons on 15 June 1921 by P. W. Raffan, through the instigation of Bankole-Bright. Churchill, answering for the British government, acknowledged that Rabbit 'at most was guilty only of excessive errors of judgement', and no steps would be taken against him. In a private draft letter to Raffan he was told that Rabbit had been censured for his excessive zeal, but he was a good police officer who had done much to improve the police force.[52]

Vergette was charge with misappropriation of funds but he was subsequently acquitted: yet Africans found guilty of such misdemeanours, such as Hyde and E. D. Morgan, to cite just two examples, were given the maximum punishment.[53] The examples of Vergette and Rabbit exposed the partiality and prejudice of the White administration.[54] The administration appeared to admit the errant ways of its white officers, but because they were doing good work in their respective jobs, they felt that their peccadilloes should be overlooked!

This 'solidarity' policy pursued by the government so incensed Bright that he used all his undoubted talents to persecute these gentlemen. His crusade was so tenacious and incisive that F. Mcdonell, the Attorney-General, had cause to explode:

> I had no conception until my arrival here of the almost fanatical bitterness of the race feeling which exists amongst a section of the Creole community of Sierra Leone, a section which is probably not large but is very vocal, and is ever on the watch for any error or weakness on the part of the European officials whom it may pillory in the column of its press.[55]

In another development, when Bright protested against military officers assaulting respectable citizens, Slater told the Colonial Office that Bankie's allegations were exaggerated. He went on, 'Bright is an extremist – he seizes on regrettable but explicable incidents of the character to calumnate British

Administration. Racial feeling in this colony – or rather in Freetown – does appear to me, as far as I can judge after such a short residence here, to be nearer the surface than in other colonies in which I have served.'[56]

However, the real racial outburst and confrontation, to be discussed presently, between Bright and the government came four years after Slater had assumed office in Sierra Leone. In that drama, which was enacted in 1926, the uglier aspects of British colonial administration were put into bold relief. For instance, while criticisms by African political activists failed to unsettle British rule, or even move the local administration from its chosen path, the letters written by white officials, reporting incidents in the colony, or commenting on Africans, revealed the depth and pervasiveness of racial bias in official circles in Sierra Leone during the inter-war years.

A young Sapper officer in Sierra Leone, who felt that the strike was 'very comic, but a bit of a nuisance', wrote home to his parents regaling them with anecdotes ridiculing African individuals. He told of a colleague who refused to go to church on the grounds that he 'had rooted objections to being preached at by niggers'. The writer, A. J. H. Dove, confessed that he fancied 'a lot of people here could go to church if it was strictly confined to Europeans, but the B. A. Durhams wandering round Freetown put them off...One can't go round shouting that the black man is just as good as the white man', he complained, 'because the whole country is run on the opposite assumption, white man prestige, or government without the use of force.'[57]

Even the Church was not free from these prejudices. While the white leadership in the Church establishment believed that ecclesiastical authority should be retained by European clerics, because their African colleagues were 'not yet' ready to assume the reins of responsibility, the reaction of the Church to the strike situation varied from individual clerics who had some misgivings about the turn of events, to full support for government measures given by the Anglican Bishop of Sierra Leone, Rt Revd George W. Wright. The situation got so bad that both the C.M.S. and Methodist Missions expressed strong fears for the future of Anglo-African relations. When it was discovered that the Bishop, who would have to preside over the celebrations of the C.M.S. Jubilee scheduled for that year, was getting very unpopular, the occasion was postponed to the following year because 'feelings were running high'. Happily, it was celebrated 'with success' in November after the strike had ended.[58]

The 1926 strike

On 14 January 1926 a 'lightning strike' broke out in the Railway Department of the Sierra Leone government. It arose out of workers' reactions to the government's policy which aimed at reorganising the railway and ensuring that it was run efficiently and economically. The implementation of the policy appeared to have affected the African employees most adversely. The labour unrest which followed lasted for over six weeks. In time the strike

69

encompassed other complex issues and assumed political dimensions. The government saw the strike 'as a political fight to the death between' itself 'and the Creoles' who had 'rebelled against the government just as the natives, in the Protectorate in 1898 had done'. Recalling his own strictures against the weakness of the previous Wilkinson Administration during the 1919 strike, 'clear-thinking' Slater had taken certain precautions to maintain order, and had indicated a determination to break the strike from the beginning.[59] He had expected the strike to last a few days because he assumed that a few tough measures would soon send the Africans scampering back to work. He was over sanguine; as the strike went beyond a week, Slater became truculent and hysterical. What particularly roused the ire of Slater's administration was the role the intelligentsia played in the episode by coming out publicly in favour of the workers.

The strike, and its significance, has been fully treated elsewhere.[60] In this section attention is being focused on the political dimensions of the labour unrest, with special reference to the intriguing interpretation given by government to the role of elected African representatives. Anglo-Krio relations, and the wider implications of the strike on future government attitude to the Colony *vis-à-vis* the Protectorate, and on the political prospects of the educated elite in the Colony, are also taken into consideration.

In 1919, the Railway and Public Works Department workers had struck, *inter alia*, on account of the nonpayment of War Bonus gratuities to African workers, although these had been paid to other government employees, especially European personnel.[61] The strike degenerated into a riot in which damages, almost exclusively suffered by Lebanese (Syrian) traders, were estimated at over £500,000. The intelligentsia, the leading citizens in Freetown, had not supported the strike or the riot. Indeed, they had condemned the violence of the civil disturbance, though they did not hide their jubilation over the misfortune of the Syrians, against whom they harboured some ill will; nor did they sympathise with the discomfiture and embarrassment of a government they were increasingly beginning to resent.[62] The government, anxious to find scapegoats to cover their own fumbling incompetence, charged the City Council, without a shred of evidence, with responsibility for the riots. A levy – a diktat – of £36,635, later reduced to £5,000 (to be paid in ten years), was imposed on the Council 'to instil into the citizenry civic and corporate responsibility'.[63] This gross miscarriage of justice rankled among the Krio elite. The administration never really trusted the Krio after this, and the Colony inhabitants in turn became more hostile to government. And when Slater kept referring to the 1919 episode in 1926, it reopened old wounds.

Compared to the 1919 strike, the 1926 industrial action was better organised, and formally led by the Railway Workers Union (founded in 1925) which, in putting the case of its workers, had gone through the established procedure of long negotiations and the submission of mem-

70

oranda. These features earned the Union respectability in the eyes of a class of people whose political training was steeped in ordered representations. Besides, violence had not been extensive. More to the point, the picture of a bullying government intimidating a poor defenceless people, who were only trying to improve their situation, seemed to the elite one more piece of evidence of the insensitivity of the administration to the sufferings of its African subjects. This was especially so when Slater made it clear that no matter what it cost the government in terms of loss of revenue he was going to break the obstinacy of the workers. Consequently, the elite, who, of course, had their own grievances against the government, saw the workers as fellow sufferers of the colonial system. They identified themselves with the cause of the strikers, thus harmonising worker and elite interests for the first time in the political history of the country.

On 21 January, a meeting of rate payers and citizens was held at the Wilberforce Memorial Hall to consider the strike situation. It was well attended under the chairmanship of J. A. Songo-Davies, Deputy Mayor of Freetown, and a well-respected veteran politician. Important decisions were taken at this meeting. For instance, it was agreed that they would not prejudge the case by arguing on the merit and demerit of the strike action, but that every effort was to be made to end the labour unrest. They offered to mediate, to be 'buffers' between the workers and government. At the suggestion of J. C. Shorunkeh-Sawyerr, supported by H. R. Morrison, a former civil servant, and Bankole-Bright, a committee of ten Africans and five Europeans was set up to deal with the situation and arrange such terms with the government as would ensure a maintenance of the status quo ante.[64] Another committee of seven citizens (including two Europeans) and seven workers' representatives was to meet the General Manager of the Railway to discuss terms for the ending of the strike.[65] All these attempts at mediation were to no avail; offers by other bodies and personalities, for example, the Bishop of Sierra Leone, to help in solving the labour unrest were spurned with supreme disdain by Slater.[66] The latter, backed as he was by a Colonial Office, fed up with constant complaints about a 'nasty turbulent' place called Sierra Leone,[67] was determined to smash the defiance of the workers, to efface 'the spirit of indiscipline which appears unfortunately, to be so ingrained in so many Sierra Leoneans'.[68] Indeed, the governor was convinced that the strikers' obduracy was sustained by the support they had received from the intelligentsia.[69] He was outraged and scandalised by the elite, who were supposed to support the government, assuming the leadership of the workers. What was even more serious, the opposition was proving 'much tougher than we expected'.[70] These rebels not only established a strike fund on 8 February, subscribed to by Sierra Leonean exiles abroad as well as inhabitants in the Colony and Protectorate, but there also appeared to have been effected a front of solidarity, unifying Protectorate and Colony peoples.[71] It signified 'the importance of unity and combined effort on the part of West Africans politically and economically at the present stage of our history'.[72] The documented case of the participation of a Mende man in the strike effort was jubilated over as a fitting reply 'to those who want the aborigines to dissociate themselves from the Creoles'.[73] It was a demonstration of 'national resistance'.

This development exercised the government no end, as the speeches made by the Executive Council members showed. In fact, since the strike had now assumed a political complexion, Slater saw it as 'a serious trial of strength', 'a political fight to the death between the government and the Creoles' and, in this confrontation, there could be only one survivor.[74]

But all this show of solidarity and demonstrations of brinkmanship, spiced as they were by ugly scenes, did not help the workers, simply because the government held the whiphand. On 26 February, after six weeks of stout defiance, the workers returned to work on the government's terms. Less than a dozen people were arrested; thirty-seven pensionable workers, some of whom had worked for twenty years, were dismissed from the railway.[75] The Colonial Office sent telegrams to Slater congratulating him for having 'successfully beaten' the strike.[76] But the ripples went beyond the Railway headquarters at Cline Town. They embraced the whole Krio community, especially the City Council.

At a post-mortem session over the strike the entire Krio Community was subjected to vituperative abuse by the Executive Council. Their denunciations of Krio disloyalty went to hysterical dimensions. Bitterness, resentment and extreme distaste for the Krio were reflected in the vitriolic comments of the government officials.[77] Dr W. D. Inness, Director of Medical and Sanitary Services, opened the barrage with this salvo: 'the disgraceful manner in which the educated Creole has, almost without exception, seized the opportunity of the strike, even if he is not *actually guilty*, as I think he is, of having engineered it from the start, to range himself definitely on the side of disorder' indicated that they were 'not yet ready for elective representation'.[78] Since they valued this highly, it must be taken away from them. P. F. Barton, the Treasurer, added that those who had benefited from the concession of elective representation had supported the strike, and had 'fanned racial hatred and defied, so far as [they] dared, all discipline, law and order'. What was even more reprehensible, this 'menace to constitutional government' had in a 'selfish and self-seeking manner' made 'an invidious attempt to stir up disaffection through the nominated Protectorate Chiefs'. Their aim, he concluded, was to 'oust the European. The broader outlook on the long view seem to be beyond their vision.'[79] Another member, Lt Col. Norton, exercised by this iniquitous attempt by Krio politicians to corrupt the Protectorate people, waded into the fray with typical military directness and bombast:

> It seems to me that the elected members have been chosen as the people's representatives in the local 'parliament' merely as a means to an end, i.e. to say, to embarrass and hinder the government in every possible shape and form. Their battle cry is 'Africa for the Africans' or being otherwise interpreted

'Sierra Leone for the Creole'[!] They devoted themselves mainly to airing some petty or alleged hardship inflicted on their fellow Creole brethren by a hard and unsympathetic government...attitude of disrespect of one elected member might influence the unsophisticated chiefs.

They had thrown down the gauntlet and challenged the authority of the government, pronounced the Army Commandant.[80] Two Krio leaders, Bright and Betts, were singled out, for obvious reasons, as targets for the most cutting comments. McDonell, the Attorney-General, the strongman in Slater's administration,[81] opined that because of the low level of intelligence of the electorate, and the paucity of qualified voters in the rural areas, 'the most undesirable representatives had been chosen'. He feared that

> elected members by providing a focus has exacerbated race feeling in Sierra Leone. The major part of their contribution to debate[s] has been concerned with demands of more and more of the loaves and fishes for their brethren, and has been rarely, if ever, directed in avenues indicating a glimmering of statesmanship in viewing the needs of the colony as a whole.
> The serious part of the situation seems to me to lie in the fact that, owing to the adventitious importance given by the new constitution to two not very successful practitioners of medicine and law, they have been able if not in the first instance, to foment, at any rate by their demagogic arts, to prolong a strike which they have used as an occasion for stirring up latent racial prejudice throughout the colony.[82]

H. C. Luke, the Colonial Secretary, performed the *coup de grâce*:

> The manner in which the Creole community has manifested its sympathies [with the strikers] renders it desirable for government to reconsider the claim of the Creoles to be a civilized people and to enjoy the privileges generally associated with such a claim. I would refer to the manner in which all organised and articulate Creole opinion has, almost without exception, used the strike as a channel for the expression of its repudiation of the methods and principles of European rule, and its anti-European sentiments. In other words, it has not only endeavoured to make of the strike a revolt against discipline, it has endeavoured, without the smallest provocation to make it a quarrel between black and white.

His remedy to this aberration was short and to the point – suspend 'for an indefinite period' the provision of elective representation in the 1924 Constitution, because the 'Creoles have been blameworthy'! This decision, he pointed out, 'will not affect the loyal aborigines'![83]

The man who had praised elected members for their constructive contributions to the debate on the 1926 Estimates a few months back, now thundered in answer to an objection raised by Slater:[84]

> I will at once agree that they have not always been obstructive, although I cannot recall any legislative pitfalls of importance from which they have saved us. On the other hand, I have a vivid recollection of their lack of constructiveness and their narrowness of outlook, particularly in connection with the Estimates, the scrutiny and criticism of which may be regarded, I suppose, as their most important function.

73

The two elected members, he insisted, were 'as unsusceptible to the processes of argument at all events, of argument from the side of the government'. Clearly Slater's Executive was out for the blood of the Krio. Typically, the administration was chasing shadows for substance, refusing to identify and acknowledge the real cause of the unrest and the reasons why the Krio elite supported the workers. These reasons were not important to the administration. As a matter of fact, as Slater's government saw it, the Krio had a narrow and parochial attitude; they had a callous disregard for truth; and their racial bias was pronounced and intemperate. Indeed, 'their intemperate and disrespectful criticism of government would have unsettling effects on Paramount Chief members'. On the latter point, notice the emphasis the government put on the absolute undesirability of allowing the degenerate Krio agitators to corrupt loyal, obedient and trustworthy members of the Protectorate. As already noted, the same preference for, and sympathy to, the Protectorate, was demonstrated by the Slater administration in 1922 on the question of the payment of the levy imposed on some towns for damages caused in the strike and riots of 1919. Slater was prepared to write off the levy because he wanted to attest his confidence 'in the Chiefs'. But he did not discountenance the suggestion from his advisers to pressurise the City Council into honouring its fiscal obligations under the Riot Damages Act, even though the government acknowledged, in another development, that the City was too poor.[85]

Such nuances, and others identified in various parts of this work, were responsible for, and sustained, the dichotomy in Sierra Leone politics. An appreciation of this feature will help to understand the political polarities of the 1940s.

As far as the strike issue was concerned, Slater generally agreed with his advisors, but he had certain reservations. He counselled caution. It was not that he did not think that the Krio deserved a salutary punishment for their temerity, but he considered that there might be some unwelcome complications arising from the decision to suspend the constitution. At one point, though, he was even prepared to go that far if the O'Brien Commission on the City Council that was then meeting in Freetown recommended the dissolution of the Municipality.[86] However, so the governor's analysis reasoned, apart from extremists in and out of the Legislative Council, like Bright, J. F. Boston, Betts and J. C. Shorunkeh-Sawyerr, some of the more solid citizens, such as C. E. Wright, a nominated member, and A. E. Tuboku-Metzger (who was ill for most of the time), were studiously moderate in their pronouncements. A. J. Shorunkeh-Sawyerr, Songo-Davies, E. H. Cummings, S. J. S. Barlatt, and A. N. Jones, two of them unsuccessful candidates at the last elections, had refrained from expressing an opinion. Barlatt was in fact currently holding a government appointment as Acting Police Magistrate. Given this substantial section of moderate citizens, therefore, 'Freetown must not be judged by its journalism, its City Council, and its West African Congresses'! Besides, other segments of the population,

74

for instance, the Chief Justice, the Bishop and the European Chamber of Commerce had advocated tempered justice for the workers also. More gratifying was the fact that the chiefs had consistently refused to be influenced 'by the windy and reckless speeches of the Urban members'. On the contrary, Slater exulted, 'their attitude seems to be one of quiet satisfaction and even amusement at the repeated defeat of these members in argument – a defeat to which the Chiefs are beginning themselves to contribute effectively, and not infrequently'.[87] Still, noting that his Executive had not advocated the removal of Paramount Chiefs from the Legislative Council, he was not convinced that the exclusion of elected members would guarantee the protection of chiefs from undue influence: 'the Chiefs would still hear the same vehement criticism of government, and their mis-representation outside the council would be much less easy to counter'. Besides, the governor confessed, 'there is already no little difficulty in selecting suitable Africans as nominated members'. Consequently, the governor advised,

> In my opinion, the harm that demagogues of the type of Dr. Bankole-Bright and Mr. Beoku-Betts can, and undoubtedly do, cause, is to some extent mitigated rather than accentuated by the fact of their membership of the Council. Their sense of responsibility as legislators is, it is true, painfully low; but it is occasionally discernible... Moreover, the character of the resolutions tabled by these members in respect of the Railway Strike have been moderate in tone, in striking contrast to their unmeasured and mischievous utterances at public meetings... Bankole-Bright was characteristically disingenuous and offensive but Beoku-Betts was evidently anxious for a restoration of good will... In my judgement to oust from the Legislative Council the members who were chosen by the people less than two years ago would, by making martyrs of them, increase their power for harm more than continued tolerance of their presence can do.

To sum up then, to avoid antagonising the moderate section 'on whose tacit, if timid support, we can now depend', by taking such acts of reprisal and thus driving 'underground the disorderly and undisciplined elements unhappily present in the colony of Sierra Leone', and 'thereby gravely enhance the danger arising from such elements', Slater advised against suspending the constitution. Furthermore, he quickly pointed out, 'it would inflict a damaging blow at the prestige of both local and Imperial governments' to withdraw, after two years of trial, a concession granted to a people whose character they had known before they agreed to promulgate the constitution. This might make an unfortunate impression on the people.[88] The Colonial Office, which, of course, shared the local government's distaste for Colony politicians, endorsed the governor's decision. Ormsby-Gore, the Under Secretary of State for the Colonies, opined, 'I am quite sure it would be impolitic to attempt to revise the Constitution of the Legislative Council even if Sir C. O'Brien makes a recommendation which I hope he will not make. Personally, I think Dr. Bankole-Bright has already overreached himself, and I believe there will be a reaction if things are wisely handled.' Other means were found to punish the Krio for impugning the prestige of the government. These included the slowing down of the rate of Africanisation.[89] Bright and Betts became *personae non gratae* at Government House; they were excluded from the list of invitees to official functions. A new set of regulations, introduced in April, made it an offence for an African Civil Servant to associate with political groups, address a meeting, or to 'take part in any demonstration or procession which has a political character or purpose'.[90] Aspiring activists who were government employees were thus effectively gagged. This affected political mobilisation in the Colony, while government assault on the City Council, an African-'controlled' institution, gave warning about the nature of future relations between the administration and the Krios.

The dissolution of the City Council

More by design than by chance the Freetown government chose at this time to investigate the City Council, set up as an elective Corporation with a Mayor and Aldermen as early as 1893. There had been threats before to do away with the Municipality, but the Colonial Office had not approved of the moves because, *inter alia*, it was thought then that at least the *raison d'être* of the Council was to give an opportunity to Britain's African subjects to learn the art of government.[91] However, the minutes of the Colonial Office staff at this time, and the thirst for blood evinced by the colonial administration after the defeat of the 1926 strike, give strong grounds to suspect that the move to inquire into the Council's affairs was not unconnected with the reprisals against the Krio. The remarks of Ormsby-Gore who wrote after his visit to Sierra Leone, on 14–24 April immediately following the strike, that the latter 'had tended to become political rather than industrial in character', and that it had become 'complicated by the intervention of a certain section of the politicians in Freetown', confirm this.[92] Besides, A. Fiddian, the official handling Sierra Leone affairs, had questioned the wisdom of investigating the Council at a time when it could 'be construed that the Sierra Leone government was determined to put the citizen of Freetown in his place, and generally speaking to get the neck of the African well under the European heel'.[93] But then he salved his conscience by arguing that since the process had started, it must go on as Slater had insisted – 'to drop the proposal now would look like backing out'.[94] It is also clear that over time official thinking was that the Council was a breeding-ground for African critics of the government, 'a nest bed for political demagogues'.[95]

In May 1926, Sir Charles O'Brien, a former governor of Barbados, was appointed sole Commissioner to inquire into, and report on, the affairs of the Freetown City Council. He was accompanied by A. J. Dawe of the Colonial Office who was sent so that he could get 'a view at first hand of Freetown and its problems'.[96] The decision to hold this inquiry partly arose from the government's dissatisfaction with the affairs of the Council, especially with the way its finances were being handled. Correspondence on the City Council revealed a depressing monetary state: at the end of October 1921, the Council had an excess of assets of £644 over liabilities, but in the fiscal year of 1919–20 there was a deficit of £2,041 on the City Fund Account, and £3,143 on the Water Works account; accumulated arrears for 1923–4 amounted to £2,469. The explanation behind this was that the City Council had not been vigorous in collecting its rates but, more important, there seemed to be utter chaos in the financial arrangements; administrative and fiscal control seemed lax.[97]

These revelations were nothing new. Indeed, even before 1926 the public had been critical of the way the Council was administering the City, although its defenders protested that it could not do much because of the constraints placed on its areas of supervision by the central government and, more particularly, that it could not give improved services without money. This was not forthcoming because the Freetown people were too poor to be able to bear further increases in rates.[98] The colonial government itself had admitted in 1922, when considering what measures were to be employed to force the City Council to pay the fine imposed on it after the 1919 strike, that

> a community such as Freetown is relatively poor. When the Riots occurred, Freetown was fairly prosperous; it is not now. With the exception of government officials (European and African) who have had substantial increases in salary, every class of the Community is poorer than before the outbreak of the war and any increase in rates would be a hardship on the poor ratepayers.[99]

Still, there was a demand for a reorganisation of the Council to make it more efficient and give it more teeth. A paper on the issue was presented at the Congress meeting in Freetown in 1923.[100] Public education on the Council led by Mayor May's paper, the *Weekly News*, and public criticisms, reached the high point of 1926 when certain disclosures came to light, namely, corruption among the Council's officials. These exposures eventually led to court cases in which the City Solicitor, J. Fowell Boston, played a dubious role. The Town Clerk was later charged with fraud, and the Mayor, Claudius May, nominated Unofficial Member of the Legislative Council, Editor/ Proprietor of the *Weekly News* and Honorary Consul for Liberia in Sierra Leone, was gaoled for nine months for conspiracy to defraud the Council of 160 corrugated iron sheets.[101]

These developments conveniently came at a time when the local government had decided, with the acquiescence of Whitehall, to investigate 'the whole question of the Council's constitution, powers, sources of revenue etc.' Had the government contented itself with this legitimate goal, it could have been argued that the reason for the government's intervention in Council affairs was the perfectly normal desire of seeing that the municipal government was being run efficiently. But, from the first, the government had ulterior motives to make the City Council a 'department of government'.

77

The colonial administration had never been happy over the 'independent' character of the Council, and it had increasingly shown marked disapproval of City Councillors playing the role of mentors of the people.[102] The government was therefore happy to confirm the recommendations of the O'Brien Commission to replace the elected African majority in the Council with an official majority. In December 1926, the City Council was dissolved and replaced by a Municipal Board, entirely made up of government nominees. And for the next twenty-two years the Municipality was run directly by government.[103]

The decision to dissolve the City Council aroused widespread public indignation and outrage. Newspapers like the *Weekly News* castigated the British authorities for this transparent heavy handedness and gross injustice. They pointed to the double standards evident in the local authorities' handling of the 1926 debacle; for instance, similar disturbances in London did not call forth as harsh a treatment as was meted out to the Freetown workers. For that matter, the British government did not dissolve a Borough Council in England after a number of councillors were proved to be corrupt or, when Fitzgerald, a former District Commissioner, defrauded the government the latter did not decide not to appoint any more white men as District Commissioners because one had betrayed the trust reposed in him! So went the comparisons. In short, the conviction of senior officials of the City Council should not be interpreted as an index of venality justifying dissolution. It was a political act then, clearly aimed at destroying the political aspirations of the Krio.

Protests by citizens presented in memorials and resolutions were brushed aside with supreme disdain.[104] Bankole-Bright thundered against British perfidy all he could, continuing his protests against the administration, when he had complained bitterly to Ormsby-Gore in 1925 that 'government appears to set out on the policy of embarrassing our corporation in that it tries to cripple its finances by bolting the door against all financial income'.[105] Later on, during the debate on the abolition of the Council and the establishment of a Temporary Board in its place, Bright emphasised the point that the Council had been established to train people in self-government, though he himself 'had never aspired to be a City Councillor because he had no wish to be a party to an organisation whose wings had been so clipped by government that it was merely a tax collector'. Even so, the work of the Council had been carried on for several years by Mayors with success. And it was unfair, he maintained, to condemn the Institution because of a 'past administration'. Admittedly, he went on, the finances were chaotic and the frauds were persistent, but these were due to collusions between the auditors and Treasurer who should have been given stiffer sentences by the Judge. As for May's conviction, he believed in the man's innocence, and he darkly hinted at his own conclusions about May's trial and conviction. On O'Brien's recommendations for a European Mayor and a European majority in the new body to be set up by government, he alleged that it was a 'colour legislation'.[106] Betts himself objected to this colour bias, and while conceding that a reconstitution of the Council was desirable he wondered whether 'efficiency could not be achieved without striking at the root of the Institution'. For, after all, the public disclosures preceding the Commission of Inquiry had been 'due to the action of the Council itself'![107]

The grand old man of politics, culture nationalist, A. E. Tuboku-Metzger, in a passionate speech, denounced his colleagues, accusing them of appearing to accept the change to the *status quo* too readily. He believed that the main point of the Council system constituted 'an important element of education and culture'. And he deprecated O'Brien's recommendations on the grounds that they would introduce 'discontinuity'. They were also destructive without being constructive.[108]

A. J. Songo-Davies, government nominee and Deputy Mayor in the just dissolved City Council, appeared to have worked closely with Slater. He and C. E. Wright, nominated member of the Legislative Council, approved the O'Brien Report with enthusiasm. Slater called Songo-Davies' stand one of 'conspicuous courage and thoughtfulness', while Wright averred that if government was going to control the new body it should have somebody at the head to put through its policies. Slater concluded from these remarks that despite the general tenor of the elected members' speeches even they had accepted the prospect of practical government control. The persistent demand for an elected majority control of a resuscitated City Council in later years does not justify Slater's over-sanguine conclusions.[109]

However, a singularly interesting contribution came from the Bishop of Sierra Leone. He expressed regret that the Commissioner had not paid tribute to the hard work which had been put in from time to time by those in authority, for example the late Mayor (May?). It was an ironic twist (if he was referring to May, and not Betts, who was acting Mayor when the Council was dissolved) that it was left to a European to call attention to this omission. It did suggest that at least some members of the European establishment did not think that the City Council, dominated by Africans for thirty-three years, was decrepit and rotten to the core. Another suggestion which the Bishop made was the possibility of bringing 'Protectorate elements' into the new body. The suggestion was not immediately accepted, but government's response to this idea was to be reflected in the reconstitution of the City Council twenty-two years later.[110]

But for now Bankie could roar and blast against British injustices for all he was worth. This made no impression on the government. Rather, the Colonial Office and the Sierra Leone government were happy over the City Council's demise; they congratulated themselves for having given the Krio their come uppance. The feelings of the Colonial Office were explicitly enunciated in the following quotes: 'The men that are chosen to work in these Councils are as a rule quite incapable of administering the affairs of any Municipality. It seems the same in many places. Had I been another month in Jamaica I would have dissolved the Kingston Corporation' (S.H.J.).[111]

A. J. Dawe, the official handling Sierra Leone affairs, observed: 'The reason why Council won't work is that the African Native is quite unfitted to discharge administrative responsibilities.' He exulted when news of the O'Brien Commission Report reached London and noted:

The government has now complete control of Freetown Municipality affairs; the City should soon begin to feel the benefit of a new regime of honesty and efficiency. So ends the experiment of 1893, and from the sentimentality which inspired it, the unfortunate Africans have had to suffer a great deal. It is a pity the history of the matter cannot be made widely known as it contains lessons which would be useful guides for bigger things.[112]

But the government did not come out of the episode untarnished, nor did the 'efficiency and honesty' of the Council improve beyond reproach under government control. Its complicity in the trial and conviction of Mayor May, hitherto a respected pillar of society, cannot clearly be proved. Nevertheless, certain aspects of the trial and the admission of government officials that they had been influenced (to pervert justice) strongly indicate a case of vendetta by officialdom against May, who was President of the local Congress at the time of his conviction. Fowell Boston, according to Cookson's evidence, certainly had a grudge against May, and helping to bring charges against him was his own way of spiting the ex-Mayor.[113]

Two positive results came from the strike however: the Mountain Railway connecting the City and the European Reserve at Hill Station was closed down in 1929 because it was belatedly realised that it was costing the government a great deal of money. In any case, it was becoming less relevant, since the European officials, for whose convenience the railway was run, now had their own motor cars. The railway was replaced by a bus service that catered for the needs of the rural inhabitants in a more meaningful way.[114] Secondly, improvements in the railway, such as the introduction of the Garratt-type engine (capable of pulling a 200–5 ton weight and 69 per cent more load) into the service, the training of deserving African mechanics who could drive the new engines 'very satisfactorily', and the setting up of a Railway Staff Committee – some sort of Arbitration Board – were all intended to make the railway more efficient and economical. But this was at the expense of a nascent trade union organisation whose members were victimised or harassed by the Administration. Not surprisingly, the Railway Workers Union declined. It is also doubtful whether the admittedly sound reforms carried out in the department made much impact on the perennial deficit of the railway.[115]

Apart from humbling the workers, the political implications of the episode point to a number of conclusions. The evidence clearly indicates that colonial administrations were opposed to organised labour, especially when such a movement resorted to industrial action. They were even more implacable to the idea of the elite making common cause with the workers, or 'subverting' British influence among the chiefs. Also the punitive measures taken by the government against the Krios retarded their political advance as Slater had boasted in an address to colonial circles in London.[116]

These points sharply illustrate the contradictions in colonial policy. A rationale of continued British presence in her colonies was the declared objective of teaching Africans the mechanics of democracy by training, through the use and experiment of British institutions, political concepts, parliamentary procedure and behaviour, so that they could be well equipped to eventually control their own future. Yet, when those sufficiently trained in these virtues, the elite, who were articulate enough to express themselves, chose those very means of protest and representation, regarded as legitimate in Britain, they were denounced as traitors and troublemakers. Colonial administrators were prepared to tolerate the elite if they identified with the colonising power, but once they stepped out of this prescribed role they were castigated as saboteurs of colonial rule. Political scientists who chide and condemn this generation of politicians for not going too far in their resistance to colonial rule, or plainly accuse them of collaboration, often appear to ignore the political realities of the period. They fail to appreciate the dilemma in which people like Bright found themselves. These activists, as Magubane has argued, in the context of the performance of the educated elite in the early struggles of the African National Congress in South Africa, appreciated the benefits of British rule, but their instincts, their commitment to their motherland, impelled them to attack the bad policies of the colonial government. Yet when they did this, they were tarred with the opprobrium of extremism.[117] The irony is that 'radical' scholars regard them as conservative collaborators.

In any case, what were Bright and Betts guilty of? In the strike action they were merely identifying themselves with public opinion. And this was solid, taking into its embrace a cross section of Freetown society. For instance, the meeting at Wilberforce Memorial Hall was addressed mostly by Congress members, but the speakers included a highly respected politician such as A. J. Shorunkeh-Sawyerr, not a member of N.C.B.W.A., and the Reverend E. N. Jones, who had changed his name to Lamina Sankoh because of white prejudice. The latter called the labour unrest a 'race Strike'.[118] Barlatt, then acting as Police Magistrate, gave £6 to the Strike Fund and acted as solicitor to the Workers' Union.[119] However, Bright and Betts, as elected leaders, saw it as their responsibility and duty to give leadership to the people, to take the brunt of the colonial assault, to act as buffers between the workers and the government. For this Bright, in particular, suffered personal insults and vindictive ostracism at the hands of Slater and his aides. But he was more than equal to the challenge.

During the debate on the strike action in the Legislative Council, Slater took gubernatorial arrogance too far when he upbraided Bright and told him to lower his voice as it was a small chamber. That stalwart promptly and aptly retorted: 'Your Excellency, I am sorry, but I have been used to speaking like this for the past twenty years and I am afraid that it is too late in the day for me to moderate my tone. I think, Your Excellency will appreciate my difficulty'![120] After repeatedly slighting the Double Bs. by excluding them from the list of invitees to official functions at Government House, the administration received a sharp rebuff when Bright and Betts refused to attend the ceremony to see the governor off.[121] Queried by the Colonial Office for this alleged disrespect to Slater, Bright's answer typically underlined his stout defence of his race's integrity against the arrogance of officialdom: 'Whilst I conceive it my bounden duty as an elected member of Council to show the usual courtesies to H.M.'s representative, equally so I feel it should be the pleasure of H.M.'s representative to show the *usual courtesy to me as the People's representative* [my emphasis].' The man's peerless fortitude and courage were irreproachable. Happily, Colonial Secretary Amery had the good grace to let go of the issue, but Bright was a marked man.[122] Governments, especially the colonial type, have long memories and they do not forget an impudence.

An opportunity to chasten Bright and to discredit him to the pubic presented itself to the government in 1929 when Bright got himself involved in a civil suit filed against him by a lady friend, but the administration let the chance go for reasons which, to say the least, are very intriguing. Bankie, who had the reputation of being a lady's man, apparently got involved with Mrs Abigail Harris Felix (allegedly an ex-patient of his) while she was staying with her father, Emmanuel Nathaniel Harris, between April 1925 and November 1928. During the course of this relationship, some money transactions took place, and Bright allegedly refused to pay back these loans. Bankie denied these charges, made by Mrs Harris and her husband, and he protested that the case was trumped up by his political enemies to embarrass and discredit him. The Chief Justice, His Honour M. L. Tew, however, ruled against Bright. The learned Judge agreed that there was evidence of a political vendetta, and that J. F. Boston, the plaintiff's lawyer, singled out as one of Bright's enemies, 'was inspired by no friendly or even unprejudiced feelings towards him'. But he confessed that the 'loose moral character' of the complainant apart, he did not believe Bright 'because his financial position did not seem to have been so satisfactory as he had represented'. 'The defendant', he went on, 'shows every appearance of being possessed of a domineering character and I do not find it the least difficult to believe that he acquired such an ascendancy over plaintiff.'[123]

Bright appealed, through his lawyer friend, Beoku-Betts, against the Chief Justice's ruling, but he lost the case the following year with costs. But Bright was a determined man; consistently protesting his innocence, he made several attempts to plead his case before the Privy Council. When these applications were refused, he asked the Colonial Office to have his case reviewed by its Legal Officers, claiming government animosity towards him, police harassment, and ostracism by government (he was not invited to Legislative Council dinners).[124] One is not sure about the correctness or constitutionality of Bright's procedure, but his persistence is typical of his dogged tenacity once he decided to pursue an issue. The length, duration, or roughness of the hunt did not matter to him. However, if Bright hoped to get sympathy from Whitehall, he was sadly mistaken, and his optimism betrays a slight suspicion of naïveté, since even Bright himself should have known that because of his activities he was not the most popular person at the Colonial Office. One official called him a 'particularly unpleasant person'. Some suggested that his name be struck off the medical register for 'infamous conduct in a professional request [sic]'. Interestingly enough, this action was discarded because of complications: for instance, the Colonial Office was not sure whether by defrocking him they might not be making a martyr of this 'positively offensive man'. The punishment might be counter-productive. Indeed, the government might even be accused of vindictive persecution of the people's leaders.[125] This admission tacitly gave recognition, if grudgingly, to the popularity of Bright and his standing among his people. More intriguing, the case of Bright is perhaps the only example of a colonial administration letting off a sworn enemy for fear of antagonising public opinion. If there are other examples, they are not many.[126]

In any case, the Colonial Office decided alternatively to invoke Article 22 of the Legislative Ordinance (1924) which stipulated that a member who absented himself from Legislative Council sittings for two calendar months without being ill, or without the permission of the governor, forfeited his seat automatically. The governor was told, in March 1932, to transmit to Bright the C.O.'s inability to concede to his request, and to inform him that because of the infraction of the above article he could no longer take any part in the proceedings of the Council.

Apparently this decision was not acted upon,[127] because Bankie continued to be an elected member of the Legislative Council for the next seven years. But such was the official resentment against Bright that even when, in 1929, he became the first Urban member, the listing gave precedence to Betts, who should, according to strict Legislative Council protocol, come after Bright.[128] It is also clear that the Administration was never happy over the runs of success of Bright and Betts. After the 1934 elections in which Betts polled 1,351 votes, and Bright 1,196 votes, T. N. Goddard, author of the *Handbook of Sierra Leone*, then acting as governor, sent character sketches of the unofficial members of the Legislative Council.[129] Betts was said to be

> a lawyer whose practice compares favourably with any Barrister of pure African blood [though] exceedingly poor lawyer [sic] according to some Chief Justices and Law Officers, but considerable facility in public speaking and his reputation as a demagogue is high. During his public career, his loyalty has been suspect on several occasions, and although during the past few years he has behaved himself he is not to be trusted and his actions are inspired by a motive no more exalted than the consideration of his personal career. He is of little use to the Council and has seldom uttered a constructive criticism worthy of the government's consideration. He is a skilled young man and will probably retain his seat for a considerable period. He will need watching.

In spite of Goddard's deprecations, it is curious that Betts' name consistently appeared in all major Committees of the Legislative Council and public ones set up by government from which Bright was invariably excluded!

The report on Bright was considerably longer. The second Urban member was

> a fire brand who is rapidly flickering to extinction. In the days of comparative prosperity he had in him the makings of a rather dangerous demagogue, but his complete lack of any kind of moral or financial integrity and his present precarious and questionable mode of life have robbed him of any kind of prestige in the eyes of all save the riff raff of the electorate. He has considerable gift of speech and an undoubted power to sway a mob, and he depends for his seat on the Council on a section of the Community that is notoriously short in memory and prone to give their suffrage to the loudest speaker. His re-election to the Council caused nobody any surprise. During recent years he has been involved in a most unsavoury case in the Courts which would have ruined any public man in a community with a high standard of public morality; he is utterly unscrupulous in financial matters and is now appearing in court in connection with sundry judgement debtor summons [sic]. He has no medical practice; it is no exaggeration to say that he lives almost entirely on blackmail and intimidation. His presence on the Council is no help to the Council or the Constituents he purports to represent; it is occasionally a nuisance but does not nowadays amount to much more than a nuisance. Everybody knows quite well that he is a worthless scoundrel, and he is well aware that every one knows it.

Predictably those on nominated members were less harsh, even admiring; for instance, C. E. Wright, of mixed parentage,

> speaks little in Council, all he says is to the point and well worthy of consideration. His criticisms of government Bills have always been of the greatest value to the law officers of the Crown. He is of independent mind and is at all times prepared to give his time and knowledge ungrudgingly to the service of the government. He is an exceptionally able lawyer, and I know of no man in Freetown who could adequately fill his place as a member of the Council in which he is by far the most useful unofficial member.

Indeed, the renomination of this model subject of the local British Administration to a third term as an unofficial member in the Legislative Council appears to have inspired this smear campaign on the other members to justify the government's conviction that Wright was an indispensable asset in the Council. Goddard and his colleagues believed that all the other nominees were 'unwantables'. 'Wright was incomparably preferable to any available.' The Colonial Office was, however, not very happy about this candidate because of precedents and complications arising from a third term of office by an incumbent who should normally serve two terms maximum. To be sure, the Secretary of State gave his approval with some reservation.[130]

J. A. Songo-Davies, a veteran of seventy-three years, was an 'indefatigable social and church worker in Freetown and the Protectorate – an African gent of the best type'. He had a marked independence of mind 'entirely fearless and pursuing what he considers to be the honest course of action in the face of bitter opposition from some of his compatriots, and in complete disregard of threats of actual personal violence. He is a very useful (if somewhat longwinded) Councillor, and his place will be difficult to fill.'

The chiefs who were not always forthcoming, according to some reports, were, according to Goddard, 'intelligent', 'level headed', 'enlightened', and they rendered good service; the utterances of P. C. Alfred Tucker, for example, 'always repay attention'. Still, they merited only three sentences each. C. F. Loxley, the European Mercantile member (1926 and 1931), made criticisms that were 'wise and thoughtful' – a very useful member who commanded the respect of every class of the Community.[131]

The point brooks no argument that this decidely biased account by Goddard patently exposes the low regard the local government had for elected members in the Council. All of them (including J. G. Hyde, the Rural Area member, whose 'contributions to debates in Council were usually thoughtful and moderately expressed') were men 'entirely devoid of any scruples', overtly ambitious and dangerous, unsuccessful professionals, whose relevance to the Legislative Council was questionable. On the other hand, nominated members, who invariably supported government measures anyhow, because their continuation in the Assembly depended on government backing, were moderate, useful and sensible representatives! If Bright and Betts were such useless miscreants one wonders why the people continued to vote them into office in 1924, 1929, and 1934. Perhaps there was nobody responsible enough to 'stand up to such creatures as Dr. B. B.'?[132] Again, it might simply be a case of there being no suitable alternatives to the Double Bs. But this could hardly be the case in an articulate and politically alert place like Freetown. And it is unlikely that the electorate was as consistently unsophisticated and naive as the Acting Governor would have us believe, bearing in mind that the franchise was limited to propertied and literate citizens. However, if we accept Goddard's assessment, then we should exclude the Double Bs. from this compliment paid to the unofficial members by a governor on two occasions:

> I have always been impressed with the care with which unofficial members draft legislation, but the vigilance of the members in this Council is exceptional. I think, almost without exception, that each of the unofficial members has contributed to our deliberations something by way of useful criticisms, suggestions and information...I have also noticed with great interest not only the vigilance of Unofficial members but their vigorous independence. More than one of the suggestions made yesterday and today by the new members came, I fancy, as a surprise to the official side. I consider it of good augury for the future that every member of the Council at its first sitting has shown himself conspicuously alive to the public interest. (Slater, 1924)[133]

> I have been struck with the care which unofficial members have taken to see that the rights of the subject are not unduly encroached upon. That is a very proper function of the unofficial members, and they have exercised it faithfully[!] (Slater, 1927).[134]

It would be unfair to dismiss Bright and Betts because of Goddard's prejudices.

If C. E. Wright was such a virtuous and useful citizen, it would have been more commendable for him to test his standing with his people by seeking election. Being occupied with his career is no excuse, for Bright and Betts were professionals too, with jobs to do! Also, if Betts was the kind of man Goddard claimed he was we are surprised that the government chose him from among twelve possible contenders, including Barstow Scholar, Henry J. Lightfoot Boston, to appoint him as the first African Police Magistrate in 1937. Was it to drive a wedge between him and Bright, or because he had mellowed, having now been satisfied that 'his personal ambitions are more likely to be realised by co-operation with, than by opposition to the government'?[135] The point that is being argued here is that one must be careful in accepting official assessments of local figures. Government's opinion changed with time, circumstances and personalities. All is not white, neither is everything black, but invariably the degree of official disapproval matched the intensity of the subject's opposition to government's policies.

5

In the Legislative Council, 1924–1939: constructive opposition

A year after the Colonial Office decision not to entertain his appeal against the judgement on the Felix case, an admiring pen portrait on Bright was published in *W.A.S.U.* the magazine of the West African Students' Union in London. While he was not blind to Bankie's obvious faults, the writer proclaimed that were West Africa a republic no one would be more fitted to be elected President as Dr Bankole-Bright.[1]

> He is ambitious enough and skilled in pushing himself up. *Without him the light of Sierra Leone would be dim and her voice mute.* It is therefore the duty of every citizen to have the fullest confidence in him for there is no gain saying the fact that he is now the best politician in Freetown.

It was the highest compliment Bright ever received in public.

This then does not suggest that the 'ardent nationalist' was solely devoted to bearding the English Lion in its den. On the contrary, he made a great deal of constructive criticism and championed issues of real importance, for instance, the Assessors' Ordinance – probably the single most vital issue with which Bright was emotionally involved or, to put it another way, a cause to which he devoted 'his professional leisure in the pages of his paper'.[2]

The Assessors' Ordinance and other issues

One of the grievances of the elite was the vexing question of the Assessors' Ordinance. It was introduced in 1895 to replace the jury (in criminal cases) on the grounds that the local juries were often partial and parochial, and that unbiased findings could not be obtained. More to the point, it was argued that juries tended to be illiterate and they could not understand the fine points involved in cases like embezzlement and fraud. Also, racial considerations were not excluded from jury findings.[3] However, the most odious parts of the Ordinance were, for example, Section 42, article 35 (of a 1905 amendment) which gave the Attorney-General the authority to demand Trial by Assessors if he believed justice could be secured through that avenue. But then it gave the Attorney-General too wide a power, liable to be abused; it made a lazy Attorney-General more likely to seek the easy way out by opting for Trial by Assessors knowing full well that the chances of getting a conviction were more than assured, particularly so since the Judge (assisted by three Assessors, handpicked by the government) was not bound to accept the Assessors' verdict, even if unanimous. The accused, if found guilty, had no right of appeal. First used in the trial of J. H. Spaine, the Krio Postmaster, Head of the Post Office, charged with embezzlement in 1895, in time the people of Freetown came to regard the Ordinance as a convenient tool used by the government to get rid of troublesome critics and objectionable individuals.[4] Many fell victim to this system, including the respected Mayor May: between 1901 and 1921, thirteen cases were tried by Assessors and the Court found them all guilty, though in twelve of these the Assessors unanimously returned a verdict of not guilty. In the thirteenth case one Assessor cried guilty while the other two declared the accused not guilty. Of these cases, eight were tried by G. K. T. Purcell, Chief Justice of Sierra Leone (1911–29).[5] Those from the January 1921 to January 1927 sessions amounted to forty-nine cases. Some of these included accused persons who had multiple charges against them; others involved several trials with more than one accused in the dock. For example, A. E. Lynch had seven charges of false pretence, and I. O. Bright was charged with Augustus Marke, Robert Palmer, Bokari Santigi, alias Kowa, Joe, Sonnifu, Abdulai, and Ansumana of larceny and conspiracy (only Marke was found not guilty). Again, in this second set of cases, the statistics show a consistency in the incidence of conviction, even though in as many as five cases there were unanimous returns by the Assessors of not guilty verdicts. On the other hand, thirty verdicts coincided with the decisions of the Judges, while in split verdicts the decision of the court went either way – guilty or not guilty.[6] The frequent used of the Ordinance, as proved by the documents cited, and the number of convictions it secured, was most worrying to citizens. And, as the names in the lists revealed, victims under this system cut across social and ethnic lines. In the case of Bright, his concern as a citizen was leavened by the fact that his half-brother I. O. Bright, a Post Office employee, was convicted and gaoled under this system in 1923. But others, too, were very much interested in the question and were fiercely committed to the abolition of the Ordinance. Prominent among these concerned citizens were F. J. Boston, a local barrister and City Solicitor who became an implacable enemy of Bright's, and E. S. Beoku-Betts. Indeed, the Assessors' question became so topical and urgent that deputations and memoranda were presented to the local government and to Whitehall through the agency of Bright or Boston; these two, sometimes, as individuals, did take up the issue with officials in the Colonial Office. And, of course, the latter hardly welcomed these importunities. Bright was a 'very ill-behaved person' to them, and at one occasion the idea did present itself to ignore him, but Fiddian wondered whether as an elected representative the Colonial Office would be wise to show such a discourtesy to him.[7]

Early in 1923 Bright petitioned the Colonial Office to grant leave to his brother to appeal against his conviction. On a recommendation by Slater this was refused.[8] Later, another petition on the general question of the

Assessors' Ordinance and trial by jury was presented by F. J. Boston after he had seen Ormsby-Gore through the help of the Aborigines' Protection Society in London.[9] The petition was allegedly signed by 445 persons including E. H. Cummings (Mayor), M. Wilson, Archdeacon of Sierra Leone, T. J. Thompson, A. S. Hebron, J. A. Songo-Davies, Bankole-Bright, Beoku-Betts, J. Fowell Boston, A. F. Rahman, Civil Servant, Dan Street, A. R. Hassan, A. A. Z. Din Gabisi, Forster Street, Fourah Bay, M. T. Sanusi, Alimamy O. Jamboria, J. P. (Headman for the Foulahs), Alimany Abdullah Fofana (Headman for the Madingoes), King George (Mende Tribal Headman), Kangbay Sesay (Loko representative), James Macfoy (Limbas), Mohamad Camara (Sarakules), Sorie Coyah (Temne), Alieu Camara (Susus) and others. The petition sought to include as wide a spectrum of the society as possible, but there were some significant omissions; for instance, the Shorunkeh-Sawyerrs, C. E. Wright and S. J. S. Barlatt did not append their signatures to the petitions. We shall return to this point later.

In the petition, after going through the usual complaints about the harshness and unfairness of the system, the memorialists hit on two important points: (1) Art. 42 of the 1905 Ordinance which took away the option of the accused to sue for trial by jury or Assessors and replaced it with the power granted to the Attorney-General to order a trial by Assessors on a criminal charge. (2) Right of Appeal: insisting that the system of Assessors was a slur on their loyalty as British citizens, they asked for what amounted to the abolition of the Assessors' Ordinance. They emphasised the point that as British Citizens also they deserved to be included in the provisions of the Criminal Appeal Act of 1908 which gave a right of appeal as a matter of course to an accused dissatisfied with the court's verdict. In the judicial system operating at that time, a right of appeal was given to an accused involved in a civil case. These three points were specifically prayed for:

(1) That the right of appeal in Criminal cases should be granted to any accused person who is dissatisfied [*sic*] with the decision of the Court.

(2) That when the Assessors are unanimous in their opinion the opinion of the Assessors shall be the verdict of the Court.

(3) That in the case where the Assessors are not unanimous and the Judge decides with the majority he should state a case for the consideration of the Appeal Court, if the accused is dissatisfied [*sic*] with the decision.[10]

Neither Bright, whose petition was regarded as 'a political manifesto against the system of trial with Assessors rather than a *bona fide* request for "Legal relief"',[11] nor Boston's memorial received satisfaction from Whitehall.

The following year, the lawyers sent a resolution on some judicial questions that touched on the Assessors' Ordinance, signed by the Shorunkeh-Sawyerrs, C. E. Wright, J. Kempson, A. S. Hebron, J. Fowell Boston, Amado Taylor, and others (except Barlatt and C. D. Hotobah-During). The resolution asked for an Appeal Court of three practising barristers from England of not less than seven years' standing, and the relief of the Police Magistrate from such duties as those of Coroner, Visiting Justice, and Registrar-General. The lawyers suggested that Justices of the Peace should sit on some of these cases. The resolution was acknowledged and the barristers were told that the matter was being looked into.[12]

It is not to be supposed from the above that the administration was insensitive and deaf to all these appeals. To be fair, the Freetown government itself, or at least certain individuals in the Sierra Leone administration – including Slater – and in the Colonial Office, were not happy over several features of the Ordinance.[13] They were, of course, convinced that the Ordinance should remain in the Statutes Book as a guarantee of fair trial, peace and order, but they believed that some gestures should be made to satisfy the grievances of the citizens, at least partly; for instance, through the granting of a right of appeal, though not in all cases. Indeed, Chief Justice Purcell himself had written a long memo as early as 1920 complaining about the embarrassment of judges in the Supreme Court having to sit on appeals from their own cases, and many other inconveniences, including trial by Assessors.[14] More important, he believed that people should not only get justice, but even more so 'they should be made to feel and see that they were getting it'. Thus, one positive recommendation was to establish a West African Court of Appeal 'consisting of all the judges in British West Africa, holding sittings twice a year at Freetwon, Accra, and Lagos, such Appeal Court being so formed at these different centres so as to ensure that no judge sat in the particular Appeal Court in which any of his own judgements come under review'. He quite accepted possible objections to this Court on grounds of expenses and the dislocation of the local courts, but he pleaded at least for a special court for Criminal Appeal. Secretary of State, Lord Devonshire, did not like the idea of a separate right of appeal against Assessors, as opposed to Purcell who wanted to retain the Assessor's Ordinance but to grant leave to appeal in cases where the judgement was against the opinion of the majority of Assessors.[15] In any case, some kind of appeal, on certain conditions, was conceded. The problem and hence the bottleneck impeding the smooth establishment of an improved system of justice centred on the structure of the New Appeal Court, the attitudes of the other West African governments and a determination to make the system as foolproof as possible. Meetings were held at Whitehall, and the governors did exchange views, but there were insurmountable problems.[16] The lawyers' resolution then was a response to the vibrations that radiated from Whitehall and Government House. More to the point, in order to fully discuss some of the problems of her West African Colonies, the British Government decided to send the Under-Secretary of State, Ormsby-Gore, on a fact-finding mission, since callers at Downing Street, complaining about the Assessors' Ordinance, had been told that he was going to look into the problem on his projected visit.[17]

Before he left England in 1926, Boston and Bright saw Ormsby-Gore in July 1924 and September 1925 respectively.[18] Bright had an interview with the Under-Secretary of State and discussed many issues with him. The Assessors' Ordinance was one of these. Here Bright recounted the onerous oppression of the Ordinance and, while he admitted, 'it may not be wise to remove the Assessors' Ordinance from the Statute Book', he went on, 'it is essential to give the prisoner the opportunity of deciding whether he wants to be tried by jury or Assessors, and not leave the handle to the Crown Officer, a handle which is frequently used to wreck the honour of men'. Concluding his interview, he advised Ormsby-Gore not to allow himself to be 'put in an official cage by the official element'. It was likely that there would be a tendency to 'allow you to visualize things from the official perspective'. But it was necessary to 'allow unofficials to bring to you their own focus – the only way to see the problems of Sierra Leone'.

Ormsby-Gore did not heed Bright's advice. He did just what he was asked not to do. He came to Sierra Leone on 14 April, met representatives of various bodies, received petitions and held discussions with official and unofficial members between that date and 24 April. He then went home and wrote what was perhaps the most prejudiced and ill-considered report compiled by a Minister responsible for the Colonies. Obviously biased over the 1926 strike of which he strongly disapproved, his report on Sierra Leone, and the Krio in particular, was replete with contempt and ridicule for these people – they were, in sum, selfish and unhelpful ingrates: 'These descendants of freed slaves, who are styled Creoles, have no tribal organisation, native custom or tradition. They might be described, to use a rather clumsy word, as "Anglicized" Africans.' Then he rather surprisingly conceded that the Krios were highly educated and were rendering legion service all over the coast, but he doubted whether 'education in England is necessarily suited for an African who is to spend his life in Africa'. As for development in Sierra Leone, undue attention had been paid to Freetown and its 'English speaking population'.[19] Consequently, Freetown was prone to believe that in Sierra Leone the interests of the Colony should come first. Conveniently forgetting that it was the European-nominated member, J. H. Phillips, who had moved a motion (and Betts, for one, had supported him because he felt officials were making too much of the differences between Colony and Protectorate) asking government to postpone the 'expensively elaborate' and 'sophisticated' Njala Agricultural Scheme, Ormsby-Gore was seriously disturbed that

> the attitude of the two Urban members has, I regret to say, been somewhat grudging towards any government project for the development of the Protectorate. For instance, the important scheme for constructing an Agricultural College at Njala was opposed; the real ground of the opposition being that the Colony members were jealous of such expenditures in the Protectorate.[20]

Tendentious statements like these, which were not free from racial bias, encouraged successive administrators, for example, R. R. Blood, to continue to subscribe to the view that the under development of the Protectorate was

Bankole-Bright and politics in colonial Sierra Leone

the result of the selfish and parochial interests of the Krios and their vigorous efforts to secure these at the expense of the interior peoples.[21] With documents like Ormsby-Gore's report, the reason why the Krios have had a poor image in their own country is easy to identify.

As regards the Assessors' Ordinance, the Under-Secretary of State noted:[22]

> I think it is obvious that in the circumstances obtaining in Freetown, which consists of a comparatively small community most of whose members are personally known to each other and where there is no possibility of transferring the case to another venue such as exists in England, some alternative to trial by jury must exist in certain cases. Further, the educational standard of many of those entitled to serve as jurors is still low, and in complicated cases dealing with such matters as embezzlement or fraud it would be very difficult for any ordinary Freetown juror to appreciate the points. Still further, and here I am frank, cases occasionally give rise to racial antagonism and in some of these cases trial by jury would lead to a travesty of justice. Consequently, I think the Assessors' Ordinance must stand.

We do not know who borrowed from whom, but it seems that Slater and Ormsby-Gore were using the same script in stating the government position on the Assessors' Ordinance.[23]

The publication of Ormsby-Gore's *Report* in 1926 caused a furore, and triggered off several consequences. Firstly, Bankole-Bright wrote and published (as it is, his only extant literary effort) a pamphlet, *The Maladministration of British Justice in the Courts of Sierra Leone* (*The Assessors' Ordinance*). First read on 28 September 1927 to students of the W.A.S.U. (at Friends House, Euston Road, London), the pamphlet caused a sensation. In his submissions Bankie gave a historical account of the evolution of the Assessors' Ordinance, citing examples of good men, Caleb Johnson and Mayor May, who had not been found guilty by the Assessors, but had been convicted by the court, Johnson 'eventually dying of a broken heart'. Bright did overstate his case, to be sure, but the document was an indictment of British justice in West Africa and a strong criticism of Chief Justice Purcell. Not unnaturally, the Colonial Office was hardly amused by all this, and it showed its spleen in the comments of certain officials in the establishment: J. Risley, the legal expert, considered the pamphlet 'full of malicious mistatements and suggestions, all intended to prejudice his [Purcell's] reputation in Sierra Leone and elsewhere'.[24] There was even a suggestion of instituting a libel suit against Bright. But it appeared that not all the officials were admirers of Purcell, the wronged party. A. Fiddian wanted him to retire (he was already sixty), but Risley disagreed. He did concede that Purcell was 'a little eccentric', but he believed him to be still, after Sir A. Coombe, 'the ablest Judge in West Africa'. Ormsby-Gore, however, did not share Risley's confidence 'after hearing Sir R. Slater's and other Senior Officers opinion of him on the spot, and I confess I was not personally impressed'.[25] Consequently, though privately the Colonial Office

92

was worried over these disclosures of Purcell's incompetence, it tried to keep a tidy appearance by telling the governor of Sierra Leone to convey its confidence in the Chief Justice to Purcell, but also they should press further for the institution of a West African Court of Appeal. As for Bankie's accusations, the governor was told that they were malicious and inaccurate.[26] But even so, the Colonial Office's admission that all was not well was a major point for Bright, because he was the one who publicised these peccadilloes in British justice.

The second major consequence of the *Report* was even more dramatic. In the Legislative Council it elicited two crucial debates covering two important matters: Ormsby-Gore's statement; and the Assessors' Ordinance. On the first matter, African members in the House took strong exception to Ormsby-Gore's inaccurate statements and aspersions on the Krios. Betts, for one, heatedly questioned the statement that the Colony had objected to the inclusion of Paramount Chiefs in the Legislative Council, and to the Agricultural College at Njala 'always believing that the interests of the Colony should come first'. The first Urban member then went on to refute these charges, showing how Colony politicians had welcomed the Chiefs, although a constitutional point had been raised previously, and how much the interests of the Protectorate had been advocated by the Colony.[27] Bright was 'never so despondent' as he was then when addressing the Chamber on the Ormsby-Gore statement. He recounted how he had pursued the case of the dismissed men from the railway and had asked the government to give their families sympathetic consideration. As for the Protectorate he declared that he had been one of those that had welcomed the discovery of iron ore, but he took the opportunity to point out that a Sierra Leonean, Walter Carew, a trained engineer, had discovered mineral deposits in Pork Lokko, the very same spot in which the Government geologist, Major N. R. Junner, had found them. Coal had also been found between Hastings and Waterloo. However, being an African, his findings were ignored.[28] What Colony politicians objected to, argued Bright, 'was the line of cleavage that government tries to draw between Colony and Protectorate'. Government, he went on, was always giving the impression to the Protectorate that the Colony was hostile to them. He dismissed Ormsby-Gore's statement that Africans trusted white medicos better as a falsehood:[29]

> If you have Nigeria today, you have to thank our fathers from Sierra Leone who were the early pioneers, and we their children are proud to think that it was under their influence that the treaties were signed by virtue of which England owns Nigeria today. One thing the government has always to think about is the link between the Colonies: I stand here today as a Sierra Leonean, but I belong to the Ikija tribe of Nigeria, I also claim a link with Oyo land.

Tuboku-Metzger corroborated Bright's claim with reference to Carew, but he was particularly put out by being called a 'Creole'. He claimed that it was slang, imported by the Nova Scotians. He preferred to be called a Sierra Leonean. This interesting contribution by Tuboku-Metzger sparked off a public debate on the accuracy of the term.[30] On the Agricultural Scheme, he was of the opinion that government was neglecting Mabang, an Agricultural Institute which was founded by the will of the Krio recluse, the wealthy S. B. Abuke Thomas, in favour of Njala.[31] Songo-Davies made a direct contribution in the debate on the governor's speech which, of course, had quoted excerpts from Ormsby-Gore's *Report*. He called attention to female education in the Protectorate advocating that efforts be made to bring girls to parity with boys. This remark pleased Chief Bai Comber of Upper Bambarra, Central Province, the only Paramount Chief to make a contribution. However, he confined himself to welcoming the governor's address and to noting the interest of Songo-Davies in Protectorate matters. C. E. Wright was generally supportive of government policy.[32]

The following year there was a debate on the Assessors' Ordinance. It was initiated by Betts who tried to introduce a novel way of attacking government policy through the ploy of tacking a motion to the Supply Bill – to withhold approval of supplies until members' demands had been satisfied. It was an ingenious and courageous, though foolhardy, move.[33] For it was clear that with the governor's presiding prerogative, his veto, and built-in majority, no unofficial member could hope to breach the government's solid defence. As it happened, the 1927–8 Estimates to which it was tacked, had been debated and passed, on the insistence of Governor J. A. Byrne, before Betts was allowed to proceed with his motion. And, as such, the second part of the above lost its meaning. But then as Tuboku-Metzger explained, though it had become an academic point, as a result of the governor's ruling, it was 'tagged on to the motion as a technical protest to express I believe, the sincerity and earnestness of the mover and to intensify the motion'. The motion read:[34]

> This Council is of opinion [*sic*] that the time has come when the law for the administration of Criminal Justice should secure to the subjects of His Majesty adequate protection against miscarriage of justice and a guarantee for the preservation of personal liberty, and in order to achieve those ends it urges that the Jurors and Assessors Ordinance (Cap. 106) be amended in order to abolish trial with Assessors, that the right of appeal in criminal cases be provided for, and that the Perjury Ordinance (Cap. 149) be amended to the effect of repealing those sections of the Ordinance which empower a Judge or Magistrate to summarily punish a witness without trial. And until these reforms are affected it feels justified in withholding its approval to the vote for the Legal Department with the exception of the Master's Office, the Registrar-General's Office, Sheriff's Office and the Curator of Intestate Estates' Office.

Further, the mover asked the government to justify the reasons for maintaining the Assessors' Ordinance given the fact that the Perjury Ordinance and the Law as it stood with reference to the Assessors' Ordinance gave no right of appeal in criminal cases to the accused; consequently there was no guarantee of personal freedom and no security against miscarriage of justice. Tuboku-Metzger seconded the motion. Being a gentleman with a tidy and orderly mind, an ex-police clerk, he started his contribution by cutting out the inessentials and slotting the motion into four neat cubicles: (1) The Jurors and Assessors' Ordinance; (2) Appeal in Criminal Cases; (3) Perjury Ordinance; and (4) Withholding of approval of the vote on expenses in the judicial department until the remedy of certain grievances was obtained. Unemotional and painstaking, he took his audience through the evolution of the Assessors' Ordinance since 1895. As it was then conceived, he believed it could be fair, but events had forced him to conclude that it was 'a horried [*sic*] machine and a dreadful engine of tyranny and danger, and a weapon of oppression which may be used at any time to deprive a man of his honour, his reputation, and his liberty, in a way the Legislature could never have intended'. Trial by Assessors, he asserted, was really trial by the judge alone (a point Purcell himself had stressed in his memo of 1920), and the Assessors, however intelligent, were of little consequence in the result of the trial, while under the Perjury Ordinance an accused was not allowed to bring in witnesses to his defence. In short, it was un-British for the administration to allow anomalies to go on.[35]

As the debate progressed it became clear that it centred on Bright's pamphlet as much as on Ormsby-Gore's statements and the Assessors' Ordinance *per se*. Bright himself regretted having this kind of debate in the initial period of the new governor's tour, but he insisted that the issue was a bitter one in the minds of the people. The Ordinance was not intended to supersede trial by jury, but over time it had become an iniquitous and unrighteous instrument of spite and envy – a travesty of justice. He then went over old grounds and concluded that the Ordinance was building up an educated class of criminals whom the people rightly believed were victims of an unjust and unrighteous law. It also made the Attorney-General lazy, since he was, almost always, sure to get a conviction through Assessors. He then launched a personal attack on Songo-Davies whose *volte face*, Bright claimed, was due to his 'personal spite and envy of the 1st Urban Member' (Betts, who was a political opponent of Songo-Davies).[36]

The contributions of Songo-Davies and C. E. Wright showed that even among the Krio elite there was divided opinion on the subject of the Assessors' Ordinance. The ultra-conservative bloc to which these two belonged was for maintaining the Ordinance as a guarantee of peace and stability. Songo-Davies himself admitted that he had signed the petition of 1923 asking for its abolition, but he was now against its abolition though he would agree to an amendment.[37]. However, he refused to suggest one when challenged by Betts. He supported the establishment of an appeal court, but advised patience until the Colonial Office gave its approval. C. E. Wright concentrated on attacking Bright's allegations in his pamphlet. With a lawyer's precision, and eye for detail and accuracy, he set out to demolish the statistics presented by bright. He asserted that only a fraction of Bright's percentage had fallen under Purcell's axe. And, in any case, one should not blame the judge since he was acting on lines laid down by law. Moreover, as a result of the Chief Justice's own representations, after 1923 judges could no longer sit in an appeal on a case which they had tried in the court of first instance. As for the conviction of Bright's brother, he could emphatically say that never was there a more clearly proved case of misdemeanour than that of I. O. Bright.[38] One could imagine the official members rubbing their hands in glee over Wright's hatchet job in what was possibly his longest speech in the chamber.[39] Bright was refused a chance to reply, but then Wright had his match in Betts who had the last word, as the mover of the motion. He could not help making a dig at Wright's background. He knew, he said, that 'Mr. Wright was trained in England, that he is a very conservative man and does not move with the people, and I will be doing no injustice to him if I say he knows very little of the customs and minds of the people.' With that broadside, Betts went on to explain that he had long been exercised over the Assessors' Ordinance and, indeed, he had attempted to write a pamphlet on it and had asked Casely Hayford to write a preface. He had not known about Bright's pamphlet; in fact he had not read it before this debate. And when the existence of Bright's pamphlet was made known to him, he decided to postpone writing his own pamphlet (he did write an article the following year) and he therefore tabled the motion so that the question could be thrashed out by both sides.[40]

In this, Betts had done a service to his people by insisting that an issue that various bodies, including the National Congress, had discussed and exchange views on, should be treated in the place, the Chamber of the Legislative Council, where it should rightly be settled. And Bright, for all the allowances he took with his presentation, as usual, like John Wilkes, the eighteenth-century English radical, managed to put into focus an issue of wide constitutional importance. The fact that he was to cry for the return of the Assessors' Ordinance should not make us overlook this public duty, for his *volte face* is another matter which will be dealt with later. As for the debate, the government merely restated its position quoting freely from Ormsby-Gore's *Report*, but then Byrne appeared to meet his government's critics halfway. He told them with unprecedented candour that they were 'flogging a willing horse', because the government had been trying to set up a comprehensive Court of Appeal for some time. The delay in its implementation was due to the attitude of the Gold Coast and Nigeria governments. He was bitter over Bright's assertion that the Executive appeared to connive with the judiciary to gaol its opponents, averring that he had rarely heard a public figure make a more mischievous and unfounded statement'.[41] The same could be said of Ormsby-Gore's *Report*. Bright's charge may be impossible to prove, but the gesticulation and manoeuvres by government officials in court cases, for instance a documented one like May's, surely gave ammunition to critics like Bright. They did not encourage the public to have confidence in the impartiality of the court and the clearness of government's intentions. When the vote was taken, the motion was predictably lost. Paramount Chief Bai Kompa of Koia Cheifdom, who appeared to be the most forward and independent-minded of the Protectorate representatives, voted with the elected unofficial members, though the government tried to confuse him.[42] This bizarre episode in the colonial experience of Sierra Leone, however, ended on a happy note, though it did not fully satisfy the complainants, when in 1928 the West African Court of Appeal was established.[43]

If an accused finds today that even in a much restructured judiciary he could appeal on a criminal charge, he should spare a moment of gratitude to the tenacity and bulldog perseverance of people like Bright, Betts, Tuboku-Metzger and Fowell J. Boston, whose continuous assault on the system forced the Administration to review its policy.

With regards to other constitutional issues, for instance, parliamentary privileges, those who are legislators in present-day Sierra Leone might do well to remember that some of the allowances, such as those for travelling, that they now receive as a matter of course, had been fought for by Bright with admirable consistency.[44] Equally so, he was vigorous and unceasing in his campaign fighting for government recognition of private medical practitioners' certificates for government employees. This question received a great deal of attention from Bright in his speeches, and questions in the Chamber of the Legislative Council. What would seem today part of parliamentary procedure was not so in Bright's days. He did, without much success, try to persuade the Colonial Office that members of Council, especially unofficial members, should first express their opinions on proposed legislation submitted to the Secretary of State before the Secretary decided on a Bill, rather than the governor first seek the opinion and approval of the Secretary of State before bringing it to the Legislative Council – upon which occasion the big stick was always used to get the Bill passed because the Secretary of State or the government wanted it.[45] He was, in other words, asking for representative government. In this case, Bankie was far ahead of his time. His attempt to secure for the Legislative Council control over government expenditure was another constitutional hurdle whose relevance was unrealistic given the political philosophy in a colonial setting at that time.[46] He, however, made tremendous contributions to the discussion and treatment of concerns which affected the everyday lives of all Sierra Leoneans.

Africanisation, employment and salaries

Employment and salary structures for Africans were areas of concern for Bright. These were very important and vital questions, given the fact that the salary structure in government service was most discriminatory. Employment was in short supply also. A look at these figures gives us a fair idea of the conditions of service for African personnel. For instance, a European doctor, Mrs D. B. Blacklock, was on a salary of £660 × 30 – × £960 p.a., while M. C. F. Easmon, after sixteen years in government service, was earning

Bankole-Bright and politics in colonial Sierra Leone

£600 × 25 – × 700 p.a. in 1927.[47] The African Assistant Director of Education, the Reverend C. A. E. Macauley, was on a salary of £360 × 20 – £500 p.a., while the Vice-Principal of the Prince of Wales School, a European, who should actually be his junior, was getting £600 × 20 – £720. When S. M. O. Broderick was African Assistant Director of Education in 1937 his salary was £310–£450 p.a. European Education Officers were senior to the African A. D. E., and they, of course, acted when the substantive D. of E. was away, not the A. D. E. Interestingly enough, the African Education Officers like C. E. Tuboku-Metzger and E. J. B. Williams were junior to Broderick.[48]

In 1925 salaries of African graduates were slashed from £78 and £96 p.a. to £54 × 9–£144, on the grounds that experience had shown that graduates did not perform any better than non-graduates and that they were not giving value for money, 'nor [is] Fourah Bay College equipped to train people for clerical jobs'.[49] Those of Europeans were not much affected. In 1924 when the Sierra Leone government happily reported a surplus (£166,926) of revenue for the 1923 fiscal year, it saw fit to reduce the entry scales of all African Senior Officers on the grounds of economy. For example, the African Assistant Colonial Secretary, African Assistant Treasurer, and Supervisor of Customs were taken from salary scale £400 × 20 – £500 to a lower entry point, £360 × 20 – £500. Others, such as Staff Superintendents (£400 × 10 – £450; £350 × 201 – £450) were brought down to £310 × 20 – £450. Reduction on European staff was £50 fixed; for example, a European Supervisor now entered at £400 instead of £450.[50]

A government statement in answer to questions raised by Bright in 1925, revealed that an establishment of 864 Civil Servants (European and African) in government service, who were eligible for medical treatment, had twelve European and eight African Medical Officers assigned to them in their respective racial group.[51] It would also appear, looking at specific examples, that African Civil Servants lost some benefits or monetary compensation when promoted. Take, for instance, the African Master and Registrar of the Supreme Court. When the incumbent was a European he was on a salary of £480 p.a. (maximum). His assistant, the Chief Clerk, was getting a maximum of £372 p.a. (264 × 12 – £372). In 1925, J. Rogers-Wright was promoted to the post of Master and Registrar at a salary of £360 × 20 – £500, and he was not given a Chief Clerk. In effect, he was doing the two jobs all by himself. V. K..Edwin was appointed Assistant Postmaster-General in 1925 at £450 p.a. (£450–£500). As Staff Superintendent, from which post he was promoted, he was earning £450 p.a. plus £18 in fees. His new position gave him added administrative responsibility and social obligations at £310–500 without fees.[52] In the case of a European Assistant Controller of Customs whose promotion caused a loss of fees, government gave him two years' increment to compensate for the loss.[53] Again, when J. H. Cheetham Smart, Chief Clerk at the Colonial Secretary's Office, was made African Assistant Colonial Secretary in 1924 he was put on a scale £400 × 20 – £500. But, in a letter to the Colonial Secretary, the acting governor explained that the government was pleased with Mr Smart's performance, and felt that he should be rewarded for this. 'In the Gold Coast', he pointed out, 'the rule is that an African appointed to hold a European post draws what the European would draw less 16⅔ L.C [sic, living cost?], so that his [Smart's] salary would be £420 rising to £800. But we need not apply this to Sierra Leone where [the cost of] living is much cheaper and qualified persons easier to obtain.'[54] The above evidence alone cries out for a paper on 'Salary differentials: the politics of employment discrimination in the Colonial Civil Service'! On the other hand, it is fair to acknowledge the fact the Slater, more than any of his predecessors, did much to advance African staff to senior positions, at least up to 1926. J. R. Wright, Cheetham Smart, Edwin and C. R. Morrison, to name a few, were beneficiaries of this magnanimity.[55] However, it is equally germane to argue that often practical implementation did not keep faith with pious platitudes. When Wright was promoted he was on probation for three years with a proviso that if he misbehaved his appointment would be reviewed.[56]

Consequently, Bankie became a vigilant watchdog over the interests of his compatriots. His interference in this matter was unwelcome, but at one point even the governor conceded that his contribution was notable. His enquiries on behalf of A. T. Summer and Miss Cole have been referred to already. There were many others, including M. C. F. Easmon, and Uel John. Interest in salaries of course, led to interest in jobs for qualified Africans. Questions raised by Bright on this subject are too many to enumerate, but his impact on this area was of sufficient note for one Colonial Official to report it as one of Bankie's specialities.[57] In 1928, he enquired about the employment of E. H. Taylor-Cummings, son of the Mayor, who had returned home a few years back with a medical qualification in health (M.B., Ch.B., Liverpool; M.R.C.S., L.R.C.P., London; D.P.H., Liverpool), the first Sierra Leonean to so qualify. The governor's reply was evasive and deprecatory. A European without Taylor-Cummings's qualifications or those of another Sierra Leonean, Dr G. C. E. Refeell, was appointed Medical Officer of Health, and then sent for training.[58] Bankie did repeat his question on the employment of Taylor-Cummings a number of times. As always the government's reply was that it could not appoint a local person in a small place like Freetown to be Medical Officer of Health since he would be amenable to all sorts of pressures. Also an African so appointed would have to deal with European Masters of Ships, Summonses, and many other matters. These, it was argued, would cause complications. Happily, the young Taylor-Cummings, who in fact entered government services as Medical Officer in 1920, was, in 1936, promoted to Medical Officer of Health. He retired in 1947 as Senior Medical Officer of Health. Bright's demands for the appointment of an African Assistant Colonial Secretary and for Africans to be appointed to other senior posts also deserve to be remembered.[59] However, the most celebrated case of this genre championed by him was that of Milton Margai, Sierra Leone's first Prime Minister, and Bright's political opponent in the 50s.

The Margai question and protectorate issues

Milton A. S. Margai became the first Protectorate graduate of Fourah Bay College, University of Durham in 1920; then he went on to be the first man from the interior to quality as a medical doctor in 1927.[60] On returning home he tried unsuccessfully to enter the Medical Service. The Sierra Leone government was unable to employ him, though it found it easy to fill vacancies in the European establishment of the Service. Bankole-Bright took Margai under his wings. The initial contact is not easy to determine although he once claimed in the Legislative Council Chamber that he had urged Margai's people to send him for medical training. However, on 16 May 1928 he enquired of the governor 'whether Dr. Margai, the first African of the Sierra Leone Protectorate as Registered Medical Practitioner, has been refused government admission into the service on grounds of no vacancy, if so, why?...Is it not government's repeated wish', he went on, 'for more Africans to be trained in the Medical profession?...Would government consider the advisability of offering this gentleman an appointment considering that *such procedure would be an encouragement to the parents in the Protectorate to educate* their sons and have them qualified for such a profession?'[61] The government's response was terse and intimidating. No, it announced, there was no vacancy because the establishment African posts were all filled, but if there was a vacancy in the future Dr Margai would have to take his chances with other aspirants. Governors either did not take the trouble to read their correspondence or they had short memories. For in 1919, when the African doctors, F. Campbell, W. O. Taylor and M. C. F. Easom complained about their conditions of service, the Colonial Office ruled that

> any qualified Medical Officer who is a native of West African and who is recommended by the governor is eligible for appointment to the government service, and indeed government is bound to offer him appointment if he applies. That is why there is no fixed establishment, and it is much better to leave the number vague so that any suitable man can be taken *regardless of whether there is a vacancy or not.*[62]

It was a position the Colonial Office, in theory, maintained with some consistency.[63] Yet Byrne told the questioner that government was unaware of having expressed 'the alleged desire' for more qualified doctors. What it wanted was African doctors to carry on practice among their own people. Furthermore, the idea must be disabused in the popular mind that people with qualifications procured by their parents were entitled to demand appointment in the government service irrespective of the existence of vacancies! With this withering *non possumus* the governor dismissed Bright's representation. But he reckoned without the terrier quality of the man. In the subsequent questions Bright was able to elicit that the established posts for European doctors were ten and those for African doctors eight![64] The statistics need no amplification. They tell of the callousness and indifference with which colonial administration treated the interests of their subjects.[65] What was more pernicious was the fact that three European doctors were appointed after Margai's application. It was due to tenacious and single-minded enquirers like Bright that some of the iniquities of colonial rule were exposed. And, indeed, 'it was mainly through the influence and indomitable bulldog qualities of the late Dr. Bankole-Bright', argues Deanna Thomas, 'that Dr. Margai was eventually recruited in the Medical Service' on 1 December 1928.[66] After Margai's appointment no African was offered a government job until 1939 when another Protectorate medical graduate. J. C. Massaly, entered the Medical Service.[67]

Contemporaries maintain that Margai was forever grateful to Bright for his efforts and, however bitter their political animosity became, that private understanding and esteem, born of this one act by Bankie, was never obliterated. The point is important not only because Bright supported Margai against another Krio doctor, G. C. E. Reffell, but also because Bright has always been described as an anti-Protectorate particularist.[68] Far from that – he was primarily interested in Colony affairs no doubt, but this concern went beyond this narrow frontier to include issues affecting the Protectorate peoples. The examples of Summer and Margai are points to his credit.

Indeed, Bankie always got his nose bruised when he poked it into government policy *vis-à-vis* the Protectorate. For instance, when the government passed the Mineral Ordinance (1927) which in effect alienated land in the Protectorate and denied the indigene from having the full benefits from the resources of his land, Bright was one of the Colony politicians who stoutly opposed this measure. A memorandum was sent to the Colonial Office protesting against the law. As usual with anything to do with the Protectorate, Colony politicians were told not to interfere. It was no business of theirs.[69] Similarly, the protests of Bright and Betts over the non-compensation to chiefs for the loss of their domestic slaves following legislation abolishing slavery in Sierra Leone in 1927 were ridiculed and disparaged.

Although slavery had been declared illegal in the British Empire in 1833, it still continued to exist in the Protectorate. Stung by adverse criticisms in the press and pressured by the London government, the Freetown administration decided to legislate to end slavery in the Protectorate. The issues as they emerged in the debate were whether abolition was to be staggered, or immediate and final. Secondly, since slaves were property, the views of the Colony politicians were that the chiefs ought to be compensated. The government, at first, were not opposed to this in principle, but as the figure of compensation would be enormous (about £800,000–£1,000,000), it became hesitant, and finally decided against compensation. Since the Colony politicians insisted on compensation as a fair solution, the government turned against them, and accused them of obstruction and interference. Thus, in the ensuing debates, none of the chiefs supported Betts's amendment to the Bill to amend the Protectorate Ordinance of 1924, even though during the debate P. C. Bai Kompa, speaking in Temne, had disagreed with the Slavery Bill and had insisted that he wanted compensation. Bai Comber, the other chief, was willing to refer the matter to the Assembly of Chiefs. And Bright, in seconding Betts' motion proudly proclaimed: 'I am the descendent of a Slave, and I have every reason not to be ashamed of it; in consequence of British philanthropy I stand here a free man.' When a division was called however, the chiefs voted with the government.[70] Acting Governor Luke who commended the elected members for making their points 'very fairly' was to express astonishment that it was Colony politicians who raised the issue of compensation. This was odd, 'given the origin of this colony proper'.[71] Eventually, the Bill was passed unanimously in 1927 because, as Betts had pointed out earlier in a debate in 1926, it would be foolish for him to vote against it when the chiefs had expressed one view and voted the other way.[72]

Still, Bright refused to be ignored or diverted from pursuing his duty. And so we find him raising objections to the government decision to sell Masanke Plantation to U.A.C. in 1938,[73] and strongly complaining about workers' conditions of service at the Delco Mines in Marampa.[74] Many would be surprised to learn that Bright asked for legal assistance for poor illiterate Protectorate people charged with murder; that he also complained that there was not 'a single lamp post or light in the streets', though a lot of produce came from the Protectorate, and that he hoped it would be possible to see lights in the Protectorate soon. Further, he supported the government scheme for training Medical Assistants for the Protectorate so that 'our Protectorate brethren [would be brought] into line with scientific education'. For that matter, Betts had strongly condemned the teaching of the vernacular in Protectorate schools, insisting that Protectorate children needed to be educated in English 'to compete on equal footing with non-Protectorate [people]'.[75]

These are interesting vignettes in Bankie's career that people know little about. Two other sides of his life that history has overlooked were Bright's advocacy for women's franchise and his contributions outside the Legislative Council, for instance, to W.A.S.U., the West African Students Union, the nursery of later political leaders of West Africa. In 1928 he asked the governor in the Legislative Council whether he would consider the advisability of extending the vote to women in the colony and their membership in the Assembly. That worthy replied that the government was not prepared to take up 'at present' the question of extending the franchise to women. For that matter, neither did the administration consider it advisable to amend the constitution to provide for an all-elected Legislative Council.[76] Bright followed the question of women's franchise with some consistency. And at a meeting of Congress in December 1928 he was warmly praised for raising the issue of the inclusion of ladies in the Legislative Council and for his stance on the Assessors' Ordinance. The Chairman of the occasion treated himself to some wry humour when he remarked that the presence of the ladies 'would create a soothing atmosphere in the Legislative Council Hall'.[77] As to this, the intensity of passion in the Legislative Chamber of Sierra Leone then and now does not support the Chairman's hope, but Constance Cummings-John, the first-ever elected woman to sit in the City Council, and the women who got the vote eventually in 1957 may have done well to spare a thought in gratitude to the pioneering effort of Bankie. They would not thank him though for opposing the employment of unmarried mothers as teachers in schools on the grounds that they would be a bad influence on young plastic minds![78]

Founder of W.A.S.U.

Bankie's pioneering contribution to the founding of the West African Students Union (W.A.S.U.) represented an enduring commitment to pan-Africanism and the stimulation of conscious African nationalism. The documents on Bankie's connections with W.A.S.U. are thin; at best they are not very clear. However, several accounts concede that Bright played a crucially instrumental role in the formation of this students' body. While one source called him the founder of W.A.S.U.,[79] another noted that Dr Bright was very popular among West African Students; 'for it was with his advice and encouragement that W.A.S.U. came into existence'.[80] J. B. Danquah, President of W.A.S.U. in 1926, referred 'particularly to the untiring energy of Dr. Bankole-Bright (SL), through whose beneficent activities the W.A.S.U. came into being'. What seems to have happened was that the West African students in London in the 1920s were going through a crisis period. Ladipo Solanke, the Fourah Bay College graduate from Nigeria, had founded the Nigeria Progressive Union in 1924 to promote the interests of its nationals. Other groups in existence at that time were the Gold Coast Union, the Union for Students of African Descent (U.S.A.D.), founded in 1917, and the African Progressive Union (A.P.U.), established in 1918 'to promote the social and economic welfare of the Africans of the World'. These groups did not seem able to co-operate with each other and provide a solid front in their attacks on racism and colonialism. If anything, they were factious and wrangling. It was at this crucial point that Bright entered the picture. In one of his frequent visits to London, Bankie was approached for advice. It was a compliment and an acknowledgement of his impact on the young African activists. His vigour and his outspokenness, and positively brilliant oratory, no doubt had a mesmeric effect on the young, and his stout defence of his race went down well with these future leaders.

Consequently, on an invitation to speak to a student gathering, Bright enjoined his audience to organise themselves. Stressing the need for greater unity, Bankie pointed out to the students that had the N.C.B.W.A. not presented a united front in its agitation for reforms, individual politicians would never have succeeded in achieving what the organisation secured for the four colonies.[81] It was at that meeting on 7 August 1925, that W.A.S.U.

was born. Bright provided the catalyst that led to its birth.[82] In effect, we may concede that he was at the very least, the co-founder of W.A.S.U. And the most recent study on the W.A.S.U. by Professor Olusanya supports this view, though he billed Bankie as the 'Founder' and Solanke, 'Co-founder'.

Bright did not seem to have been closely involved with W.A.S.U. politics after this date, but he consistently supported the ideals and aims of W.A.S.U. He did make contributions to its funds and addressed audiences at W.A.S.U. meetings as 'father of the Union and one of its Chief "Ogboni Agba"'[83]. In 1937 he sought to commit the Sierra Leone government to give a subvention for the funding of the W.A.S.U. Hostel without much success.[84] However, what is important for us to remember is that W.A.S.U. was Bankie's bequest to a generation of African political leaders, including Danquah, Azikiwe and Nkrumah, that continued the job begun by Bankie's peers, and who eventually wrested control of their countries from the hands of the former colonial masters.

Other African Legislative Council members

Other elected members did speak on many issues and with equal vigour. For instance, the elected Rural Area member, A. E. Tuboku-Metzger, the grand old man of politics, was always guaranteed to speak on Protectorate affairs. Nor should this be surprising, for in his various positions in government as Treasury Clerk (five years), Police Clerk (thirteen years), during which he helped draft a number of Ordinances, for example, the Magistrate Courts Ordinance (1905), and African Assistant District Commissioner (Bonthe District, 1908–17), he acquired a wide experience and an encyclopaedic knowledge of the Protectorate – an accomplishment that was publicly recognized by Governor Moore.[85] Tuboku-Metzger was also outstanding in two other ways. He was the first Sierra Leone graduate to enter the Colonial Civil Service in 1885 – at the ridiculous salary of £45 per annum. Secondly, among Colony inhabitants, he made a break with tradition. He did not send his sons to the C.M.S. Grammar School, his Alma Mater, the nursery of the elite in Freetown, but to the Albert Academy, founded in 1904, reportedly for Protectorate boys' schooling in the city. One recommendation that lent the Albert Academy to Tuboku-Metzger was the emphasis on technical education implicit in the school's curriculum. The training in carpentry and other technical subjects the Metzger boys received in this institution served them well. One of them. S.J.C. Tuboku-Metzger, was until recently the Managing Director of a successful furniture construction company – Faremi Works, Kissy Road, Freetown. The example of Tuboku-Metzger debunks the myth that Krio elites looked down on technical professions; and his strong links with the Protectorate is another dimension documenting relations across the boundary line of the two sections of the territory.[86]

The nominated members, including the Paramount Chiefs supported government measures generally but, in some instances, they did speak their own minds. One of this latter category who expressed his views even against heavy-handed attempts by the official members to muzzle him, was P.C.Bai Kompa of Koia Temne. Examples of these incidents have been given in previous pages.

A. J. Shorunkeh-Sawyerr, a nominated member in the Legislative Council for thirteen years before it was reconstituted in 1924, is perhaps the best example of an independent-minded and fearless critic of government. Indeed, on Sawyerr's retirement from the Legislative Council in 1924, the government was sufficiently impressed by his legion service to recommend the award of an O.B.E.[87] On the other hand, the courage and independence of other nominated members like J. A. Songo-Davies and C. E. Wright were sometimes suspect because the praises showered on them by the government were based on dubious foundations. E. S. Betts, the other elected Urban member and Bankie's ally, usually associated with Bright. In most cases he supported Bright's stances in the Legislative Council, though there were a few significant instances – for example, during the Prince of Wales affair – when he actually voted against his colleague. The other instance of disagreement was over the V.D. Bill of 1933, aimed at forcing patients to be attended by qualified doctors instead of druggists. Bright 'supported it with such unnecessary force as to make it suspect'. Betts considered the Bill premature, though his criticisms were moderate. The government in an unprecedented show of positive response to public opinion, was persuaded by popular outcry to shelve the Bill. Though Bright and Betts took different positions on these two issues, the clashes did not seem to have affected their harnessed efforts, for we find them asking questions for the other when the one was absent from the Chamber. Again, Betts had his own pet interests – for instance, Immigration and Labour. Betts raised many questions on Syrian immigration, and was in favour of imposing restrictions on it. However a policy statement of 1926 made it clear that the government saw 'no reason whatever for the exclusion or restriction of this useful and energetic community'.[88] He was equally vigorous in demanding legal reforms in the Protectorate. His signature was to be found on any memorandum on legal issues. He was appointed a member of a committee to consider and recommend law reforms in 1931 and subsequent years, in particular the Supreme Court Ordinance, the Imperial Status Law Adoption Ordinance, the Companies Ordinance, the Protectorate Courts Jurisdiction Ordinance, and a few others. And in 1933 he was made a member of the Rule Making Committee under the Supreme Court Ordinance.[89]

Although Betts was under a cloud for some time for his part in the 1926 confrontation with Slater's administration, in point of fact he was not considered as objectionable as Bright. He was often included in Sub-Committees of the Legislative Council. In 1934, he, Dr G. C. Reffell, A. K. Fraser (money lender), J. G. Hyde (lawyer), N. J. P. Metzger-Boston, T. E. Nelson-Williams, C. E. Wright, C. D. H. During and E. H. Taylor-Cummings were invited to the exclusive (and all European) Freetown Rifle

Club in order that 'they may form the nucleus of the African personnel required for a Defence Force Scheme when the time is ripe'.[90] He had a line to officialdom. He was awarded an M.B.E. in 1934 and sent to represent Sierra Leone at the coronation of King George VI in 1936. Beoku-Betts, in short, was getting all the honours and all the accolades. It was as if government was deliberately baiting Bright, spiting him, and trying to drive a wedge between the Double Bs. The message was on the wall: unceasing opposition would reap no rewards, but flexibility (a virtue Bright did not possess in abundance) might pay dividends. If that was the plan, the administration succeeded. In 1937 Betts, on firm recommendations from the Colonial Office, was appointed Police Magistrate, the first Sierra Leonean to be given a substantive appointment to the magistracy.[91] He was picked out of twelve applicants (and a short list of three: himself, H. J. Lightfoot-Boston and T. E. Nelson-Williams) not because he was the most qualified or the most brilliant jurist, but because he possessed 'more than sufficient knowledge of the theory and practice of the law to enable him to perform with credit and efficiency the duties of Police Magistrate'. Although the Attorney-General was reluctant to recommend him because of his political activities, it was on this point, ironically, that he was preferred to H. J. Lightfoot-Boston. The latter's connection with his uncle, F. J. Boston – the enemy of the Betts/Bright combination – made him a political risk, whilst Betts was still popular with his countrymen. Furthermore, in recent years, Betts 'has always been most respectful and reasonable...I can only conclude', commented Governor Moore, 'particularly since the award of the M.B.E., made to him in the New Year honours of 1934, that he is now satisfied that his personal ambitions are more likely to be raised by co-operation with, than by opposition to, the government'.[92]

Be that as it may, Betts decided to accept the appointment though his friend had tried to dissuade him. Bright felt that Betts was selling himself short. Contemporaries say that Betts was ambitious, and that he was looking for security. After all, argued one informant, one could not eat on opposition alone.[93] Still, Bright gave an all-night party at his home, Whitehouse, in his friend's honour, to celebrate his elevation.[94] It was a courageous thing to do, and Bright must have summoned all his strength to conceal his disappointment. Giving a vote of thanks at a meeting called by the local Congress to welcome Betts and his wife back from attending George VI's coronation, Bankie confessed that it was with 'mixed feelings' that he rose to speak since he was losing a collaborator of thirteen years and the Colony was losing a valuable asset. It was this matter that pained him most. He conceded that no man was indispensable, but, he asked, 'who is there to succeed Mr. Betts?' He wished Betts and his wife well, and he expressed a conviction that 'Mr. Betts was second to none in fitness for the post.'[95]

Nevertheless, whatever papering effort was made, the split between the Double Bs., a companionship that had gone through many vicissitudes for over twenty years, was complete in 1937. This rift continued to widen as the one advanced in society and the fortunes of the other, perhaps the more courageous and indomitable fighter, went lower, buffeted by legal fights with political enemies and also his wife from whom he was separated.[96] In the Felix case he just managed to clear himself from criminal complications. He was almost struck off the Medical Roll. Politically, he was a lone wolf, gradually ageing, whose style of politics was fast becoming less relevant to a more democratic and constantly changing society. When he sought election into the Legislative Council in 1943, Lamina Sankoh had this to say: 'I am in sympathy with Dr. Bright who, like many aged Africans [he was sixty then], do not know when to keep off the stage.'[97] The observation had an ominous ring to it. There is an implicit note of finality, or rather, impatience with an old order.

6

At the crossroads: the flickering flames of Congress and the challenge of W.A.Y.L., 1936–1939

The interwar years were a period of global depressions, trade recessions, inflation, massive unemployment, political upheavals, social and labour unrest. If these years had profound and wide-ranging consequences for the developed world, they had a disastrous impact on colonial economies. The labour unrests of 1919 were only two of the most dramatic manifestations of these social, political, and economic ills. In the 30s, while Britain was wrestling with her economic problems and contending with the threats posed by Hitler's grand design, there was little time to pay attention to the demands of her subjects. On the other hand, developments in her colonies compelled the attention of Britain. While activists continued to rail against the colonial system in increasingly loud tones, the colonial authorities worked out strategies to exploit the newly discovered mineral resources so that the sagging economy of its African empire might be boosted. Some commentators on African affairs in Britain, such as Lugard, Professor W. M. MacMillan, Rita Hinden, the South African-born economist, and Lord Buxton, sought to influence government policy in a positive way, even though not all of them may have been liberal in their attitudes towards the African.[1] Nevertheless some of the reforms of the 30s and 40s can be traced to the activities of these people, as, for instances, the Colonial Development Act (1929), set up to finance and supervise development projects in the colonies. Furthermore, research and empirical experience in her Empire indicated to Britain the need to overhaul the administration in her possessions, to streamline her bureaucracy.

In 1926 iron ore was discovered in Marampa, Port Loko District and, six years later diamonds were found in Kono District. The Mining Ordinance (1927) nimbly side-stepped the inconvenient traditional land-tenure system which recognised the communal ownership of land in the Protectorate, and declared the minerals to be the possession of the government. Next, the latter set up the Protectorate Mining Benefits Fund (1932) to develop the mineral-producing areas and the Protectorate in general.[2] Over the protest of Colony politicians, government went ahead and gave liberal mining concessions on a 99-year lease to European companies such as Delco (the Sierra Leone Development Company, 1930 – iron ore) and S.L.S.T. (the Sierra Leone Selection Trust, 1935 – diamonds). And they latched on to these a punitive law which made it criminal for Sierra Leoneans to mine their own minerals.

It was not until 1957 that licences were given to indigenous alluvial diamond miners.[3]

Labour in the thirties was cheap, and employers exploited this ruthlessly; the conditions of service were inadequate and, as investigators later discovered, workers at the Delco Mines, for instance, were herded together like cattle in miniscule concrete blocks that passed for residential quarters, in unhealthy and unsanitary conditions. Wages were as low as possible; for instance, a labourer was paid 1/6d. per day, sometimes as little as 9d. per day. These wages were higher than those in the diamond mines where an unskilled labourer earned 6d. per day (skilled ones 3s. 6d., though the average was 11½d. per day), but they compared unfavourably with government rates in the various departments. For instance, locomotive drivers in the Sierra Leone Government Railway earned 3s. 6d. – 8s. 0d. per day (actual rates ranged between 3s. 6d. and 4s. 9d.), and artisans at the P.W.D. averaged between 2s. 0d. and 5s. 0d. per day. Mercantile firms paid 'starvation wages' to their clerks at the rate of 10s. 0d. to 30s. 0d. per month. Working hours were long in both private and public sectors. House rents were beyond the means of many. Though rice, the staple food, was subsidised at Delco, the diet was less than satisfactory. Employers claimed that they could not give more, and that earnings were subject to the vagaries of the international market that tended to slump and rise with bewildering consistency. Furthermore, they argued that the efficiency of the African workers did not merit more financial consideration.[4] Still, these companies were able to give employment to thousands of labourers though, in times of recession, retrenched workers added their number to the mass influx of shiftless, jobless, and hungry crowds that fled to the urban centres in search of work. All this was bad for an economy that was largely agrarian and trying to adjust to the new extractive industries. It was a ready-made situation for industrial and social unrest.[5]

As another way of gingering the economy and reforming some of the more blatantly oppressive features of chiefly rule, the government introduced the Native Administration (Indirect Rule) in 1937, following a report by J. S. Fenton, then a Senior District Officer in the Protectorate. Under this system, administrative and organisational structures like the Tribal Authorities were established. They consisted of 'Paramount Chiefs, Councillors, and important men, elected by the people according to Native Law and Custom'. These collected taxes, paid salaries and organised the chiefdoms, the political units into which the Protectorate was divided. What it all meant was that there was closer supervision of the chiefs, who now became salaried officials though in some cases it would seem that under this system chiefs arrogated more power outside the traditional system, secure under the protection of the government.[6] Indeed, the heavy handedness of chiefly rule and the deteriorating economic and social conditions, as well as the erosive nature of colonial rule, had led to the Haidara Kontorfilli Rebellion of 1931, which quickly expired after its leader, Haidara Kontorfilli, had been killed by British forces.[7]

Bankole-Bright and politics in colonial Sierra Leone

While it may be said that the administrative reforms of the thirties did not solve all the problems of the Protectorate (if they didn't accentuate some of them), no such reforms were made in the Colony. The City Council, as was noted, was dissolved in 1926, and the Municipality continued to be ruled by the Central government. The Krios had no political institutions they could call their own. Official opinion now deemed the Colony as 'relatively unimportant' and believed that its constitutional position was adequate. In fact, in reply to clamours for constitutional change from Colony politicians, it was explicitly stated that further constitutional progress in the Colony would depend on economic, social, and political progress in the Protectorate. As for the latter, the signs were not very encouraging according to Governor Jardine's report in 1938.[8]

A new wave of anti-Colony feeling began to reveal itself in the 30s. A good representative of this was Hilary Randolph R. Blood, Colonial Secretary in Sierra Leone, 1934–42. He proved to be another Cardew. His comments on Krio activists and interests reflected nothing but contempt for Krio politicians. To quote but a few examples to illustrate the point: 'Their [the Krios] tradition has been one of dependence upon a philanthropic government.'[9] And this, their dependence on the benignity and largesse of Britain, he continued, had rendered them incapable of doing anything for themselves, while the Protectorate, the larger unit of the possession, had long been neglected, owing to the demands of the colony. Blood felt it was time to change this trend. According to Mayhew of the Colonial Office, both Blood and Jardine believed that the Protectorate had been neglected owing to the 'rather extravagant claims of the intelligentsia in the Colony'. And, as such, 'it was their intention to do much for the Protectorate in the near future'.[10] And yet, when Karefa-Smart applied for a scholarship in 1937 to study medicine under the Protectorate Mining Benefits Fund Scheme, set up specifically to develop the Protectorate, the Executive Council refused him an award.[11] Thus the anti-Krio policy of the government was compounded by contradictions even in its pro-Protectorate policy. Logie Wilson, another senior administrator in Sierra Leone, was gratified to note that resentment against the Krios had reached such a point that 'with the introduction of N[ative] A[uthoritie]s, in 1936 a new political consciousness arose in the Protectorate and towards the end of World War II the anti-Creole feeling was beginning to find expression in various ways'.[12] Further, Amolo's study on Trade Unionism in Sierra Leone has told us about the determined efforts by colonial officials, such as the Trade Union Adviser, Edgar Parry, to destroy the influence of 'the politically conscious Creoles over the Trade Unions', and to put up Siaka Stevens 'to do something about the Wallace Johnson influence.'[13] It was a classic case of *divide et impera*.

The Colonial Office was not immune to these prejudices or a feeling of smug satisfaction over the reversal of policy *vis-à-vis* the Colony. Thus, on receiving information in London that the government headquarters of the departments of Forestry and Agriculture, for very good reasons, had been

110

moved to Njala, A. J. Dawe remarked: 'I should like to see more of this *drang nach osten* in Sierra Leone. The Protectorate is more important than the Colony.'

But some of the officials did begin to feel some concern over the lack of progress, and the evidence of stagnation in Sierra Leone. Noting that promotions seemed static, O. G. R. Williams wondered why with all their education Krios were finding it difficult to get government posts.[14] Reverend H. M. Grace, member of the Colonial Office Advisory Committee on Education in the Colonies, expressed concern over the future of the Freetown Krio – 'he is a definite problem and few seem to realise it. And he will increase as a problem to the discomfort of the government sooner or later. I suggest a small commission to enquire into the whole Creole question on the West Coast, chiefly Freetown, but also Bathurst and Lagos.'[15] No such commission was appointed, but as far back as 1936 the Colonial Office had agreed with Governor Moore that the Colony, especially its rural areas, had been badly neglected. This conclusion led to the construction of the Peninsula Road, girting the city, and a Maternity Hospital from grants under the Colonial Development Fund. An attempt at agricultural planning for the peninsula was also made.[16]

Nevertheless, prejudice, as much as government's pro-Protectorate policy, made the Colony a backwater, or, more correctly, put the political aspirations of the people in suspended animation. As for the politicians, wrote I. J. F. Turbett, the Attorney-General, only retired old gentlemen and older-generation activists paid much attention to politics. The younger generation were much more interested in football, cricket, and tennis![17]

As if to refute this view the local Congress, still the most active of the branches, held a Conference in 1936.[18] This event is very significant because it debunks the assertion by writers that the Congress collapsed after Casely-Hayford's death in 1930.[19] Further, it demonstrated a resilience that was not expected from a body considered moribund. And the discussions which took place showed a positive response by Congress to the urgent economic, social, and political concerns of the country as a whole without reference to ethnic, class, or regional self-interests. A discussion of the Conference which lasted for fifty-four days – 15 March–8 May 1936 – can be followed in this author's article in *I.J.A.H.S.*[20] But, to underscore our premise, references will be made to the papers presented.

Dr Bankole-Bright, current Vice-President of the branch, prefaced his paper on *Legislative Council Reforms* with brief remarks on the idea of self-government for a colonised people and the efforts made by Congress to secure constitutional rights for the people. One point he emphasised was that nominated members of the Legislative Council were in an anomalous situation, because they were both representatives of the people as well as supporters of the government, even though this support might be prejudicial to the interests of the people. Although he conceded that City Council members had, through corruption and incompetence, lowered the status of

111

their institution, he was convinced that the government had never been happy over the 'independence' of the City Council, and so it had done away with it. Concluding, he asked for the restitution of the privileges and status of that body, and an elected Legislative Council, controlled by an unofficial majority. While Betts conceded that British justice was better than most, he still felt that there was a large room for its improvement in the colonies. Specifically, he would like to see the end of the Assessors' Ordinance, and the functioning of a West African Court of Appeal that would protect the interest and liberty of the accused. He also wanted reform in the Protectorate, for instance, the separation of the judiciary from the Executive (i.e., District Commissioners should cease doubling as magistrates), improved facilities for granting bail, and a right of appeal by indigenes against the decision of the District Commissioner.[21]

Betts appealed to government to give jobs to Africans with the necessary legal qualifications, and to repeal the Perjury Ordinance. However, it was not until 1946 that the government made plans for overhauling the legal system 'for the whole of Sierra Leone which [will] provide a common system of magistrate's courts throughout the territory and empower the Supreme Court to exercise jurisdiction throughout Sierra Leone'.[22]

The paper on Colony/Protectorate relations was of absorbing interest to the audience. Originally scheduled to be read by the Reverend Max Gorvie, a man born in the Protectorate, but who grew up in Freetown and had travelled widely, it was presented by Reverend E.I.C. Steady, General Superintendent, A.M.E. Mission. The speaker confessed that Congress was not satisfied with the situation, and would welcome efforts through inter-marriages, a more equitable land-tenure system in the entire country of Sierra Leone, the abolition of differentiation of legal status between Colony-born and Protectorate-born, education, religion and culture, that would ensure a more harmonious relationship. To be sure, some of the suggestions made above had already been effected: people of the interior had been coming to Freetown over the years; friendships had been formed, marriages, whether regular or not, had been taking place. But, he warned, people should stop being narrow minded and to pray that 'the effusion of time and evolution would transmute all the tribes and peoples of Sierra Leone to a homogenous whole as in other civilized countries'. A lively discussion took place afterwards. A former Minister of government, Dr John Karefa Smart, then a student at Fourah Bay College, was given plaudits when he put the Protectorate's case in 'a forceful and humorous' manner (The *Weekly News* did not elaborate).[23]

Venereal disease, blocked drains and their consequent hazard on health, the lack of medical facilities in the country as a whole, and the high mortality rate in some areas, were the concerns of Dr A. F. Renner-Dove. He called for the exemption of duties on drugs, and the maintenance of a good supply of anti-tetanus injections; also anti-toxin serum for the use and sale to private medical practitioners.[24]

112

The flickering flames of Congress and the challenge of W.A.Y.L.

Three more papers should detain us further – French's 'Agricultural Outlook', Aymer's 'Commerce and the encouragement of combination and co-operation in private enterprise', and Williams' 'Unemployment in Sierra Leone'. The first speaker suggested establishing a plantation-type of agriculture for Sierra Leone where cash crops, such as coconuts, oil palm, and cotton would be cultivated with useful adjuncts such as sheep and cattle rearing, as well as poultry. As for capital and other technical details, which would make the scheme successful, a discussion, in which Karefa Smart participated, came up with suggestions that an Agricultural Bank be formed to supply the capital, that model farms be set up, supervised by travelling inspectors, and that youths should be sent overseas for training.

Aymer believed that what was needed for development was a co-operative group – a wholesale central body to supply goods to retailers – controlled by a 'Christian dictator with a sledge hammer'. It was obvious that what the speaker was proposing was a Co-operative Institution, and this is significant, for this thinking seemed to have anticipated the government's tardy decision to introduce co-operatives in the 40s. When Aymer's other suggestions for a co-operative banking system and drug store appeared to require a large capital (about £23,000, in shares of £10 payable in instalments), his audience balked at his 'grandiose plans'. To the faint-hearted doubters, he gave a sharp rebuke, telling them that nothing was too big for Sierra Leoneans if they put their minds to it. And he gave examples of substantial establishments, for example, the Bata Shoe Company, which had had humble beginnings but grew to be thriving businesses.

Dunstan Williams lamented the absence of unemployment bureaux in Sierra Leone; also he felt that the emasculation of the Trade Unions did not make for a vigorous development of the movement. He therefore pleaded for a Labour Bureau to be established. This anticipated the government initiative by ten years. Williams also believed in the right of women to work, and he was also of the opinion that a fishing industry, properly set up, would ease unemployment and boost the economy.

Other papers discussed a few questions of relevance to the Society with equal force and conviction. For instance, O. J. V. Tuboku-Metzger averred that the Congress was the only organ to express the people's grievances intelligently, and he appealed to the youths to wake up to their responsibilities. Lerina Bright-Taylor read a good paper on education. She believed that a recognised native language should be used to teach children in the kindergarten and primary levels of the school system. The Principal of the Prince of Wales School, W. J. Davies, praised her for the 'high quality' of her paper. S. Adole Hughes, the Congress Secretary, also provided a blue print for education called 'Education – sound and academic, and suggestions for a more progressive Educational policy'. These papers not only reflect the all-embracing interests of the Congress, they also offer a different interpretation to that contained in the literature on Sierra Leone, by demonstrating that interests such as agriculture, education, unemployment,

113

and legal reforms affected both the elite as well as the common man.[25] Indeed, on balance, they were of more immediate concern to the man in the street. The problems of the Colony were viewed from a national perspective, expressed in this resolution 'that future relationship between the colony born and protectorate born should tend towards a similarity of interests, and that every effort should be made towards promoting co-operation between the two'.[26] Again it was announced that Congress was going to extend operations into the villages and the Protectorate of Sierra Leone 'with a view of forming branches in those places'.[27] The records do not show whether this latter objective was effectuated, but the foregoing does not support Padmore's slanderous remark in 1957 that 'until recently, politics in Sierra Leone have centred around personalities, most of whom have been demagogues using their professional and social status to bamboozle the illiterate masses for their own personal aggrandizement'.[28]

It is possible to hold reservations about the strategies of the Congress; and it could certainly have shown more energy in advertising its activities and emphasising its relevance. Nevertheless, the identification of the country's problems, the quality of the discussion, the wealth of suggestions, and the commendable initiative taken by the delegates on the issues treated above surely sustain the claim being posited in this work, that is, that Congress politicians were concerned and positive citizens. Historians have not given them the sympathetic consideration they merit.

The government, too, did not treat the conference with much seriousness. As if surprised by the 'spark of life' shown by a body they considered moribund, the government ordered an investigation into the activities of the local branch because it seemed 'desirable to keep a record of the organ'. Furthermore, the covering letter of Acting Governor H. R. R. Blood, and the reaction of the Colonial Office, leave little doubt that the hostile attitude of the British Administration in Sierra Leone sabotaged and undermined the effectiveness of the Congress.

The Colonial Office comments were in marginalia:[29] the demand for an elective representation to be made universal in the Legislative Council, or the calling for an unofficial majority, were deemed to be premature. The view of London was that there was little hope of the Colony acquiring this 'in the present rate of development'. This position was held consistently; for, in subsequent demands for an all-elected Legislative Council or an official majority, it was clearly stated that such a concession would only be of advantage to Colony inhabitants. Indeed, as late as 1945, the Colonial Office laid down that 'the political and social development of the Protectorate is an essential condition to further constitutional advance',[30] in Sierra Leone. Thus it was not until 1948 that a reconstituted Municipal Council was restored, even though Colony inhabitants had urged this to keep in step with the development of local government institutions in the Protectorate in the 1930s and 1940s.

As for the rest of the resolutions, the Colonial Office did not agree that judges of the West African Court of Appeal should be independent of the Supreme Courts of West Africa in order to guarantee impartiality; it refused to concede that a unanimous decision of Assessors must be taken as the judgement of the Court; its response to the idea to separate the judicial functions of District Commissioners from administrative duties, and the appointment of qualified Africans to judicial and legal posts, as in Nigeria and the Gold Coast, was negative.

There was, however, some favourable response to the resolutions on unemployment, and the suggestions for the creation of jobs, medical reforms and facilities, and those on founding Agricultural Banks to encourage *bona fide* farmers, and the training of African Agriculturists. These, and the request for a shorthand writer to take evidence in court, were put down as noted or under consideration.

What the above analysis suggests is that while it may be conceded that government had the onus of deciding the priorities of the dependency, it is clear from its response that it was opposed to any political concessions and that it still saw the Colony and Protectorate as two separate units with differing needs and relevance. Blood, for one, told the Colonial Office that Congress was 'entirely limited to Freetown and the immediate surroundings' and that their demands did not reflect the needs of the rest of Sierra Leone.[31] This equivocation by officialdom is responsible for the dichotomy in Sierra Leone history.

On the other hand, Blood's bland comment on the 'exclusiveness' of Congress needs a further look, because this inability to spread was the greatest weakness of Congress. The government never failed to exploit the absence of an identifiable link with the Protectorate in terms of organisation and membership, if we overlook the odd ones like Max Gorvie. This point was forcefully brought home by the columnist, Rambler, at the close of the year when he observed: 'The Sierra Leone branch – surely, though silently – is working for the public good, but if Congress is to become effective it must spread, it must be popular, not merely sitting in conclave and publishing minutes of proceedings, but go to the highways and hedges, and compel people to come.'[32] Congress, he insisted, must engage in active propaganda; it must divide the country into districts with organising Secretaries, a full-time Secretary-General (although this had been done in 1922 it would appear that the reorganisation was not very effective); and members could pay monthly subscriptions as low as 1d. Once this had been achieved, he reasoned, Congress would gain the Protectorate and the Colony; then 'its representations will receive respect from the government'. Ade Sawyerr, another columnist, put it another way two years later, in the heat of Wallace-Johnson mania. He argued in an article entitled, 'The Sierra Leone Youth League, as I see it, present and future', that the only political organ that had done much for Sierra Leone was the Congress. Unfortunately, he lamented, it failed to have a hold on the people and to impress them with much of its work, because 'they are spasmodic in their activities, heard at election time and during big controversies'.[33]

And that was the weakness of the Congress. It never became a popular party. But then Congress was hardly in a position to make profound structural changes in 1936. The total membership was forty, most of whom were self-employed professionals with full-time businesses of their own to attend to, and a few pensioners. Congress met only occasionally, at most every six months, to discuss topical issues. The branch was starved of funds, and the active participants seemed always to be Bright, Betts, and Tuboku-Metzger. Besides, the movement was rent by feuds and personality clashes. In short, Congress was going through the trauma of emasculation by the end of the thirties.

The consistent rejection of their suggestions and demands by the British government gave rise to a feeling of frustration and despair. Politicians got fed up with hitting their heads on a blank wall. Apathy and lethargy set in. Freetown was in some kind of political stupor. Moreover, the ranks of active politicians were sadly depleted in the years before the Second World War. Many went to other pastures, celestial as well as material: Mayor May, 'an unselfish paradigm of the ideal citizen', A. J. Shorunkeh-Sawyerr, 'a conservative mind with indomitable courage', and his brother, J.C., 'a brilliant and radical mind', died within months of each other in 1929.[34] Tuboku-Metzger left the Legislative Council as Rural Area Member the same year when he was defeated by his successor, J. G. Hyde. But this 'poor man's Lawyer' and patriot lost his freedom nine years later for an alleged misdemeanour.[35] Betts became a Police Magistrate in 1937. E. T. Nelson-Williams, urged by Herbert Macauley, had left to go to Nigeria by the end of 1939.[36] Public figures like the inimitable and eccentric socialite, William Rainy Lumpkin, known as Alimamy Bungie, the Sympathetic Undertaker, and Professor J. S. T. Davies, a former Assistant Postmaster-General and amateur Historian and Agriculturist, took their exit from this world in 1935. A. J. Songo Davies followed them on 27 July, 1938.[37] Those who remained in the political field were divided among themselves. C. E. Wright tended to be more on the conservative side, and was apt to support government policy. He could not work with the elected unofficial members.

The feuds between Bright and his political enemies, for instance, Fowell Boston, certainly contributed to the disarray in the ranks of the Krio politicians. Indeed, Bright's high watermark of popularity was in 1936 when he won a libel case against Boston, who had called him a bankrupt. The courts were packed full, and when Bankie emerged as victor there was a sigh of relief from his public supporters. Turbett's prognosis on the increasing popularity of Bright did not, however, stand the test of time.[38] Three years later Bright was forced to resign the Vice-Presidency of the Congress. He was ostracised. Thus by 1938–9 the Kiro leadership had been emasculated. A near

vacuum was created. It was not for nothing that the *Weekly News*, in
lamenting the passing away of May and the Shorunkeh-Sawyerr brothers,
noted that the 'rank of tried leaders is depleted to a great extent'.[39] Wallace-
Johnson tried to fill this vacuum and inject new blood into the tired veins of
Colony body politic.

L. T. A. Wallace-Johnson is perhaps the best-known Sierra Leonean
politician in history, because of the studies that have been done on him and,
possibly, because his elan had some kind of fascination for certain writers
intrigued by the man's professed socialism.[40] Consequently, positive things
have been said about him: the only Colony politician to bridge the gap
between the Colony and Protectorate, to attempt collaboration between the
two; the radical African nationalist who spoke for independence against the
conservative elitism of Bankie's clique; a workers' man, a socialist Trade
Unionist, and many more. These assessments are contained in 'Studies on
Sierra Leone History' and do not need any citation. Indeed, Wallace-Johnson
mania has reached such a point that it has threatened to become a cult.
Honours have been heaped on him posthumously. A statue of this hero
stands prominently in the street which is named after him, in front of City
Hall – the old Wilberforce Memorial Hall. Such effusions are heartwarming,
but perhaps some people who now extol Wallace-Johnson's virtues could
have done a better service to the nation if they had given him their support
when he most needed it. In fact, he and Siaka Stevens were bitter rivals for
the Trade Union leadership. Stevens, writing to Rita Hinden of the Fabian
Bureau, disparagingly referred to Wallace-Johnson

> who is a political leader and who wants to dominate the Unions and push them
> into his party...[he] goes to the lowest depths of journalistic irresponsibility
> possible. But he certainly does not now hold the sway he used to hold a few
> years back. The people simply will not swallow all the rubbish that he tries to
> dish out to them now.[41]

Be that as it may, the point is that while a case could be argued for each of
the characterisations referred to above, it is quite another thing to suggest,
as the impression is given in a few studies, that Wallace-Johnson initiated
politics in Sierra Leone and that before his time it was all placid complacency,
and unmitigated loyalty to the British Raj.[42] To say the least, such an
interpretation of the political history of Sierra Leone is not only an unhealthy
distortion, it is also a disservice to the legion of activists who had been
plodding the field long before Wallace-Johnson appeared on the scene.
However, this passage is not to detract from Wallace-Johnson's own useful
contributions to political awareness and popular organisation, but an
attempt to put them in perspective, in relation to the work of others. Of
course, his international activities are too well known to need recounting
here.

Isaac Theophilus Akunna Wallace-Johnson was born in 1895 to a working-class family at Wilberforce Village. Educated at the local school, he ended up at the Collegiate (W.A.M.) School. While at school he tried his hand at journalism, a field for which he was well equipped; and he was encouraged in this by Bankie who was his hero then.[43]

He soon left school and, when he started work in the Customs Department of 1913, he immediately came up against authority because of his tendency not only to raise uncomfortable issues that were of concern to his peers, but also to encourage them to make representations against their conditions of service. Between 1913 and 1938, when he made his dramatic entry into Sierra Leone politics, Wallace-Johnson had moved from job to job, including a stint in the Carriers Corps during the war and a brief spell at the Freetown City Council from where he was sacked in 1926;[44] then he had some experience as a seaman. By 1928 he was associating with a mixed bag of socialists: that year he attended the Comintern Conference in Moscow; allegedly he studied Trade Unionism for some time at Kutvu University in Russia; and, in subsequent years, he was attending conferences organised by socialist bodies where he met other Africans like Jomo Kenyatta and E. F. Small.[45] Between 1931 and 1937 he worked in Nigeria – where he founded the first Labour Union in 1931 – and the Gold Coast, mobilising the workers, editing papers and generally being a thorn in the flesh of the colonial authorities. As a consequence of these activities he had to flee the Gold Coast in 1937. By the time he finally came home in April 1938 Wallace-Johnson had been exposed, more than any of his contemporaries, to varying types of societies and ideologies and he was therefore justified in calling himself an 'International African'.[46] Wallace-Johnson's political philosophy was strongly influenced by socialism, though, oddly enough, contemporaries deny that he was a socialist or even knew what Socialism meant.[47] He also had a strong anti-establishment mentality, and what can be termed as an instinct for grass-root solidarity. In presentation he was crude and coarse, even unashamedly scurrilous in his denunciation of his opponents.[48] Yet he was eloquent and charismatic. His humble background lent him an edge over his peers – an earthy commonsense that appealed to the masses. He was their own man. Wallace-Johnson brought with him a new type of populist leadership which sharply contrasted the 'drawing room politics' of Bankie's generation. Also, the advertised virtues of socialism were like a heady tonic to his audience. In the Sierra Leone setting, socialism was paraded as the panacea for all the ills of the society. Using blitzkrieg tactics, Wallace-Johnson, from the beginning, kept up a continuous assault on the establishment. He ridiculed and dismissed the conservatism of Bright and others as irrelevances.[49] Consequently, Wallace-Johnson's ringing denunciations did evoke an empathic, even enthusiastic response from young intellectuals; for instance, R. Sarif Easmon (Black Tulips); older folk like the respected F. A. Miller, former Clerk of the Legislative Council, who lent respectability to Wallace-Johnson's movement by consenting to be Vice-President; the lawyers: C. D. Hotobah-During, Oyekan Otto During,

Metzger-Boston, and a host of others; angry and disgruntled people like the activist feminist, Mrs Edna Elliot Horton, reportedly the first woman degree holder in West Africa, and S. M. O. Boyle. The latter was so mesmerised by Wallace-Johnson that he worshipped him; and when Boyle got himself elected Secretary of the Freetown branch of W.A.Y.L. he resigned his £6 per month job as Senior Customs Clerk for U.A.C. To these devotees were added a group of young men who were denounced by the *Weekly News* for living a reckless life, 'absorbing slogans and stage habits'.[50] The impact was intoxicatingly dramatic.

On the other hand, the type of leadership represented by Wallace-Johnson was not peculiar to Sierra Leone. Bankole-Bright's response to these new men was not singular either. Comparing the politics of Congress with that of the Radicals in the 30s, Post cites the example of Kitoye Ajasa who disparagingly referred to radicals as 'water rate agitators'. Bankie called them the 'oi Polloi'. In fact, in the late 30s, a body of more militant activists emerged in West Africa demanding independence now rather than in the distant future. In the Gold Coast and Nigeria, as well as francophone West Africa, radicals like Nkrumah and Azikiwe had been exposed to different educational systems than the British. They had learnt a different kind of political ideology. These 'New men' injected an immediacy into politics that became impatient with the evolutionary strategy of British colonial policy.[51] They demanded and advocated direct action. The circumstances for the efficacy of their tactics were auspicious: the Soviet Union, angling for opportunities to spread her influence and export her brand of socialism world wide, offered advice and training on strategies for rebellion through such organs as the Comintern (Communist International), the L.A.I. (League Against Imperialism and for Colonial Independence), I.N.W. (International Negro Workers) and I.T.U.C.N.W. (the International Trade Union Committee of Negro Workers). Individuals like R. Bridgeman, A. Sorenson, and Ellen Wilkinson appeared to be the links between emergent African radicals and the Socialist International headed by Russia.[52] In the metropole, too, one of the major parties, the Labour Party, was increasingly identifying itself with the interests of the toiling masses in Britain's colonies. It appeared to be more willing to listen favourably to the anguished cries of the colonised. Institutions like the Fabian Colonial Bureau (14 October 1940) were set up 'as an invaluable organ for research, factual information and constructive proposal' with a Secretary, Dr Rita Hinden, the South African-born economist and confidante of African politicians.[53] Arthur Creech Jones, the Labour Secretary of State for the Colonies in the middle of the forties, and Reginald Sorenson, were parliamentarians who were known as people who championed the cause of the Africans. Many questions were now asked, more than ever before, on behalf of the black peoples of the colonies. The links these people had with Africans (and Wallace-Johnson had personal contacts with, for instance, Creech Jones and Sorenson),[54] and their pressure on the government in London, brought forth a more conducive atmosphere

119

for the conceiving and implementing of ameliorating measures in the colonies. This background then encouraged the growth of much more radical movements that had better chances of success than Bright's memo-sending brigade.

In Sierra Leone, the personalities and activities of Bright and Wallace-Johnson reflected the change of climate, moods and attitudes – the end of an era that was becoming less relevant in a society that was experiencing a new economic situation of high prices, low wages and escalating unemployment for an enlarged labour market. And it was to this sector that Wallace-Johnson made his appeal.[55] When Wallace-Johnson focused attention on the labour and industrial conditions of Delco workers in 1938, he was not the first to raise the issue. A few months back there had been a call to investigate conditions at Delco. The *Weekly News* itself filed a report on the unhealthy and inhuman conditions of the workers in Delco. An open letter was sent to Major J. M. Campbell, Managing Director of Delco, to look into questions of ill treatment, poor salary, summary dismissals of workers and the inefficiency of his management staff.[56] Earlier, the same paper had publicised the existence of a Commercial Pool which it claimed was deliberately aimed at 'smothering African enterprise'.[57] An editorial also complained bitterly against a decision to import workers into Sierra Leone to work in the mines. Not that it begrudged assistance to sister colonies, but it insisted that this should not be done at the expense of Sierra Leoneans. The paper believed that the scheme would increase 'unemployment in our midst'.[58] In other words, there was no lack of public concern, nor was there any lethargy in speaking out against these things, but it was a question of style and approach. Wallace-Johnson believed in immediacy and direct action. He was an effective propagandist and agitator with great ability to communicate with, and appeal to, the masses through his speeches and writings.' He had the 'ability to spot grievances, articulate them, and foment discontent among all kinds of sufferers', writes Martin Kaniki.[59] These characteristics stamped all the issues he championed: workmen's pay and compensation, discrimination, women's franchise and many other complaints that had all been raised before by Bright, among others.[60] But then Wallace-Johnson had a knack of injecting fresh breath into old questions, bringing them alive, as if they appeared only yesterday. Indeed, his very first broadside against the establishment was unleashed from London when he ridiculed the ludicrous suggestion by Alex D. Yaskey (who became his Treasurer at W.A.Y.L. to name the Institution for the Destitute (the later King George VI Home), Henry Moore's British Museum. 'Why not', he asked, 'name it after Africans like Cornelius May or E. H. Cummings?'[61] It was using little things like this to make the older people look foolish which endeared him to the populace.

However, he made two major contributions to the development of politics in Sierra Leone – the establishment of the first popular party in the country, the West African Youth League (W.A.Y.L. on 29 April/2 May 1938) set up

120

under the auspices of the West African Civil Liberties and the National Defence League (29 April 1938);[62] and the reactivation and mobilisation of Trade Unions that were more mass organised than those before the 1926 Railway Strike. Between September 1938 and the end of 1939 Wallace-Johnson had succeeded in establishing three major unions, the Postal Workers Union, All Seamen's Union, and the War Department Amalgamated Workers Union, under the umbrella of the Trade Union Congress (T.U.C.). He had also organised, incited, or associated with, strikes and sit-ins at Mabella Coaling Depot and Marampa Mines and a Mutiny (the Mutiny of the Gunners). And, as a consequence of these activities, he forced the government, under pressure from London, to legalise Trade Unionism in November 1939.[63] Meetings called by his W.A.Y.L. were packed full, and, though the claim that membership in Freetown alone had reached 25,000 by 1939 is doubtful, the impact of W.A.Y.L. is attested by a contemporary columnist, Rambler. Enthusing over W.A.Y.L.'s popularity, he proclaimed that 'to ignore it is to pretend to ignore the existence of a wave of consciousness that is sweeping the country and affecting old and young alike'.[64] This euphoria is understandable given the issues raised by W.A.Y.L. More important, these, including the wholesale condemnation of colonialism, bad roads, inadequate hospital and social services, and the advocation of the participation of women in national affairs, reflected the depressing economic situation of the interwar years and the disillusion of the articulate citizens. The virulence of the denunciations gave hope to the aspirations of the down trodden. Consequently, in addition to the middle- and lower-middle-class elements of pensioners, clerks, teachers, artisans, lawyers, and self-employed people like Lisk-Carew, the photographer, and C. Tregson-Roberts, a surveyor, his movement attracted a large mass of the working people. A greater proportion of the latter came from the Protectorate, their number swollen by the jobless and the hungry.[65] The visual presence of these Protectorate people in W.A.Y.L., and the establishment of branches in the Protectorate, formed that identifiable link between the Colony and Protectorate with reference to political mobilisation which the Congress had not been able to effect. The link has been singled out as the first attempt made by Colony politicians to bridge the gap between, and to integrate, the Colony and Protectorate.[66] The evidence suggests that this is an exaggeration. Wallace-Johnson was not the first Colony politician to stretch a hand across the divide. As has been argued in the foregoing pages, A. J. Shorunkeh-Sawyerr, A. E. Tuboku-Metzger, Betts, and Congress had made pronouncements on this issue and, for a short while, such a body (S.L.A.S.), comprising members from both sides of the territory, existed.[67] Wallace-Johnson succeeded thus far because apart from his own flair and undoubted talent at propaganda, the conditions were favourable; the issues advanced, advocated earlier by Congress, cut across ethnic and social lines but were more insistent in the hungry 30s. And, most of all, Wallace-Johnson addressed himself to the bread and butter issues that were calculated to impress and interest the workers who felt the economic pinch the most.[68] On the other hand, Wallace-Johnson's rapport with the Protectorate was confined to the urban working mass, and was never with the educated protectorate elite, for reasons which are still elusive; but one which can be identified is that the elite held back: they did not respond to the stretched hands. Kaniki's study even questions the impact of W.A.Y.L. in the Protectorate because, he argued, with an Executive almost entirely Krio in membership, it was regarded as a Krio party.[69] And, in any case, Protectorate inhabitants were still suspicious of the Krios. Further, if Wallace-Johnson did in fact establish this rapport it needs to be explained why this cooperation was not sustained beyond 1939. Neither Margai, nor Kasrefa Smart, nor Siaka Stevens, appeared to have shown any positive response. In the Legislative Council, hardly any chief spoke in defence of this integrationist during the debate on the Three bills. The point is that the evidence supporting the integrationist effort is not very strong. Wallace-Johnson certainly made the attempt, but the evidence does not indicate that he succeeded in bridging the gap. The 'alliance' was one of convenience. A generous view on this issue would therefore be that his influence was too brief for us to come to any definite conclusions. Nevertheless, Wallace-Johnson's abrasiveness, his direct approach, and his forceful drive, dismayed and ruffled the government, and old-style politicians who believed they were threatened by this maverick. African politicians were partly resentful because they were being supplanted by this vigorous fellow from an obscure background, but they also harboured genuine fears that Wallace-Johnson wanted to force communism down their throats; and given their own political ethos this fear was not unreasonable.[70] The government, on the other hand, were scared out of their complacency by the fear of the potential of Wallace-Johnson's following.[71] His promises raised the hopes of workers; they gave pride to the low. And when, as a result of his agitation, a mutiny by some soldiers occurred in January 1939, and strikes were erupting everywhere at a time when the war clouds were gathering, it became imperative for the government to take up the challenge posed by Wallace-Johnson.

In 1938–9 war was imminent. Freetown was a naval base and the government was afraid, for security reasons, or so it argued, that W.A.Y.L's campaign would cause unrest and instability in the Colony and, more seriously, weaken a strategic link in Britain's imperial defence. The fact that Wallace-Johnson unashamedly flirted with communist and socialist contacts, who were presumably backed by expansionist Soviet Russia, may have coloured the imagination of an administration that feared a dastardly plot against its rule.[72] And the mutiny in the colonial army stationed in Freetown led by a Krio gunner, Emmanuel Cole (allegedly a member of W.A.Y.L.), protesting against low wages, in January 1939, merely served to heighten reasons for disquiet.[73] But there is no doubt that Douglas Jardine, the governor, was excitable and prone to panic, and that Blood, his Colonial Secretary, was an imperious authoritarian of the first order. Throughout

1938 and 1939 correspondence streamed into the Colonial Office reporting Wallace-Johnson's activities. Blood, for one, scarcely able to contain his rage, watched impotently as Wallace-Johnson went from success to success.[74] In June 1938 Wallace-Johnson embarrassed the government by causing the publication of a purloined correspondence from the governor to the Secretary of State stating that the average family could live on 15s. 0d. per month. The governor later had to admit his mistake when the Colonial Office ordered an investigation into the cost-of-living index and labour conditions in Sierra Leone. But, in the subsequent court action against Wallace-Johnson, nearly the whole Sierra Leone Bar associated itself with the defendant. A further correspondence revealed that eighteen out of the twenty-one African barristers in Freetown were members of W.A.Y.L.[75] Later in the year W.A.Y.L. upset the pattern of the local City Council elections when it fielded candidates for all the wards and swept the polls, scoring a historical point in that for the first time a woman, Constance Commings-John, was elected into a local assembly, getting the greatest number of votes cast in the whole election. O. J. V. Tuboku-Metzger, originally a Congress member, was elected unopposed for the Eastward.[76]

Added to these, the rest of 1938 and 1939 witnessed a series of strikes and civil disobedience, all traced from the impact and influence of W.A.Y.L. This was too much for Blood, and he wrote what was even regarded at the Colonial Office as a very strong letter, advocating that Wallace-Johnson be contained. He complained that events had convinced him that W.A.Y.L. could not 'be diverted into constitutional and useful channels so long as Wallace-Johnson remains in Sierra Leone as its organizers and that his continued presence in this country is a menace not only to local interests but also to the Empire'. He was sure that 'Johnson's concern is not with the economic and political betterment of the workers but with real sedition, violence and revolutionary activities'. He must be banished from Sierra Leone. Exposing the fear (of the Colony and Protectorate presenting a common front by the merging of their interests) that had always haunted officials in Sierra Leone, Blood expressed grave concern lest 'such a person exploiting a simple and unspoiled people' as the Protectorate inhabitants, should threaten the peace in Sierra Leone and undermine the prestige and power of the government.[77] With sentiments like these one does not need to look far for a reason why co-operation between Colony and Protectorate was always stillborn.

However, concern and worry did not come from official quarters alone. In July 1938, after a mammoth meeting held by W.A.Y.L. and noting the whirlwind success of the party, Ade Sawyerr offered some kind words of advice to Wallace-Johnson. He suggested that, among other things, W.A.Y.L. changed its motto, 'Liberty or Death', because it savoured too much of revolution, although he was sure that was not the aim, to 'For God, King and Country' or 'For Our Country's Sake' or 'Service for the Good of All'. It must educate the masses towards constitutional protests and the

League must co-operate with the other organs. Wallace-Johnson's denouncement of the Church, had alienated many; and it was wrong of him to regard prominent men as hypocrites because they did not rush to his bandwagon. If W.A.Y.L. could see to these and lead people to co-operate with their native industries it would become a strong political party, he prophesied.[78]

Another correspondent, Speedo (M.G.M. Cole, whose silvery voice was to charm Sierra Leone listeners to the 'B.B.C. Calling Sierra Leone' programme in the fifties and sixties), chagrined by Wallace-Johnson's allegations, denied that the predecessors of Johnson had been idle. Issues affecting Paramount Chiefs, and those on the franchise, higher appointments for Africans, reform of the Assessors' Ordinance, withdrawal of the Criminal Code, and the V. D. Bill, were advanced by 'patriotic bodies and individuals who have not been idle; and though they may not have done all we may say they should have done, yet the fact remains that they did something, and a sweeping statement that they have let us down would be a lie'. He strongly denounced 'uncivility under the guise of bluntness, soap box oratory which leads the rabble like unthinking horses into battle, the untutored mind, abusive and insulting, the uncultured mind, antagonistic to criticism however honest, eloquent ribaldry misleading the rabble. We want a leader not a Irascible Bobadil or a Migratory Monomaniac.' He advised, '*Festina Lente*. If you can get a thing without abusing A, for God's sake, do so and get one enemy less. You may even get him as a valuable ally later.'[79]

This angry retort by a citizen underlines the fact that Bankole-Bright was not the only one who resented W.A.Y.L.'s methods of protest. Other people were very much concerned about the activities. The *Weekly News*, too, though an organ of Congress, had welcomed W.A.Y.L. with enthusiasm but, by the turn of the year, had changed its opinion, because of what it deemed the League's excesses. By April 1939, commenting on the trial and conviction of Emmanuel Cole and During, the leaders of the soldiers' mutiny, it was denouncing the result of 'the pernicious influence of Youth League'.[80] The above, then, is the background to the passing of the Three Bills. These, on Sedition, Undesirable Literature, and Deportation, were introduced in the Legislative Council in May. And by 21 June they had been passed into law.[81]

The details of the Bills need not detain us, for they were aimed at suppressing sedition, muzzling opinion, and getting rid of critics of the government in order 'to maintain the safety of the realm'. There was strong opposition to these bills in and out of the Legislative Council. While the government kept on insisting that these were passed for the security of the state, to re-establish peace and order, the African members in the chamber denounced them as oppressive, vindictive, and a slur on the ancient loyalty of the people of Sierra Leone. With reference to the Deportation of Undesirable British Subjects, J. C. O. Crowther, the newly elected Rural

The flickering flames of Congress and the challenge of W.A.Y.L.

Area Member, called it a 'Trojan Horse' that was going to 'induce its red warriors in the heart of the loyal and amenable people in Sierra Leone'. And, in any case, how could it be proved who was a Sierra Leonean or not? he asked. And the vagueness of the definition of undesirable person – it was such that it could be construed from anything from casting glances at the Police Commissioner or failure to take off one's hat before a European. In other words, 'if the words peace, good order, good government and public morals had been properly defined one might know where in he offends'. The provision for taking evidence at trials of the accused were other areas of grave concern to members and, on this, Chief John Mana Kpaka, on behalf of the chiefs, made a special plea for the open and fair trial of an accused. He appreciated the necessity of the Bill, though he did not necessarily like it. T. E. Nelson-Williams, the new Second Urban member just come back from a visit to Nigeria, attacked the Bills with a lawyer's repugnance for any restrictions on the liberty of the people through legislative action. He told the House that he could not with conscience assist the government with the Bill.[82] Outside the Legislative Council, opposition came to such a dangerous point that the nervous and panic-prone Jardine, unnerved by large crowds of 'Mammies (with children) and their menfolk demonstrating their disapproval', chanting 'we wont's be slaves till we're in our graves', frantically telegraphed the Naval Commander-in-Chief to allow H. M. S. *Rochester* to remain in Freetown until the situation was clarified.[83] The Committee of Citizens, a middle of the road group, was formed in September 1938 with the pharmacist, E. D. Morgan, as Chairman, and the following foundation members: Otto I. E. During, S. C. C. Pyne-Bailey, A. Benka-Coker, T. J. Shorunkeh-Sawyerr (grandson of the bookseller), C. V. Jarret (Secretary), George C. Thomas, C. Wallis Smith, Ulric Coker, and E. R. Palmer. The Committee sent deputations and protested loudly against the Three Bills.[84] W.A.Y.L. of course, believed the bills were directed against them, and Wallace-Johnson, who was ill for sometime ('not half as ill as I could have wanted', observed the malicious Jardine), used all his undoubted talent as a lampoonist to ridicule the Bills, especially the one on Deportation which called forth the bitterest resentment.[85]

However, one man, a former uncompromising critic of government, stood squarely behind the administration, even seconding the Bills. This volte-face by Bright has been the subject of much speculation. Was it a mere case of pricked *amour propre*? Was it fear and jealousy of Wallace-Johnson?[86] Or was it a dramatic bowing out of public affairs (for Bright was also a showman in his own right), having sensed that he was no longer as popular as he had been before 1938? Could it have been just plain vindictiveness directed at an ungrateful public who failed to show appreciation for his efforts? There may never be correct answers to these questions. All we can do is perhaps partly explain this transformation without necessarily condoning or even applauding Bright's postures. Some element of jealousy does come in. According to a contemporary, Bankie was, after all, an older man and this counted for a lot in a gerontocratic society.[87] He had been slogging it since the twenties without making much dent on the shield of the establishment, and then suddenly a younger man came almost from nowhere and, without so much as asking the blessings of a pioneer fighter, proceeded to damn all the work Bright and his peers had done, to call them names. Wallace-Johnson's tasteless lampoon of Bright and his supporters after the W.A.Y.L. victory in the City Council elections did in fact lead to a libel suit filed by Bright. The latter did not, of course, enjoy an experience in which he found it difficult to secure the services of a lawyer to defend his case. He did not win the suit.[88] Another filed against Otto Oyekan During, a supporter of W. A. Y. L., was dismissed by his former friend and associate, E. S. Beoku-Betts, the presiding magistrate. He narrowly got out of a criminal summons for false pretences, purportedly engineered by Wallace-Johnson, before the same judge.[89] These personal indignities apart, he suffered physical assaults from W.A.Y.L. supporters; his house was stoned and his chauffeur was manhandled.[90]

Beyond all this was also the political dimension of Bright's change; as he told his detractors:

> I should state that the ethical mind is subjected to variations conditioned by circumstances and that such procedure is not incompatible with progress; nay more, that the Sierra Leone of yesterday with its policy for order and good government is now converted by a new organisation and its environment to a Sierra Leone of disorder and lawlessness backed up by some members of the local branch of the National Congress. Consequently, there should be no surprise if I have had to revise my views on certain policies to meet present emergencies.[91]

Bankie believed that the Sierra Leone of yore was not the same as that in 1938–9. Now it was being ruled by the mob, inexorably prodded on by a 'galaxy of irresponsibles driven to thoughtlessness by seditious propagandists of the Youth League and by a frenzied display of the lawless man'.[92] The antics of these people were 'undermining authority and vilifying and frustrating British rule' in Sierra Leone.[93] To hastily dismiss this as a contradiction for a man who, in his earlier days, had also vehemently attacked the British administration would be less than fair to him. For even in his most extreme denunciations, Bankie had always believed in the organic connection with the British Crown, and he showed this on many occasions.[94] More to the point, he believed in constitutionality (in everything you do, be Constitutional'). Therefore, he had rejected an offer by Bolsheviks in 1920 to help the Congress secure its demands from Britain. The latter, he was always saying, had its faults, but it was the best colonial government one could wish for. And then came this Bolshevik with his anti-British slogans and his socialist rhetoric promising the world to workers and disrupting the equilibrium of society. He was outraged at Wallace-Johnson's deception of the people. As a veteran agitator he knew full well that government would not give concessions unless they were of a mind to do so.[95] Finally, in

126

Wallace-Johnson he saw the embodiment of an evil destroyer of all the things he stood for.

Thus, his stand in 1939 was on a political issue. This is clear from the speeches he made both in and out of the Legislative Council. Beginning his contribution to the debate on the Bill for the Deportation of Undesirable Subjects with the Krio proverb 'who wowo go bring wata en babu cry' (lit. 'He who is ugly should fetch water, baboon cries.' Cf. 'If the cap fits' in English),[96] he assured his audience that nobody needed to anticipate falling a victim to the law if he did not misbehave himself. These were not normal times, he elaborated: Sierra Leone was an important part of imperial defence, the international scene was uncertain; and, in the face of all this, a rowdy mob was running amok. The niceties of constitutional procedure were unknown to them, the press had been corrupted; people were afraid to speak for fear of being mobbed; and juries would free any W.A.Y.L. member – the country was in chaos. Why? 'Because of an unscrupulous individual backed up by the rabble and the oi polloi with a few intelligentsia who are only there with no object in view but cheap popularity.' A patrician to the last, he refused to represent 'a community of such degenerate hooligans. I would rather sit at home than come here as their representative. I refuse to be gagged by the rabble and the oi polloi. I deal with educated and law abiding citizens. I listen to the intelligentsia of the community.' For these reasons he supported the Bill. He went further, he suggested, in a letter to the governor, that the Assessors' Ordinance (an iniquity he had fought against for over ten years) be invoked against such disturbances of the peace; he also suggested the suspension of the elective provision of the Constitution because, given the consequences of W.A.Y.L.'s activities explained above, 'I stand for an organic connection with the British Empire and anything that savours of disconnection must be repugnant to me.' He may have been chagrined by all these unusual phenomena but, in making these submissions, he appeared to have overstated his case. Happily, Bright failed to impress the officials with his argument. Jardine was convinced he was inspired 'solely by political spleen and the fear of seeing the three elected members drawn from ranks of what he would style the rabble instead of from the small professional class'. Another official in the Colonial Office expressed contempt for the political maturity of the citizens of Freetown.[97] The local Congress was not convinced by the sincerity of Bankie's politics, either. In December 1938, the Committee of Citizens, politically a centrist group, with overlapping memberships with W.A.Y.L. and the local Congress, passed a vote of non-confidence on Bankie for his pro-government stand.[98] The next year, on a motion moved by O. J. V. Tuboku-Metzger, a W.A.Y.L. member of the City Council, and a member of Congress Executive, Bright was condemned for anti-Congress activities derived from 'a poisoned and vengeful mind'. He was asked to resign as Vice-President of Congress. But Bright was more than equal to the situation. He gave as good as he received. Telling them that he had anticipated their move long ago and, for that matter, had stopped attending meetings months previously, he slammed the Executive for their ingratitude. Parts of his letter are worth quoting:[99]

> I am amused at the paradox disclosed in your letter, tinctured with the essence of personal invectives, assuredly characteristic of some of the type of men forming the body politic of the Congress at present. I am further amused at the panaceal stream of self-conceit which the mover of the Resolution was apparently summoning when he was moving Resolutions couched in such insipid effusion.

Recounting his association with Congress for the past twenty years, with people like Casely Hayford, Malamah Thomas, William Dove, Leslie Macarthy and Betts, little did he think that the basic principle of Congress which was 'to maintain inviolate its organic connection with the British Empire' would have been so flagrantly violated by those who today formed the local body politic. He did not need their resolutions, moved by a 'puerile pseduo-politician', asking for his resignation, because he had long ago decided to have less to do with the body and to found his own party. However, to satisfy the mover, he was resigning his post as Vice-President and his membership of the Congress, but he would remain an independent supporter of the party principle, i.e., to maintain the organic connection with the Empire. Thus existed Bankole-Bright, certainly one of the most colourful figures in colonial Sierra Leone politics.[100]

Bankie's politics may not bring forth cheers, while his actions could have been more circumspect, but the courage of the man is another matter altogether. He stood by what he believed. These letters explained his political philosophy – he was a conservative, albeit a radical conservative, a Tory,[101] not a follower of men; certainly he was not going to be dictated to by the oi polloi. And it was this, his inflexibility, his rigidness, which was his undoing. As Wallace-Johnson observed, Bright believed in aristocracy, however decadent. Some say he was a very stubborn man, while others called him a brave activist.[102] Indeed, he received a left-handed compliment from the government when he retired from the Legislative Council in 1939:

> A vigilant and vehement critic of the government during the 15 years that he was a member of the Council, Dr. Bright always had the courage of his convictions, and when at long last the day dawned when he found himself in full agreement with government's policy, he did not hesitate to speak and vote as his conscience dictated, despite the unpopularity which this course was bound to entail.
> I cannot believe that Dr. Bright's temporary eclipse will mean his disappearance from the public life of this town; and I bespeak for him many years of useful public service to come.

But one wonders what value one can attach to this encomium coming as it were from a government, Jardine, the incumbent governor, in particular, who had watched with ill-concealed glee and amusement the loss of popularity of one who had been a thorn in the flesh of the administration. For, while saying one thing in public, he told the Colonial Secretary that Bright's criticisms of government had been outspoken to a degree verging on vulgar abuse:

> In latter years, he has toned down a great deal; and during the political disturbances which arose from Wallace-Johnson's incursion into local politics, he was a strong supporter of government measures. How far this change of heart was due to a campaign of abuse directed against him by the Youth League, surpassing even his own first efforts, or to a certain mellowing which often accompanies political maturity, I do not pretend to know.
>
> It is, however, interesting to note that he appears to have steadily lost ground with the public since Mr. Betts, his coadjutor in Legislative Council, left that assembly for the government service. This change of form has isolated Dr. Bright from his followers.[103]

The Bills, we know, were passed.[104] And when Wallace-Johnson was charged with libel for a publication in his paper he was tried and gaoled for twelve months. Before this, he was detained under the Defence Regulations Act (1939) for activities 'aimed at bringing all forms of authority into disrepute', and which had 'continuously endeavoured to undermine the loyalty of government African servants, civil and military'.[105] As events were to show, Wallace-Johnson's wings had been effectively clipped. His colleagues, S. M. O. Boyle and George C. Thomas, were also detained for publishing seditious articles in the *African Standard*. These, noted an official in the Colonial Office wryly, 'if published in this country [England] would do no harm [but they] might have a different effect in the atmosphere [much more excitable Africans] of Freetown'.[106]

But Wallace-Johnson's brief career did bring dividends to the people of Sierra Leone. For instance, the violent publicity his agitation gave to the poor labour, industrial, and economic conditions in Sierra Leone, and the subsequent public disorder which these gave rise to, induced a cynical and unsympathetic Colonial Office to order an investigation into Sierra Leone. Even Blood did admit that the Government was not blameless. The inquiry was carried out by Professor W. M. MacMillan, a Scottish-born political scientist from South Africa, with a keen interest in the environment of colonial peoples and the effect this had on their political and economic aspirations.[107] He arrived in Freetown towards the end of 1938, had discussions with local officials, and visited important places in the country. In his report, MacMillan, apparently, did not think much of Jardine's competence in handling the situation in Sierra Leone, and he made some pointed remarks about certain features of industrial policy in the country. He believed that industrial management was generally bad, though S.L.S.T. was better than Delco. Conditions, he insisted, ought to be improved and this would, for example, determine the way the political agitation engineered by Wallace-Johnson might or might not develop to some serious dimensions.[108] In a later publication, Professor MacMillan emphasised his earlier points on management, but he also insisted that the poverty and scantiness of African natural resources gave rise to the material and spiritual backwardness of the people.[109] On the troublesome problem of the Krio, the professor had a few penetrating remarks to make. Dismissing the bland accusation that the bookish education given by missionaries had created badly adjusted persons who failed to fit into their own society, he pointed out that 'the truth is that, though slow and hampered, the pace of educational advance, as in Sierra Leone, had far outstripped that in the economic field which was more peculiarly the sphere of governments; so that in spite of clamant need for their services the openings for educated men have been deplorably few'. Poor communications and resources and an unhealthy soil threw the Krio to their own devices. To those who blamed the Krios for all the trouble in Sierra Leone and pointed fingers at their so-called white-collar orientation, MacMillan had this to say:

> This aloofness is made a charge against them, even by officials who might find the co-operation of Creole and 'Native' critics embarrassing. Their attitude is no more than a reflection of the fact that in the tribal peasant setting of Sierra Leone as a whole the Creoles are to all intents and purposes a 'middle' class, with essentially middle-class occupations, interests and outlook

In sum, the Krios were a problem. Apart from the fact that there was now less demand for their services, British policy of Indirect rule left little room for educated natives, and 'none for outsiders like the Creoles'.[110] Rarely has a government-sponsored report given such an objective analysis of the peculiar problems of the Krio. Where Ormsby-Gore's was emotional, biased, and ill considered, the professor gave a clinical and professional assessment of the situation and, in the process, an indictment of government policy. Possibly, it was as a result of MacMillan's report and a tacit admission on the part of the governor (who claimed to have a sneaking regard for the Krio) that conditions did in fact need amelioration, that a series of reforms were introduced by 1939. But then these were in the best tradition of British policy of 'the carrot and stick' variety – they were aimed at deflecting Wallace-Johnson's influence, to reduce it, by making concessions that would be of immediate relief to the people.[111] Consequently, at the time the Three Bills were passed, the Trade Union Ordinance was introduced and passed. Trade Unionism was legally recognised. Workers' Compensation, an Arbitrational Tribunal and a Bill to inquire into the Economic and Industrial Conditions in the Colony and Protectorate, were other ordinances that were passed into law. Bright gave his support to all of them. The Delco management was pressured into improving conditions in their company. And H. A. Nisbet was seconded from Kenya for a temporary post of Labour Secretary in Sierra Leone to establish a machinery for labour matters.[112]

The alacrity with which these measures were passed, giving relief to certain questions that had been raised and fought for by Bright and his peers much earlier than Wallace-Johnson, may have encouraged W.A.Y.L. supporters to believe that their tactics were more successful than the 'personal manifesto and appeal' of Bright's days but, as has been argued, it was really a question of timing, relevant immediacy, and official attitudes. Indeed, it can be argued that the policy of firmness the British demonstrated in 1939, modified by conciliatory tit-bits, was occasioned by the approaching Second World War. While it was strategically imperative to plug any suspicious chinks in the imperial defence likely to be exacerbated by disaffection and labour unrest, it also made tactical sense not to alienate Britain's colonial subjects by being insensitive to their genuine industrial and economic concerns. And, for that matter, the local administration tried not to antagonise the articulate citizens during the war. Still, even these minor concessions were a measure of success for Wallace-Johnson's politics. On the other hand, the 1938–9 episode left some bruises and nasty after-effects in the body politic of Sierra Leone: for example, Betts was under a cloud of official displeasure for sometime because he apparently failed to convict Wallace-Johnson on a libel charge filed by the government. Betts also antagonised his people for being part of the establishment, especially when he temporarily acted as Solicitor-General, and helped to prosecute Wallace-Johnson and his colleagues, Boyle and Thomas. More than one informant claimed that Betts was hunting with the hounds and running with the hares because he wanted to ingratiate himself with the establishment for political honours.[113] As to this, the evidence is not conclusive, but an official document did reveal that government deployment of Betts in 1939 was not unconnected with the impression it got from the public's attitude to Betts who had been 'ineffective on the Bench by reason of his fear of public opinion and his proneness to intimidation'.[114] Furthermore, the spectacle of his friend, Bankie, appearing before him on a criminal charge must have been an agonising experience for Betts.

The Legislative Council elections of 1939 were another example of the fragmentation of the politically articulate members of the Freetown public. The fight between Otto Oyekan During, C. D. Hotobah-During and Dr W. Ojumiri Taylor (formerly of Congress), chosen as W.A.Y.L.'s candidates, led to a 'split in the ranks which is so common a feature of Sierra Leone public life'. And Boyle was led to complain bitterly about 'splitting domestic votes'.[115] The results were C. D. Hotobah-During 504; Otto Oyekan During 445; G. W. S. Ladepon 405; S. Deen Alharazim 364; and Reverend Dr W. Ojumiri Taylor 154. Contempt and disdain suffused the covering letter from Jardine to the Secretary of State: Ojumiri Taylor was financing W.A.Y.L.'s activities 'from his government pension, no doubt'; Hotobah-During was generally popular – he once had, at least, a fairly extensive practice at the Bar, but he had exhausted the meagre facilities Providence had endowed him; however, 'this [will] not deter him from filling many pages of Hansard and from wasting the valuable time of others'. Otto During came into prominence as a result of his role in the Wallace-Johnson libel case in 1938; and he was a former clerk of Hotobah During. 'On the whole', said the governor witheringly, 'I find it hard to congratulate the electorate either on

Bankole-Bright and politics in colonial Sierra Leone

the field from which it had to choose, or on their choice.' On the other hand, the same governor, in putting the case for a fourth nomination of C. E. Wright (1924–9, 1934, 1939) enthused:

> [he has] always been of the greatest possible assistance to me, criticizing with cogency on the one hand, and with moderation on the other hand, whenever he has considered criticism is due, and being always ready on such occasions with a reasonable alternative to the government's proposals [?? !!]. I can give you an assurance that it is not possible to suggest any other person whose services as a Legislative Council would be at all comparable with those of Mr. Wright.

This so astounded O. G. R. Williams that he lamented thus: 'It's unfortunate that Sierra Leone should provide such a small proportion of suitable persons for nomination in [the] Legislative Council.' The evidence speaks for itself. The British administration clearly had a low estimation of Krio politicians. Thus, hatred, disunity and resentment inexorably worked into the body politic and sapped its energy further. Bankie, for instance, faced no less than four court cases between 1937 and 1939, both with his family and his political enemies. These, and his struggle with Wallace-Johnson, must have had their effect on Krio politicians and Bankie himself. For, in the changes on the political front and the alignment of groups, friends took sides against old friends. New alliances were forged. For example, O. J. V. Tuboku-Metzger, son of Bankie's Congress colleague in the Legislative Council of 1924–9, who had, in fact, defended Bright in the libel case against J. Fowell Boston, was now an enemy of Bright. He moved the motion of non-confidence on Bright. The king maker, F. A. Miller, joined W.A.Y.L. and became Chairman. Many others deserted Congress. The ranks of the Krio were split down the middle. To this end, then, if blame is to be apportioned, both Wallace-Johnson and Bankole-Bright must answer for their part in destroying the fragile solidarity which had been nursed by Congress, through their inability to come to an understanding.

Wallace-Johnson did not unite the Colony and Protectorate either. On the contrary, the Unions he created, which had large followings from the Protectorate, were threatening to disintegrate even before Wallace-Johnson's detention, because, noted Blood with malicious satisfaction, the representatives of the Union and their members were completely at variance. There was a split between the officers of the union 'who are Creole and the rank and file who are Protectorate [people]'.[116] Wallace-Johnson, 'a spent force' after 1939,[117] did not fill the vacuum left by an emasculated Krio leadership in 1938, but opened the chasm wider. Even those who had supported him in the heady atmosphere generated by the euphoria for W.A.Y.L., had to regret identifying themselves with Wallace-Johnson's cause.[118] In the end, Bankie and Wallace both lost in the political stakes.

132

7

In the political wilderness: the turbulent years, 1939–1951

While Britain was struggling for survival during the 1939–45 war years, her African possession remained relatively quiescent; at least, there were no violent eruptions.[1] In Sierra Leone, there were a few spirited mutterings, over issues like a reconstituted City Council controlled by an elected African majority, an expanded Legislative Council and responsible government, and the Africanisation of the Civil Service.[2] But there was hardly any call for the overthrow of the British colonial government; though, of course, the Sierra Leone government believed that Wallace-Johnson had, just before the outbreak of war, told the chiefs that the advent of the 'capitalistic war' provided the opportunity for them to throw off the British yoke.[3]

On the contrary, Sierra Leoneans did their duty to God and King. Krio men enlisted in the armed forces. Rambler, the columnist, repeating his 1914 call for a Territorial Army (for Krio boys), regretted that Government policy was discouraging Krios from enlisting. Still, he was happy to note that some adventurous Krio boys did get into West African Regiments under Protectorate names, for example, John Roberts became Momo Kamara, 'finding perhaps the lure of music some compensation for going without his accustomed footwear'.[4] Some, like E. A. Thomas, were trained as pilots,[5] and others, for instance, the 'tall, straight and dignified Flight Lieutenant J. H. Smythe' acquitted themselves well and were mentioned in despatches and secured decorations.[6] The Sierra Leone Infantry, a great number of them from the Protectorate, did legion service in Burma and other theatres of war, and received glowing tributes from their commanders.[7] Contributions were also made to the Imperial War Effort. The Sierra Leone Bomber Fund stood at £26,376 16s. 3d. in January 1941.[8] The elite did their own share of work, collecting funds through social occasions and dances, for example. The Colony and Protectorate collaborated through organisations committed to supporting the war effort. C. E. Wright moved a motion urging the Sierra Leone government to contribute £100,000 to the British Imperial War Fund, and Paramount Chief Albert Caulker gave his unstinted support on behalf of his Protectorate colleagues with this statement:

> From my experience I think the people in the Protectorate have realized the benefits of the British Empire, perhaps more than the people in the Colony, because before the advent of the British government our lives in the

Protectorate were more miserable than we could be able to express...and it is my firm belief that we shall sing on Britannia rules the waves'.[9]

Sierra Leoneans believed that the war was their own. In this regard, the fears which Wallace-Johnson's activities had given rise to, that had led to repressive legislation, were proved unfounded. The government, on their part, did try not to antagonise the people. It frowned on any overt display of racial arrogance by white troops such as marred Black/White relations after the First World War.[10] Still, Jardine and his successor, Hubert Stevenson, refused to release Wallace-Johnson from detention because he was considered a person of 'thoroughly bad influence'.[11] When he was finally released, together with another martyr of the popular cause, the leader of the mutineers, Gunner Emmanuel G. Cole, in November 1944, he was still his defiant self, though now a 'spent force'.[12] During the course of the war, then, there was a tacit and undeclared truce between the administration and the governed.

However, after the conclusion of the war, when it seemed that European powers wanted to renege on their promises contained in the Atlantic Charter of 1941, African activists redoubled their efforts to demand independence 'now', not in the remote future.[13] In London the League of Coloured Peoples of the United Kingdom formulated in 1944 a Colonial Charter asking for economic, educational, legal and political rights for all males and females irrespective of colour. It also had plans for self-government for colonial peoples.[14] African soldiers returning home after 1945 also brought with them radical ideas which they had imbibed while serving in various theatres of war. Their activities in the 40s added weight to the agitation for independence.[15]

Nationalist efforts were given a psychological lift by the anti-colonial stance of the leading great powers – the U.S.A. and Soviet Russia.[16] In Indo-China and continental Asia, the first salvoes had been fired against the imperial powers by nationalist movements. In 1947, India achieved independence, followed by Pakistan. And, although Winston Churchill was quoted as saying he would not preside over the liquidation of the British Empire,[17] the truth of the matter was that once political self-government had been conceded to other colonial peoples in the British Empire, however staggered the timetable was, it was only a matter of time for the same concession to be given to Africans.

Already Africans had been given a glimpse of the centre of power when, in 1943, in order to harness all the resources available for the war effort, to present a visual partnership, the British administration appointed to the Executive Councils of their West African colonies a number of African members.[18] In Sierra Leone, J. Fowell Boston, a respectable citizen who carried 'some weight in the Creole community' and proprietor of the *Daily Guardian*, 'a very moderate Journal', and Paramount Chief A. G. Caulker, senior nominated Protectorate representative in the Legislative Council for three years, were appointed to the Executive Council to represent their respective regions.[19] Before that, in 1938, Jardine had established a Standing Finance Committee comprising two officials and all the Unofficial Members (seven Africans and three Europeans) to act as a watchdog over the finances of the country.[20]

It would be wrong to read too much into these developments. It is clear from the documents studied that the Colonial Office moguls, especially A. J. Dawe, conceded with ill grace to the suggestion of including African members into the Executive Council.[21] Indeed, the joint pressure of Sir Alan Burns and Sir Bernard Bourdillon, governors of Nigeria and the Gold Coast respectively, who were firmly convinced that such a concession was advisable 'to offset agitation in African Colonies already beginning to be expressed through irresponsible agitators', went a long way to overcome the opposition, not only of the Colonial office, but even of Lord Hailey.[22] Even so, Dawe was adamant to the last, making it clear that the capacity of the Africans was advisory rather than executive. Governor Hubert Stevenson, first demurring that for security reasons he could not recommend this development for which Sierra Leone had not agitated anyway, then claiming he could not find suitable persons to nominate into the Executive, had to toe the line when the other colonies appointed African members to the Executive.[23] In short, the reservations and misgivings shown by Whitehall, and its obvious reluctance to grant this concession, is a good example of that sleight-of-hand illusion, well practised by the British, of appearing to give away a point, but keeping the substance of the concession in tight control. This trick of the eye, this illusion, may have made J. M. Rose wonder aloud whether there was any point in voting for representatives in the Legislative Council since it was a mockery; the franchise was a farce and people had no faith in 'our present government'.[24] Rose's point was in fact underscored by Stevenson's real feeling about the experiment. He felt that it 'would neither benefit the African community, nor the government', while Dawe did not think that chief Caulker would introduce 'a very dynamic element into the counsels of Government'.[25]

Nevertheless, in spite of the wide margin between pious pronouncements and the realities of the colonial situation, statements had been made both by London and Freetown officials, and investigations had been carried out, which, if they did not suggest immediate self-government, gave hopes that there would be further reforms. For instance, Hubert Stevenson, on assuming office, assured his subjects that he would be 'accessible to all reasonable representations' and would always give 'careful consideration to all interests'. Recalling that the Secretary of State for the Colonies had promised that His Majesty's Government would continue to encourage and to assist all schemes of social development in the Colonies, he proposed to examine the local problems thoroughly to get a 'far greater knowledge of them'.[26]

In 1943 Colonel Oliver Stanley, Secretary of State, visited the four British West African Colonies to get some 'first-hand knowledge of the colonial

Bankole-Bright and politics in colonial Sierra Leone

empire'.[27] Before he left London he and his permanent officials had some meetings with Stevenson, who was home on leave, to brief the Colonial Secretary about problems in Sierra Leone. The most important questions earmarked for discussion were constitutional reforms, development projects, education, and the appointment of Africans to higher posts, the income tax issue, medical facilities, and agriculture.[28] And, true enough, when Stanley arrived he was greeted by the *Weekly News* with these desiderata: local government reforms to march with those in the Protectorate; reform of the Legislative Council; posts for Africans and medical facilities for the Protectorate.[29] Reports from Sierra Leone gave a gloomy account of conditions in the Protectorate and concern for this area was of high priority,[30] but then, to cover their own shortcomings, governors of Sierra Leone consistently accused the Colony of causing this state of affairs. So Stevenson warned Stanley:[31]

> When considering the development of Sierra Leone, the backward state of the Protectorate population must be borne in mind. A disproportionate attention has been paid to Freetown, and the Creoles have enjoyed far greater opportunities and advantages than the Protectorate natives. The comparatively small Creole community can most easily make itself heard and it has a preponderating influence over the unofficial members of the Legislative Council, but the Creoles have no firm roots in the country outside the Colony peninsula and although they profess to have [the] interests of the Protectorate natives at heart, in reality they consider them an inferior race and their real interests lie in Freetown affairs and the welfare of their own kindred. The natives of the Protectorate do not take kindly to supervision or direction by the Creoles; for this reason, among others, it will be necessary to educate and train Protectorate natives to provide staff for the different departments to work in that area which is by far the largest part of the dependency, and which contains the bulk of the population.

As a consequence of this state of affairs government policy in the 40s was distinguished by its concentration on the Protectorate, to swing the pendulum the other way:[32] the rationale behind this was that the Colony had had more than its fair share of British largesse and, as the Protectorate was still economically and socially disadvantaged, it needed more developmental engineering to bring it at par with the Colony. In broad terms this did not run counter to Lord Hailey's recommendations for African development. Following his visit to West Africa in 1940 he drafted a programme for eventual self-government for the African colonies. Briefly, the thrusts of this staggered schedule were social and economic development before political advance.[33] As he saw it, the British government should not rush to bring Africans into the decision-making process, but they should be trained in the science of government through participation in local administrations and then gradually brought into the centre of affairs. In short, independence was to be a long process. 'The solution', noted an official,

> suggested in this memorandum, is, on the one side, a resolute development of local institutions, combined with the progressive admission of Africans to all

branches of the government services, and on the other, a policy of caution in political matters which, while leaving an opening for advanced opinion to play its part, would keep the substance of power in the hands of the official government, until experience has shown us under what constitutional forms the dependencies can move most securely towards the final stage of responsible government.[34]

That was the prescription of Hailey. And it was its adoption which led to the establishment of the Protectorate Assembly in 1946.

An interesting dimension in government policy at this time was that both the local administrators and certain officials in the Colonial Office managed to inject into this programme of development what appeared to be an anti-Colony colour.[35] When Otto During, first Urban elected member in the Legislative Council, perhaps encouraged by the vibrations in the air, moved a motion on 16 November 1944, Stevenson brought pressure on him to withdraw it. The motion was,

> that this Council is of the opinion that the time has come when the people of Sierra Leone should take a more effective part in the government of the country and in order to harmonize with the principle of self government which is the prevailing policy of His Majesty's Government respectfully request that a humble petition be submitted by this Council to H.M. the King through the Rt. Honourable Secretary of State for the Colonies that the Constitution of the Legislative Council be amended to provide for an unofficial majority in the Legislative Council.[36]

Explaining his decision to the Colonial Office, Stevenson confessed that he did not consider that 'the provision of an unofficial majority in the Legislative Council at this junction [is] in the true interests of the African people as a whole'. Conceding that there must be political progress, he opined,

> side by side with this political advance must go social development, and in this term I include advance in education and progressive measures for training and employment of Africans from the Protectorate as well as from the Colony in higher government posts...It is my considered opinion that, pending the social development of the Protectorate it would be clearly premature to consider the wish of an unofficial majority in this Council, and furthermore I am quite honestly convinced that precipitate action to this effect would impede the orderly advance in political development in the Protectorate.[37]

The expression 'the political and social development of the Protectorate is an essential condition to further constitutional advance'[38] was to be repeated often in the succeeding years in answer to demands made by Colony politicians for constitutional reforms. Reacting to the governor's explanations, O. G. R. Williams admitted that the differences between Sierra Leone and the Gold Coast were marked. In the latter, the social advancement, though patchy, both in the Colony and Ashanti, was much more widely spread in these two areas compared with the Protectorate and Colony of Sierra Leone respectively. Nevertheless, he confessed that Stevenson's

137

proposals appeared reactionary having regard to what was going on elsewhere; on the other hand, he reasoned, 'I think it would be a great thing for the political minded elements of the Colony to have the realities of the position presented to them rather emphatically'.[39] In further exchanges with Wallace-Johnson in their meeting in London in 1945, where the latter had gone to attend a T.U.C. Conference, Williams told him that if unofficial majority was given the 'Freetown community would be completely swamped by representatives from [the] Protectorate – a large mass of illiterates unlikely to appreciate the nature of the proceedings in the Legislative Council'! Wallace-Johnson then retorted that if the Colony was to wait until the Protectorate people were brought to the educational standard of the Colony person it would take many years before this could happen; he was not even sure that if education was speeded up it would not take more than fifty years for education in the Protectorate to come at par with that in the Colony!

Alternatively, according to Williams, Wallace-Johnson suggested an electoral college of chiefs to vote for representatives, not necessarily Paramount Chiefs, to be elected into the Legislative Council. That, he believed, would limit the representation of the Protectorate to a small number of persons. But then Wallace-Johnson was considered by Colonel Stanley, the Secretary of State, 'a bad influence', and so his staff decided that he must be discouraged from corresponding with the Prime Minister. This is just one more example of how the British deliberately refused to entertain opinions, naive, or otherwise, from leaders among the Krio.[40] On the same issue of representation, the *Weekly News* agreed that the Protectorate was larger in size and population than the Colony, but it pointed out that there were 'other weighty factors than mere number for [the] Colony's present quota just as there were other important factors to warrant the "disproportionate" representation of European non-official representatives in [the] Legislative Council'.[41] Logie Wilson, then Acting Chief Commissioner in the Protectorate, admitted the disadvantageous position of the Protectorate *vis-à-vis* the Colony but he gleefully reported when the Protectorate Assembly was set up that the Protectorate people were taking full opportunity to voice their opinion and to call attention to the financial and other advantages which the 'Creoles were enjoying at the expense of the Protectorate'.[42] Another official maliciously noted that 'there was an excellent Anti-Creole undercurrent' in the first District Chief's Conference.[43]

More examples of this anti-Krio stance of the administration can be given, but what is being argued here is that those who contend, as *West Africa* of the period seemed to do, that independence could have come earlier but for the exclusivist, parochial and inflexible attitude of Colony politicians, would do well to read Hailey's recommendations and the official correspondence of this period. They would find that the British government planned its work according to a timetable; inbuilt in that timetable was the implicit assumption that for the Protectorate to catch up with the Colony, the latter was to remain in some sort of suspended animation.[44] But what was astonishing was that they failed to follow their own timetable, and long-range policies had to be contracted to short-range expediences because developments elsewhere and pressures from both the Colony and by now a vociferous Protectorate forced the government to trim its sails and bring forward constitutional reforms in 1947.[45] Perhaps this reading explains the contradictions in an administration which loudly protested that the Protectorate was still not yet ready to march with the Colony but proceeded to introduce a constitution which gave that same disadvantaged section majority control! On the other hand, it could be argued that the administration had always insisted on the prior claims of the Protectorate, being the larger of the two units, and therefore it was logical that in a democratic setting it should be given majority rule. There is a third possibility. It could be that pressures were such that it was simply a case, as suggested by Wilson, of 'find a leader and hand over to him'.[46] These are possibilities which the documents suggest, though we cannot claim them to be conclusive.

However, what is beyond doubt is that the anti-Krio sentiment of the administration did play a role in the sordid drama of 1947–51. Colony people have always claimed that white administrators put up the Protectorate people against the Krios.[47] While it may not be easy to prove convincingly that the Sierra Leone administration deliberately worked to frustrate the aspirations of the Krio, the papers of some officials who held key positions in the Protectorate administration, and copies of official correspondence, too, clearly show that individuals in the government did disparage the Krio to the Protectorate people and incited them to make anti-Krio pronouncements. Indubitably, the anti-Krio sentiments encouraged by members of the European establishment did influence people's attitudes.[48]

In July 1946 the Protectorate Assembly was inaugurated.[49] It was a development of the Chief's Conference initiated by Paramount Chiefs to exchange views on issues of mutual interest. The government adapted this institution to give practical effect to the policy of developing the Protectorate.[50] According to Logie Wilson, it accorded a training ground for membership in the Legislative Council by 'offering Protectorate representatives an opportunity to express their views and to consolidate opinion'. It functioned mainly to advise on matters relating to the Protectorate, particularly on Bills which would be presented to the Legislative Council.[51] Thus, as planned, matters directly affecting Protectorate interests were discussed at the Assembly before being brought to the Central Legislature. The Protectorate Assembly was composed of forty-two seats: twenty-six for Paramount Chiefs indirectly elected by the Native Authority Administration and District Council, eleven officials, one representative for European interests, and one representative of Krio business interests, one missionary representative and two Educated Protectorate Africans elected by the Native Authorities. The idea was to get the Protectorate used to the ways of a Westminster model parliament as a precondition for eventual integration with the Colony but, in working towards this integration, government continued to pursue a policy of dualism.[52] Subtle and not so subtle overtones conveyed the idea of separateness.[53] By discussing Protectorate matters in this Assembly before taking them to the Legislative Council, while matters affecting the Colony went straight into the Central Legislature, an impression was given that Protectorate interests were contra Colony or vice versa. It contributed in no small measure to the polarisation of forces in the forties.

Still, Colony people welcomed the establishment of the Assembly and wide coverage was given to its deliberations in the Freetown press. Congratulatory messages were sent to the Protectorate people, especially since its inauguration fortuitously occurred on the fiftieth anniversary of the Proclamation of the Protectorate.[54] Colony people were not found wanting in active participation in the celebrations of the golden jubilee.[55] Also the District Councils, set up in the same year as local government administrations to help in advising on, and providing, essential services for their locales, were received with warmth. When P.E.P.U. (the Protectorate Educated Progressive Union) was founded in 1945 by educated and traditional elites in the Protectorate, the *Weekly News* wished it every success. The *Daily Guardian*, on the other hand, proclaimed the decision by P.E.P.U. and the Moyamba Chiefs' Conference to give ten scholarships to their students to train as teachers at Fourah Bay College for two years[56] an object lesson at co-operation for the Freetown Colony to learn. The chiefs of the Port Loko District Conference also offered a scholarship to S. I. Sise to study medicine in the United Kingdom.[57] These developments were praised as timely and progressive. At the same time Colony opinion did complain about the continuing influence of the local officials over the chiefs, especially in the District Councils and the Protectorate Assembly where the District Commissioners and the Provincial Chief Commissioner were chairmen, respectively. The illiteracy of most of the chiefs was another issue of awkward concern.[58]

The chiefs on their part, enthusiastically welcomed the opportunity for ventilating their grievances in their own legislature, as it were – and they made full use of this in the opening sessions.[59] Their complaints ranged from the obvious developmental backwardness of the Protectorate to roads for this district, schools for another, the need for better health facilities, and schemes for agricultural improvement and education. The more courageous of the chiefs complained about the role of the white officials in the political development of the Protectorate.[60] And an interesting exchange between a chief and the Chief Commissioner on this point supplied a humorous if poignant anecdote:[61] complaining that it was not convenient to have a lorry shared by two chiefs, each having a wife, four hammock boys, horn blowers, etc and twelve loads, the chief was asked by the Chief Commissioner (J. S. Fenton) 'What would you do if you had to travel by plane?' The chief returned: 'When time comes we shall adjust accordingly.' Fenton: 'How could you when you have not adjusted yourselves to lorries?' Chief: 'When a road goes right up to my town I shall do away with hammock boys and that will be less four'! The Chief may have been illiterate but he had an intelligent grasp of essentials!

Other chiefs were to complain resentfully about being ill used by the District Commissioners. Siaka Stevens also talked in derogatory terms about the District Councils and the Protectorate Assembly.[62] So, at least on this one point, the baneful role of administrative officers in the Protectorate, the educated elites in the Colony and Protectorate were in agreement.

But, more important, the above indicate a revolutionary spirit in the Protectorate, a will and a determination to articulate their grievances and aspirations. Thus, in his speech at the Protecterate Jubilee Celebrations on 2 December 1946, Paramount Chief R. B. S. Koker proclaimed,

> By all means we must intermingle with our Freetown brothers... Our brothers and sisters in Freetown are going forward. We are keeping them back, and it is time we all moved as one Sierra Leone. We know your difficulties, your disadvantages, but do not lose hope. We shall at all times cry to the government as Churchill in 1940: Give us the tools and we shall do the job, and do it well.[63]

The tools were being given and a few cosmetic changes had been wrought by the government to ginger up the Protectorate, but it would be some time before the required results could be secured. By 1949 the number of primary schools in the Protectorate was 190 and the school-going population was 16,700; those in the Colony were 74, and over 12,000, respectively.[64] As for degree holders and professionally qualified people, only three doctors (M. A. S. Margai – 1927, J. C. Massally – 1937 (died 1943) and J. Karefa Smart – 1943) had been produced by the Protectorate by 1950. Its first qualified lawyer was Albert Margai, in 1948. I. B. Taylor-Kamara and A. J. Massally were called to the Bar in 1949 and 1950 respectively. In the field of education, A. T. Sumner, his son, Doyle Sumner, R. B. Kowa, W. H. Fitzjohn, F. S. Anthony and Amadu Wurie had carved niches for themselves. The most prominent non-degree holders were Siaka Stevens, the ex-policeman turned Trade Unionist, who was sent to Ruskin College, Oxford to study Trade Unionism in 1947, and A. J. Momoh, veteran Civil Servant and President of the Sierra Leone Civil Servants Association. In 1953 a government survey revealed that fourteen out of eighteen medical students on government scholarship came from the Colony; all the six dentists and six of the seven privately sponsored medical students were Colony-born.[65] Thus, though in terms of educational output the Protectorate was qualitatively and quantitatively weak, it had great potential strength in its numbers and, perhaps, time in its favour to make up the deficits.[66]

It is true that there was an open feud between the Protectorate-educated elite and the traditional elite derived from the resentment felt by the former over their exclusion from the centre of the institutional structures being erected in the Protectorate. But a modest accommodation of their grievances was symbolised by their inclusion in the membership of the Protectorate

Assembly and District Councils and, more important, the moderating and shrewd influence of Dr M. A. S. Margai and progressive chiefs like Julius Gulama ensured that some kind of solidarity was reflected in the Protectorate leadership.[67] This was cemented by the S.O.S. (the Sierra Leone Organisation Society) founded at Moyamba on 28 June 1946.[68] According to the *Daily Guardian* the name was changed from the Protectorate Organisation Society to the above, because it was 'ruled in the end, that in view of the long association between the Colony and Protectorate people which had broken down all but the artificial political barrier, and in view of the scope of the Society that was envisaged, the name of the society should be Sierra Leone Organisation Society'. The aims were spelt out thus:

1. To develop an enlightened public opinion in all matters affecting the people of the country.
2. To foster the spirit of co-operation among all the peoples of the country, regardless of age, sex, religious creed, social status, occupational interest or tribal origins.
3. To be a clearing ground for all civic and social projects.
4. To encourage a close study of the facts in all issues affecting the welfare of the country and to stimulate research work.
5. To seek the co-operation of existing organisations in the country.
6. To sponsor a programme of self-government aiming at raising the standard of living of the country in all its aspects. Membership was open to all natives of Sierra Leone on payment of a fee of 2s. 0d. and an annual subscription of 2s. 0d (S.O.S. = Save our Sierra Leone).

We do not have the papers of this organisation to confirm whether it lived up to its promise to establish a national political movement cutting across administrative, political, and cultural barriers, but the published works give a definite impression that the organisation was specifically Protectorate. The postures and sympathies of the organisation in 1947, and the constitution of the executive itself, lend credence to this view. And this, of course, raises the question of why it was unable to establish a national movement. Was it that because it was founded in the Protectorate, that that fact alone disqualified Colony people from joining it, as it were, playing the reverse of Congress? if we do not accept this view, then it is odd that Wallace-Johnson was not associated with the movement. Everybody agreed that he had done the impossible by establishing some form of national movement that brought the two peoples under one umbrella. That being so, one might have expected that some effort should have been made to bring him in. If he was approached, did he turn it down, and why?[69] What about Lamina Sankoh, the maverick Anglican priest? Christened E. N. Jones, he changed his name to Lamina Sankoh in the twenties in protest against white racism, not, as has been suggested in many publications, to dramatise his sympathy for, and association with, the Protectorate people.[70] But he certainly related with them and his Peoples Party, which eventually merged with the S.O.S. to form the Sierra Leone Peoples Party, was open to all Africans. He also had some interesting schemes, such as a co-operative movement for the development of the country. But, apart from this visual partnership with Protectorate organisations, the practical demonstration of this integration eludes assessment.

If political co-operation between the Protectorate and the Colony, through association, was frowned upon by the Administration there certainly were other avenues and institutions, which, given the political will and the dedication, could well serve as some basis for co-operation.[71] And for some inexplicable reasons these abound in the period just before political rancour and dissension set in. Take, for instance, the African Civil Servants Association. The President was A. J. Momoh. He could sufficiently relate with his Krio colleagues to agitate for better conditions of service for the members of the association, and he was popular enough to be elected to a seat in the Freetown City Council in 1948. Yet this collaboration could not be translated to political integration.[72] Nor, for that matter, was it the case of the Bo African Club. The executive comprised E. B. Williams, President, A. Karim, Vice-President, J. E. Williams, Financial Secretary, T. P. Tucker, Treasurer, J. Tambi, J. M. Macfoy, Auditor, A. L. Hume, Literary Secretary, G. E. Davies, Social Secretary, S. T. Matturi, Librarian, Y. D. Seisay, Caterer, J. H. Thomas, Games Captain, A. E. John, R. B. Kowa, H. T. Johnson, Unofficial members. Social Committee: A. Bakarr, A. M. Browne, and A. S. Koker.[73] Among these people no less than two became members of Milton Margai's first government. E. B. Williams, Acting Principal of Bo Government School, the father of Professor Awadajin Williams of Fourah Bay College, appeared to be a highly respected member of the Krio Community in Bo. He was Honorary Treasurer of the Protectorate Jubilee Celebrations Fund, to which eminent Colony citizens like J. Fowell Boston and Dr R. S. Easmon contributed liberally.[74] M. A. S. Margai had a line to Krio society through his friendship with M. C. F. Easmon and his close relationship with the Tuboku-Metzger family. And Dr W. H. Fitzjohn, too, tells us that his father had 'come from Freetown but lived in the Protectorate for forty years, married a Mende woman…and for all intents and purposes I was a native of the Protectorate, but had cousins (Mende, Sherbro, Creole).[75] When the brilliant Sierra Leonean surgeon, R. B. Wallesley Cole, 'Kossoh Town Boy', returned to Britain from a visit home he wrote enjoining his compatriots to work for a 'social fusion' and co-operation between the Colony and Protectorate.[76] The *Daily Guardian*, guided by Thomas Decker, preached the ideal of one Sierra Leone, and prescribed a recipe for 'oneness' through exchanges of visits, education, inter-marriages and the learning of languages.[77] When the Protectorate celebrated its jubilee in December, people in the Colony joined hands with their compatriots to give thanks to God. E. S. Beoku-Betts and Fowell Boston addressed mass meetings during the celebrations.[78] The Colony/Protectorate annual football match also provided lively relief through friendly rivalry.[79] Colony and Protectorate citizens fought shoulder to shoulder to protect and maintain West Africa's oldest institution of higher learning, Fourah Bay College, when its existence was threatened by the Elliot Commission on Higher Education in 1943–4. A Fourah Bay College Fund was set up and, in the executive committee of the Fund, no less than four Paramount Chiefs were Vice-Presidents.[80]

In other words, what the above suggests is that the links were there that could have forged a viable structure for co-operation but they appear not to have been used. And it would be invidiously futile to argue about which side should have made the first move. Things were allowed to drift until government policy and certain developments made the Colony people feel that they were being elbowed out; while, it would appear, the Protectorate leadership read the signs of the times more accurately and decided it was tactically wise to consolidate their interests rather than pool their resources with their Colony brethren. Time and the dictates of a democracy, they reasoned, were on their side. These points come out very clearly in the furore over the 1947 Stevenson Constitution.

In 1945 the Labour Party succeeded the Conservatives in office. It tended to be more flexible in responding to African demands, for it had demonstrated during its opposition days a keen interest in African colonial matters through affiliated agencies like the Fabian Colonial Bureau; more important, the Party included in the government individuals who had had a long association with African activists and had exhibited some sympathy for their causes. One such individual was Arthur Creech Jones, Under-Secretary for the Colonies in 1945 and substantive Secretary for the Colonies from October 1946 to February 1950. Believing that the central purpose of British colonial policy was to guide the colonial territories to self-government, taking cognisance of developments elsewhere, he instituted certain reforms that were aimed at bringing the West African Colonies a step forward towards representative government.[81] Consequently, constitutions designed for that purpose were introduced in the various West African Colonies after 1945.

Though this accommodating disposition was advertised as a policy of commitment, it is pertinent to point out that both in the Colonial Office and among its proconsuls there were strong reservations about the independence timetable.[82] The general belief was that self-government would only be achievable in the next thirty to forty years. In Sierra Leone, Governor Hubert Stevenson, who had never shown any particular belief in the capacities of the African, had strong doubts about the preparedness of the people for majority rule (one source quoted him as expecting this to happen in centuries!)[83] but, as instructed, he introduced in 1947 a Constitution that provided for an unofficial majority. The unofficial members were increased to sixteen, broken down thus: ten from the Protectorate (nine elected by the Protectorate Assembly and one nominated by the governor) and four to be elected by the Colony; two Europeans were to be nominated by the governor to represent commercial interests. Though the number of officials was reduced from twelve to eight, these still retained executive power and control

144

in the Executive Council. Two nominated Africans were, however, to be added to the membership. It did not amount to much and, as a newspaper later charged, nothing was said about the Executive Council which was the real issue.[84] But the most significant feature of the Constitution was the provision which gave unofficial majority to the Protectorate.[85] Indeed, the preamble of the constitutional proposals anticipated this, for it stated that the Colony was over represented, but perhaps this was understandable in view of existing conditions twenty years before –

> The Colony members have exercised very considerable influence in the Council and have given valuable service, but the time is now come to start to redress the balance between the Colony and Protectorate. Sierra Leone is now ready to take the first step to constitutional progress.

To this end, the governor proclaimed that he was satisfied with the performance of the Protectorate Assembly and the District Councils. In the Colony the franchise was extended to all adults (male or female) of twenty-one years and above, British subjects or protected persons, having resided for six months in premises whose annual rateable value was £6, and who earned £60 p.a. In the Protectorate the vote was given to the Protectorate Assembly. As for the Executive Council, pressure mainly from the Colony members induced the administration to allow the Select Committee appointed in 1948 to discuss the modalities for the inclusion of African members in that body.[86]

Another intriguing aspect of the new constitution was that it was introduced a year after Colony politicians had been told that '[we] are not yet ripe for the reconstitution of [the] Legislative Council on a scale that [we] could consider worthwhile', at a time when demands by the Colony for the restoration of the City Council, to match with local government reforms already effectuated in the Protectorate, had not yet been met, but were being considered.[87] The sudden changes and somersaults were too bewildering for the people to comprehend. Small wonder then that when they were asked to discuss the constitutional proposals, articulate opinion was cautious, and then, as the implications of the provisions became clear, there were loud protests. These objections, raised mainly by Krio politicians, both in the Legislative Council and outside it, reflected their frustrated hopes and aspirations, but they also expressed real concern over certain aspects of the proposals which appeared to retain power in the hands of a European government. Issues, such as the preeminence of the Paramount Chiefs and the criteria for eligibility for membership in the Legislative Council, were other areas of concern. On these two main points even the Protectorate elites found themselves supporting the position of their Krio counterparts; and, all things considered, this could have provided the basis for political co-operation.[88] But the excesses of Krio particularism, and arrogance towards the Protectorate people, or so argue writers of this period, alienated the Protectorate and made such co-operation impossible.[89] However, reasons for this missed opportunity went beyond Krio attitudes and must be sought

145

elsewhere. There were excessive claims on both sides. The sinister influence of officials must also be taken into account. Private papers of individuals do strongly suggest that the establishment anticipated a clash between the two sides, and it is possible that some may have even wished for it. The examples of Wilson and Bailey have been given and others can be found in private papers when these are opened to the public. Wilson, for one, was suspected of having incited Bai Koblo to make a hostile anti-Krio speech.[90] In other words, reasons for the poisoned atmosphere of the 1940s do not exclude the baneful influence of some administrative officers on the politics of the period. On the other hand, the Protectorate politicians proved to be better strategists and more astute tacticians by muting their denunciations, except for a few outbursts, confident that number, links with traditional authority, and time were on their side. Certainly, Bai Koblo, Paramount Chief of Marampa – Massimera Chiefdom, who had spent some time with Krio families in Freetown in his younger days, saw this plainly when he claimed in 1948: 'I want to state that I make no apologies for openly stating that we intend to use our majority to safeguard our interests whenever and wherever possible.'[91]

Apart from Koblo's statement of intent, discussion in the Legislative Council was much more restrained. The Protectorate Assembly, for their part, though it balked at some of the provisions of the constitution, for example, the governor's reserve powers, did, by resolutions, approve the constitutional proposals providing the following were conceded:

(1) Protectorate representation should be increased to thirteen, elected by District Councils, and these people should automatically become members of the Protectorate Assembly;
(2) One of the two members to be nominated by the governor from the commercial and industrial sections of the community should be an African;
(3) The period of membership of the Legislative Council should be five not four years; each member should hold his seat for the normal life of the Council;
(4) The Assembly accepted the principle of governor's reserve powers but insisted on prescribing these powers after consultations with Colony representatives.[92]

Outside these institutions, no restraint governed the passions of speakers. For one thing, the Colony was outraged that consultations were first made with Protectorate institutions and various bodies before Freetown was approached. And this led Thomas Decker to ask whether there were two Sierra Leones or one![93] The press was partisan: the *Weekly News*, generally moderate in striving to reflect Protectorate views faithfully, became pro-Colony; the *Daily Guardian*, a pro-Protectorate paper before 1947, tended to become critical after 1947; and so was the *African Standard*.[94] The *Sierra Leone Observer*, the first Protectorate weekly, edited by A. B. Cotay, which professed, in its inaugural publication (27 August 1949), 'to bridge the gap between the Colony and Protectorate, and thereby make real a national spirit embracing the whole compass of Sierra Leone', hardly kept faith with this pious proclamation.[95] *West Africa*, the international magazine, was pro-government and pro-Protectorate. Anybody reading *West Africa* for this period would come to one conclusion, that the Colony was particularistic, inflexible and intolerant. But the magazine was severely criticised by a correspondent for this lopsided presentation.[96]

The image of intolerance and unreasoned bigotry put out by writers and publications of this period was hardly merited. On the other hand, Colony politicians themselves did not help matters. Certain of them, such as the lawyer, J. C. Zizer, one of the most extreme Colony activists, but an agitator of international repute in the 1920s, gave unrestrained release to their feelings. However, if Zizer's articles were stripped of their rhetoric and inane slogans they were not unworthy of consideration. For instance, arguing that if the new constitution was meant to unite the two people then it was 'absolutely desirable to give them the same laws, the same status, and the same government during this transition', he suggested that the Protectorate be declared a British Colony and be united with the Colony of Sierra Leone under one settlement, designated the Colony of Sierra Leone.[97]

This dualism was a fundamental issue in Colony/Protectorate relations. Interestingly enough, although the colonial administration was not unaware of this problem, this has been glossed over or ridiculed by writers, who perhaps agreed with the view of the editor of *West Africa*, that 'the unification of Sierra Leone can be achieved by any party that considers that the present interests of the Colony and Protectorate are more important than the historical division between them'.[98] But it was precisely because the Colony people, rightly or wrongly, were convinced that their interests in one section of the country had not received fair attention, while those of the other side in the Colony had been recognised and guaranteed, that they protested so vigorously. And this, of course, according to a contemporary observer, smacked too much of 'me-too-ism'![99]

Curiously enough, Wallace-Johnson, the soi-disant national bridge, was oddly reticent at this time. Was he already embittered by his experiences? Or could he not work with his colleagues anymore? And who were these anyway? Sidney Boyle and George Thomas had received gaol sentences for their W.A.Y.L. activities, and they could hardly join somebody whom they believed had let them down. In fact, Boyle immediately went to England on his release, and he has stayed there since![100] Young radicals like Easmon, Cox-George, Harry Sawyerr and Eldred Jones were more intellectual in their approach to policies. They were not professional politicians. The teeth of Congress had been drawn out when activists of the twenties and thirties had withdrawn from active politics or had been transported to the great beyond. Among the elites, names like Taylor-Cummings and C. E. Wright were, too, associated with the establishment to provide opposition leadership; while many of the respectable citizens who had welcomed Wallace-Johnson in 1938 had been turned off by his extremism. Crowther proclaimed that Wallace-

147

Johnson could have made a better politician (than Bright), 'but he lacked culture'.[101] Other interested citizens like Pa F. Miller had died (in 1943).[102] Lamina Sankoh could not work with his Krio counterparts for a number of reasons, for instance, his religious apostasy.[103] Thomas Decker, young, earnest and a keen believer in one Sierra Leone, was a lone voice in the wilderness. In other words, Krio leadership was in disarray; it had disintegrated. It could not, and it did not, have the cohesion of the Protectorate leadership, despite the differences between the traditional and educated elements in the latter. And so one cannot talk of a Protectorate challenge in 1948–51.[104] On the contrary, the Krio were in a quagmire, as it were, groping for an acknowledged leader with enough stature and courage to articulate their fears and channel their grievances, actual or imagined – Bankole-Bright became that leader by default.

Cohen offers an interesting insight into this period. He argues that 1947–52 was a period of traumatic experience in the psychology of the Krio, because they had been rudely shaken from their security by the turn British policy took in the forties and, to compensate for this, they sought refuge and consolation in Freemasonry, 'an almost exclusive Creole bastion of status symbol'. This may have been one response of the Krio to the situation, but I do not think that was true for all Krios. Besides not every Krio wanted to be a Freemason.[105]

Bankole-Bright was a stormy petrel in the twenties and thirties, but he had been in the twilight since 1939. Apart from irregular appearances on public platforms he hardly took part in public issues, except for his spirited attack on the government in 1942 for its reluctance to appoint nominated members to the Executive Council on the grounds that it might cause a security breach.[106] But, looking at the documents for 1940–7, Bankie could not be found to have said anything profound on such topical issues like the future of Fourah Bay College or the reconstitution of the City Council.[107]

Bright did, however, try to enter the Legislative Council in 1943 through an election contest with Dr G. C. E. Reffell, against whom he had supported the candidature of Milton Margai for employment in government service in 1928.[108] In his manifesto, written in flamboyant style, Bright listed his achievements and explained that he had received the clarion call to his duty; for since he left the Legislative Council, he had been dismayed by the destruction of 'barricades built by [my] comrades and [myself], due to the inertia of some of the present elected members'. Promising, if elected, to continue his fight for Africanisation, the extension of the franchise 'whereby the finance of this country [would] be controlled by unofficial majority', the giving of the vote to women, and the Rice question, he ended with a flourish' I am still young and active, and my brain power, I believe, is at its highest. I now stand at the public bar of your conscience for my trial...If I pass favourably under the political limelight of your searching exam...I am content to await with composure your verdict on the polling day.'[109] The verdict was given in favour of his rival, G. C. E. Reffell, whose manifesto was not much different from Bright's in essence, except that it was simply and clearly stated.[110] Indeed, certain people in the society had not forgotten or forgiven Bright's past 'mistakes' and they made sure that the public was aware of this. T. J. Shorunkeh Sawyerr (grandson of the famous bookseller, deceased), and Treasurer of the Committee of Citizens, warned the electorate that a vote of no confidence had been passed on Bankie in June 1939. Lamina Sankoh dismissed him as a has-been that did not know when to 'keep off the stage'.[111] Not satisfied with the verdict of the electorate, Bankie went on to file an election petition against Reffell for alleged bribery, infringement of secrecy, treating and undue influence. He, of course, by this action, secured the dubious distinction of being the first man in the history of Sierra Leone to file an election petition. He lost the suit and received a roasting from the trial judge for his pains. His Honour told him: 'I feel I must say that more reckless allegations than some of those contained in the Petition, and abandoned, I cannot conceive; and these were made without the slightest foundation.'[112] Bankie's defeat was complete.

In the light of the above we must ask ourselves these questions. Why did a man who appeared to have been out of touch with current politics, who had been spurned and rejected twice (in 1939 and 1943) by his own people, who even in retirement was hounded by law suits, decide to come back to politics?[113] Why did a man no longer his fighting self, having languished in obscurity for eleven years, loom so large in the scheme of things in 1947–57? Why was he catapulted into the Krio leadership? We can hazard a few answers here. Over the years the Krio leadership had gone through a series of traumatic experiences. Its fragmentation created a vacuum which needed to be filled. The candidates were not many. However, there was one man, Bankole-Bright, whose past fame as a dauntless critic of government recommended him as a good choice. Quite a few Krios believed that a man of his stature and undoubted courage would be able to speak for his people. But it was a lost cause. Much had happened in the intervening years. For instance, Government policy had clearly indicated that power would devolve to the Protectorate. For that matter, individuals like Thomas Decker, Cox-George and others, who could not assume the leadership of the Krio for reasons already explained, accepted Protectorate majority, but hoped to prune the constitution so that they could secure some kind of 'guarantee' for the Krio minority.

Their optimism had no basis. At the same time, as the indications were that the Krio had been abandoned politically by their benefactors, they appeared also to have been invested with a belated recognition of their abilities, though inadequately rewarded. In a way, this reflected the ambivalent experience of the Krio in their relations with the British. This intriguing feature was demonstrated in the dramaturgy of the 40s: the down trend in the political fortunes of the Krio was contrasted by an apparent uplift of their social and professional aspirations. Major appointments made by the government among the Krio created an illusion of influence, power and prestige.

The year 1944 was good for the Wrights. Miss Frances Wright, a daughter of C. E. Wright, nominated unofficial member of the Legislative Council, was appointed the first woman temporary Police Magistrate on 26 January 1944, scarcely a year after she began practising law in October 1943.[114] Her uncle, E. Jenner Wright, an authority on dietetics, was appointed to an additional post as a specialist physician. He was the first Sierra Leonean to be so appointed.[115] E. S. Beoku-Betts was elevated to the rank of Puisne Judge on 10 February 1944, while O. J. V. Tuboku-Metzger was given permanent appointment as Assistant Magistrate, with effect from 15 June 1942. E. F. Luke secured the post of Temporary Magistrate.[116] M. C. F. Easmon and E. H. Taylor-Cummings were made supernumerary Senior Medical Officer (Sierra Leone) and Senior Medical Officer (Health) with effect from 10 January 1942, after twenty-nine and twenty-two years' service, respectively. The *Weekly News* had to comment that this 'belated recognition of their worth...would have been better appreciated if made earlier'. The paper also reported the appointment of Alfred A. Short as Collector of Customs.[117] In 1949 Dr E. A. Renner, the son of an ill-used former Acting Principal Medical Officer, Dr W. Awunor-Renner, became Acting Director of Medical Services (justly reclaiming what was denied his father),[118] and was given a seat in the Executive Council as an ex-officio member, the first African to be given that honour since the days of Sir Samuel Lewis.[119]

This policy of reward, contrasted with one of denigration, has led some observers to conclude, on the one hand, that the loud protests by Krios in the 40s demonstrated a selfish desire to maintain their privileged position and elitist status and, on the other, to see it as corroborating evidence supporting the claim by the government that the Colony had always monopolised its attention to the neglect of the Protectorate.[120] The reality was different.[121] But these promotions, coming at a time when the atmosphere was beginning to turn ugly, have not helped the Krios in making their position on the Stevenson constitution – why they had to oppose its introduction with such hysteria – understood by outsiders.

At this point, it is necessary to recall that the Colony people were the first to demand an all-elected Legislative Council, and an unofficial majority, when Bankie raised these questions in 1925, 1928 and 1936, while, in 1943, Paramount Chief A. G. Caulker, on the side of the Protectorate, expressed some hopes for a more liberal constitution after the war.[122] Thus, in October 1943, when Colonial Secretary Stanley visited Sierra Leone, he was presented with a number of proposals for a reformed legislature which provided for seven elected members to represent the Colony; one representative each for an area or district to be elected by the chiefs of the District, or Area or Tribal Authorities to represent the Protectorate (twelve or thirteen?), and two nominated Europeans to look after commercial and banking interests.[123] Implicit in these suggestions, be it noted, was a concession by the Colony to the principle of Protectorate majority; but, in subsequent arguments, the

In the political wilderness

impression was given that it opposed the view taken by the administration and the Protectorate that numbers or the size of population were the sole determinants for representation.[124] Consequently, between 1943 and 1947 and beyond, there was much speculation and figure juggling over the issue of what was fair representation. This situation was reflected in an interesting exchange between two people whom one can only assume were Protectorate citizens. One, calling himself Ansumana M'Paki of Rosanda, near Magburaka, Tonkolili District, proclaimed that since the populations of the Colony and Protectorate were 70,000 and 1¾ million respectively, and that the greater part of the wealth of the dependency came from the latter, it was but fair that the representation be worked out thus: fifty elected (Protectorate); two Urban (Freetown) elected and two (Rural) elected, plus ten nominated official members. He doubted, though, whether the Protectorate could field fifty educated people, and that might be the reason why 'the Protectorate are not so enthusiastic about an elected majority until... they are in a better position to insist on their representation'. But he blamed 'the hot heads of Freetown' for the disadvantaged state of the people of the interior.[125]

This brought forth angry reactions from the Colony, and even from another correspondent from the Protectorate. This writer, identifying himself as Kohn Bap, from Mokelleh, via Mattru Jong, denounced M'Paki for his slanderously ungrateful remarks about Colony representatives who, he claimed, 'have in the past advocated for, and secured, progressive measures for the Protectorate'. He was not impressed by M'Paki's argument either. He professed not to have confidence in the chiefs to represent the views of their people freely without bias, and what he wanted was an opportunity for Protectorate people to vote for their own representatives. He contended that the 'basis of population and wealth should not be the only consideration for representation in Council; such a situation would be simply absurd. The idea of democratic representation is not limited to wealth and population only.'[126] The editors of *Weekly News* and *African Standard*, on their part, lectured M'Paki on his errant ways; and the first paper, for instance, admitted that the Protectorate merited fairer representation but, at her present stage of development, it was being recommended that she should have six elected representatives.[127] The suggestion was ridiculous given the realities of the Protectorate's potential, but the Colony was to go on raising points of contention over literacy as a criterion for membership in Council, the preponderating influence of the chiefs whom they claimed were tools of the government, the duality in the land-tenure system, the differentials in legal status and the awkward technicality of protected persons sitting in, and legislating for, British subjects in the Legislative Council. Certainly, these concerns, including the land-tenure system, had a great deal of historical and constitutional significance which were not unperceived by local administrators, for example, Governor Beresford-Stooke himself. And they were of sufficient degree for the Krios to ventilate their fears about the future. But,

151

in putting across arguments to support their contentions, some amount of disingenuity and melodrama crept in. No doubt the Colony protagonists were naive to make a point about the legality of Protectorate people sitting in the Legislative Council. This issue had been raised before and the Administration had not answered it satisfactorily. Rather, it sought refuge in legal gobledegook, explained thus: the Protectorate citizens were aliens, but since they were in the Legislative Council they could legislate for British subjects. This legal point was never clarified; nor, for that matter, did the British, for reasons that are still not clear, agree to the demand, made more than once by the Colony, to declare the people in the Protectorate British subjects so that everybody could have the same rights. And, in this regard, it is a matter of opinion whether the British Nationality Act of 1948, inviting citizens of the U.K. and its dependencies (i.e., residents in the Protectorate or Protected persons) to apply for British citizenship, did clarify this twilight area of legalism.[128]

Again, the differentials in legal status and designation which referred to people in one part of the territory as 'Natives' and others as 'Non-Natives', and the requirement of passports from Protectorate citizens who wished to travel out of Sierra Leone, and none from Colony residents, continued to give the impression of two communities unconnected with each other. Furthermore, prior consultations with the Protectorate on a number of major issues, for instance, the 1947 Constitution, before these were discussed with the Colony, concretised this belief.[129]

The issue of the Reconstitution of the City Council in 1948 provides a good example of this dualism. As proposed, the government argued that over time more people, not natives of the area, had come to settle in the city, and a reconstituted City Council should reflect this cosmopolitanism. The argument was fair enough, but the government would have saved the country from a lot of acrimony if, in reorganising the Protectorate, a similar argument could have been used in making provisions for non-natives of the Protectorate, i.e., Krio residents, to participate fully in the affairs of the District Councils or Protectorate Assembly as their Protectorate counterparts had every right to do constitutionally in Freetown's local government, the City Council. Krio residents had no right to vote in the Protectorate, and were subjected to a number of disabilities. One of these was their ineligibility to buy or own lands in the Protectorate, while a citizen from the latter could have landed property in Freetown. Though it is fair to note that, much later, reforms on such disabilities like the settlers' fees, among others, were intended to ameliorate the situation, in 1947–51 these concerns rankled.

All these were fears which Colony representatives sought to have dispelled, but this was impossible to secure given the psychology of the period. Colony politicians believed that they had fought for the constitutional development of the country, and that they had not gained anything enduring from this, while the Protectorate, largely under the paternalistic rule of the District Commissioners all this time, had suddenly emerged as the gainers of the devolution of power. And, indeed, though the reconstitution of the City Council was given as a 'sop to the demand for a reconstitution of the Legislative Council, made by the Colony', it did not dispel this resentment because it was interpreted as a ploy to deflect the Colony's agitation for an African-controlled legislature.

The new City Council was organised this way: nine councillors were elected by rate payers – three for each of the three wards for three years; three Aldermen (one each ward) were elected by Council from among serving elected members for six years – total twelve. The governor had the right to appoint seven Councillors: three officials in the Technical departments (P.W.D., Education and Health), one Commerce and three others (two must be Africans) including one for Labour – the latter to cover relief and Trade Union questions, wages and labour. He would also represent non-Krio interests. And, for that matter, special representation for non-Krio interest was rejected. The new council's expanded functions included street lighting, markets, slaughter houses, cemeteries, food inspection, poor relief, the fire brigade, water supply, control of building, street maintenance, housing, sanitation (street cleaning), conservancy, prevention against epidemics and infectious diseases, municipal trading and transport and, finally, dog licensing. To help finance the operation of all these responsibilities the government offered to give loans and subsidies. An African – S. B. Jones[130] – was eventually selected to train as Town Clerk. But then certain sections (16, 43, 53, and 61) made sure that government retained effective power in its hands, because Freetown, the argument went on, was an important port with imperial interests, and it played a preponderating part in the affairs of Sierra Leone. The government, therefore, did not think that a body which had such important functions to perform must be 'entirely free of any sort of control by the governor'.[131] Krio political aspirations were blocked everywhere by these institutional prunings.

The Protectorate, on the other hand, appreciated the potentials of the Stevenson Constitution; it gave them power and hegemony; and it was unreasonable to expect them to forego such a useful instrument. In this regard a clash between the two halves of the territory was inevitable, though its consequences could have been minimised, and even contained, if the British administration had tried to be less clever and had shown more constructive concern.

To be sure, two of the Colony's concerns were shared by the educated elite in the Protectorate. These were literacy as a requirement for membership of the Legislative Council, and the prepondering influence of the chiefs. The letters of Kowa, Albert Margai and Siaka Stevens cited in this work support this contention.[132] For a time it did look as if some understanding could be arrived at on this common basis of hostility to illiterate chiefs, but this entente did not get off the ground because of 'Krio arrogance' and 'intransigence' – an attitude which repelled the Protectorate educated elite.[133] This interpretation is too facile. Writers put all the blame on Krio politicians

153

for this impasse and, more significantly, they do not give credit to the political acumen of the Protectorate leaders. Certainly, they resented the influence of the illiterate chiefs and they were alienated because the establishment did not provide them a role in the political structure existing in the Protectorate but, in the final analysis, there were links, consanguineal ties with these ruling houses, which no amount of common understanding with Colony politicians could hope to match. In any case, any 'alliance' with Colony politicians would, at best, be temporary, because the logic of political developments would eventually submerge the Krio minority, and power would pass on to the Protectorate majority. It therefore made political sense for the Protectorate educated elite to identify themselves with the Protectorate side.[134] This brought them much more quickly to the centre of the decision-making process.

Indeed, to appease the educated elite, reforms were later carried through in the District Councils in 1950 which enabled educated Protectorate people to have a role in local government. This made it possible for Siaka Stevens and Albert Margai to be elected into the New Legislative Council.[135] Also, because of protests by both the educated elites in the Colony and Protectorate, the government set up a Select Committee of the Legislative Council comprising the Unofficial Members and seven extraordinary members (four Protectorate Paramount Chiefs and three representatives from the Colony) to discuss the proposals of the Protectorate Assembly, asking for thirteen members and seven members to represent the Protectorate and Colony respectively.[136] The meeting was abortive since the Colony extraordinary members – Easmon, Cox-George and Barlatt – walked out, allegedly because they took exception to the presence of the Acting Chief Commissioner whom they suspected might influence the Chiefs.[137] Past experience may have warranted this strange protest; but it is an open question whether it was wise of them at that point in time to have left the Select Committee,[138] because their exit, apart from supplying fuel to the detractors of Krio politicians, may have hastened the decision of the Select Committee to accept the proposals unchanged. The decision was later endorsed by the Legislative Council, including Colony representatives.

Furthermore, Cox-George's impulsive departure robbed him of the chance of putting across his ideas. It is not being suggested that they would have been accepted or even well received, but their discussion might have given a new insight, and might have gone some way in meeting the claims of the two sides in the sense that both the Protectorate and the Colony would have got their majority in two different houses. As proposed, there was to be a bicameral parliament: (a) an Upper House of representatives from the Districts in the Protectorate, the Freetown City Council and Rural Areas and the Sherbro Judicial Council, elected by an electoral college on nomination by the Lower House; (b) a Lower House of representatives from the Colony and Protectorate based on a ratio of their educated (articulate) population thus: Colony eleven, Protectorate eight (to embrace non-chiefs as far as possible); and four ex-officio. The Lower House had competence over legislation, subject to confirmation by the Upper House, which would have a suspensory veto for one year. One important provision was that a law was to declare a Sierra Leone Citizenship that would do away with the status differential. Another was that the governor would retain reserve powers over legislation in both houses; but these were to be limited to external affairs. The Executive Council must have an unofficial majority who would elect a prime minister among themselves; he, in turn, would select his colleagues and assign portfolios to them.

Cox-George, a lecturer in economics at Fourah Bay College, did not envisage the constitution as a permanent arrangement, but 'a case of expediency', to answer, as far as possible, the demands of both sides. The usefulness of his suggestions was that there would be one country once a Sierra Leone citizenship was declared and, more important, they allowed 'the most educated and developed elements in the country...to be real legislators'. He did not discuss in detail the mechanics of selection and voting, but one thing his constitution would have done would have been to get rid of the obnoxious questions of the preponderating influence of chiefs and illiteracy. It was not a radical constitution, and it did not seek to give the vote to everybody; nor would that have been a wise thing, given the level of literacy of the mass of people. Indeed, Cox-George's proposal was not so strange as it may look; for, as Akintoye has observed: 'In practically all other African countries, the independence legislature was made up of two Chambers – a lower chamber called House of Assembly or House of Representatives, and an Upper Chamber called the Senate'. Sierra Leone was the exception. 'It created a one-chamber legislature in which the chiefs were given a guaranteed number of seats. This made the chiefs very powerful in the national political system, since they had so many effective votes.'[139]

We do not know how much support Cox-George would have generated for his proposal but, in an earlier pamphlet of his, 'Crucifixion of Sierra Leone: an Examination of the New Constitutional Proposals', he had argued in favour of a greater representation for the Protectorate. That this was not possible, he reasoned, was because of the level of literacy in that area.[140] His latest effort, therefore, was an attempt to supply an answer to that problem. However, his departure from the Select Committee, which was bitterly criticised by Decker, made the usefulness of his suggestion an academic point.[141]

Still, opinion outside was unreconciled to the provisions of the constitution and, as a result of demonstrations and protests made by the Colony, the governor attempted to have another conference to iron out these differences. It never met because his 'advisors [have] failed to reach agreement on the composition of the Committee'.[142] By this time the polarities had almost been established. In 1949–50 the atmosphere was tense; the government was impatient, wanting to break the impasse. And this was given some urgency by a spate of violent unrest in the Protectorate at this time.[143] More important, the Protectorate now began to show signs of impatience, believing, as it were, that the recalcitrance of the Colony politicians was a sinister plot to deny them of their hegemony promised by the new constitution. This is suggested by the correspondence between Siaka Stevens and Rita Hinden. The letters read like a barometer monitoring the political temperature in Sierra Leone; and they give us an insight into the thinking of the Protectorate educated elite at this time. On 17 January 1949 he told Dr Hinden:[144]

> to my mind the whole thing hinges on the one question that is troubling most parts of British West Africa today – the position of chiefs in the Legislative Council. This is the burning question. *I, for my part, agree with the colony people that an unofficial majority made up mostly of chiefs from the Protectorate, who, likeable people in themselves, are but part of a government and hold their position at the will of government, and above all illiterate (most of them); such an unofficial majority would be nothing but a farce...* Many people cannot help feeling that government with the wealth of experience and knowledge at its disposal, *if it seriously wanted representatives other than chiefs to be elected to these District Councils, it could have them...* So there we are, the 'New Constitution' was turned down in the last Legislative Council by an overwhelming majority – only the unofficial side of the Council voting, officials refraining from voting. So we have to start it all over again. I sincerely trust that the root of the difficulty will be tackled and not just the top. Once this difficulty is cleared, once the Colony people can see at least 50% Protectorate representation consisting of literate Protectorate men, I think their talk about the Colony getting more representation than the Protectorate will blow away.

Stevens' sanguine hopes soon disappeared; for his next letter on 15 March reported:[145]

> beginning to think government is acting slow on constitutional matter...Speech of one of the P.C.s on the occasion started some bitter feelings here. Some people have the feeling that the speech was inspired. The man attacked the Colony people, said they were slaves and were incapable of governing themselves etc. The Colony people had some hard things to say in the Press about this

A ray of hope appeared in his next letter of 3 December 1949:

> some colony people now coming round to accepting Protectorate Majority...Wallace-Johnson is urging that the governor's proposal for (a) Committee be accepted as a suitable basis for Constitutional discussions. The strongest advocate now against [*sic*] acceptance is L. Sankoh, an Oxford man, and his ideas are sound, even if one does not always agree with them.[146]

But in July 1950 a very angry note crept into the letter; he expostulated that the

> Colony people, a mere 24,000 out of a total population in Sierra Leone of a little over 2 million [?] – now claiming 50/50 representation when they had agreed to seven Colony representatives and thirteen (Protectorate Representatives) in 1948. Sir George Beresford Stooke, the governor, has now threatened to implement the Constitution if both sides refused to come to terms, but the

governor had made this over 3 months ago, but [had] not carried out the threat. [It has been] interpreted as a sign of weakness in most quarters in [the] Protectorate. In fact some quarters are even going so far as to suggest that the government *deliberately created the deadlock that has arisen*: also government has not yet selected Committee to study proposals.[147]

Space does not allow us to quote Stevens' letters *in extenso*. They clearly show the development of attitude among the Protectorate elite, from empathy to resentment and hostility, and we are also reminded of the sinister role of the establishment in the affair. But if Stevens was exasperated by the recalcitrance of the Colony, observers outside Sierra Leone could find no good word to say in defence or sympathy of the Colony.[148] It was all-round condemnation – some even likened their attitude to the exclusivist outlook of White Colonists in South Africa or Australia.[149] The view of one international figure, George Padmore, reflected the change of feelings towards the Krio. In 1936 he said of the Krios that they were long used to freedom and they fought for it: 'These ideas of freedom reinforced by western education' put them 'among the most progressive and aggressive natives in Africa'; but, in 1957, commenting on the 1950–1 episode, he dismissed them as 'demagogues using their professional and social status to bamboozle the masses for their own personal aggrandizement'.[150]

Milton Margai also had some biting comments to make too. In 1950, moving a motion for the acceptance of the Constitution and praying for its implementation, he denounced the Krio thus:[151]

Sierra Leone, which has been the foremost of all West African Colonies is still saddled with an archaic constitution with an official majority. The reason for this backwardness is evidently due to the fact that our forefathers, we regret very much to say, had given shelter to a handful of foreigners who have no will to co-operate with us and imagine themselves to be our superiors because they are aping the western mode of living, and have never breathed the true spirit of independence.

Margai's outburst was unhistorical, because the situation was different from his account. He was also less than frank to say they never breathed the true spirit of independence because, as Bright told the governor of Sierra Leone, the renown of Sierra Leone and of West Africa in the nineteenth century was the handiwork of the Krio.[152] Be that as it may, a speech of this kind made by a man of such standing and prestige as Margai, by now the acknowledged leader of the Protectorate, dramatically symbolised the irreversible polarisation of the two factions.

In the Colony, various political groups organised themselves into a single political party, the National Council of Sierra Leone, in August 1950, under the leadership of Dr Bankole-Bright, committed to defending the interests of the Colony inhabitants *vis-à-vis* the Protectorate.[153] However, according to the late Pa Rogers Williams, N.C.S.L. spokesman for financial matters in the Legislative Council, what became the N.C.S.L. was never intended as a political party. It was intended as an exclusive Krio movement, and the

157

original name chosen was Ogboni Society but, in deference to Bright's suggestion for a broad-based organisation, the name was changed to the more innocuous National Council of Sierra Leone.[154] It did not make much difference anyhow. It was regarded as a Krio party, just as the S.L.P.P., made up of the Krio, Lamina Sankoh's People's Party, P.E.P.U., and S.O.S., was identified as the Protectorate Party. These two parties were to lead their respective people in their bid for control of the Legislative Council.

Launched with the determination not to be swamped by the Protectorate majority, the National Council of Sierra Leone resorted to obstructionist tactics and protests to put off the introduction of the Stevenson Constitution. Otto During and his faction, the Positive Action Group of the Council, even filed court actions against the governor for alleged illegalities in the constitution and for an unconstitutional action.[155] Protests continued after 1951 to the extent that Bankie and Wallace-Johnson went to England to demand the rescinding of the 1947 Constitution; failing that, to declare a separate existence for the Colony.[156] If the National Council focused attention on the political question, another Krio movement not only committed itself to defending the virtues of their traditions, but also to contest the legality of the British action in ceding their Colony to a much larger entity, Sierra Leone, which was to be dominated by 'foreigners'. On this latter point, an impassioned pamphlet was published in 1956 by Ahmed Alhadi, former Master and Registrar of the Supreme Court, a Muslim Krio. Making copious references, he argued that 'in the first place, transplanting the Free Settlers here and purchasing Sierra Leone for them, their heirs and successors forever constitute a compensatory gift for the part the Free Settlers played in defence of British lives in the war of American Independence. The gift is inalienable'.[157] The Settlers Descendents Union (S.D.U.), a political/cultural movement, based its programme on proving the legality of the ownership of the peninsula by the settlers and their descendants. It was founded by its President, J. C. Lucan, in 1952, with an executive which included E. J. Robinson, Vice-President, and Leslie Asgill, retired Collector of Customs, Secretary. The movement drew support from the lower strata of Krio society. The elite, complained Pa Lucan, when he was interviewed in 1974, held themselves aloof, or gave lukewarm support. Even Bankie did not become a member until the very end of his career when he paid the nominal membership fee of two shillings in his sick bed – he 'eventually saw the rightness of our case', Pa Lucan said.[158]

The S.D.U. mounted costly suits against the British government, carrying them even to the highest court in the land, all to no avail. Some people, however, believed that the S.D.U. won its case but the political implications of this deterred the court from giving a verdict in their favour.[159]

Be that as it may, we are anticipating the story here and it will be returned to later. The fact of the matter was that neither the trapezing acts of N.C.S.L., nor the antics of S.D.U., shifted the government from its mapped course. In September 1951 Governor Beresford-Stooke (known as a wan yai guvnor because he sported a monocle) proclaimed the implementation of the Stevenson Constitution.[160] Only one concession was given to educated opinion: a provision requiring literacy in English for membership in the New Legislative Council was added to the constitution. Otherwise it remained unchanged as it was approved by the Protectorate Assembly and the Legislative Council.[161] But it is a point for debate whether the government by its prevarication, and its alienation of Bankie (by not consulting with him when, in fact, by 1950 he had emerged as the leader of the Colony politicians), did not contribute to the bitterness of the period.[162]

In November 1951 elections were held on a limited franchise in Freetown and the Sherbro Urban District, and in the Protectorate the voting was indirect. The picture is not clear as to how the elections were conducted and the issues that the two groups championed. Contemporary reports are confusing. The S.L.P.P., for one, was formed in April 1951 and, according to *West Africa*, it claimed in a manifesto issued in August that it hoped to contest every seat in the Colony and Protectorate, and would sponsor candidates who would give a written pledge to support the party's policy of political unification of the two units in the dependency and self government within the British Empire.[163] But it did not contest the election on party lines, though, of course, successful candidates who declared for the S.L.P.P. were members of the party.[164] Indeed, the party came to power 'not as the result of victory at the polls, but following a committee meeting'.[165]

The National Council, on the other hand, contested the elections on party lines and the returns gave the following results: N.C.S.L. three: Dr Bankole-Bright, C. M. A. Thompson, and J. Rogers Williams; S.L.P.P. two: A. G. Randle and M. S. Mustapha; Independents two: I. T. A. Wallace-Johnson and J. C. O. Crowther. From the Protectorate the District Councils elected twelve representatives and the Protectorate Assembly two, thus: Bo District – P.C. R. B. S. Koker; Bonthe District – M. A. S. Margai; Bombali – P.C. Bai Farima Tass II; Kailahum – P.C. Bockari Sambi of Daru; Kono – Reverend Paul Dunbar; Koinadugu – Lansana Kamara; Kenema – P.C. Kenewa Gamanga; Port Loko – P.C. Alkali Modu III; Pujehun – P.C. Jaia Kaikai; Moyamba – W. H. Fitzjohn; Tonkolili – P.C. Bai Kurr. Protectorate Assembly: Siaka Stevens and A. M. Margai. In this list only four (the two Margais, Stevens and Fitzjohn) were party members.[166] On the basis of the directly contested seats in the Colony, the National Council won the elections; however, if the two independents joined the N.C.S.L., that party would have a clear majority.[167] But then party politics had not developed on clearly defined lines, and one delicate question was where did the indirectly elected Protectorate members fit in? There were no guidelines on this and, in 1967, it was to rear its ugly head again over the issue of whether Paramount Chiefs must declare for the government party after the latter had won a clear majority in the General Elections, or should identify themselves with a party thus ensuring majority seats to the party before a government was appointed. This was one major issue which caused the crisis of 1967.[168] In 1951, however, given the state of Colony/Protectorate relations, and the fact that despite its advertised image of a 'unifier' the S.L.P.P. was a Protectorate party at daggers drawn with the 'separatist' National Council, a Colony party, and also given Milton Margai's assiduous canvassing of the Protectorate members, eventually all of them, including the chiefs, declared for the S.L.P.P.[169]

What follows has never been satisfactorily explained in the literature; and, even now, because some of the submissions cannot be substantiated by hard-core evidence, we can only make conjectures here until various archives are fully open to the public.

After the elections, Dr Bright, the leader of the 'majority party in the limited field of declared party contest', for reasons derived from his meeting with the governor, appeared to have entertained the belief that he was going to be appointed leader of the government. Possibly he was misled by the results of the polls and the kite-flying suggestions of the governor. Or, again, as has been suggested, he had been assured by Columbus Thompson (the Colony representative in the Protectorate Assembly) that the elected Protectorate members would declare for him.[170] Dr Fitzjohn appears to have agreed with Thompson; though his statement that 'they would have accepted Creole [sic] leadership' was vague enough to refer to any period in time, one doubts whether he was specifically referring to 1951.[171] In post-election discussions with the governor, Bright was given the impression that he would be in government. On the other hand, if it came to a head count, as indeed it turned out, the S.L.P.P., with its lines to the traditional elite, would gain the upper hand. Moreover, certain officials, for example, the Chief Commissioner, Hubert Childs, were not in favour of the governor handing political power to the Colony; and the Commissioner, for one, appeared to have exerted some influence on the Protectorate's behalf.[172] There is even a suggestion that he put up Protectorate chiefs to make anti-Colony statements. Records are not easy to find to elucidate these points, but it would appear that government attitude changed between Bankie's meeting with the governor, the intervention of Childs, and the official opening of the New Legislative Council the next day.[173] This is important to remember in analysing Bright's 'two hills speech'.

On 28 November 1951, His Excellency Sir George Beresford-Stooke formally opened the New Legislative Council. In his address he took great pains to point out that party politics was still in its infancy, and that it was not well developed and this being so he put out a veiled suggestion for a coalition. The relevant portions are worth quoting *in extenso*:[174]

> where there is a well developed 'party system' it is the practice of His Majesty the King or representative to send for the leader of the party which commands a majority and invite him to form a government. Here in Sierra Leone today I am not sure that the party system is yet quite sufficiently developed for me to introduce a procedure modelled *mutatis mutandis* on that which I have described. I propose therefore on this occasion to consult unofficial members

at a private and informal meeting on the choice of those who are to be invited to join the government. I want to make two points clear: (1) that this should not be regarded as establishing a precedent; (2) that in following this procedure this year, I am guided solely by the overriding necessity to ensure that the Executive Council has the support of a working majority in this Council.

After this, the governor asked the elected members to wait behind for a closed session. There are no minutes for this extraordinary session and the proceedings are not recorded in the *Hansard* but we can fairly guess what happened from the claims made by both sides during debates in 1952 and 1953. At this meeting the governor reiterated his remarks and, stung by what appeared to him as a volte face, bearing in mind what had transpired before, Bankie was moved to say 'we are like two hills that will never meet, but if you with your experience could get us together'.[175] The first part of the statement is often quoted; the second part never, because it modifies the first and suggests flexibility not intransigence. Even more intriguing is Margai's own statement which is seldom quoted, if ever. According to his biographer, after the governor had suggested a discussion, Margai exploded and refused a meeting – 'we have had four years of this'. It was then that Bankie made his observation.[176]

There has been much speculation about the meaning of Bankie's statement. Many see it as a symbol of Krio ultramontanism, and that once it was uttered it cooked the goose of the Colony people and the latter lost their chance for some consideration in the sharing of political power. More important, it is interpreted as an ethnic slur, that it represents Bright's arrogance and hostility towards the people in the interior.[177] Bankie had his prejudices, no doubt. He was contemptuous of the oi polloi, and the possibility that he may have resented people from the Protectorate or, at worst, he was ambivalent towards them cannot be dismissed. On this there is no general agreement. There are those who swore that Bankie disliked the Protectorate people,[178] others say he accepted those he believed fulfilled his own requirements of a civilised being, for instance, Milton Margai. There is a further opinion that avers that Bankie, a man free from rancour and vindictiveness, had a warm and open-hearted relationship with people in the interior. It is not unlikely, also, as was the case of quite a few Krio families, that the Brights may have had familial links with Protectorate peoples.[179] And if it is remembered that he had fought for Protectorate interests despite the discouraging noises from the establishment, then we need not see this slur as the only interpretation. More to the point, if kept within its context, it was a political statement, that is 'we are seeing two sides of the coin, but if you could get us to see the same side then I would be willing to accommodate you'. That is a reasonable explanation if we take into consideration the modification of the second part of the quotation and Margai's own statement. This interpretation is further supported by a statement Bankie made in conversation with his Krio peers during this period of rancour and dissension in the 50s: 'We have no right to say that we have the right to be the leaders of this country. But we have the right to choose our leaders, and to ensure that the country is led properly.'[180] If we accept the validity of this statement, and my informant was emphatic on the accuracy of his report, then Bankie was not the rigid exclusivist the literature has given us but a pragmatist, who was willing to show flexibility in politics. Further, he had a wider breadth of politics and a greater concern, all embracing, for the country of Sierra Leone than he has been given credit for. Professor Canon Sawyerr, former Principal of Fourah Bay College, has attested that Bright was a man without rancour and a mature politician. On two separate occasions widely apart in time and space, Professor Sawyerr has proclaimed to me that Bankie was a 'most fascinating man', the 'greatest politician he had ever known'.[181] And, of course, his niece has always insisted that Bankie was not opposed to the idea of the Protectorate getting political power, but that he felt it should be better prepared to exercise it.[182] And this is supported by his advocacy for infrastructural development in the Protectorate, examples of which have been cited in this work.

There is another explanation of Bright's Legislative Council statement. Bright was given to melodramatic rhetoric; he loved to use metaphors and flowery language. Examples of these have been given in this work, and it is possible that his two hills speech was just another example of his speech style.

In any case, once Bright made that statement, so popular belief has it, the governor was compelled to ask the leaders to stand, and to suggest that those who supported either should join the leader of their choice.[183] The majority joined Margai. The two independents, Wallace-Johnson and Crowther, identified themselves with Dr Bright. And so, in this strange and curious way, Sierra Leone's first 'representative government' was appointed.

Krio people and writers have blamed Bright for his intemperateness and extreme language.[184] One even maintained that because of that the Krio are suffering today.[185] But this criticism is unjust. Bright's language was no more reprehensible than Margai's or Bai Koblo's. But the truth of the matter is that the logic of British policy presupposes that power had to be handed over to the Protectorate. Even if it is argued that there was goodwill on the part of some Protectorate people, and that they were ready to accommodate the Colony politicians, it is difficult to imagine what formula the British administration could devise that would assuage the outraged demands of the Colony and satisfy the rising expectations of the Protectorate. In the Gold Coast and Nigeria, the leaders of government were appointed directly without fumbling over technicalities. The British government could not do otherwise in Sierra Leone. Besides, even if a formula was found, for instance, giving some kind of guaranteed participation in government to the Colony, experience within our times leads us to the conclusion that given the character of African politics, it would have become a dead letter, within a few years of independence once the British presence was removed. Examples abound of firm promises given in entrenched clauses only to be given legal clothing and over-turned when convenient for the regime in power.

In this regard, on the impasse of 1951 Stooke really behaved like Pontius Pilate. He refused to give a judgement and he sought refuge in ponderous constitutionality. Thus Milton Margai, through a decision by the governor and not by 'an overwhelming electoral victory',[186] became leader of government business and later Chief Minister. He chose the following as colleagues in the Executive Council:[187] his brother, Albert Margai, Siaka Stevens, P.C. Bai Farima Tass, A. G. Randle, and Sanusi Mustapha. Power still remained in the hands of the governor who was president of the Legislative Council and ex-officio member of the government. Bright became leader of the Opposition, and he spent the rest of his parliamentary life moving unceasing motions of censure that were largely ineffectual. It was living the inter-war Legislative Council life all over again. Wallace-Johnson, though a member of Bright's party, was too much of a rebel to remain attached for very long. He was virtually an independent member in the Council. Eventually he severed his links with Bright's organisation; so did Crowther. Columbus Thompson and Rogers-Williams continued to support their leader.[188]

8

Second innings in Parliament: the twilight years, 1951–1957

In the 1950s Bright was a tragic figure. Over his long political career he had received many bruises; he had fought against the British; he had crossed swords with his peers; he had fought for parliamentary freedom and for the dignity of the African; and he had contributed a great deal to the development of politics in Sierra Leone. Yet he had nothing to show for all these. His friend, Betts, became a Puisne Judge in 1944 and, two years later, he was appointed a Judge of the West African Court of Appeal – an institution he and Bright had fought to have the British government establish. In 1953 he became Vice-President of the Legislative Council where he and his comrade-in-arms had bearded the British lion. And, no doubt, it must have been a harrowing experience for the two to face each other in the chamber on different levels! Betts received the supreme accolade of a distinguished public career when the Queen knighted him in July 1957, 'the first Sierra Leonean to be knighted after 61 years'.[1] Sir Ernest died within three months of receiving this singular honour, while he was in his post as Speaker of the new House of Representatives. Bright mourned his death. A little over one year later Bankie also died.[2]

Meanwhile Bright had to go through an agonising chain of events. Domestic happiness eluded him: separated from his wife Ada, his children left home (and it is this writer's understanding that they have never returned to Sierra Leone), and Bankie went through a number of court cases, which, fortunately for him, did not land him a prison sentence. His medical practice, too, was not as successful as it used to be; some even claim that it was non-existent in the forties and fifties.[3] A flamboyant and incisive speaker in his early days, Bankie had in the fifties lost the effectiveness of the inter-war years, though young men continued to be mesmerised by his platform performance. But the hostile *West Africa* refused to be impressed by his 'jaw breaking words'.[4] Nevertheless, he retained some of his undoubted charisma. In 1951, Bright was sixty-eight years old and was possibly, the oldest member in the new Legislative Council. The Leader of government business, Milton Margai, was thirteen years his junior. In terms of political experience he had no equal. He was definitely the 'doyen of West African politics'.[5] But this hardly served him well. And given the backlash of 1947–51, and the consequent bitterness, his efforts to retrieve his lost glory and contribute

164

positively to the development of the nation were a trying experience even for a veteran parliamentarian.

The government of Margai was an association of interest groups from divergent power bases, and each of them had to be satisfied – it was a fragile structure kept as a unit only by Milton Margai's own cautious and accommodating leadership and the common hostility towards Krio politicians. Again, though it was a government conducted by an African majority, real power was still exercised by the governor, the representative of the British government, which in itself imposed constraints on the power and effectiveness of the Margai regime. Certainly, problems it had to face, such as unemployment, labour unrest in the mines and a rising population that always seemed to be on the verge of hunger, were beyond its competence. Moreover, evidence of financial irregularities, and possibly corruption, in Margai's government did not help his image.[6] Consequently, the poor performance of Margai in his first years gave ammunition to Bright to launch his salvoes against the regime. But then the National Council, Bankie's party, and its supporters, wasted valuable time in legal tussles with the British government which had no chance of success, because no British government would admit that it was wrong in handing over political power to the Protectorate.

Thus, in the first few years of opposition, the N.C.S.L. wasted its energies in needling the Margai regime and pursuing a policy of obnoxiousness. Bright, for one, moved, on 29 July 1951, a motion which was in effect one of censure on Margai's party, asking for independence for the Colony area. It was ignored, but the opposition leader persisted in pursuing the matter; and, in an unlikely combination with Wallace-Johnson, he went on a mission to London the same year to plead with the British government to establish a federation in the dependency. The Colony's standpoint was restated and it was pointed out that the Stevenson Constitution, instead of uniting the country, was splitting it. For instance, the franchise disqualified many Krio living in the Protectorate from voting. Consequently, they asked that if it was not possible to federate the territory, the colony must be given autonomy. London refused to commit itself, but advised the delegation to go back and try out the Constitution and, if it proved unworkable, the Colony could then make further representations. In fact, although W. L. Gorell Barnes, an official at the Colonial Office, appeared to be sympathetic to some of the concerns of the Colony, Governor Beresford-Stooke firmly discouraged his suggestions for accommodation, claiming that they might invite a reaction that might lead to complications between London and Margai's government.[7]

As it turned out, the London Mission was the last time Bankie and Wallace-Johnson co-operated on any issue. There have been suggestions that the latter had betrayed his leader, even going behind his back to the Colonial

Office to explain that though he had come with the delegation he was not in sympathy with the contents of the resolution.[8] One source maintains that he severed himself from Bankie because he was exasperated by Bright's inflexibility.[9]

Indeed, one finds it difficult to explain away the naiveté of Bankie, the utter loss of balance in tilting at the windmill. His futile efforts only gave ammunition to one critic who accused him of 'turning democracy into an obstacle race, the sole duty of the N.C.S.L. being to provide the hedges and ditches [i.e., English language and culture] on the course'.[10] Frank Inkumsah's reference may have been frivolous, 'incapable of visualizing things from the right perspective', but the only excuse we can offer for Bright's postures is that perhaps his ego refused to accept reality.[11] On the other hand, a reasonable explanation may be that Bright and his party were still suffering from shock – for the Colony people could not get over the stark fact that the British had sold them out. Yet the curious thing was that they continued to believe that the British would play the game, that they would go through the practised procedure of petitions, memoranda and even the law courts to make their point. But all along Britain had made it clear that it played the game according to rules which she alone could interpret. The British had given all indications that they did not need the Krio. They had been dropped like hot potatoes.[12]

It is perhaps invidious to draw parallels between the white colonists in Kenya and Rhodesia (Zambia and Zimbabwe) because they were not on all fours with the people in the colony of Sierra Leone, but it is significant that when black majority rule was demanded, the same British government, including individuals who may have denounced the Krio as separatists, stood arguments on their heads in trying to make a case for some consideration for the white minority.[13] In the case of Sierra Leone, the S.D.U., taking up the Krio cause after the demise of N.C.S.L. in the late fifties, claimed that the Colony was the home of Sierra Leoneans (that is Colony inhabitants) by cession, and that no subsequent act or legislation had invalidated the legality of that claim of ownership. Court cases pursued by an array of prominent Krio public figures – J. Holland Rose (the columnist), Balogun Palmer (the pharmacist), J. C. Zizer and J. C. Lucan, leaders of S. D. U., and Dr Prince Buck and others – went to the highest bodies in the British judicial system. All to no avail.

On the other hand, there was a belief that certain high officials in London and Freetown held that the Colony had a case, that its contention could be sustained. But such a decision was politically explosive and so, for that matter, no court could give a judgement in support of the S.D.U.[14] Two letters purportedly initialled and signed by Ian Macleod, Secretary of State for the Colonies, and Sir Maurice Dorman, governor of Sierra Leone, as well as a letter from the Attorney-General's Office in London, substantiate the belief that for political reasons the S.D.U. could not win the case against the British government.[15]

To take the letter from the Attorney-General first. Apparently addressed to the Colonial Secretary on 26 August 1960, it revealed that the Attorney-General had talked with the governor of Sierra Leone and he had looked at the relevant papers. He believed the S.D.U. had at least up to 90 per cent successful action 'except and unless any unforeseen circumstances occur'. 'I can assure you', he went on, 'that I will do my uttermost. I cannot hold out any promise of any high degree of success. You may inform the governor of this my studied opinion not bothering you with legal technicalities and authorities' (not signed by hand: addressed to Sir Ian Macleod). The latter forwarded the above to the governor, Sir Maurice Dorman, with this comment:

> Taking seriously the opinion of the learned lawyer's, one can almost predict what the outcome shall be. Consequently, in the light of current events (I refer particularly to Siaka Stevens' E.B.I. [Election Before Independence Movement] which is gaining momentum and [the] sympathy of the British Public and Press and in some official quarters also), I believe the time has come for you and your cabinet to think of making a two way constitution – one for the Colony and one for the Protectorate with a Common House where matters of common interest on both sides would be discussed and decisions reached. Although the success of this would mainly depend on what attitude the representative body of the Union shall adopt. In view of the discussion now taking place between the Secretary of State, the Attorney-General, the British Representative in the U.N. and my humble self, it is patently clear that the S. Union are staging an all out fight of the U.N.O. I shall therefore warn that you advise your P.M. to adopt a moderate attitude over things in general until the whole issue is settled.
> (Addressed to Sir Maurice Dorman, dated 29 August 1960, initialled by Ian Macleod, Secretary of State for the Colonies.)

The governor of Sierra Leone, writing from the Colonial Office on the same date, told the Commissioner for Sierra Leone in a letter that he had met the Secretary of State and the Attorney-General:

> the learned Attorney-General is of fixed opinion that the colony of Sierra Leone is a private property, that of the Sierra Leone Settlers, their heirs, and successors, based on a detailed study of the treaty side by side with the charter of 1829 [sic] granted the Sierra Leone Company by the British government which was never amended or dissolved at the time it was returned by the Sierra Leone Company. Both documents therefore give the S.D.U. of Sierra Leone an indisputable claim to the territory.
>
> Their case now pending is unbeatable. It seems now purely a battle of endurance. In the interval I strongly recommend that you accept the advice of the Secretary of State as contained in the last paragraph of his letter (enclosed). I must warn you that only projects that are of paramount nature already started and likely to benefit the country when government assumes power in the near future need be continued.

The governor then went on to warn the Sierra Leone government that if the S.D.U. action was successful H.M.G. would grant their prayers set out in their petition.

'It must be remembered', he continued, 'that with this case of the settlers on the one hand and the E.B.I. movement led by Siaka Stevens which is fastly gaining the sympathy of the British public and other governments, the position of the present set up of the Sierra Leone government is questionable' (signed Maurice Dorman).

While other documents do not corroborate these statements, the 'unforeseen circumstances' did occur. The independence of Sierra Leone on 27 April 1961 made the settler case a non-issue which was finally laid to rest by the Justice Wilberforce decision on 5 May 1964.[16]

The S.D.U. episode is history now; and one is not qualified to engage in legal disputation on the constitutionality and legality of the Wilberforce judgement, but it is important to state here that not all Krio were members of the S.D.U. or even sympathised with their cause. Bright's attitude to the S.D.U. was at best ambivalent. Blyden gives an account in his thesis of instances when Bankie publicly ridiculed Balogun Palmer, one of the extreme rightist leaders of the S.D.U. And Bright, popularly regarded as the chief protagonist of Krio values and culture, did not become a member of this organisation until a few months before his death.[17] G. Coleridge Taylor, in an article in the *Daily Mail* of 8 July 1958 entitled 'National interest should prevail', was bitterly critical of the Union: 'They are stupid, narrow minded attempts to perpetuate disunion when wiser heads are finding a cure for the deadly wound of dissension that is sapping the very life blood of our country's progress. Thus they are not only unprogressive but retrogressive.' S. A. J. Pratt criticised from Geneva both the N.C.S.L. and the S.L.P.P. for being non-parties, since their influence was felt only in Freetown and a few 'dormitory' villages.[18] He urged Bright and Wallace-Johnson to adopt an active programme of educating the citizens of the Protectorate about the popular phases of 'our constitutional advance', and to stop being defeatists. Quite a substantial number of Krios, either because they genuinely believed in the S.L.P.P.'s professed programme of 'One Country, One People', or because they were realistic enough to read the shifting of forces more clearly, decided to positively associate themselves with the S.L.P.P.[19] The case of Lamina Sankoh is well known. Not as well known are the cases of J. M. Rose, the columnist, who in fact defected back to the N.C.S.L. in 1958, N. D. J. Smart, deputy Secretary-General of the S.L.P.P., who advertised his sympathies with a series of articles critical of the social stratification in the territory, and J. Galba-Bright, the cousin of Bankole-Bright.[20] *West Africa* of 6 September 1952 also has a list of young educated Krio Colony supporters of the S.L.P.P. They included H. E. B. John, a tutor at the C.M.S. Grammar School (Secretary-General of the Party), Miss Lettie Stuart, Mr. W. Conton, Reverend Harry Sawyerr – all members of staff at Fourah Bay College; Mr Singer Betts, nephew of E. S. Beoku-Betts, Miss Lottie Hazely, acting Principal of the Freetown Secondary School For Girls, Mrs Constance Cummings-John and S. M. Broderick, ex-assistant Director of Education (retired). To this may be added M. S. Mustapha – a Muslim Krio (at this time referred to as Aku Mohamedan). One leavening factor which facilitated this rapprochement was the links which some of these people had with the Protectorate. H. E. B. John, for instance, was associated with the Protectorate Teachers' Union.[21] And Mustapha, a Muslim, contested for an area that was dominated by immigrants from the interior. At that time, it was fashionable for people like Mustapha to pass themselves off as non-Krio and, by identifying with his Muslim co-religionists, he gained acceptance. Hence he polled the highest number of votes cast in Freetown.[22] Harry Sawyerr grew up in the provinces, and was the playmate of contemporary educated elites from the Protectorate. He could speak Mende very well. He understood the culture, and so, naturally, he came out with a book years later on *The Springs of Mende Belief and Conduct* (1968). Certainly in the Reverend Prof. Sawyerr's career we can find evidence of his contention that Krio contact with the Protectorate is more than can be accounted for. It is deep and subtle. Many families, for example, the Williamses and Fergussons, have Sherbro blood; provincial rites have been adopted in Krio customs. And, in this regard, to show that the split between the two areas was artificial, and that there had been occasions of long harmony, M. C. F. Easmon wrote an article on Paramount Chief Bai Kurr. This man, given the name Samuel Edward Carew, not only lived with a Krio family but he also went to school with Bright, I. G. Cummings and V. K. Edwin.[23] This was not an isolated case. Such invisible links may have had a bearing on the founding of the U.P.P. (United Progressive Party) with a largely Krio leadership and a respectable Protectorate following. Founded in June 1954 by Wallace-Johnson and C. B. Rogers-Wright, 'unquestionably Sierra Leone's most eminent lawyer', it appeared to have been given a lift by the legion work its leader, Rogers-Wright, did for Protectorate clients in the aftermath of the 1955/6 disturbances. Assuming an anti-authoritarian and anti-establishment stance, and showing a willingness to woo Protectorate supporters, it soon replaced N.C.S.L. as an alternative party. It was certainly regarded as a Colony party, a 'Creole government', but it was much more broad based than the N.C.S.L. and more populist.[24] Other parties founded in the Colony were the Sierra Leone Labour Party led by Ronald Beoku-Betts, the lawyer son of Justice E. S. Beoku-Betts, and Marcus Chamberlain Grant, the Trade Unionist, which tried to cash in on the latter's reputation derived from his heroic role during the 1955 strike.[25] The Sierra Leone Independence Movement (S.L.I.M.), founded in November 1956 by the activist lecturer, Edward Blyden, grandson of the Black patriot, Edward Blyden, borrowed large doses from the philosophy of foreign parties, for instance, Eric Williams's National Unity Movement of Trinidad. Its strong denunciation of colonialism and uncompromising condemnation of Britain's betrayal of the Colony people endeared S.L.I.M. to young Krio intellectuals who nurtured this resentment against the British without going to the extremes of N.C.S.L. or S.D.U. It did not make much headway in Freetown or the provinces, though in 1962 it merged with Tamba S. Mbriwa's Kono Progressive Movement (1955) to form the Sierra Leone Progressive Independent Movement.[26]

In the Legislative Council Bright continued to criticise the government, but he was largely ignored. Rather, the administration went about consolidating its power bases and strengthening its hold, especially in the provincial administration where several reforms were instituted.[27] In 1953 Milton Margai assumed the designation of Chief Minister. Three years later he was elevated to the rank of Premier, and his colleagues were named Ministers with cabinet ranks and were given responsibilities for a range of executive functions, though the European executive heads of government departments were outside Ministerial control.[28] In 1958 the first African Minister of Finance, Sanusi Mustapha, was appointed, though he had to go through two years of apprenticeship under the European Financial Secretary.[29] By this date Margai felt confident enough to ask London for full independence.

In the face of all this, the futility of Bright's opposition has led Professor Hargreaves to comment: 'but it is hard to see, in the motions of censure on Ministers which he regularly and conscientiously tabled, even the seed of a national programme'.[30] This is a less than fair comment on Bright. By raising certain questions and making some useful criticisms and suggestions, he did make some contributions to parliamentary government.[31] Bankie's objection, in 1953, to the governor's participation in politics, which earned him the rebuke that he was seeking to 'apply to Sierra Leone rules of constitutional practice' that were 'appropriate to a colony with a more advanced Constitution', may have been precipitate, but it served to illuminate the point that Africans, despite the window dressing, were still far from the centre of the decision-making process.[32] No doubt this realisation may have inspired the African members of the government to press for more say in policy- and decision-making – and, as we have seen, this was gradually conceded in the next six years. But, in looking at the debates in the Chamber between 1951 and 1957, we cannot but admit that these years were the least creditable epoch in the otherwise enviable constitutional and parliamentary history of Sierra Leone. Bright and his colleagues put an incessant number of motions in the Council, designed to discredit and frustrate the Margai administration. And, of course, these were predictably lost.[33] Indeed, motions moved by the opposition, however well intentioned, were bound to be opposed by the government side, ridiculed or invested with base motives. For instance, a motion by Wallace-Johnson calling for compulsory education 'with a view to combating the menace of mass illiteracy especially among the female element in the Protectorate', was queried by the Protectorate members, insisting that it was full of hidden meanings. Siaka Stevens declaimed that the Protectorate did 'not want anybody to shed crocodile's tears for the education of the Protectorate. We have been watching to see that we get our just due.' Happily, the motion, after it was amended by the S.L.P.P., was carried over.[34]

Equally, the opposition consistently voted against government measures. According to Blyden, parliamentary deliberations were 'tribal and sectarian rather than political'.[35] If the government rejected an appeal it was because 'I am a Creole'; and if the opposition made a useful suggestion to improve the economic and social condition of the Protectorate, it was labelled as one more instance of 'Colony superiority'. It was all bitterness, rancour and recrimination. Bankie complained, without success, that his position as Leader of the Opposition was not given the honour and recognition it deserved. Hon. P.C. Jai Kaikai preceded him in the Legislative Council listing, and when Margai was elevated to the rank of Chief Minister, his salary rose from £720 p.a. (as leader of government business) to £2,200 p.a. Bright's salary as Leader of the Opposition remained at £600 p.a. He claimed that his salary should have been increased correspondingly as was the convention in other parts of the Commonwealth, for instance, Britain.[36]

This unattractive side of the new Legislative Council notwithstanding, the debates and personal encounters served a useful purpose, because they induced members, given the contemporary polarities in the political fabric of the territory, to identify their roots. A. G. Randle, for instance, in making a case for cooperation between the two units, admitted that he was Krio (though he represented Bonthe Electoral District). His father came from Regent, and his uncle was the early African activist, Dr J. K. Randle (of Lagos). Columbus Thompson told Paramount Chief R. B. S. Koker that the latter was a product of a Liberated African. This was not denied. Bankie acknowledged that he was the grandson of a Foulah Town Imam, and Mustapha added that since Bankie was a nephew of Alpha Z. Deen Belal, to whom he was related, Bright and Mustapha may be kinsmen.[37] Siaka Stevens, too, denied that he disliked the Krio, claiming that he was 'brought up by a Creole woman'.[38] The papers also tried to outdo each other in publishing cases of Colony/Protectorate marriages. For example, P.C. Maria Bunting Williams of Mattru Jong Chiefdom, elected in 1947, was married to James R. Zizer of Freetown, a cashier at C.F.A.O. Another reported a Miss Thompson marrying a Mr Kamara. In short, despite the bitterness and acrimony, there was some attempt to 'bury the hatchet', and work together for the good of Sierra Leone, phrases that were current in the media at this time.[39] And enlightened reforms did away with such obnoxious laws as Settlers' Fees. Also an amendment of the Aliens (Expulsion) Ordinance made Protectorate citizens no longer aliens in the Colony as far as practical politics were concerned.[40]

More important, the deliberations in the Legislative Council were not limited to cutlass-slashing and name-calling encounters. There were some positive contributions. The effort by the Colony legislators to promote education in the Protectorate has already been referred to. The mineral resources of the country were another important concern for all, especially in the fifties when smuggling of diamonds in Sierra Leone and the resultant short fall in revenue became legendary.[41] The opposition supported a motion by the Bo District representative, R. B. S. Koker, that in view of the prevalence of the illicit mining of diamonds and the grave economic and social consequences of this, the government should 'enter into negotiations with S.L.S.T.' – the concession company with a monopoly in the diamond industry. Though the House had rejected a similar motion by C. M. A. Thompson, N.C.S.L. members voted with the government.[42] Thompson abstained. However, when Siaka Stevens, as Minister of Lands, Mines and Labour, signed an agreement, the Diamond Agreement of September 1955, with S.L.S.T., which provided for the payment of £1,570,000 compensation by the government to the company, Bankole-Bright and his party were bitterly critical. Apparently, their objection was that the deal was one-sided, that the government had not fought hard enough to win concessions from the company. The government, on the other hand, claimed that it did its best since the original demand by S.L.S.T. for compensation was £10 million. The pleas made by the government did not impress the opposition. They slammed it as shameful and insulting, wicked and inimical to the interest of Sierra Leone. They walked out of the Legislative Council, an action criticised by Ronald Beoku-Betts and Sam Metzger; and the 'rump parliament' of S.L.P.P. legislators approved the agreement.[43] This open rupture did not, however, stop Margai and his party from supporting Bankie's motion asking the government to pass laws restricting the purchase of land in the Colony by aliens.[44] The attempt by the *Sierra Leone Observer*, the organ of the S.L.P.P., to make an issue of the legislation was ignored by the parliamentary party. The motion was passed by an overwhelming majority.[45]

This co-operation and mutual goodwill went back to the previous year when it seemed that each side could not do enough to assist and support the other side. Bright 'ably seconded' W. H. Fitzjohn's motion calling on the government to accelerate Africanisation in the Civil Service, especially the Education Department, though he had opposed a previous motion by the same mover asking for more scholarships for students studying in America. On the latter, he objected to the introduction of American Culture in Sierra Leone, a 'defiance of British culture which we cannot afford to dispense with'! He supported the Africanisation motion, insisting that he was not against expatriates when no Africans were available, but 'when we find qualified Africans that spirit of antagonism is created in us…in my opinion I may say that I support Africanization of the Civil Service, because I appreciate the fact that from the psychological standpoint, the African could only be his own teacher'.[46] The motion was passed. In moving to other matters we need to note the consistency of Bright in his attitude to the needs and interests of his African compatriots. To this end we may also take notice of his support for Fitzjohn's motion asking the government to tar the main roads in the Protectorate.[47]

Finally, when in July 1955 Wallace-Johnson moved that the government take immediate action to implement the government's statement for a new constitution, Bright supported Milton Margai's standpoint that they should not rush things. Insisting that the government needed to sound opinion before putting its cards on the table, Bankie added that it was dangerous for government to submit a draft constitution for the people without consulting them. This co-operative episode, coming after such a record of abuse and antagonism, so amazed Wallace-Johnson that he sourly observed that he was 'much pleased to hear the observations which have been made, and to know that the Leader of the Opposition and Leader of the Government side are now political bedmates, and they are moving on real good terms of political relationship'. He was so bitter and abusive that Beoku-Betts, the Vice-President of the Legislative Council, had to ask him to withdraw his statement.[48] This honeymoon between the two parties did not last.

Notwithstanding Bankie's statement on the issue of the Constitution, the N.C.S.L. took the initiative in making positive proposals. It suggested 1961 as the date for independence for Sierra Leone; and accepted a 'unicameral system of government' instead of a federation, in deference to 'public opinion'. Even the blasé Sam Metzger was suitably impressed to comment favourably on the N.C.S.L.'s 'masterly handling' of the Constitution that made 'the People's team of experts and University men look like literary puppets'.[49]

This more positive outlook in N.C.S.L.'s political programme did not change the fixity of the political situation, however, because it seemed that the government had decided to ignore Bankie, whatever the merits of his arguments. Even in the opposition benches he could only rely on Rogers, Williams and C. M. A. Thompson. According to his own evidence; J. C. O. Crowther virtually stood alone; and, of course, he later joined the S.L.P.P.[50] Wallace-Johnson had severed links almost from the beginning in 1952. Hence Bankie's record in Legislative Council was a catalogue of defeats. The unkindest irony of all was that Sierra Leone's most experienced politician and legislator did not attend the closing session of the old Assembly in 1957 because he was ill. He was destined not to sit in the new House of Representatives in 1958.[51]

On the other hand, although there were a couple of efficient and hardworking individuals in government, the latter did not requite itself well. There were problems, no doubt, but some of these were handled with ineptitude and incompetence; others were not of their making but consequences of the world economic situation and current trends in the country. In the 50s, Margai had to contend with the problems of ensuring the survival of his regime and, at the same time, wrestle with the social and economic questions that seemed to be piling up during this period.[52] The diamond boom of the mid 50s diverted a great deal of labour from the agricultural sector. People, thousands of them, risked life and limb to get rich quick. Consequently, agriculture suffered, and there were resultant phases of food scarcity. More than that, the rush to the diamond areas brought in its train many undesirable consequences – smuggling and other illicit activities which taxed the resources of the security agents of the government. Boom towns such as Koidu sprang up over night and, as mining frontier towns, they brought their own social and developmental problems. These, which specifically emanated from Kono, the diamond belt, and the suspicion that the government was not doing much to help the area that was contributing as much as 43 per cent of the total export of Sierra Leone, led to the founding of the Kono Progressive Movement (K.P.M.) in 1955 by Tamba S. Mbriwa. The party, drawing its support from young men determined to exploit the mineral resources of their district in the interests of Konos, also articulated the grievances of farmers whose lands had been expropriated by mining interests. The party did cause a stir and drew attention to the plight of the Konos.[53]

As the affluence of the people became more visible, taxation was increased. This increase, for instance, in the provinces, was accompanied by extortion and oppression by Paramount Chiefs, who, apparently convinced that the government would protect them (since Margai had always insisted that the institution of chieftaincy would be respected by his government), made endless illegal demands, including forced labour, on their subjects.[54]

In Freetown, the economic position of the workers was characterised by low wages and rising costs of essentials and this led to demands for more pay. The discussion of this pay demand in 1954, and the disagreement resulting from it, gave rise to a general strike by workers called out by their leader Marcus Grant on 9 February 1955. It lasted for several days and was accompanied by looting and damage to property, including residences of Ministers. The army had to come in to establish order. Many deaths occurred.[55] In November 1955 demonstrations against taxes and the heavy-handed rule of chiefs began in Port Loko. By 1956 the unrest had engulfed the entire Protectorate. Order was eventually restored, after much killing by the army units. Chiefs who were found guilty of abuse of power by a Commission of Inquiry were punished. And reforms that would reduce the powers of chiefs were introduced.[56]

These two events are important. In the first place they drew attention to the fact that all was not well and they forced the government to be more alert to the problems of the common people. Secondly, they contributed to the alignment of political forces and the identification of interests among groups that were politically and culturally apart. And, of course, while Cartwright and Kilson have fairly well treated these episodes, it is important to say that these events brought certain Krio leaders much closer to the masses in the Protectorate. C. B. Rogers-Wright established his credentials through the counselling work he did for those involved in the disturbances. The membership of his party increased correspondingly. Bright's party, too, did gain from the spin-offs of the 1955–6 disturbances.[57] For instance, N.C.S.L. got the sympathy of a local leader of some prominence in Kambia district because of some help it had given to the group. This help, Bright's sister, Lerina, told the author, was given to the people in their fight against their chief, Yumkella. They were sufficiently impressed to even invite her to stand for their constituency in the next general election. The invitation was responded to, but the anti-Krio feeling whipped up by the S.L.P.P. in 1957 was such that Lerina was prevented from filing her nomination paper through the active opposition of I. B. Taylor-Kamara (who told her she was not a Temne and she could not stand for Temne people), Mahmoud Ahmed and Bai Farima Tass.[58] So ended an attempt at rapprochement.

In one way, the 1955 strike in Freetown did promise to lift the sagging fortunes of Bankie. The workers turned to him for advice and he did speak to them in front of his house at Garrison Street. He asked them not to loot, but to go and sit down until the government answered them. Spies were sent to monitor the meeting, and, as a result of the garbled account they took back to the authorities, Bright was accused of having incited the workers. It was claimed that he exploited the situation and even actively engineered it to embarrass the government and discredit Margai. He did not have to do that to dishonour his political foe, because revelations after 1958 proved that though Margai himself may have had clean hands, those of his colleagues were not half as clean.[59] As for Bright's involvement, the Commission of Inquiry set up to look into the riot could find no evidence to implicate the Opposition Leader in a diabolical plot against the government. The Commission comprised Sir John Shaw (Chairman), the Hon. Mr Justice C. S. Acolatse, G. G. Honeyman, C.B.E. Q.C., and J. P. L. Scott (Administrative Officer, Sierra Leone), Secretary. Various lawyers held briefs for the interested parties. The Solicitor-General, S. A. Benka-Coker, and J. H. Smythe, Crown Counsel, held briefs for the government. After sitting for over a month, the Commission concluded, with reference to Bright's implication in the strike, that

> Dr. Bright's speech was not, according to the terms reported to, and accepted by us, on the face of it an inflammatory speech. It encouraged the strike in emotional terms, it attacked the government in general and certain Ministers in particular, and offered support of his Political Party; but it did not actually exhort to violence. Indeed, he made some reference to the importance of peaceable behaviour.

And, of course, this was more in the nature of Bright; for all along his career, as we have shown in previous pages, he eschewed violence as a means of protest. Nevertheless, a man of his position and political experience should have informed himself of the issues involved. Rather, by complacently accepting the possible break down in sanitation and electricity, which he said was of no interest to hungry men, the Commissioners considered that in their view 'the speech was unwise'. Not satisfied with giving him a mild ticking off, the Commission made a great point of insisting that 'we do not think, however, that it was his intention to incite to violence; and, indeed, there is no evidence that his speech had that effect'. Marcus Grant, the strike leader, was not so lucky; he came in for some severe roasting from the Commission, who felt that he had abused his power of trust, while Beoku-Betts, A. B. Magba Kamara, and Kandeh Bureh were showered with warm praises for their initiative in negotiating for the end of the strike. The government and its coercive forces were exonerated from blame. It was a neat job of rehabilitation and restoration of confidence.[60]

For Bright, the clock had turned full circle. Exactly nineteen years previously he and Betts had identified with, and championed, the cause of workers in a similar labour protest against a European colonial government. They burnt their fingers badly, and the colonial administration could not find enough expletives to condemn them. This time, he was not railed against by the establishment. He was exonerated of any charge of subversion, but he was told that he ought to have known better than to have got himself involved in a quarrel about which he did not know much. On the other hand, his former friend once again picked up the plaudits and his fortune sparkled blindingly. The episode is just one example of the unrelenting catalogue of misfortunes experienced by Bright in the latter part of his political career. However, the fact that the workers consulted him and asked him to speak to them suggests that he still commanded the respect of the ordinary folk, for whom he still had some relevance.

The S.L.P.P. weathered these storms, slightly battered, but resilient and determined enough to take all comers in the election of 1957. As they told their audience, they had been ruling since 1951 and they had had the experience of governing. The S.L.P.P. had not been happy with the 1951 Constitution and had made this known to the British government.[61] And, quite apart from this, and the N.C.S.L.'s own loud complaints, normal constitutional procedure and developments elsewhere ensured that the constitution would be revised to make for more control by Africans and eventual independence. Thus, in July 1954, the Keith Lucas Commission (chaired by Bryan Keith Lucas, Nuffield College, Oxford) was asked to look into the electoral system and to make recommendations. Other members of the commission were Bankole-Bright, A. T. A. Beckley, Y. D. Sesay, Banja Tejan-Sie, and P. C. Kai-Samba. They presented a unanimous report which made a few broad reforms. The most important ones were that universal adult suffrage was given to the Colony and Bo, provided voters had been resident in their areas for six months. In the rest of the Provinces the vote was given to all adult males over twenty-one years who paid the local head tax and also to women over twenty-one who paid tax. Full universal adult suffrage for the whole country was expected to take effect in 1961.[62]

Bright subsequently felt that the recommendations were not faithfully carried out. And the acrimony which these allegations produced delayed the implementation of the report and the first general elections.[63] In the meantime, suggestions for a new constitution were submitted by the two main parties and individuals. There were not many major differences in the submissions of the S.L.P.P. and N.C.S.L. Both argued for majority control by Africans and the exercise of power by the Prime Minister, moderated by the presence of the governor in the executive and the retention of his Reserve

Powers.[64] On the question of the distribution of seats, N.C.S.L., still insisting that mere numbers were not an exclusive factor in democracy, proposed giving fifteen seats each to the Colony and Protectorate. What they sought was democratic self-government.

> Not democracy as a matter of forms and institutions, but that democracy of a set of determined values, real and useful, whereby the dignity of each group is accorded an equal respect and from which the rights to freedom of speech, conscience and association can be enjoyed equally by both communities but which is now denied one group owing to the unbalanced majority constituted under the Constitution, which has been a complete failure.[65]

The S.L.P.P., naturally, disagreed and counter-proposed a 52-seat legislature called the House of Representatives, which would give thirty seats to the Protectorate and twelve to the Colony.[66] However, one recommendation made by Bright's party which, whether by design or fortuition, was realised, was 'that the year 1961 be the determining date for democratic self-government for Sierra Leone as a whole within the British Commonwealth'.[67]

In the final analysis the 1957 Constitution provided for fifty-seven seats: four ex-officios; two nominated members; fourteen elected by the Colony; twenty-five elected by the Protectorate and twelve Paramount Chiefs indirectly elected. The franchise was still different for the two parts, though it was planned to be uniform by 1961.[68]

The old Legislative Council was dissolved on 8 April 1957 and an election took place on 3 May 1957. A good account of this first National Election can be read in Scott's article. However, one or two features of the election need mentioning here.[69] The 1957 election, more than the 1951, as reflected in the newspapers, the scurrilous songs and menacing postures of the crowds, was fought in an atmosphere of vilification and unbridled tribalism.[70] The S.L.P.P., of course, as a government party, aided by its stranglehold in the District Councils, clearly had the edge over the other parties. And the N.C.S.L., much as it did try, could not adapt itself to mass politics, the haranguing and the hustling of such activities. Bright ridiculously continued to address his audience in English! The Krio tag did harm his party though some Protectorate people had become members of the N.C.S.L.[71] The parties fielded the following number of candidates: S.L.P.P. – fielded for all seats; N.C.S.L. – eleven; Labour Party – six; S.L.I.M. – four; U.P.P. – twelve in the Colony, six in the Protectorate.[72] The S.L.P.P. won twenty-five seats (four unopposed); U.P.P. five seats; N.C.S.L. – none; Labour Party – none; S.L.I.M. – none; Independents – nine. It was an overwhelming victory for the S.L.P.P. and, in some way, vindicated its claim to be nationally representative, though certain irregularities and patterns of voting might raise some question marks on this claim.[73] One major disaster was Bankie's failure to retain his seat. He lost his deposit, polling 316 votes compared with the S.L.P.P. candidate, P. W. H. Wright's 2,642 votes; even Blyden beat him. This rejection of Sierra Leone's 'doyen politician' was the unkindest cut of all, though inevitable. In August he had been forced to give up the leadership of the Council in favour of Columbus Thompson.[74] Many claim that the mental anguish and heartbreak drove him to the grave.

Milton Margai was appointed as Prime Minister in 1958. He narrowly escaped a palace coup in that same year, dodged the vicious swipes and blows Siaka Stevens aimed at him with his P.N.P., E.B.I.M., and A.P.C. parties and, in 1960, he succeeded in attracting opposition members such as C. B. Rogers-Wright and John Nelson-Williams to his side. A United National Front of all parties was formed. Sir Milton Margai (knighted in 1959) led his country to independence on 27 April, 1961, the year chosen by Bright; but the date also commemorated the outbreak of the Hut Tax War (1898) in the South.

9

Bankole-Bright and colonial politics: an assessment

On the death of Bright, Sir Milton Margai gave a generous tribute and carried his appreciation further by making substantial contributions to the funeral of Bankie.[1] Even his brother, Albert Margai, proclaimed that Bright's death was 'one of the outstanding events of 1958'.[2] Indeed, the S.L.P.P., holding its convention at that time, sent a message of condolence to Bankie's family 'for the irreparable loss not only to them, but to the entire nation, of one who played a most distinguished role in the awakening of National consciousness not only in Sierra Leone, but in the whole of West Africa, and who was always ready to defend the cause of justice and freedom'.[3] The *Daily Mail* reviewed his achievements over the years, while *West Africa*, still impenitent, recalled that 'Sierra Leone's great veteran politician' had hindered the introduction of the 1951 Constitutional Changes 'fearing that the values of the Creoles of the colony would be obliterated by the peoples of the Protectorate'.[4]

The last word came from his gad fly, Wallace-Johnson. He confessed that Bright had inspired him to follow the career of journalism. But he went on to say that Bright had his faults, and that he had crossed swords with him many a time; W.-J. was still convinced that Bright's attitude had delayed the country from freeing itself from the tentacles of British colonialism.[5] Bankie was a patriot of his race and country no doubt, 'but it is also a fact that his patriotism was narrow minded'. His Sierra Leone was distant from the common man and his attitude could rightly be applied to his view of the whole African continent.

> Dr. Bright believed in aristocracy however decadent and out of date. To him the term 'British Subject' was a great honour and for any one to think of changing the nomenclature for something else that one could not be regarded as a patriot. *And yet throughout his life Dr. Bankole-Bright was not considered a worthy competitor for a British Empire title.*

Dr Bright was a philanthropist, insisted his erstwhile opponent, and he had demonstrated this a number of times; for example, he was one of the founders of W.A.S.U.; he championed the cause of Margai in 1928; and, W.-J. reminded his audience, if Bright had had his way, education would have been free and compulsory in Sierra Leone. However,

one of Dr. Bright's greatest drawbacks, which in my opinion, led him to that
position which made his life in these latter days to become a bit hazardous was,
that he was not only a *positive man* but almost an impossible type of politician:
he appeared to see everything only from one angle. He was rather a one way
traffic dramatist in politics. Thus in most instances, he had to play the solo
music which attracted no dancer.

   Dr. Bright has lived his life. He played his part and he has reaped his reward.
He is dead but it certainly would not be easy to forget such an individual whose
life and activities in the community will go into historical record for better or
for worse.

Years after his death it has been heard said by A.P.C. leaders that Bright
was one of our most courageous nationalist fighters and builders of our
nation, though the ruling regime has done nothing to give practical
expression to this appreciation. As late as 1983 Professor Canon Sawyerr
could still have fond memories of 'the best politician he had ever known',
who talked a lot of rubbish, of course, but had a 'grasp of politics'.[6] Thomas
Decker recalled in 1975 that Bankie was 'one of the bravest persons' he had
ever come across,[7] while one of our historians has been courageous enough
to state that fears which Bright had articulated were, in retrospect, not
unfounded.[8] Finally, Dr Fitzjohn, who, by his own account had no cause to
admire Bright, said: 'But we will always say of Dr. Bright, who earned the
distinction of honourable gentleman by service, that although he was in every
respect Victorian, he was one of the most brilliant politicians and Statesmen
that West Africa ever produced.'[9]

   So in spite of all these encomia, what made Bright such a tragic figure? The
Daily Mail for 17–20 December, for instance, gave more space to the death
of Pope Pius XII and the lawsuit between M. S. Mustapha and John Nelson-
Williams than to somebody who was, by the admission of his contemporaries,
a national hero.[10] It would seem that even as early as this contemporary
writers had begun to neglect Bright. Historians have not respected Sir
Milton's fervent wish either.

   However, the purpose of this assessment is to identify his bequests to
Sierra Leone, to place him among our nationalist heroes. Many questions
would, of course, arise, such as, for instance, whether some of his fears for
democracy were proved justified, but these may take more than this work to
answer satisfactorily. Indeed, the analysis suggested here places the man in
the context of Sierra Leone history.

   A crucial factor in the biography of Bankie was the man's personality. He
was very much attached to his elitist background. He could not suffer fools
(black or white) gladly. He was consumed by his own sense of omniscience.
He was conceited, and he tended to be inflexible – these made him unable to
relate with many people. And, in an increasingly populist world, he was out
of rhythm with his contemporaries – this harmed his political life. One judge
described him as a bully. Certainly, he had strong, maybe overbearing mien;
and so he sometimes tended to be impervious to suggestions. While Betts'

suave urbanity and *gentil* humour invited confidence and acceptance, Bright's forbidding countenance and hectoring manner inspired fear and awe. People became uneasy in his presence. Again, Betts and Wallace-Johnson could trim their sails and adjust to new situations, the latter to the extreme point of founding and changing about four to six parties within twenty years. But Bright was the proverbial oak. He stood his ground until uprooted by the storm, though, as has been cited earlier, there were occasions when he showed a surprising capacity for flexibility.[11]

But Bright was not without some good and attractive qualities. He was a good dresser, neat and fashionable. His bowler hats, well-tailored suits and inevitable cigars may have supplied ammunition to his critics with which to ridicule him, but they were also points of reference to the sophisticated young gentlemen; they certainly must have lent some colour and interest to the drab walls of the Legislative Council Chamber. One gift which everybody aspired to emulate was his peerless ability as a public speaker. On this point there is no disagreement. Many people recall how Bankie could keep his audience spellbound by his absolute wizardry with words. Even a person as blasé as Wallace-Johnson was impressed. Bankie's speeches in parliament were classics – none could beat him. Records of these are a study in parliamentary diction. His contributions to debates, even in the twilight years of the fifties, were monumental.

In a parliamentary career that totalled twenty-one years, he gave the legislature a positive position in Sierra Leone politics. The issues he raised there, from inquiries into salary differentials to motions of censure on the government for its racialist-motivated policies, from sensitive subjects like the Assessors' Ordinance and the V.D. Bill furore to women's suffrage, all underlined his firm belief that matters which affected the common weal must, and should, be decided in the Legislative Council. The powers of the members might be restricted, but nonetheless they were there to look after the public interest. Our experience of post-independence parliamentary usage, practice, and performance surely elevates Bright's parliamentary accomplishments to a pedestal of incomparable distinction – a paradigm of legislative competence, devotion and commitment, and fearless independence.

One quality not possessed by many of his contemporaries was his indomitable courage. He spoke what he believed in and damned the consequences. In a profession where a man's word was not taken at face value, it was a quality worth emulating. In a positive way he used this to defend his race and people. This is important because, though people like Bright are often caricatured in the literature as collaborationists only interested in securing their privileged position in the colonial setting, it is necessary to remember that we are talking about a time when the whiteman's position was virtually impregnable, when blackmen had to salute whitemen, no matter their status. And it took a lot of courage to say 'Boo' to the whiteman; it was courageous of Bright to tell the governor, who was *in loco regis*, to his face that he had iron lungs, or to tell him that if he wished to be respected he must show the courtesy that Bright's position as the people's representative merited![12] Again, it was a demonstration of incomparable courage and audacity for him to go on to move a motion after he had been threatened by His Excellency. Betts tried to upstage this once, but it did not quite come off.[13] The cases of Barber, Rabitt and many others clearly established Bright as a dauntless fighter for the respect and dignity of his people's race. He encouraged others to have self respect and to demand consideration from the white colonialist.

Bluntness, forthrightness and an irrepressible courage were part of Bright's make-up, and so when he did take a position he was just being his natural self; but it could also be argued that had he been better able to dissemble his feelings, he might have got on with the establishment and with his colleagues.

Another accomplishment which many activists of Bright's genre did not seem able to attain was to escape the punitive clutches of the establishment. Stories abound of people who became too loud in their criticisms of the administration and were conveniently found guilty of this or that crime and received gaol sentences. May, Wallace-Johnson, Thomas George and S. M. O. Boyle are nearer examples. Bankole-Bright, for one reason or another, was never incarcerated, though he had a few close escapes. Was it just luck? Or, as his nephew suggested, was he such an astute linguist, so able to express himself, that he did not fall foul of the authorities?[14] Hardly; May and Wallace-Johnson, for example, could express themselves with equal facility and yet they became victims of the system. Should one then conclude, from an admittedly small evidence, that Bankole-Bright escaped the wrath of the government because the latter was sometimes wary of the political capital that could be made out of any overtly vindictive retribution inflicted on its enemy, especially when that enemy was as popular as Bright was in the 20s and 30s? It may just be possible, and we may not be able to supply a more convincing answer based on present available evidence, but Bright's case is unique in the history of political radicalism in Sierra Leone. In any case, there were more ways to skin a cat. Bright was never convicted of any crime, nor was he ever gaoled by the colonial authorities because of his political activities, but the administration made sure that he was kept out of the centre of power. Most often he was not even included in select committees or public bodies. Betts' name seemed to adorn these. One important committee to consider the Revision of Salary of Government Employees (clerical and others) to which he was appointed had its meetings suspended because of the outbreak of the Second World War in 1939.[15]

Still, Bright did leave an impressive record of achievements. These may be summarised here: he founded W.A.S.U. – the nursery of latter-day African political leaders. This, and his leadership role in the N.C.B.W.A., are significant dimensions of his pan West African Nationalism. Significantly, also, his contributions to journalism as a medium of criticism and protest against colonial rule, and his role in the institutional development of the Legislative Council, are major points to his credit. More important, his contributions to the development of politics generally in Sierra Leone are without equal. For, whether one liked his politics or not, he raised issues whose solution or discussion laid the foundation of politics in his country. Parliamentary conventions and traditions are built on test cases and precedents – and Bright supplied many of these. His belief in constitutionality as a module for protest and reform left a tradition of constitutionalism in Sierra Leone, which, except for a few aberrations, has fairly been sustained.

Bright's fight against officialdom and the defence of his people were major contributions to the growth of nationalism and political awareness. His patrician disposition is not overlooked, but his denunciation of the oi polloi, the unthinking masses, does not disqualify him as a concerned and sympathetic leader of his people. Ideologically, he was a constitutionalist, even a liberal, but he was not a democrat.[16]

His championing of legal causes, for example, the Assessors' Ordinance, did go a long way in improving the judicial system of the country. Equally, if doctors are enjoying certain privileges today they might do well to spare a moment of thought in gratitude to the man who harassed the administration to give recognition to the just demands of their profession. Many who got promoted in the Civil Service owed it to Bright for calling attention to their merits in government service.

Finally, by securing an appointment for Milton Margai, he perhaps gave the first Prime Minister the opportunity of establishing his credentials among his people which were to serve him well when he made a bid for political power. Margai did not forget this.

These achievements were secured over time; and set against the harsh realities of politics under colonial rule, they are a remarkable coup by any standard. And another facet of the Bright tragedy that we need to bring into focus was the times he lived in: given the development of British policy by the turn of the century, which clearly indicated that the Krio had been abandoned, and given the imponderables of a developing democracy such as existed in Sierra Leone, it is evident that Bright could not have become the leader of an autonomous Sierra Leone. Other Colony leaders, such as W.-J. and Lamina Sankoh who had such aspirations, were disqualified because one was discredited, and the other did not quite establish himself in the S.L.P.P. leadership. As for the latter, it had several advantages over the Colony leadership. Margai, for instance, lived an almost sheltered life, given the occupational hazards of activists in a colonial setting. He did not have to work under such adverse circumstances as Bright and his peers experienced. More to the point, he had all the advantages and none of Bright's disadvantages. This point is underscored by the British government's programme for the devolution of power to majority rule, in this case, the Protectorate. Granted that the scales were heavily tipped in favour of the chiefs, the important point to note is that Margai's own shrewd diplomacy, his behind the scenes efforts among the traditional elites, and his links with that stratum of society, added to the administrative reforms in the Protectorate, made it possible for Milton Margai to assume the leadership among the Protectorate elites. He had one more recommendation which made him preferable to the government. He had not blotted his copy book throughout his career, whereas, among the Colony elite, even those that had not been political activists, for example, M. C. F. Easmon, there were many who had black marks against their names.[17]

On the other hand, Bright may have been an accomplished politician, a fact acknowledged even by his opponents, but the rewards hardly corresponded to this estimation. Furthermore, Bright was not a good organiser, at least, he was not in the same league as Wallace-Johnson. Bright understood the fine points of politics and aspired to play the game as it was supposedly done in Britain, but he seemed to have misunderstood the rules as they applied to a colonial dependency. It was not that he was unaware of the contradictions between the ideal, the concept, and what was possible, but he believed so much in the sportsmanship of the British to play the game (according to the rules) that in the stark realities of colonialism he appeared to have confused fantasy with reality. Again and again the minutes of Colonial Office mandarins, cited in various parts of this book, showed that what obtained in Britain did not necessarily apply to Sierra Leone, especially as the Colony had been joined to the Protectorate, where a different set of laws had operated. This was made clear in the strike of 1926, in the dissolution of the City Council, in Ormsby-Gore's statement and, more dramatically, in the words of W. H. Crocker, Government Printer in the 1930s: 'Africans do not think like Europeans – no amount of education could make them understand European civilization – it is not a matter of intelligence, they are highly intelligent, it is just that they do not think as the European does.'[18] Put in another way, the African could not be assimilated, and so, therefore, they could not expect to have the same rights and privileges as obtained in Britain. This was underscored by a government statement in 1953. When Bright challenged the interference of the governor in the government led by Africans, he was told by the Attorney-General: 'The Honourable Leader of the Opposition seeks to apply to Sierra Leone certain rules of constitutional practice which are appropriate to a colony with a more advanced constitution ... My submission is that the rules which are applicable to the Governor-General of a Dominion are not applicable to the Governor of this Colony ... The Governor of this colony is both in form and in fact the Executive.'[19] The distinction has a ring of finality. But Bright, who was nurtured in British institutions and civilisation, could not understand why a distinction should be made between black and white British citizens of the Imperial Power.[20] He believed in that power, but he died very much disappointed in Britain.

The Krio contemporaries of Bright also must take some responsibility for the Bright tragedy. While they could not have done much or changed the inexorable path of fate, if they had given the support Bankie deserved they could have impressed the local government more to respect a solid representation of Krio views. The government, of course, was always happy to note the deep fissures in Krio ranks, which they were willing and able to exploit. This is not to say the Krios could not unite. They could show a solid front when the interests of the group were threatened, as they did in 1919 (Criminal Code Campaign and the 1919 strike), in 1926, and even in 1947–51, but Krio solidarity never had any sustaining effort. It was episodic. Also, the Krios are too individualistic, and too full of their own wisdom, knowledge, and expertise, and are not willing to concede leadership to others among themselves. There is always a struggle, a competition for recognition of leadership by the rest of the group. This characteristic of individualism, admirable in some respects, has been politically suicidal. It may have been a throwback to the individuality of their Nova Scotian ancestors and the ethnic diversity of their Liberated African forebears, but it helped the Colony leadership to lose in the political stakes of the dependency.

Writers have always tried to show that the Krio were a privileged group who had 'shared power with the British government through most of the colonial period'; they had dominated the Legislative Council and had exercised 'a tremendous influence on many of the final decisions in the constitutional structure' until they were challenged by the Protectorate people in the 50s.[21] However, when viewed closely against the political realities and contradictions of the British administration in Sierra Leone, the evidence does not support these claims. At the very least they need qualification and contextual perspective. Indeed, the writers themselves are not unaware of these contradictions of Anglo–Krio collaboration and Krio 'power'. For instance, Kaplan and others have argued that 'the Creoles... enjoyed maximum participation in governing the colony'.[22] Furthermore, 'it was only slowly and spasmodically that, in anticipation of independence the Creoles and the Colonial government began to adapt to the likelihood that the Colony and the Protectorate would have to be integrated politically'.[23] The suggestion is implicit that there had been a collusion between the Krios and the British government and that this pre-determined the rate of political development of the then Protectorate peoples.[24] Thus, in the early 1950s, so their arguments go, as Sierra Leone moved towards a degree of self-rule and, ultimately, independence, the indigenous peoples seeking access to power and its rewards 'began to challenge the political primacy of the Creoles'.[25] Yet, Kaplan and his colleagues did admit that once the Protectorate had been declared in 1896, 'the new British nationalism was accompanied by a belief that only the British were qualified to guide and rule the indigenous peoples. Thereafter the Creoles were excluded from the posts of power and influence they had previously held. Their self esteem and society suffered a major decline.'[26]

Of course, the statement cited earlier, suggesting 'Krio power', cannot be supported by historical evidence, but the visible evidence of Krios in positions of 'authority' and 'influence' perhaps needs an explanation. A simple one is offered, and that is, these' positions' did not necessarily reflect the realities of the Krio position in the colonial system, but they created an illusion of power. This was deliberately fostered by the British administration for obvious political reasons, to play off one side against the other. Statements made by Ormsby-Gore, Lord Hailey, and successive governors, focusing on the benefits that the Krio had derived from association with the British compared with the neglect of the greater portion of the dependency, and the similar experiences of the elite in other British territories, support this interpretation.[27]

Steady, a Sierra Leonean sociologist, contends that 'in many instances, Creoles served as assistants to, or co-administrators with, the British Colonial Officers. Consequently they became identified with the ruling group.'[28] But it was precisely as subordinate functionaries that they performed, not as initiators of policies or decision-makers. These were the preserves of the British raj. And they were jealously guarded.

All the posts Krios were appointed to were junior to those held by Europeans, even in a case when the designation of African Assistant Director of Education appeared to be more senior to that of the Senior Education Officer. When the substantive holder was away the European Education Officer acted, not the incumbent's putative deputy, the African Assistant D.O.E.[29] Similarly, the post of Deputy Postmaster-General was created to supersede that of the African Assistant Postmaster-General. It was filled by a European.[30] In fact, it was not until the late 30s that the discriminatory prefix 'African' was dropped from designations held by non-Europeans.[31] Nevertheless, the Krios had to be used because they had the requisite qualifications; they had the education that was acquired for them by their parents, not by government patronage. The pre-eminence these attributes gave them was brought about 'not by sinister design but by the undeniable fact of a longer, much longer association with western education which meant an ability to use a major world language'.[32] If non-Krios had possessed these facilities they would have been used. And, in this regard, Gaffney's monumental work on the Civil Service and his observation that the 'Creoles have not dominated the political and economic activities of Sierra Leone, although they have played a role disproportionate to their share of the population', is worthy of close study.[33]

The point of self-education needs emphasising in view of the claim by the colonial government that it had paid much attention to the Colony and had neglected the Protectorate. This myth, that the Colony was developed out of the wealth of the Protectorate, is still echoed in certain circles today. The truth of the matter is that Bright's generation was educated by its parents, not by the government. In fact, as late as 1937, Bright was urging the government to offer scholarships to Sierra Leoneans.[34] Educational institutions were largely established by Missionary bodies, with Krios themselves playing an active contributory role. For example, the efforts of Reverend J. C. May in founding the M.B.H.S. in 1874 and Ezzidio in building the Wesleyan Methodist Church, are cases in point.[35] Abuke Thomas left money to found an Agricultural College for Krio boys; Obadiah Johnson and John Randle provided money to establish a Science Faculty at Fourah Bay College.[36] The government established its first school, the Bo School in the Protectorate in 1906, and it was not until 1913 that the Government Model (Secondary School) was established in Freetown. This later developed into the Prince of Wales School, founded in 1925, primarily to provide science education; and it was not exclusive to the Colony. Interestingly enough, there was much opposition to the Prince of Wales School from Krio bodies because they resented its privileged position as a government-financed school.[37] It was not until the 1940s that the government began to give scholarships to deserving Sierra Leoneans for further studies. In short, the evidence to support the claims of the C.E.A. in 1922, echoed by R. B. S. Koker in 1953, and subsequently cited by researchers, that their education had been wilfully neglected by the Colony, whose schools were kept with money which should have been spent on introducing compulsory elementary and intermediate education in the Protectorate, is difficult to find.[38] In several passages in this work reference has been made to agitation in the Colony for the educational development of the interior.[39]

But this question needs a further look. The bulk of the revenue of Sierra Leone for long was derived from its agricultural produce and the value of this suffered under the vagaries of the world market. For years, successive administrations bewailed the consistent deficits in Sierra Leone.[40] In the 30s, minerals were discovered, but it was not until the early 40s that their exploitation was begun. Proceeds from this extractive industry beefed up the economy. A special Fund was set up to develop the Protectorate from the revenues from the mines. The Colony was excluded from this. If one takes a look at the statistics one will find that a great percentage of the money spent was for the upkeep of the British administration.[41] Indeed, on several occasions, Bankie raised the question of local employment, when there was a surplus in the Estimates, as, for instance, in 1927, not only to encourage parents to send their children to school, but also to reduce the overheads of the government.[42] He was given all sorts of evasive answers. Figures of African doctors employed in relation to European doctors have been given in a previous section, and also we noted that it was not until 1937 that an African was appointed to the substantive post of Magistrate. Elsewhere in the Civil Service, promotions to senior posts meant loss of salary, and it did not mean increased authority. To cite one example, the Civil Service List for 1930 shows a top heavy European establishment:[43] in the Education Department two of its eleven staff members were Africans: C. A. E. Macauley, African Assistant Director of Education, and A. T. Sumner, Vice-Principal, Protectorate Central College; the Medical Services had twenty-eight doctors – twenty were Europeans, seven were from the Colony and one from the Protectorate; the Law Officers – four – were all white; agriculture was all white; survey, all white; in the Railway Department only one African, James C. Hamilton, Staff Superintendent, held a senior post out of twenty-two in the staff. When one recalls that European expatriates averaged £650–1,400 p.a., compared to their African counterparts' £360–£720 p.a., then it is not difficult to guess where the money went. Thus, what is being suggested here is that the Krios did not have any exclusive benefits, if indeed they had any benefits at all, from the wealth derived largely from the Protectorate. The Krios were able to sustain their educational and social needs through thrift (in some cases parsimony – Abuke Thomas was noted for that eccentricity), private employment, or trade, to some extent, and money earned from services in the other colonies. Evidence pointing to the financial contributions of exiles in the Congo, Nigeria, the Gold Coast, and the Gambia, to the economic position of their group abound. Fyfe, for instance, cites many examples of Krio exiles who worked in the neighbouring colonies, sent their children to schools in Freetown and returned home to die in their country. The Sierra Leone Friendship Society did not forget to send money for the strikers of 1926. In the 20s about half of the lawyers in Calabar were Sierra Leoneans.[44] And these, of course, would remit money for the upkeep of their families and to build houses. Krio wealth was externally generated. In short, what is being suggested here is the hope that some day somebody might do a thorough investigation into the economic power base of the Krio *vis-à-vis* the Protectorate in the colonial setting. It will throw some light on this aspect of Sierra Leone history.

The same government that had talked of its exclusive attention to the Colony did confess to having neglected the Colony. An official conclusion after looking into City Council affairs in the 1920s, was that the citizens of Freetown were too poor since the end of the first World War to afford increased rates. Yet they did nothing for the Council, until they took it over in 1926, not because they wanted to bail the Council out but because the 'independence' of that institution had become intolerable. It had to be ended.

And this leads a return to an area that has been mentioned earlier, but which needs reemphasising, i.e., the so-called 'political power' and influence of the Krios. There is much talk about Krio dominance in colonial Sierra Leone. But what did this mean in practice? The Krios were allowed only one institution, a local government – the City Council in 1893; thirty-three years later, it was taken from them and, until independence, they could not point to any local government they could call their own. Certainly, they filled the Legislative Council, because the provisions of the constitution, such as they were, made it possible for these people to be there. Moreover, they were educated, westernised, they were trained in the ways of the white man, having learnt about their institutions and political customs. And so they could articulate the rising expectations of their people; they loomed large in the affair and, for reasons of their own, the British encouraged them to believe that they had the making of a modern elite. And yet, as Marcus Jones graphically puts it, 'the Aristocrats of the old Legislative Council never enjoyed the privilege or had the opportunity of exercising effective power. Always in the minority, their role was a frustrating one. They appeared to be a miniature opposition, criticizing but never initiating policy.' They were perpetually in opposition and permanently excluded from power.[45] The Legislative Council, then, was a forum for the ventilation of grievances to which the colonial power responded as it considered opportune or adequate. When some measure of political power was conceded in 1951 the gainers were not Krio. There is no evidence, therefore, to support the claims of some writers that the Protectorate challenged Krio power in 1951. 'Krio power' was non-existent. On the contrary, the Protectorate had always had political power, fractured though it might have been during colonial rule, but it had potentials. And these revealed their true nature in the fifties.

Be that as it may, the British policy of divide and rule was so successful that it created and perpetuated a dichotomy in Sierra Leone. Peoples on either side tended to regard each other as different; politics was seen in terms of them against us. And these differences were institutionalised and perpetuated in legal status, land tenure, and administration, as well as in many covert ways. Despite these 'iron curtains', however, there were meeting points between the two areas. These have been identified already. And so the picture of Krio exclusiveness is certainly not supported by evidence. Protectorate and Colony issues were equally advanced by the enlightened Colony leaders though, in some cases, preferences were shown for one side against the other. But, positive outreaches made by the Colony politicians have not been given the exposure they merit, rather the historiography tends to overlook these and to articulate the negative ones to the ridiculous extent that one writer claimed 'Creoles rarely appeared in the Protectorate except on short term of official service – rarely settled in the Protectorate rather they migrated to Gold Coast and Nigeria.'[46] A look at Chalmers' *Report*, the newspapers of this period, memorial tablets in Freetown churches, and the autobiographies of a few Sierra Leoneans will quickly dismiss this assertion.[47] And, as for the negative points, for instance, the objection of the Colony to chiefs entering the Legislative Council, or the ultramontanism of the 40s, these have to be put in perspective to explain why they did happen.

If, as has been argued in these pages, the Krios never had the power they had been alleged to possess during the colonial period, why did they fight as it were to keep what they did not have in the first place? As Professor Ballandier has argued, colonial regimes very often allow some role to the educated elite, some area in which to manoeuvre, although the rewards remain far behind the demands of such a social category. Above all, they usually impose a ceiling to advancement.[48] Their protégés, for this is what they really are, are allowed to go thus far and never beyond a specific point. It is within this prescribed arc that the Krios operated and secured their achievements. To this end then, one can argue in the context that because developments in the 40s and 50s appeared to threaten to destroy even these minor benefits in the colonial reward system, the colony citizens reacted the way they did.

When Eldred Jones joined the Civil Service in 1943, S. A. D. Peters, as Chief Clerk, was a 'distantly elevated figure in the hierarchy'. And the latter was overjoyed to be made Administrative Secretary, the first African to be so appointed in 1951 – thirty-one years after joining the Civil Service![49] These things appeared big in their eyes yet in terms of power and status they were relative *vis-à-vis* the white colonial establishment and the potential of the Protectorate. And so, when one talks about 'Krio Power', it must be seen in this limited circumscribed context, not, as the literature suggests, as co-regents of the British raj. They were not allowed that much latitude. The foundation of their position was always weak. Britain could always crack the whip when it suited her. Thus, in the case of the Krios, they were given this much allowance – they were next in the social hierarchy, but they were bound to the system by a promise implicit from the founding of the Colony. 'Under the British', says Gershon Collier, 'the Creoles had been led to believe that as the most educated and "prepared" element in the country they were eminently suitable to assume the responsibilities of leading Sierra Leone to independence.'[50] This point has been repeated by other writers including Roy Lewis in his semi-official publication.[51] And the genuine belief in this manifest destiny can be gauged from Alhadi's pamphlet.[52] To this end Kilson's remarks that 'Creoles were less concerned with the political reality they confronted than with ritualizing the values and position associated with their past ascendency. As with primitive peoples, ritualization of life's circumstances becomes life (reality) itself 'are both unfair and unkind.[53] It is true that there was an element of false reality in their hopes, but it was a feeling based on the visible evidence of the commanding positions the Krios seemed to hold – the illusion of power – in the colonial setting. And they were too British to disbelieve the promises of their benefactors. Yet the signs were there; they failed to recognise the evidence that they had been disinherited. And when it finally dawned on them that they would not succeed the British raj they were shocked out of their dreamland. They could not believe that after over a hundred years of apprenticeship they would be left out in the cold, hence the melodrama of the 40s. However, this et tu Brute syndrome apart, they did have real fears about their future position in an independent Sierra Leone. Milton Margai did try to allay these fears by appointing Krios to important positions, but it was a stop-gap policy. Soon it was made clear that the Krios could not expect to have any special consideration in a 'united' Sierra Leone. Nor is it being argued here that they should demand and expect special treatment, but the continued discrimination against Krios, with special reference to the land-tenure system, is one major factor that perhaps inhibits total integration in modern Sierra Leone. In post-independent Sierra Leone the Krios have been used more than once as the whipping boys for the misfortunes of the nation. Gershon

Collier's apologia for the S.L.P.P. regime forcefully suggests this view.[54] And indications do give the impression that the situation of the Krio is not much different in post-independent Sierra Leone from what it was during the colonial period.[55]

Notes

INTRODUCTION

1. *Daily Mail*, 15 and 17 Dec. 1958.
2. Quoted in Miles F. Shore, 'Biography in the 1980s', in Theodore K. Rabb and Robert I. Rotberg, *The New History: The 1980s and Beyond. Studies in Inter-disciplinary History* (Princeton, 1982), pp. 89–113.

1: GROWING UP: BACKGROUND TO HIS FAMILY AND EARLY LIFE

1. They were also to be found as far South as the Congo Free State (Zaire) and South Africa. See S. J. S. Cookey, 'West African immigrants in the Congo, 1885–1895', *Journal of the Historical Society of Nigeria*, 3, 2 (December 1965), pp. 261–70; *Sierra Leone Weekly News*, 25 May 1901; C. Fyfe, 'Reform in West Africa: The Abolition of the Slave Trade', in J. F. A. Ajayi and M. Crowder (eds.), *History of West Africa* (London, 1974), 2, pp. 30–56.
2. On the Krio diaspora the following are authoritative: J. F. Ajayi, *Christian Missions in Nigeria, 1841–1891: The Making of a New Elite* (Evanston, 1965); E. A. Ayandele, *The Missionary Impact on Modern Nigeria: 1842* (London, 1966); J. H. Kopytoff, *Preface to Modern Nigeria: The 'Sierra Leoneans' in Yoruba, 1830–1890* (Wisconsin, 1965); J. U. J. Asiegbu, *Slavery and the Politics of Liberation, 1787–1860* (London, 1969); A. J. G. Wyse, *Searchlight on the Krio of Sierra Leone* (Institute of African Studies, Fourah Bay College, Occasional Paper 3, 1980) and 'The Sierra Leone Krios: A Reappraisal From the Perspective of the African Diaspora', in J. E. Harris (ed.), *Global Dimensions of the African Diaspora* (Washington, 1982), pp. 309–40; Pauline H. Baker, *Urbanization and Political Change: The Politics of Lagos, 1947–1967* (Berkeley, 1974); Elizabeth Isichei, *The Ibo People and the Europeans* (London, 1973). The term Krio, used throughout this study, refers to the people known as Creoles. Whenever the latter word appears it is part of a quotation or a direct citation. For an explanation of the use of the more current term, Krio, see, for example, this author's article 'On misunderstandings arising from the use of the term "Creole" in the literature on Sierra Leone: a rejoinder', *Africa*, 49, 4, 1979, pp. 409–15.
3. The authoritative works on the founding of Sierra Leone and its subsequent history are: C. Fyfe, *A History of Sierra Leone* (London, 1962); Arthur Porter, *Creoledom* (London, 1963); J. E. Petersen, *The Province of Freedom: A History of Sierra Leone 1787–1870* (Evanston, 1969); C. Fyfe and E. Jones (eds.), *Freetown: A Symposium* (Freetown, 1968); I. Geiss, *The Pan-African Movement* (London, 1968); D. A. Vonque Stephen, 'A history of the settlement of liberated Africans in the Colony of Sierra Leone during the first half of the 19th century', M.A. thesis, Durham, 1962; A. B. C. Sibthorpe, *The History of Sierra Leone* (London, 1970) first published in 1868; M. Kilson, *Political Change in a West African State* (Harvard University Press, 1966); L. Spitzer, *The Creoles of Sierra Leone: Responses to Colonialism 1870–1945* (Wisconsin, 1974); cf. Wyse, 'The

192

Sierra Leone Creoles, their history and historians', *Journal of African Studies*, 4, 2, Summer 1978, pp. 228–240; A. P. Kup, *Sierra Leone: A Concise History* (London, 1975).

4. Interview with Mrs Lerina Bright-Taylor, sister of Bankole-Bright, 5 August 1974. Since frequent references will be made to this informant, all subsequent citings will take this form: Interview: LBT, and date. Mrs Bright-Taylor died in February 1976. See also CO267/633/9567/31/1, Cookson to Passfield, 23 January 1931 enclosing a petition by Bankole-Bright (N.D.). A thesis on Dr Bankole-Bright, the first serious attempt to study his career, erred in stating that he was born in Freetown. See M. A. Bah, 'Dr. Herbert C. Bankole-Bright and his impact on the growth of constitutional government and the development of political parties in Sierra Leone, 1924–1957', M.A. thesis, Howard, 1977. On the history of the Oil Rivers and nineteenth century commercial rivalry, the following are standard works; K. O. Dike, *Trade and Politics in the Niger Delta, 1830–1885* (Oxford, 1956); G. I. Jones, *The Trading States of the Oil Rivers* (London, 1963); J. C. Anene, *Southern Nigeria in Transition, 1885–1906* (London, 1966); J. E. Flint, *Sir George Goldie and the Making of Nigeria* (London, 1960); Isichei, *Ibo People* pp. 61–108.

5. CAI/0178n MSS Rev. James Quaker: Quaker to Venn, 25 March 1865 (C.M.S. Archives, London).

6. Fyfe, 'Reform in West Africa', pp. 30–56; Peterson, *Province of Freedom, passim*; T. F. V. Buxton, 'The Creole in West Africa', *Journal of the African Society*, 12, 1912–13, pp. 385–94; K. L. Little, 'The significance of the West African Creole for Africanist and Afro-American studies', *African Affairs*, 49, 197, 1950, pp. 308–19; T. C. Luke, 'Some notes on the Creoles and their land', *Sierra Leone Studies*, (O.S.), 21 (Oct. 1939), pp. 101–2. H. M. Awoyo Johnson's article, 'The vocational outlook of the Sierra Leone Creole', *S.L.S.* (O.S.), 22 (Sept. 1939), pp. 52–7, even with his limited definition of 'a Creole', subscribes to the popular view of an elitist deskborne vocational orientation of the Krios – an outlook that shuns manual labour. Yet he ends with an optimistic note that the Krios of the 1930s were showing a positive interest in industrialisation and economic expansion. This observation by Johnson was late by fifty years at the very least.

7. Note 6 above; A. Ijagbemi, 'The Freetown Colony and the development of "legitimate" commerce in the adjoining territories', *J.H.S.N.*, 5, 2 (June 1970), pp. 234–65.

8. J. D. Hargreaves, *A Life of Sir Samuel Lewis* (London, 1958), p. 4.

9. Fyfe, *A History of Sierra Leone*, p. 348.

10. *S.L.W.N.*, 20 December 1902; CO267/633/9567/31/1, Cookson to Passfield Jan. 23 1931 encl. petition by Bankole-Bright (n.d.).

11. Note 5 above; CAI/O 178 Quaker to Venn, 18 Feb. 1865. Sometimes John Bright donated to the Church sums as large as 25 guineas. Apparently, the case of Bright, a Methodist Wesleyan, giving money to the Anglican Church, is not unique. Samuel Lewis's father also gave donations to the C.M.S. at least until 1866, before the rise of militant Methodism in Sierra Leone made such a practice unwise. See Hargreaves, *Sir Samuel*, p. 8.

12. Sibthorpe, *History of Sierra Leone*, p. 42; Porter, *Creoledom*, p. 92.

13. C. Fyfe, *Africanus Horton: West African Scientist and Patriot, 1835–1883* (London, 1972) and *A History of Sierra Leone*, p. 346–349; M. C. F. Easmon, 'Sierra Leone doctors' *S.L.S.* (N.S.), 2 (June 1956), pp. 8–96 is an attempt to list the number of Sierra Leoneans who qualified as doctors since 1787 (*sic*).

14. Fyfe, *A History*, p. 748; *S.L.W.N.*, 10 Oct. 1910.

15. Fyfe, p. 471.

16. Note 4 above; Dike, *Trade and politics*, p. 50ff gives these figures for the palm oil trade in the Delta, 1827–34, as between 4,700 and 13,495 tons; the latter figure was estimated at £450, 185. But the data supplied by Dike also show that the slave trade had increased tremendously.

17. *S.L.W.N.*, 15 Oct. 1910.

18. Interview: LBT, 5 Aug. 1974. When exactly Jacob left Nigeria is not clear. His third son, Jacob (Jun.), was born in Freetown in 1886; so he could have come back either in 1884 or 1885.
19. Interviews: LBT, 5 Aug. and Pa J. C. Lucan (aged 86; now deceased), 21 Aug. 1974.
20. Interview: Pa J. C. Lucan, 21 Aug. 1974.
21. *Ibid.*; interview: LBT, 5 Aug. 1974; Alex D. Yaskey, *Thoughts on Sierra Leone* (Sierra Leone Guardian Printing Office: Freetown, 1929), pamphlet, 34 pp.
22. *S.L.W.N.*, 2 July 1892. Other foundation members included T. Bishop, J.P., T. C. Bishop, C. J. Barlatt and a number of European firms. See also *S.L.W.N.*, 15 July 1893.
23. Interview: LBT, 5 Aug. 1974; *S.L.W.N.*, 15 Oct. 1910; CO267/633/9567/31/1, Cookson to Passfield 23 Jan. 1931 encl. a petition by Bright.
24. *S.L.W.N.*, 20 Dec. 1902.
25. *S.L.W.N.*, 15 Oct. 1910; 28 Nov. 1936.
26. For instance, the brothers Shorunkeh-Sawyerr had a total of eighteen children (six and twelve) between them.
27. N. 25 above. I was told by Bankie's niece that her grandfather, Jacob Bright, had many children outside the marital home.
28. Figures culled from adverts in the *Weekly News* and trade reports by the Sierra Leone Chamber of Commerce, *S.L.W.N.*, 27 Aug. 1892; 11 Feb. 1899.
29. Interview: LBT, 5 Aug. 1974. The example of Francis (Frans) Dove, the erudite lawyer, from the celebrated Dove family 'of Freetown and Accra', who educated his three brothers and their children up to post-secondary school level, is another good case demonstrating strong family ties. See K. A. B. Jones-Quartey, 'Sierra Leone's role in the development of Ghana, 1820–1930', *S.L.S.* (N.S.), 10 (June 1958), pp. 73–83. See *S.L.W.N.*, 9 Sept. 1904 for a defence of polygamy as an African institution.
30. The word 'Aristo' needs an explanation here. In the Western context, people in this social category, i.e., the professional men and wealthy merchants, are middle class. But in the social stratification of Freetown society, these people were at the top of the social and economic pyramid, hence 'Aristo', the 'nobility', the leaders of the common folk. For a critique of this stratification, see N. D. J. Smart's articles in *Daily Mail*, 20 and 24 July 1954 and J. Nelson-Williams' rejoinder in issues of 25 and 27 August 1954; Patrice Vautier, 'Creoles of African soil: The saga of the Krio of Sierra Leone', *Balafon*, 445, (July 1979), pp. 4–9. However, C. L. Pitt, a columnist on *S.L.W.N.*, insisted in 1910 that money alone did not make one an 'aristo'. See issue of 31 Dec. 1910; Hargreaves, *A Life of Sir Samuel.*
31. Interview, S. J. C. Tuboku-Metzger, 9 Sept. 1977.
32. Tribute by I. T. A. Wallace-Johnson on the death of Bankole-Bright, *Daily Mail*, 24 Dec. 1958; interviews: LBT, 7 Aug. 1974; Pa Lucan, 21 Aug. 1974; Pa Rogers-Williams (now deceased), 23 Aug. 1974; cf. J. C. O. Crowther, 9 Sept. 1974.
33. Interview: LBT, 5 Aug. 1974.
34. See *A Booklet of the Entrance Register of the C.M.S. Grammar School* (1935).
35. The admission number of Bright is 609 and that of his younger brother is 610. But the register of the M.B.H.S. was haphazardly kept. The names of the entrants and their admission numbers are in one column, their parents/guardians and their addresses are listed under other columns, but there are many gaps, and the date of admission is not · always given. One register gave the date of admission of Jacob Bright the younger brother, as 1904, but his admission number was 610, the one following Bankole. The latter's admission date is not given, but the above date is therefore computed from his first public appearance in 1899 and the date of leaving school, which could not have been later than 1904. When he registered for his medical course in 1905 he was slightly over 21 years old. The assistance of Mr Willie Pratt, the then Vice-Principal of M.B.H.S., in locating the registers is gratefully acknowledged here.

36. Capt. F. W. Butt-Thompson, *Sierra Leone in History and Tradition* (London, 1926), pp. 204–6; G. A. Gollock, *Lives of Eminent Africans* (New York, 1928); reprinted 1969, pp. 138–41.
37. Advert in *S.L.W.N.*, 25 Feb. 1899; cf. the Syllabus of the M.B.H.S., Lagos, in G. O. Olusanya and A. B. Aderibigbe, *A Hundred Years of the M.B.H.S., 1878–1978* (Lagos, 1978), pp. 9–10.
38. Interview: Pa E. J. Robinson (aged 81 years), 25 Aug. 1975.
39. Interview: LBT, 5 Aug. 1974.
40. Interviews: Pa J. C. Lucan, 21 Aug. 1974; J. C. O. Crowther, 9 Sept. 1974; Dr H. W. Fitzjohn, 2 Oct. 1974; Pa Robinson, 25 Aug. 1975.
41. *S.L.W.N.*, 16 Dec. 1899.
42. Obituary on Dr W. A. Renner, *Supplement to the African World*, 7 April 1917; interview: LBT, 5 Aug. 1974; M. C. F. Easmon, 'Sierra Leone doctors', p. 51.
43. Interview: Ms. D. U. Wardle, Librarian, Royal College of Surgeons, Edinburgh, 16 Dec. 1976; Exam. schedules and the academic record of Bankole-Bright are deposited in the Library of the Royal College, Edinburgh.
44. *Ibid*; Bah, 'Dr. Herbert C. Bankole-Bright', p. 4. However, Adda Bishop's father was not a doctor. He was a merchant.
45. Note 43. According to the records he did not repeat any year, unlike his compatriot Ishmael Pratt. Bankie's marks in Surgery and Midwifery in his final exam in 1910 were between 60 and 70 and 60 and 65 respectively.
46. *The Student*, 426, 24 Jan. 1908. I am extremely grateful to Professor Shepperson of Edinburgh University for not only drawing my attention to this material, but also for his helpful suggestions for my research.
47. Henry Pelling (ed.), *The Challenge of Socialism* (London, 1954), p. 352. The letter from Bright was not printed. I am grateful to Professor John Hargreaves for telling me about the existence of this letter.
48. Professor Shepperson, who is interested in the careers of Africans who studied in Edinburgh in the early twentieth century, confessed to me that he was finding it difficult to lay hands on material on Edinburgh African students. However, what follows in this section was derived from a conversation with Professor Shepperson, and a visit to the library at the University. Omoniyi's book is certified in the card index as having existed but it was not available when it was requested. Conversation with Professor Shepperson, 16 Dec. 1976.
49. *S.L.W.N.*, 10 Sept. 1910.
50. Interviews: LBT, 5 Aug. 1974; Pa J. C. Lucan, 25 Aug. 1974; *S.L.W.N.*, 15 Oct. 1910.
51. *S.L.W.N.*, 9 Feb. 1918 and 7 Nov. 1914. Apparently, Jacob went on to add Olukutun to his name while he was practising in Nigeria.
52. *Ibid.*
53. *S.L.W.N.*, 9 March 1918; 24 June 1920; 26 July 1920.
54. *S.L.W.N.*, 15 Oct. 1910.
55. *S.L.W.N.*, 21 Jan. 1911.
56. *S.L.W.N.*, 22 Oct. 1910.
57. *S.L.W.N.*, 2 July 1892; Yaskey, *Thoughts on Sierra Leone.*
58. Interview: LBT, 5 Aug. 1974.
59. Bah, 'Dr. Bankole Bright,' p. 5; cf. interviews: Pa A. M. Fergusson (aged 83 years), 14 Oct. 1974; Dr W. H. Fitzjohn, 2 Oct. 1974. This informant admitted, however, that Bankie's involvement in politics could have greatly affected his practice as a doctor. For when he was a boy he knew Bright as a 'renowned doctor and politician'.
60. Easmon, 'Sierra Leone doctors', pp. 8–96.
61. CO267/613/4084, Governor of Sierra Leone to Secretary of State, 20 April 1926. Minutes by members of the Executive Council.

Notes to pages 13–15

62. A report on native medical practitioners was asked for by the Colonial Office in 1913. The report eventually sent covered the following: A. W. Easmon, Michael L. Jarrett, Bankole-Bright, Thomas Clarkson Maxwell and Ishmael Charles Pratt. Nothing was said on Bright because an earlier confidential report on him had been sent to London. I could not find it among the documents consulted. The report and the covering letter of Dr J. Wallace Collett, Acting Principal Medical Officer, make it plain that the local administration was contemptuous of local practitioners. See CO 879/112 document 133, Gov. to S of S, 21 April 1913, with enclosures. An American scholar, Dr Adel Patton, who has been researching on West African doctors who were political activists, told me about an application sent by Bright for a Colonial Medical Appointment in 1912. I was unable to consult the document, but I understand that the government response was unfavourable.
63. Colonial and Provincial Reporter (C.P.R.), 4 May 1918.
64. Interviews: LBT, 5 Aug. 1974; Pa Robinson, 25 Aug. 1975; S.L.W.N., 9 Jan. 1926. The advert informed the public that resident cases would be admitted, surgical operations would also be carried out; and attendance on Gynaecology cases would be 'a prominent feature' in the Home.
65. Interviews: Pa Rogers-Williams, 23 Aug. 1974; Pa Fergusson, 13 Oct. 1974; Pa Robinson, 20 Aug. 1975.
66. Spitzer, Creoles, ch. 1.
67. S.L.W.N. 23 Dec. 1916 and 5 April 1924.
68. Fred I. A. Omu, 'The dilemma of press freedom in Colonial Africa: the West African example', Journal of African History, 9, 2 (1968), pp. 279–98; Bah, 'Bankole-Bright', p.5.
69. S.L.W.N. 16 Nov., 21 Dec. 1901; 22 Nov. 1902, Gustav K. Deveneaux, 'Public opinion and Colonial policy in nineteenth century Sierra Leone', The International Journal of African Historical Studies, 9, 1 (1976), pp. 45–67; Omu, 'Press Freedom', J.A.H., 9, 2 (1968), pp. 279–98; Jones-Quartey, 'Sierra Leone and Ghana: Nineteenth century pioneers in West African journalism', S.L.S. (N.S.), 12 (December 1959), pp. 230–44; C. Fyfe, 'The Sierra Leone Press in the nineteenth century', S.L.S. (N.S.), 8 (June 1957), p. 234; Bankole Timothy, 'The Sierra Leone news story', West Africa, 7 Feb. 1977, pp. 248–51.
70. CO267/590/9213, Wilkinson to Milner, 8 Feb. 1921. Minutes by officials in the Colonial Office.
71. CO267/586/20495, Wilkinson to Milner, 28 April 1920.
72. Omu, 'Press Freedom', pp. 279–98.
73. Daily Mail, 24 Dec. 1958.
74. At the Newspaper Library, Colindale, London, the extant copies of the Aurora are scattered and incomplete. J. Ayodele Langley, Pan-Africanism and Nationalism in West Africa, 1900–1945. (Oxford, 1973), p. 121, wrongly states that the Aurora was founded by E. S. Beoku-Betts and that it 'flourished briefly after a fiery start in 1919'. On the contrary it began publication before 1919 and, in 1925, the ownership and editorship passed from the hands of Bankie to E. T. Nelson-Williams. See S.L.W.N. 31 Oct. 1925.
75. George Padmore, 'Democratic advance in Sierra Leone', The Crisis, 64, 3 (March 1957), pp. 149–52; J. D. (Hargreaves), 'Political prospects in Sierra Leone', World Today, 9 (1953), pp. 208–17; J. H. Price, Political Institutions of West Africa (1967), p. 153. See also West Africa, 20 Jan. 1951; 4, 18 Aug., 27 Oct., 1 Dec. 1951; 10 Nov. and Editorial of 8 Dec. 1951 etc. Other references will be given as the discussion develops. For the purpose of identifying source material for these contentions, the following are sufficient to indicate a pro-Wallace-Johnson orientation: W. J. S. Marcus Jones, 'The protection of fundamental rights and freedoms of the individual in Sierra Leone', LL.D. thesis, Yale, N.D.; cf. W. E. Blyden III, 'Sierra Leone: Pattern of constitutional change, 1924–1951', Ph.D. thesis, Harvard, 1959; F. A. N. Lisk, 'Industrial relations in Sierra

196

Leone', M.Sc. Econ. thesis, Queen's University, Belfast, 1970; M. R. Dumbuya, 'National integration in Guinea and Sierra Leone: a comparative analysis of the integrative capacities of single and dominant party regimes', Ph.D. thesis, Washington, 1974; L. Spitzer, *The Creoles*.

76. Dr W. H. Fitzjohn, J. C. Crowther, and Wallace-Johnson, all three elected members of the new Legislative Council under the 1951 constitution, rather curiously asserted that were it not for people like Bankole-Bright, Sierra Leone would have got its independence long before 1961. Such a view obviously ignores the determinant role of the colonial government. Even up to the late 1940s the timetable for independence in West Africa had nowhere taken any clear form. But see W. H. Fitzjohn, *Ambassador of Christ and Caesar* (Ibadan, 1975), p. 28; *Daily Mail*, 24 Dec. 1958.

2: BACKGROUND TO POLITICS IN THE TWENTIETH CENTURY

1. The following deal with these points: C. Fyfe, *A History of Sierra Leone*; Roy Lewis, 'Creoledom revisited', *The Geographical Magazine*, 37, 1 May 1964, pp. 9–19; Richard West, *Back to Africa: A History of Sierra Leone and Liberia* (New York, 1970); Leo Spitzer, *The Creoles*; C. Clapham, *Liberia and Sierra Leone: an Essay in Comparative Politics* (London, 1976); J. D. Hargreaves, 'Assumptions, expectations and plans: Approaches to decolonization in Sierra Leone', Paper presented at the Anglo-French Colloquium on Independence and dependence: The relation of Britain and France with their former territories, Paris, 6–8 May 1976; Ellen Gibson Wilson, *The Loyal Blacks* (New York, 1976); James W. St George Walker, *The Black Loyalists: The search for a promised land in Nova Scotia and Sierra Leone, 1783–1870* (London, 1976). 'History', said the *Daily Mail*, 'has not dealt kindly with Sierra Leone, yet its astonishing influence on the rest of West Africa remains a fact of history.' Quoted in Blyden, 'Pattern of constitutional change', page immediately preceding the introduction.

2. See Ahmed Alhadi's impassioned protest, *The Re-emancipation of the Colony of Sierra Leone* (1956) pamphlet in the Sierra Leone Collection, Fourah Bay College Library, Mt Aureol, Freetown, 23 pp.; M. Crowder, 'An African aristocracy', *The Geographical Magazine*, 31, 4 (Aug. 1958), pp. 183–90; Roy Lewis, 'Creoledom revisited', pp. 9–19; and *Sierra Leone: A Modern Portrait* (London, 1954), p. 35, noted with profound insight that 'The Creoles followed the English tradition with fatal fidelity'.

3. Hotobah-During MSS. 'My life history' (courtesy of his son I. C. Hotobah-During); *S.L.W.N.*, 9 April 1924 reporting a speech by J. C. Shorunkeh-Sawyerr.

4. *Memorial of the Celebration of the Jubilee of Her Majesty's reign and of the Centenary of Sierra Leone, 1887* (London, 1887). Lamina Sankoh, however, calls it 'spiritual slavery'. He said: 'The Creole element is the one who has been doped the most by the whiteman's religion and civilization.' *S.L.W.N.*, 6 Oct. 1951.

5. See, for example, the Hon. W. G. A. Ormsby-Gore's diatribe in his *Report of his visit to West Africa during the year 1926* (H.M.S.O., 1926), 188 pp.; Spitzer, *The Creoles*; cf. A. J. G. Wyse, 'Sierra Leone Creoles, their history and historians', *Journal of African Studies*, 4, 2 (Summer 1978), pp. 228–40; *S.L.W.N.*, 22 April 1893 for a critical comment on the use of the phrase 'Black Englishmen' by A. J. Shorunkeh-Sawyerr and his brother, J. C. Shorunkeh-Sawyerr's comparisons between the Krio and the English in *S.L.W.N.*, 9 Aug. 1924. See also *S.L.W.N.*, 6 Oct. 1951 for Lamina Sankoh's withering comment on the acculturation of the Krio.

6. Note 5 above.

7. Fyfe, *A History*; J. E. Peterson, *Province of Freedom*; Porter, *Creoledom*; Paul Hair, 'Africanism: The Freetown Contribution', *Journal of Modern Studies*, 5, 4 (1967), pp. 521–39. Quote is from P. N. Davies, *Trading in West Africa, 1840–1920* (London, 1976), p. 155.

8. Walker, *The Black Loyalists*, p. 86.
9. See, for example, *Sibthorpe's Oration on the Centenary of the Abolition of the Slave Trade by the British Government*. Delivered at Hastings Village, Sierra Leone on 2 April for 25 March 1907 (London, N.D.); *S.L.W.N.*, 21 June 1887; *The Methodist Herald*, 8 June 1887.
10. Interview, J. C. O. Crowther, 9 Sept. 1974; *West Africa*, 9 April 1955 (refs. for quotes); *S.L.W.N.*, 5 Nov. 1892. See issue of 7 Nov. 1914 for an appeal made to the administration by Rambler, a columnist, to create a regiment of 'The King's Own Creole Boys'; Luke, 'Some notes', pp. 53–66; Lewis, *Modern Portrait*; G. Collier, *Sierra Leone: Experiment in democracy in an African nation* (New York, 1970); Spitzer, *The Creoles*, ch. 2, pp. 40–3.
11. Note 11 above; L. Probyn, 'Sierra Leone and the native of West Africa', *Journal of the African Society*, 23 April 1907, pp. 250–8; R. W. July, *The Origins of Modern African Thought: Its development in West Africa during the 19th and 20th centuries* (New York, 1967), pp. 302–4.
12. Isichei, *The Ibo People*, p. 91.
13. CO 267/438/13266 Cardew to Chamberlain, 28 May 1898; Fyfe, *A History*, p. 580.
14. Fyfe, *A History*, ch. 21–23.
15. Collier, *Experiment in Democracy*, p. 3.
16. See cited works of the following for background information Fyfe, Peterson, St George Walker, Collier; Marcus Jones, 'Fundamental rights'; Blyden, 'Constitutional Change'; C. Allen, *Constitutional Change, 1863–1967*, pamphlet in the Sierra Leone Collection, Fourah Bay College Library (N.D.), 12pp.
17. Note 16 above; M. Wight, *The Development of the Legislative Council, 1600–1945* (N.D.); T. O. Elias, *Ghana and Sierra Leone: The Development of their Laws and Constitutions* (London, 1962).
18. Allen, *Change*, pp. 1–8; J. D. Hargreaves, 'Colonial Office opinion on the Constitution of 1863', *S.L.S.* (N.S.), 5 (1955), pp. 2–10.
19. C. Clapham, *Liberia and Sierra Leone*, p. 26.
20. There seems to have been a useful relationship between F. A. Miller, for many years Clerk of the Legislative Council, and Governor Nathan of Sierra Leone (1898–9), suggested by the letters he wrote to Nathan in London. Sir Samuel Lewis and Dr Edward Blyden were also regular correspondents with Nathan (Nathan MSS) pp. 248–9, Rhodes House Library, Oxford. Fyfe, *A History*, has a few examples of amicable relations between officials and citizens.
21. Hargreaves, *Sir Samuel Lewis*, and 'Sir Samuel Lewis and the Legislative Council', *S.L.S.* (N.S.), 1 (1958), pp. 40–52 and 'Colonial Office', *S.L.S.* (N.S.), 5 (1955), pp. 2–10; C. Fyfe, 'The life and times of John Ezzidio', *S.L.S.* (N.S.), 4 (1955), pp. 213–23.
22. Note 21 above; C. Allen, *Change*.
23. See list of unofficial members of the Legislative Council in *Legislative Council Debates*, Sierra Leone (hereafter cited as *Debates*), 1924–5 Session. Fyfe, *A History*, 471, pp. 512–13, attests that Daniel Jarrett, a fierce critic of the government, was appointed as a nominated member of the Legislative Council possibly to 'muzzle a tiresome critic'. The *Debates* did not include his name in the list.
24. Quotes are from Wight, *Legislative Council*, p.100 ff.; Fyfe, *A History*, pp. 538–40, respectively. See the introductory chapter, and the article by A. H. M. Kirk-Greene, 'On governorship and governors in British Africa' in L. H. Gann and Peter Duignan (eds.), *African Proconsuls: European Governors in Africa* (New York, 1978), pp. 209–64.
25. Tekina N. Tamuno, 'The role of the Legislative Council in the Administration of Lagos, 1886–1913', *J.H.S.N.*, 4; 4 (June 1969), pp. 555–70.
26. See Note 21 above.

27. Hargreaves, 'Sir Samuel and the Legislative Council', pp. 40–52; M. Kilson, *Political Change*, pp. 100–1.
28. Notes 21 and 26. For Lewis's views on some questions, see his article, 'The wants of Sierra Leone: a few suggestions', written for the information of an M.P. in 1879 while Lewis was on a visit to Britain, and revised in 1885. Deposited in the Royal Commonwealth Society Library, Northumberland Avenue, London.
29. Fyfe, *A History*; K. W. J. Post, 'British policy and representative government in West Africa, 1920–1951', in P. Duignan and L. H. Gann (eds.), *Colonialism in Africa, 1870–1960* (Cambridge, 1970), pp. 31–57; Webster et al., *West Africa since 1800*, pp. 142–6; Geiss, *Pan-African Movement*, p. 50.
30. Quoted in Fyfe, 'John Ezzidio', p. 278; Tamuno, 'The role of the Legislative Council', pp. 555–70 and 'Some aspects of Nigerian reaction to the imposition of British rule', *J.H.S.N.*, 3, 2 (Dec. 1965); Baker, *Urbanization and Political Change*, discussing Nigerian parallels.
31. On the Native Pastorate controversy of the 1860s, see Hollis R. Lynch, 'The Native Pastorate controversy and cultural ethnocentrism in Sierra Leone, 1871–1874', *J.A.H.*, 5, 3 (1964), pp. 395–413; Ayandele, *Holy Johnson, passim*.
32. *S.L.W.N.*, 18 Dec. 1887; Spitzer, *Creoles*, p. 115 ff.
33. Hargreaves, 'Colonial Office', pp. 2–10.
34. *S.L.W.N.*, 2 July 1892. To name just a few: C. J. G. Barlatt, T. Bishop, T. C. Bishop, Samuel Lewis, J. A. Grant, F. A. Noah, and J. Galba Bright.
35. *S.L.W.N.*, 4 Nov. 1899. Letter to the editor from A. J. Shorunkeh-Sawyerr (Honorary Secretary of the Association); *S.L.W.N.*, 8 Feb. 1919.
36. C. Fyfe, 'The Sierra Leone press in the nineteenth century', *S.L.S.* (N.S.), 8 (June 1957), pp. 226–36; Charles A. Orr, 'Trade Unionism in Colonial Africa', *Journal of Modern African Studies*, 4 (1966), pp. 65–81.
37. *Sierra Leone Blue Book* (1919 and 1927). See also Kilson, *Political Change*, pp. 100–3; P. O. Esedebe, 'The independence movement in Sierra Leone', *Tarikh*, 4, 1 (1971), pp. 15–26, for a discussion and a full list of what follows.
38. *S.L.W.N.*, 1, 22 Oct. 1910.
39. For instance, one angry correspondent, J. T. E., berated the 'Untemperedness of the monster from which our social and political organizations are reared – lack of continued interest in public venture. Our efforts are mostly ephemeral and short-lived', *S.L.W.N.*, 24 July 1919.
40. But the protest against the Criminal Code alone secured over 3,000 signatures. Bankie was seventh in the list. CO 207/578/55303, Wilkinson to Long, 28 Oct. 1918.
41. The *S.L.W.N.* made this terse comment in its issue of 24 February 1917 apropos the City Council: 'It is our misfortune in Sierra Leone – an utter lack of organised leadership – wanted a leader to teach the "masses"'.
42. Omu, 'The dilemma of Press Freedom in Colonial Africa', p. 279.
43. Fyfe, *A History*.
44. A brief sketch on May is in Capt. F. W. Butt-Thompson, *Sierra Leone in History and Tradition*, p. 206; G. A. Gollock, *Lives of Eminent Africans*, pp. 138–41.
45. Fyfe, *A History*. See also his 'Sierra Leone Press', pp. 226–36; Fred I. A. Omu, 'The "New Era" and the Abortive Press Laws of 1857', *S.L.S.*, 23 (July 1968), pp. 2–14; Bankole Timothy, 'The Sierra Leone news story', *West Africa*, 7 Feb. 1977, pp. 248–51; M. L. Kilson 'Social forces in West African Political Development', in P. J. M. McEwan, *Twentieth Century Africa* (New York, 1970), pp. 1–16.
46. Fyfe, 'Sierra Leone Press', pp. 226–36.
47. Note 44; *S.L.W.N.* issues of 1884 ff.
48. *S.L.W.N.*, 2 Sept. 1922.
49. CO267/590/9213, Wilkinson to Milner, 8 Feb. 1921.

50. Butt-Thompson, *History and Tradition*, p. 206; Kilson, *Political Change*, p. 75.
51. CO267/588/58875, Wilkinson to Milner, 13 Nov. 1920.
52. Cf. Ayodele Langley, *Pan-Africanism*, p. 121, who claimed that the *Aurora* was founded by E. S. Beoku-Betts.
53. See note 73 in Chapter 1 of this work.
54. *S.L.W.N.*, 29 April 1922. However, in his letter to the editor, a correspondent, S. Ogubaje, complained that *Aurora*'s editor 'had occupied eminence in the minds and good judgement of the common people or the lower class; he has been hailed as the champion for his outspokenness where others had been playing the unnecessary duplicity; he has exhibited masculine courage in a crowd of coward politicians... but he was losing touch with the common people'.
55. *S.L.W.N.*, 31 Oct. 1925.
56. Omu, 'Abortive Press Laws of 1857', pp. 2–14.
57. *S.L.W.N.*, 22 Jan. 1916; Fyfe, 'John Ezzidio', pp. 213–23; Omu, ref. cited in note 56 above.
58. Hans Kohn and Wallace Sokolsky, *African Nationalism in the 20th Century* (London, 1965); W. Arthur Lewis et al., *Attitudes to Africa* (Middlesex, 1951); J. W. de Graft Johnson, *Towards Nationhood in West Africa* (1928), new impression with intro. by F. K. Drah (London, 1971).
59. R. L. Buell, *The Native Problem in Africa* (London, 1928) 1, pp. 882 ff.
60. Spitzer, *Creoles*, ch. 1 and 2; Baker, *Urbanization*, pp. 27–56.
61. 'Dove Papers' MSS. Afr. S399. Rhodes House Library, Oxford, Dove to his father, 13 June 1926.
62. Reacting sharply to these aspersions, J. E. Casely Hayford put up a stout defence of these people in an address to *W.A.S.U.* 5 Nov. 1926. He objected that 'in Sierra Leone and the Gambia these (people) should be reminded of circumstances in which, if blame be apportioned fairly, they played no ignoble part. Besides, whatever connection they may have had with slavery has ceased to exist long, long ago.' *W.A.S.U.*, 2 (December 1926).
63. CO267/539/10737, Mereweather to Harcourt, 25 March 1912, reporting on an alleged improper relation between a Mrs Taylor and Dr Awunor Renner, noted: 'As regards Dr. Renner's conduct, I am aware that the standard of morality among the Sierra Leone Creoles is not very high'.
64. Spitzer, *Creoles*, pp. 50–8.
65. *S.L.W.N.*, 11 March 1916. Open letter by H.K.K. Familiar Talks, a *Weekly News* column, complained in a series of issues about Black/White relations and the unwillingness of Europeans to concede equal treatment to Africans. 'They would seem', the author charged, 'to be expecting the old *dobaleh* attitude and the self-humiliation of Yes, Massa, even at this hour of the day', *S.L.W.N.*, 25 Sept., 30 Oct., 6 Nov. 1915; see also MSS Brit. Emp. S. 296 'Autobiography of Alfred Claud Hollis, Colonial Secretary in Sierra Leone during the governorships of Mereweather and Wilkinson'. Of course, Mereweather's construction of Pademba Road Prison, Mereweather's palace (opened in 1915), and his further association with another institution of correction, the new Law Courts, were black marks against his name.
66. T. S. Gale, 'Official Medical Policy in British West Africa, 1870–1930', Ph.D. thesis, London, 1972. For an official view on the competence of African doctors, see CO 879/112 No. 133, Mereweather to Secretary of State, 21 April 1913. Enclosures. See also petition by Native Medical Officers for better conditions of service in 1919, CO267/581/33027 7 May 1919. A Colonial Office minute stated: 'any qualified Medical Officer who is a native of West Africa and who is recommended by the governor is eligible for appointment to government service, and indeed is bound to offer him appointment if he applies'. *S.L.W.N.*, 16 Jan. 1915; T. S. Gale, 'The disbarment of African Medical

Officers by the West African medical staff: a study of prejudice', *J.H.S.S.L.*, 4, 1 and 2 (Dec. 1980), pp. 33–4.

67. Gale, 'Official medical policy', p. 164; *S.L.W.N.*, 16 Aug. 1913, article by Nembana. Fyfe, *A History*, pp. 538–44 has examples of Krio staff replaced by Europeans during Cardew's administration.

68. CO267/573/12234, E. J. Wright to C.O. 9 March 1916; CO267/573/14193, C.O. to E. J. Wright, 16 March 1916. C.O. Mins.

69. Gov. to Col. Sec. Harcourt, 18 May 1914, Governor's Conf. Despatches, Jan.–Dec. 1914, deposited in the Sierra Leone National Archive, Mt Aureol, Freetown.

70. Jones-Quartey, 'Sierra Leone's role', pp. 73–83; *Aurora*, 23 April 1921.

71. CO267/576/8993, Awunor-Renner to C.O. 16 Feb. 1917; C.O. to Awunor-Renner, 21 Feb. 1917; CO267/576/12415, Awunor-Renner to C.O. 6 March 1917; C.O. To Awunor-Renner 14 March 1917. He was told that the post of Assistant District Commissioner was not of Native grade. Yet a European, Colonel Hart, who had no professional qualification, his only recommendation being that he had fought in the war and had served in Boundary Commissions, was advised to re-apply for the post of District Commissioner after the war. See CO267/576/52579, C.O. to Colonel Hart, 3 Nov. 1917; CO267/588/63717, Wilkinson to Milner, 12 Dec. 1920 ref. Awunor Renner's application; *Aurora*, 23 April 1921.

72. C.S.O. 1918, S.L. National Archive, *M.P.N.N.* 16, Acting Colonial Secretary to the Secretary, Northern Provinces, 23 Oct. 1918; same to same, 10 Feb. 1919. See also Henry Harold Gaffney (jun.), 'Administration and the administrative service in Sierra Leone', Ph.D. thesis, Columbia, 1967.

73. CO267/576/4915, Colonial Office Minutes on Awunor-Renner's application; CO267/ 604/32100, Slater to Sec. of State, 17 June 1924; CO267/604/38500, Acting Governor to Sec. of State 28 July 1924; CO267/576/8993, Awunor-Renner to Colonial Office, 16 Feb. 1917; and CO267/576/12415; *S.L.W.N.*, 15 July, 30 Sept. 1922; M. Crowder, 'The White Chiefs of Tropical Africa', in Duignan and Gann, *Colonialism*, pp. 320–50.

74. Mins. by Ellis on CO267/576/4915.

75. *S.L.W.N.*, 1 Dec. 1945; Gaffney, 'Administrative service'; R. S. Jordan, 'The Creoles and the Civil Service in Sierra Leone, 1957–1969', paper presented at the Sierra Leone Symposium, University of Ontario, 7–9 May 1971 (in Inst. of Commonwealth Studies Library) 28pp.

76. Fyfe, *A History*; J. D. Hargreaves, 'The establishment of the Sierra Leone Protectorate and the Insurrection of 1898', *Cambridge Historical Journal*, 12 (1956), pp. 56–80.

77. T. F. V. Buxton, 'The Creole in West Africa', *Journal of the African Society*, 12 (1912–13), pp. 385–94; George Padmore, *How Britain Rules Africa* (London, 1936), ch. 9; Fyfe, *A History*.

78. Clapham, *Liberia and Sierra Leone*; Spitzer, *Creoles*; Collier, *Experiment in Democracy*; Sir Harry Luke, *Cities and Men: An Autobiography* (London, 1953), 1, 159 ff.

79. Dick Simpson, 'Ethnic conflict in Sierra Leone', in Victor A. Olorunsola (ed.), *The Politics of Cultural Sub-Nationalism in Africa: Africa and the Problem of 'One State, Many Nationalisms'* (New York, 1972), pp. 153–88; Geiss, *Pan-African Movement*, p. 50.

80. Buell, *The Native Problem in Africa*, 1, pp. 864–8; T. N. Goddard, *The Handbook of Sierra Leone*: Marcus-Jones, 'Fundamental rights', *S.L.W.N.*, 18 March; 20 March 1916; 18 Aug. 1918 etc. for complaints against ill treatment meted out to Krio immigrants in the Protectorate; Fyfe, *A History*, p. 545.

81. Luke, *Cities and Men*, 1, p. 159; N. C. Hollins Paper, Sierra Leone, 1921–36, MSS Afr. S. 672; L. W. Wilson Papers, Box 1, MSS Afr. S. 388, Rhodes House Library, Oxford. The comment by the District Commissioner of Moyamba, W. D. Bowden, on a complaint by Dr W. C. E. Bowen against a Krio cleric is typical of the jaundiced attitude

of the establishment towards Colony inhabitants. Bowen reported a Mr Williams, a U.B.C. Missionary, for insolently disregarding his instructions not to ring the Church Bell (a railway sleeper, really) because of a sick European patient of his who needed rest and quiet (though the doctor did not insist on a similar order to two white trading companies that rang the same sort of bell). The District Commissioner praised the sub-chief (who had acquiesced in the directive from the doctor) for his courteous and prompt response to the doctor's orders. But, as for Williams', behaviour, he waspishly observed that he could not be responsible for an 'alien population (the Krio immigrants) who claim to be possessed of Christian principles and European education. That they should have so lamentably failed in this most elementary test of both claims is sufficient commentary on their value as neighbours or citizens.' C.S.O.M. 203 S.L. National Archive, Bowen to Colonial Secretary, 9 Nov. 1913, with enclosures. On Bo School, see the following: CO267/570, Acting Gov. A. C. Hollis to Bonar Law, 3 March 1916 (enclosing Protectorate Education Report of 1915); CO267/539/11455, Gov. to Sec. of State, 3 April 1912 (enclosing Bo School Report, 1911); Fyfe, *A History*, p. 616; Henry S. Wilson, *The Imperial Experience* (1977), 7, p. 262.

82. See series of articles written by J. S. T. Davies, African Assistant Postmaster-General, on 'Agriculture in Sierra Leone and the Protectorate', *S.L.W.N.*, 10 Sept. 1910; also C. L. Pitt's suggestions to the Colony people 'to carry on extensive agriculture and so better our condition', and 'educate and civilize the natives of the Protectorate – living among them (and establishing) schools where "country" children would share the same privileges with Creoles' *S.L.W.N.*, 10, 17 Sept.; 3 Dec. 1910; Wyse, 'Some thoughts on themes in Sierra Leone History', pp. 228–40 and 'Politics in Colonial Sierra Leone: the example of the Sierra Leone Branch of the National Congress of British West Africa, 1918–1940', *Public Lecture*, 25 Oct. 1978, and *Searchlight on the Krio of Sierra Leone*. *The West African Mail and Trade Gazette* had a column devoted to Protectorate News and Notes; *S.L.W.N.* carried reports and articles on personalities and institutions in the Protectorate.

83. *S.L.W.N.*, 26 Oct. 1912; 4 July 1919; 15 July 1922; 23 Sept. 1922; 27 Oct. 1923; etc.

84. Basic texts on Sierra Leone history treat this fully. However, see C. Fyfe, *A History*; C. Marke, *Origin of Wesleyan Methodism in Sierra Leone and History of its Missions* (London, 1913), pp. 156–9. Memorial tablets in many Freetown Churches bear testimony to the large number of Krios, especially clerics, killed in the 1898 Hut Tax War.

85. N. O. Leighton, 'The Lebanese community in Sierra Leone: the role of an alien trading minority in political development', paper presented at the 15th Annual Meeting of the African Studies Association, Pennsylvania, 8–11 Nov. 1972 (Inst. of Commonwealth Studies Library, London); Marwan Hanna, 'The Lebanese in West Africa: How and when they came', *West Africa*, 19 and 26 April 1958.

86. A. J. G. Wyse, 'The 1919 railway strike and anti-Syrian riots: A Krio plot?', *J.H.S.S.L.*, 3, 1 and 2 (Dec. 1979), pp. 1–14.

87. *Debates* (Session 1923–4), 5 Dec. 1923 and 21 May 1924.

88. Wyse, 'A. J. Abayomi Cole' in *The Encyclopaedia Africana*, p. 35; *S.L.W.N.* 7 and 14 Jan. 1905; 7, 10, 17 Sept. 1910; *S.L.G.F.M.*, 16 Sept. 1910.

89. Wyse, 'S. B. Thomas', *The Encyclopaedia*, p. 154; *S.L.W.N.*, 25 May 1910; 8, 15, 29 June; 17 Aug., 28 Sept. 1901.

3: POLITICS IN EARNEST: THE SETTING UP OF THE N.C.B.W.A., 1919–1924

1. See articles on Africa and the First World War published in J.A.H., 19 (1978), especially David Killingray's 'Repercussions of World War I in the Gold Coast', pp. 39–59; M. Crowder, 'West Africa and the 1914–1918 War', *Bulletin D'ifan*, Series B, 30, 1 (1968),

pp. 227–47; Akinjide Osuntokun, 'Disaffection and revolts in Nigeria during the First World War, 1914–1918', *Canadian Journal of African Studies*, 5, 2 (1971), pp. 171–192.
2. Crowder, '1914–1918 war', p. 230.
3. Letter by Rambler, *S.L.W.N.*, 7 Nov. 1914; 9, 16 Jan. 1915.
4. *S.L.W.N.*, 12 Sept. 1914.
5. Crowder, 1914–1918 war', pp. 227–47; G. I. C. Eluwa, 'The National Congress of British West Africa: A pioneeer nationalist movement', *Genève-Afrique*, 11, 1 (1972), pp. 38–51; Langley, *Pan Africanism*, ch. 3.
6. W. K. Hancock, *Survey of British Commonwealth Affairs; Problems of Nationality, 1918–1936* (London, 1937), 1, ch. 1.
7. Langley, *Pan-Africanism*, ch. 3; Killingray, 'World War I', pp. 39–59; S. O. Arifola, 'Pan-Africanism and the organisation of African unity', in R. Olaniyan (ed.), *African History and Culture* (London, 1982), pp. 127–49.
8. Eluwa, 'The N.C.B.W.A.', pp. 38–51.
9. Langley, *Pan-Africanism*, ch. 3; Eluwa, 'The N.C.B.W.A.', pp. 38–51; D. Kimble, *A Political History of Ghana: The rise of Gold Coast Nationalism 1850–1928* (London, 1963); Kilson, *Political Change* and 'The National Congress of British West Africa, 1918–1935', in R. I. Rotberg and A. Mazrui (eds.), *Protest and Power in Black Africa* (London, 1970), pp. 571–88; M. Crowder, *West Africa Under Colonial Rule* (London, 1968), pp. 419–28; J. B. Webster, 'Political activity in British West Africa, 1900–1940', in J. F. A. Ajayi and M. Crowder (eds.), *History of West Africa*, 2, pp. 568–95; Magnus Sampson, *Makers of Modern Ghana* (Accra, 1969), pp. 131–41.
10. *S.L.W.N.*, 6 Nov. 1915; 27 April 1918.
11. *S.L.W.N.*, 15 Dec. 1917, reporting the *Gold Coast Leader*.
12. See, for example, *S.L.W.N.*, issues of Jan. 1918–Jan. 1919.
13. *Ibid*; G. Olusanya, 'The Lagos Branch of the National Congress of British West Africa', *J.H.S.N.*, 4, 2 (June 1968), pp. 321–33; J. Ayodele Langley, 'The Gambia Section of the National Congress of British West Africa', *Africa*, 39, 4 (Oct. 1969), pp. 382–95; cf. A. J. G. Wyse, 'The Sierra Leone Branch of the National Congress of British West Africa, 1918–1946', *I.J.A.H.S.*, 18, 4 (1985), pp. 676–98.
14. *S.L.W.N.*, 4 May 1918.
15. *S.L.G.F.M.*, 11 Jan. 1918.
16. Wyse, 'Sierra Leone Branch of N.C.B.W.A.,' pp. 676–98.
17. *S.L.W.N.*, 18 May 1918, my emphasis.
18. *Ibid.*
19. *S.L.W.N.*, 15 Dec. 1917; 27 April 1918; 14 Dec. 1918, letter by E. S. Beoku-Betts; 24 April 1920. For similar developments in Accra, Lagos and Bathurst, see works by Kimble, Olusanya and Langley cited above.
20. *S.L.W.N.*, 4, 11 May 1918; *S.L.G.F.M.*, 3 May 1918; *S.L.W.N.*, 30 Nov 1918; 15 Feb. 1919; *S.L.G.F.M.*, 21 Feb. 1919.
21. *Gold Coast Spectator*, 29 Aug. 1936 enclosed in CO267/655/32157. Minutes by Turbett on memo on N.C.B.W.A., 18 Sept. 1936, *ibid.*
22. *S.L.W.N.*, 4, 11 May 1918; *S.L.G.F.M.*, 3 May 1918.
23. *S.L.W.N.*, 30 Nov. 1918; 15 Feb. 1919; *S.L.G.F.M.*, 21 Feb. 1919. Quoted from Ayandele, *Holy Johnson*, p. 43.
24. *C.P.A.*, 1 June 1918. George Padmore asserts in *How Britain Rules Africa*, 372, that the Governor of Sierra Leone asked J. C. Shorunkeh Sawyerr (*sic*) – I think he meant A.J., a senior nominated unofficial member of the Legislative Council – to denounce Congress, but he refused. J.C. though not a member of Congress, did speak on its platform. *S.L.W.N.*, 9 Aug. 1924. An interesting discussion on the relevance of youthful

representation in the Conference was publicised in *C.P.R.* of June 1918. See issues of 1 June and others.

25. *C.P.R.*, 4 May 1918; *S.L.W.N.*, 25 May 1918; 12 April 1919; Interviews: Pa J. C. Lucan, 21 Aug. 1974; E. J. Robinson, 25 Aug. 1975.

26. A. T. Sumner wrote *A Handbook of the Mende Language* in 1917 for which he was praised in the *Weekly News* (15 Sept. 1917). He became Inspector of Schools in 1923 and in 1931 he was appointed Vice-Principal of the Protectorate Central College. *Colonial Office List* (H.M.S.O. London, 1923 ff).

27. *S.L.W.N.*, of 5 April 1924 reported on the Urban Working Class (the Woroko Woroko) seen on Congress Day (28 March) with Congress flags 'pinned on their tattered hangings' – a symbol of united efforts and common goal. See also issues of 24 April; 31 July 1920; 27 Jan. 1923; cf. Langley, *Pan-Africanism*, p. 159.

28. Note 25 above. A hostile critic, J. F. Knox wrote, 'The Editor [of the *Aurora*] is credited with the fact that he is the only one who has successfully wrested the right of being a member of the local Committee for the proposed Conference by means of casting on it certain insinuations which, for a time, threatened to retard its progress, if not frustrate one of the most important items set forth in its programme.' Obviously Knox was referring to some questions raised by Bright at one of the first meetings which he attended. Indeed, Knox claimed that 'since *Aurora*'s criticisms' people had kept away. See *S.L.W.N.*, 12 April 1919 and *C.P.R.* 4 May 1918.

29. *Ibid.*

30. Eluwa, 'N.C.B.W.A.'; Langley, *Pan-Africanism*, for detail accounts.

31. A. J. G. Wyse, 'The 1919 railway Strike and anti-Syrian riots: A Krio plot?' *J.H.S.S.L.*, 2, 1 and 2 (Dec. 1979), pp. 1–14.

32. Eluwa, 'N.C.B.W.A.', p. 42.

33. *Ibid.*, p. 44.

34. Cf. Langley, *Pan-Africanism*, 133.

35. Langley, pp. 128–33; Eluwa, 'N.C.B.W.A.', pp. 43–4.

36. *S.L.W.N.*, 27 March 1920; Langley, *Pan-Africanism*, pp. 125–6.

37. Eluwa, 'N.C.B.W.A.', p. 44; Langley, ch. 5. In the election for delegates to represent Sierra Leone at the London Conference, the following polled these votes: R. C. P. Barlatt 2; Prof. J. Abayomi Cole 3; J. Fowell-Boston 4; E. S. Beoku-Betts 6; F. W. Dove 14, and Bankole-Bright 24. *S.L.W.N.*, 3 July 1920.

38. Quote is from Langley, *Pan-Africanism*, p. 131. See ch. 3 of his work for a detailed account; cf. Eluwa, 'N.C.B.W.A.'. There is evidence of discord and lack of co-ordination among members in the delegation as well as personality clashes, for instance between Bright and Dove, in the Herbert Macauley Papers (Ibadan University Library) Box 18, File 3 of 1920.

39. Quoted in Kimble, *Political History of Ghana*, p. 392.

40. Langley, *Pan-Africanism*, ch. 3.

41. Cited in Drah's Introduction to J. W. de Graft Johnson, *Towards Nationhood in West Africa*, pp. 1–22. Guggisberg, Governor of the Gold Coast, for instance, told the Colonial Office that self-government would be fatal to the native races, and to the development of the colony which was not ready for it. He believed that the delegates did not represent the Chiefs. 'I have suspicions', he went on, 'that a bad influence is being exercised by the Congress over the semi-literate young men with the result that the formation of a trade union is in progress and strikes are impending. At present the situation is well in hand.' CO554/46/52395, Guggisberg to C.O., 23 Oct. 1920 (tel.).

42. *Ibid.* Quote is from W. Arthur Lewis et al., *Attitude to Africa* (Middlesex, 1951), p. 34; Olusanya, 'The Lagos Branch of N.C.B.W.A., pp. 321–33.

43. Note 41 above; CO554/46/58090, Clifford to Sec. of State, 25 Nov. 1920 (tel.); Langley, ch. 6; de Graft Johnson, *Nationhood*, pp. 13–15; Kimble, *Political History*, pp. 38 ff.; J.

Osuntokun, 'Post First World War Economic and Administrative Problems in Nigeria and the response of the Clifford Administration', *J.H.S.N.*, 7, 1 (Dec. 1973), pp. 35–48.

44. *Ibid*; CO554/50/233, Guggisberg to C.O., 2 January 1921 (tel.); CO554/50/22290, Wilkinson to Churchill, 24 April 1921. Officials in Whitehall noted in minutes on Clifford's telegram: 'The signatories on behalf of Nigeria are, Mr. Shyngle, the black barrister – not I think a Native of Nigeria – and that ridiculous petty Chief Oluwa who is masquerading as a Nigerian potentate with his exconvict Secretary, Mr. Macauley.' CO554/46/58090, Clifford to Sec. of State, 25 Nov. 1920 (tel.); Kohn and Sokolsky, *African Nationalism*, p. 9.

45. Ormsby-Gore, *Report of his Visit*, p. 23; see J. C. Shorunkeh-Sawyerr's scathing comments on the animosity of Europeans towards educated Africans, with particular reference to the Krio. *S.L.W.N.*, 9 April 1924. In one of the most penetratingly perceptive and unbiased observations made by a British permanent official in Whitehall, Ellis deprecated Flood's sneering comment on Congress's demand for a West African University as 'mischievously premature', thus: 'As regards the University proposal I should not regard it as premature if private generosity were successful… After all there were Universities in England and in every other European country, as far as I know, centuries before there was any talk of educating the masses.' C.O. Minutes on CO554/50/27392, Guggisberg to Churchill, 10 May 1921. Harold Laski's 'The Colonial Civil Service', *The Political Quarterly*, 9, (1938), pp. 541–51, is a good critique of the Colonial Service mentality.

46. de Graft Johnson, 16; Lewis et al., *Attitude*, p. 34; cf. Herbert Macauley Papers, Box 18, File 5. Dr O. Johnson to Morel, 18 Nov. 1912.

47. *S.L.W.N.*, 1 Feb. 1923. Bankole-Bright was snubbed by the Colonial Office when he asked to be allowed to lay a wreath on behalf of Congress at the Cenotaph on 11 November 1920, in memory of West African soldiers killed in the First World War. The Colonial Office replied that a government representative had already been chosen, but if Congress so wished it could join the public after the ceremony. CO554/49/54091, Bankole-Bright to Curzon, 25 Oct. 1920; C.O. to Bright, 3 Nov. 1920. For a similar snub to the Nigerian people, see Osuntokun, 'Post First World War', 35–48.

48. Minutes on CO554/49/53561, Bankole-Bright to Sec. of State, 30 Oct. 1920; Eluwa, 'N.C.B.W.A.', p. 46. Letters pertaining to the London Mission are among the Macauley Papers, Box 18, File 3, especially that signed by H. J. Reade to Bankole-Bright 26 Jan. 1921 informing Congress that H.M. Govt did not think the time had come to introduce 'the principles of election to the Legislative Councils and of unofficial majorities on these councils. Nor does [he] consider that the legal changes suggested in the petition could improve the administration of justice and be in the interest of the great bulk of the native populations'; H. J. Reade to Bankole-Bright, 17 Feb. 1921; Bankole-Bright to Churchill, 19 Feb. 1921.

49. CO554/49/46935, Bankole-Bright to Milner, 21 Sept. 1920. Enclosing N.C.B.W.A. Committee Resolutions etc; CO554/49/53561, Bankole-Bright to Sec. of State, 30 Oct. 1920. One C.O. functionary, probably Ellis, offered this sour witticism 'demands are those of Europeanized natives – nothing said about non-Europeanized natives, a long time before any of our West African Colonies are ripe for an elective franchise or an unofficial majority – a case for Tin Tailors of Tooley Street.' Mins. on 53561.

50. Langley, *Pan-Africanism*, pp. 265 ff.; also T. O. Elias, *The British Commonwealth; The Development of its Laws and Constitutions – Ghana and Sierra Leone*, pp. 29–33, 242–6.

51. CO267/613/4084, Slater to Amery, 20 April 1926. Strachey, a Senior Official, recalled that the Constitution had been granted not 'to risk an insidious rapprochement between the local "reformers" and the extremists of the Marcus Garvey type', Colonial Office minutes; Langley, *Pan-Africanism*, pp. 265 ff.

52. *Ibid*; T. N. Tamuno, 'Governor Clifford and Representative Government', *J.H.S.N.*, 4, 1 (1967), pp. 117–24.
53. Langley, *Pan-Africanism*, p. 279.
54. *Aurora*, 16 April 1921.
55. *S.L.W.N.*, 14 Jan. 1922.
56. *S.L.W.N.*, 13 May 1922.
57. CO554/50/22290, Wilkinson to Churchill, 23 April 1921.
58. CO267/576/4915 (1917); CO267/596/51428 (1922); CO267/605/45973; CO267/605/46192 (1924); Wyse, 'The Sierra Leone Branch of 'N.C.B.W.A.', pp. 675–98.
59. *Aurora*, 16, 23 April 1921 including letter by Buyufu; Langley, *Pan-Africanism*, pp. 160–1.
60. *Aurora*, 7 May 1921; *C.P.R.* 1 June 1918. Langley, *Pan-Africanism*, hits out on page 159: 'but there was no attempt by the Creole-dominated leadership, with its excessive legalism, to represent the mass of the peasantry in the Protectorate through its Chiefs'. See also Spitzer, *Creoles* p. 175.
61. 20 July 1921.
62. CO267/596/51421, Slater to Sec. of State, 26 Sept. 1922; *S.L.W.N.*, 9 Sept. 1922.
63. The latest in this genre is George O. Roberts, *The Anguish of Third World Independence*: *The Sierra Leone Experience* (University of America Press, 1982).
64. To illustrate this point further, the Boys at Bo School were required to wear their ethnic costumes to school and to go barefooted (or be laughed into ridicule, if caught!). They were discouraged from entering the Civil Service, 'even in the Protectorate', because 'they will probably in course of time degenerate into petition writers, of whom there are quite enough already. The best employment for them would undoubtedly be that of teachers...Other suitable employment can be found for them in the Agricultural, Forest and Roads Departments.' CO267/570/12946, A. C. Hollins to Bonar Law, 3 March 1916; CO2678/576/169, Bo School Syllabus of Instructions, forwarded by Governor of Sierra Leone, 13 Nov. 1917; CO267/539/11455, Bo School Report for 1911 enclosed in Govt to Secretary of State, 3 April 1912; Fyfe, *History of Sierra Leone*, p. 616.
65. *S.L.W.N.*, 18 Nov. 1922.
66. *Ibid.*; *S.L.W.N.*, 30 Dec. 1922; 13, 20 Jan. 1923. The African members of the Committee were A. J. Shorunkeh-Sawyerr, E. H. Cummings and C. May. CO267/690/21616, Slater to Devonshire, 16 April 1923.
67. *S.L.W.N.*, 2, 9, 16 Dec. 1922.
68. *S.L.W.N.*, 27 Jan, 3 Feb. 1923.
69. Herbert Macauley Paper, Box 18, File 2; See Olusanya, 'The Lagos branch', pp. 321–33; Langley, 'The Gambia Section of the N.C.B.W.A., pp. 382–94 for comments on these branches.
70. *S.L.W.N.*, 3, 10 Feb. 1923.
71. *Ibid*; see also his 'The failure of the jury system in Sierra Leone' in *Supplement to the African World*, Sept. 1928.
72. *S.L.W.N.*, 2 Feb. 1923.
73. *S.L.W.N.*, 17 Feb. 1923.
74. *Ibid.*
75. *S.L.W.N.*, 24 Feb. 1923.
76. A supplementary session was held on Saturday 17 February to finish some outstanding matters, for example, the Laws of the Congress.
77. However, see Fred Omu's comments in his review of Langley's book: 'theoretical and practical experience indicates that the direction of the political process is often a function of the values and interests of the political leadership'. *J.H.S.N.*, 8, 3 (Dec. 1974), pp. 594–7.

78. K. W. J. Post, 'British policy and representative government in West Africa, 1920–1951', in Duignan and Gann, *Colonialism*, pp. 31–51.
79. *S.L.W.N.*, 8 April 1922. Slater secured his B.A. in 1897 (80th Wrangler) at Cambridge. He was Acting Governor, Gold Coast, May to November 1915; Nov. 1916–April 1917; Colonial Secretary, Gold Coast, August 1914.
80. Indeed, a *Weekly News* editorial acknowledged his association with Clifford and warned him 'not to bring new ideas which happened to have succeeded in Gold Coast (*sic*) to Sierra Leone'. There were more pressing issues, such as the financial situation in the country, than elective representation, he was told. *S.L.W.N.*, 6 May 1922. CO267/595/10618, Maxwell to Churchill 23 Feb. 1922; C.O. to Maxwell, 25 March 1922; CO267/596, Slater's Confidential Despatch of 26 September 1922.
81. *Ibid.*; CO/267/613/4084, Slater to Sec. of State, 20 April 1926: *Debates*, March–April 1926; Kilson, *Modernisation*, p. 105.
82. *S.L.W.N.*, 15 July 1922; cf. 1 July 1922.
83. CO/267/597/53938, Slater to Churchill, 12 Oct. 1922; CO/267/597/61062, Slater to Devonshire, 24 Nov. 1922; CO/267/599/16273, Slater to Devonshire, 15 March 1923.
84. Lord Hailey, *African Survey*, (Oxford, 1957), p. 325; CO/267/596/51429, Slater to Sec. of State, 26 Nov. 1922.
85. *S.L.W.N.*, 9, 16, 23 Sept. 1922; CO/267/596/51428, Slater to Sec. of State, 26 Sept. 1922 (Confidential); Kilson, *Political Change*, pp. 126 ff.; Langley, *Pan-Africanism*.
86. ÇO/267/596/51429, Slater to Sec. of State, 26 Nov. 1922 (enclosures); Fyfe, *A History*, p. 541 asserted that the Foreign Jurisdiction Act of 1890 empowered the British Crown to exercise any jurisdiction claimed in a foreign country as if by right of cession or conquest. In 1895 an Order-in-Council empowered the Sierra Leone Legislative Council to legislate for the Protectorate in the same way as for the Colony. These laws were not made by the Krio. They were legislative Acts promulgated by the British Government.
87. *S.L.W.N.*, 9 Sept. 1922.
88. *S.L.W.N.*, 11 March 1916.
89. During Wilkinson's administration, the first motor roads linking Freetown and the Protectorate were built. The *Weekly News* praised him for this, as well as his interest in the people and education. *S.L.W.N.*, 6 Jan 1917; 1 March 1919.
90. *S.L.W.N.*, 23 Sept. 1922; editorial of 16 Sept. 1922.
91. *Ibid.*; *Debates*, 26 November; 5 Dec. 1923.
92. Notes 68 and 90; *S.L.W.N.*, 29 Sept. 1923.
93. *S.L.W.N.*, 14 March 1925; cf. Kilson, *Political Change*, p. 131.
94. This episode in Colony/Protectorate relations is often overlooked in the literature. See *S.L.W.N.*, 8 August; 5 Oct. 1918; 4 Jan. 1919; *S.L.G.F.M.*, 5 Dec. 1919; *C.P.R.*, 27 June 1918; 10 August 1918; 17 August 1931; 14 Sept. 1918.
95. *S.L.W.N.*, 14 March 1925; cf. Kilson, *Political Change*, p. 131.
96. Kilson, pp. 131 ff.
97. Interviews: T. A. L. Decker, 12 Aug. 1975; Revd Isaac Ndenema, 31 March 1978; T. A. L. Decker, *Our Paramount Chiefs of the Sierra Leone Protectorate* (Freetown, *c.* 1948), 15 pp and *Counter Proposals for a new constitution for Sierra Leone* (1948), 16 pp.; Webster, 'Political activity in B.W.A.', in Ajayi and Crowder, *History of West Africa*, 2, pp. 578–9 and 583; Collier, *Experiment in Democracy*, p. 56; cf. Richard W. Hull, *Modern Africa: Change and Continuity* (Englewood Cliffs, N.J., 1980), pp. 175–6. However, one must be careful about writers like Hull, who in one breath noted that 'the colonial governments of British west Africa were hostile to any African movements which sought to foster political unity among the various colonies. Colonial authorities had convinced most African Chiefs that Western-educated Africans were a threat to the status quo'; and, in another, makes a generalisation that was quite uncalled for, a

statement that could not be supported by historical evidence, at least in the Sierra Leone context. To quote him, 'Unfortunately, most black Americans living in Liberia and Sierra Leone proved to be anything but Pan-African indeed. They conquered and exploited the indigenous African population with a ruthlessness comparable to the white colonists elsewhere'! See pages 170, 236, note 90, 314 and 467, note 90, for Bai Koblo's 'Civis Romanus Sum' speech and Siaka Stevens's rebuff to overtures from Colony representatives in the Legislative Council. The *Sierra Leone Observer* of 27 March 1954, in a review of Roy Lewis's book on Sierra Leone, commented that for 'many years [the Krio] were the leading Africans on the coast... but their political importance has diminished with the rise of the educated people of the Protectorate. It is the latter who will have the main responsibility for Sierra Leone's future and for solving her problems'.

98. *S.L.W.N.*, 20 Jan. 1923. The European members of the Colonial Secretary, Attorney-General Fawcett and the District Commissioner for Headquarters. The Committee recommended a franchise for the Urban and Rural Areas of Freetown based on ownership of houses with a rateable value of £10 (urban) and £6 (rural), and an annual income of £100 or £60 respectively. *S.L.W.N.*, 30 Dec. 1922; 16 April 1923.

99. CO/267/595/10618, Maxwell to Churchill, 23 Feb. 1922 enclosing letter of Chamber of Commerce, dated 3 Feb. 1922; CO/267/596/51429, Slater to Sec. of State, 26 November 1922. Colonial Office Minutes.

100. *Ibid.*

101. CO/267/595/10618, Colonial Office to Acting Governor Maxwell, 25 March 1922. See T. N. Tamuno *The Evolution of the Nigerian State: the Southern Phase, 1898–1914* (New York, 1972), ch. 5 for a discussion of Colonial Office attitude to Unofficial Representation in the Executive Council.

102. CO/267/595/51429, Slater to Sec. of State, 26 Nov. 1922; C. Allen, *Change*.

103. *S.L.W.N.*, 23 Aug. 1924. Betts argued that it was invidious for Protectorate persons (foreigners) to legislate for British subjects.

104. Ellis observed 'the late governor's suggestions that a native chief should be appointed is not practicable as the chiefs are not British subjects'. But Fiddian pointed out: 'There is no objection to appoint Protected persons if they take the oath.' CO/267/595/51444, Maxwell to Churchill, 6 Oct. 1921. Colonial Office Minutes; CO/267/592/61947 dated 26 January 1922. The contradictions in British Colonial policy were not exclusive to Sierra Leone. Herbert Macauley once complained in 1928 that if British Protectorate persons were not British subjects why were local officials giving orders to the people in the King's name? Herbert Macauley papers, Box 87, File I.

105. *S.L.W.N.*, 20 May 1916; 18 March 1916; 23 March 1929 etc.; cf. Kilson, *Modernization*, pp. 131 ff. Sir Samuel Lewis himself had suggested Protectorate representation in the Legislative Council as far back as 1898. But Sir David Chalmers to whom this was put, doubted whether it was possible to find representatives that 'would be both suitable and capable of understanding the proceedings, even the language'. See Kup, *Sierra Leone*, p. 198. Documents on the legal disabilities of the Krio are in the CO267 series, for example: CO/267/613/X2692 (1926); CO267/620/4474 (1927) etc.

106. *S.L.W.N.*, 23 March 1929. In a speech during the agitation over the Criminal Code, Abayomi Cole told his audience about Chiefs in the Protectorate who were descendants of Liberated Africans. This has been confirmed by a researcher on Sierra Leone history, Dr S. A. Ijagbemi. He told me that while collecting evidence among the Temne in Magbaily, he met a local chief who was descended from a Liberated African Yoruba. He was well received as one of their own. Conversation with Dr Ijagbemi, Ibadan University, 9 March 1983; *C.P.R.*, 10 Aug. 1918.

107. *S.L.W.N.*, 15 July; 9, 23 Sept. 1922; *Debates*, 21 May 1924; 5 Dec. 1924. Note the government's tortuous argument: Protectorate peoples were aliens, and they did not

cease to be such even after taking the oath of allegiance; but once they became members of the New Legislative Council their rights would not be limited to Protectorate matters.
108. *S.L.W.N.*, 17 Aug. 1929; see also ch. 6, note 66 in this work.
109. CO270/62 Executive Council Minutes, 12 May 1924.
110. Tamuno, *Evolution of the Nigerian State.*
111. *Debates*, 1924–5; 9 Dec. 1926; cf. Ormsby-Gore's malicious aspersions on Krio reaction to the inclusion of Chiefs in the Legislative Council, in *Report of his Visit to West Africa.*
112. *Ibid.*
113. *Ibid.*
114. *Ibid.*
115. CO/267/605/55095 Slater to Thomas, 6 Nov. 1924; C. Allen, *Constitutional Change, 1862–1967.*
116. *S.L.W.N.*, 23 Aug. 1924.
117. Note 115 above.
118. *Ibid.*
119. *Ibid.*
120. CO/267/604/24832 Slater to Thomas, 12 May 1924.
121. Jardine told Dawe, an official from the Colonial Office, that the Chiefs were 'little more than figure heads who seldom expressed any opinion of their own'. Yet the government did try to influence the voting of the Chiefs in the Legislative Council. Examples of this are in *Debates*, 14 June 1926; 30 Nov. 1927, etc. Bai Kompa appeared to be the most independent-minded Chief of the first three nominated Protectorate members in the Legislative Council. See CO/267/667/32032, Notes by A. J. Dawe, on conversation with Governor Jardine, 17 Jan. 1939.

4: IN THE LEGISLATIVE COUNCIL, 1924–1939: THE DRAMA OF CONFRONTATION

1. Pen portrait of E. S. Beoku-Betts, 'He didn't like Law', in *West Africa*, 30 June 1951.
2. *Ibid*; *S.L.W.N.*, 10 Nov. 1917.
3. *S.L.W.N.*, 16 March 1918. The other was S. T. Jones, *S.L.W.N.*, 5 Jan. 1918.
4. *S.L.W.N.*, 14 Dec. 1918.
5. *S.L.W.N.*, 1918–26; *West Africa*, 30 June 1951.
6. CO207/616/Z F 6906, Report on Affairs on Freetown Municipality.
7. *West Africa*, 30 June 1951.
8. *S.L.W.N.*, 9 March 1918; 22 Nov. 1919.
9. Cobina Kessie, 'Pen-Portrait of the Honorable Dr. H. C. Bankole-Bright, M.L.C.', *W.A.S.U.*, 2, 2 (April–June 1933), pp. 42–43; Interviews; Hannah Neale, 2 Aug. 1974; Dr Shola Chinsman, 10 July 1979.
10. CO267/658/32092 Moore to Ormsby-Gore, 26 April 1937. Minutes by O. G. R. Williams.
11. Interviews: Pa J. C. Lucan (aged 86 years, uncle of Betts), 21 Aug. 1974; J. C. O. Crowther (aged 81 years, maternal uncle of Betts), 9 Sept. 1974; Sidney Boyle (former W.A.Y.L. member and a relative of Betts through marriage), Birmingham, 23 Dec. 1976.
12. He published the following: *Sierra Leone Law Recorder* (1931) 1; *Sierra Leone Law Record* (1934) 2; 'The failure of the jury system in Sierra Leone', *Supplement to the African World*, Sept. 1928.
13. See E. A. Ayandele, *The Educated Elite in the Nigerian Society* (Ibadan, 1974); Arif Hussain, 'The educated elite: collaborators, assailants, nationalists: a note on African Nationalists and Nationalism', *J.H.S.N.*, 7, 3 (Dec. 1974), pp. 485–97; Kohn and Sokolsky, *African Nationalism in the Twentieth Century*, for a discussion.
14. Interview: J. C. O. Crowther, 9 Sept. 1974.

15. Interview: LBT, 5 Aug. 1974.
16. Interview: Dr W. H. Fitzjohn, 2 Oct. 1974.
17. CO267/633/9567: 31/1, Cookson to Passfield, 23 Jan. 1931.
18. *W.A.S.U.*, 2, 2 (April–June 1933), pp. 42–3; see also Bah, 'Bankole-Bright', especially pp. 70–1.
19. Quoted from Tamuno, *Evolution*, p. 137, referring to J. J. Thomas, a nominated member of the Lagos Legislative Council.
20. CO267/64, Legco Minutes for 1924–5; *Debates*, 3 Dec. 1924.
21. *Debates*, 4 Dec. 1924.
22. *Aurora*, 6 Aug. 1921.
23. CO270/62 Executive Council Minutes (1924–31). Minutes for 21 Feb. 1927; 13 Jan. 1928.
24. *Debates*, 25 Nov. 1925. Other volumes are also instructive.
25. A ten-page foolscap account of Bright's discussions with Ormsby-Gore was sent to the latter. CO267/612/44387, Bankole-Bright to Ormsby-Gore, 28 Sept. 1925. Colonial Office Minutes.
26. CO267/613/X968, Slater to Amery, 14 Jan. 1926 reporting a meeting of the Select Committee of the Legco on the 1926 Estimates. Nevertheless, the intervention of the elected members led the government to examine the emoluments of the Senior Clerk in the Governor's Office and to recommend that the incumbent should rank as a Chief Clerk at a salary of £264 × £372 p.a.
27. *Debates*, 1925–32. Between 1929 and 1932 Betts asked a total of sixty-nine questions and Bankie fielded forty, but he was absent for almost the whole of the 1930 session. Some of these questions were repeats. Nominated members hardly ever asked questions, but C. E. Wright did ask four questions in 1930 and Loxley four in 1931.
28. CO267/607/7355, Slater to Amery, 30 Jan. 1925. The visit lasted for six days, from 22 January to 27 January, while that of the Prince of Wales was a mere one day. Much earlier, when the Duke of Connaught visited Sierra Leone in 1910, he was addressed by the Mayor. *S.L.W.N.*, 17 Dec. 1910.
29. *S.L.W.N.*, 28 Feb. 1925.
30. *Debates*, 27 Feb. 1925. The Committee included the Attorney-General, McDonell, Beoku-Betts, C. E. Wright and J. H. Phillips, nominated African and European members, respectively.
31. I think Slater's speech needs quoting *in extenso*: 'I am very jealous of the reputation of this new Council which has come into being very largely on my representations, and I feel that it will be nothing short of deplorable if our minutes are to record that so preposterous a motion was moved ... I have no doubt that if the resolution is moved, and if it should chance to find a seconder, it will be overwhelmingly and ignominiously rejected.' Those members who moved and seconded it 'will only make themselves the laughing stock of West Africa ... but they will indelibly besmirch the records of this new Council and the fine traditions of the old Council, and what is far worse, they will inflict on the high reputation of the colony for loyalty a grievous blow, from which it will take many years to recover'. *Debates*, 27 Feb. 1925.
32. Blyden, 'Pattern of constitutional change', p. 157.
33. *S.L.W.N.*, 7 March 1925. Patrick Cole's *Modern and Traditional Elites in the Politics of Lagos* (Cambridge, 1975), pp. 97–8, reports a similar episode in Lagos. He argued that the demise of J. K. Randle's People's Union came about because the elites feared that 'they would be accused of disloyalty or of sedition'. The fiasco of the Water Rates agitation of 1916 justified those fears.
34. *S.L.W.N.*, 11 April 1925. Interestingly enough, this stout stand by Bright, and his support for compensation to Chiefs for losing their slaves in 1928, were remembered with

pride by a critic even in the height of Protectorate/Colony animosity in the 1950s. See article by 'Sherbro Boy' in *Sierra Leone Observer*, 4 Dec. 1954.

35. CO270/64, Legco Minutes, 29 Dec. 1925; *Debates*, 29 Dec. 1925.
36. *C.P.R.*, 7 Dec. 1918.
37. *Ibid*; *S.L.W.N.*, 15 March 1919.
38. *Ibid*; *S.L.G.F.M.*, 7 Feb. 1919; *C.P.R.*, 3 Feb. 1919.
39. *S.L.W.N.*, 15 March 1919.
40. *Debates*, 29 Dec. 1925.
41. *S.L.W.N.*, 16 Jan. 1926; *Aurora*, 31 Dec. 1925.
42. *S.L.W.N.*, Jan.–April 1926.
43. *S.L.W.N.*, 6 Feb. 1926.
44. *Debates*, 24 March 1926.
45. *Ibid.*, 30 March 1926.
46. *Ibid.*
47. *Debates*, 3 Dec. 1925.
48. *Ibid.*
49. *Ibid.*
50. *Debates*, 24 Dec. 1924. See also Notes 83 and 84 below.
51. CO267/590/9029, Wilkinson to Milner, 21 Feb. 1921. A case of unlawful arrest was filed against Rabbit by Alimamy Bunjie, the sympathetic undertaker, known for his 'convivial and noisy habits', for arresting him on Christmas Day while singing 'Christians Awake' near the European Nursing Home. The judge, His Honour Sir George Purcell, gave judgement against Inspector Rabbit. Bunjie was awarded £20 plus costs: CO267/590/24052.
52. CO267/594/29526, Raffan to Churchill, 21 Aug. 1921 encl. letter from Bright, copy of *Aurora* of 16 July 1921 and Colonial Office Minutes; CO267/590/9213 Wilkinson to Milner, 8 Feb. 1921.
53. CO267/586/20495, Wilkinson to Milner, 28 April 1920. Compare the case of E. D. Morgan, Vice-Principal of the Government Model School, convicted of embezzlement at the Supreme Court and jailed for nine months, or the case of Mayor May. See CO270/62, Exco Minutes for 5 Aug. 1924.
54. It must be pointed out, however, that the Executive Council looked into Vergette's alleged misdemeanour. It was not satisfied with the Curator's explanations, and the matter was supposed to have been referred to the Secretary of State. Later Vergette was interdicted after a Commission of Enquiry, and it was suggested that he be suspended. This was the last document on the case. Apparently, Vergette's case was allowed to drag on and then forgotten. His death a few years later made the case academic. See CO270/48, Exco Minutes for 14 April 1919; 28 April, 28 July and 10 Dec. 1919.
55. CO267/586/20495, Wilkinson to Milner, 28 April 1920.
56. CO267/596, Slater to Churchill, 26 July 1922.
57. The papers of some officials who served in Sierra Leone are deposited in Rhodes House Library, Oxford. See A. J. H. Dove Papers (MSS. Afr. S.399) of 16–29 Jan. 1926. See other papers in the same archive, for example (MSS. Afr. S. 323) W. H. Crocker – notes on the Gold Coast and Sierra Leone, 1913–58. Peter White, a Topographical Surveyor in Sierra Leone 1927–30, vowed not to repeat his experience in 'that country...most disappointing and candidly I do not like it. The natives are a poor lot and the Freetown Creoles most objectionable. I shall leave Freetown without one single regret.' (MSS. Brit. Emp. S. 280) Box 1. For a spirited defence of the Krios by Gurney Nicol against European aspersions, see R. W. July, *The Origins of Modern African*, pp. 302–4; *S.L.W.N.*, 6 Nov. 1915.
58. G3. A1/0 folios 4, 6, 9, letters by J. Denton, local secretary of the C.M.S. and Principal

of Fourah Bay College to the C.M.S. in London, dated 1, 11 Feb. and 3 March 1926 (C.M.S. Archives, Waterloo Street, London); Revd R. E. Newton to Revd E. W. Thompson, 8 Jan. 1927. Box 1924–7, Sierra Leone, Methodist Missionary Society Archives, Marylebone Road, London.

59. Dove Papers (MSS. Afr. S. 399) letter to his mother, 31 May 1927; A. J. G. Wyse, 'The 1926 Railway Strike and Anglo-Krio relations: An interpretation', *The International Journal of African Historical Studies*, 14, 1 (1981), pp. 93–123; F. A. N. Lisk, 'Industrial relations in Sierra Leone' M.Sc. thesis, Belfast, 1970, pp. 95–8; R. Buell, *The Native Problem* 1, pp. 888–9; Padmore, *How Britain Rules Africa*, pp. 351–2.

60. See note 59 above.

61. A. J. G. Wyse, 'The 1919 strike and Anti-Syrian riots: A Krio plot?', *J.H.S.S.L.*, 3, 1 *and* 2 (Dec. 1979), pp. 1–14; Kilson, 'N.C.B.W.A., 1918–1935', in Rotberg and Mazrui, eds., *Protest and Power*, pp. 571–88; M. H. Y. Kaniki, 'Attitudes and reactions towards the Lebanese in Sierra Leone during the colonial period', *The Canadian Journal of African Studies*, 7, 1 (1973), pp. 97–113; R. J. Best, *A History of Sierra Leone Railway, 1899–1949* (Sierra Leone, 1949), pp. 45ff; H. E. Conway, 'Labour protest activity in Sierra Leone during the early part of the twentieth century', *Labour History*, 15 (Nov. 1968), pp. 49–63.

62. CO267/582/56723, Evelyn to Milner, 13 Sept. 1919, enclosing Memorial of Citizens of Freetown.

63. CO267/583/48071, Evelyn to Milner, 31 July 1919; CO267/583/68973, Wilkinson to Milner, 14 Nov. 1919; also CO267/583/71853, 22650 and 58875.

64. CO267/615, correspondence on the Strike of 1926; *S.L.W.N.*, 23 Jan. 1926. The members of the Committee (later designated the Committee of Citizens) were Messrs A. J. and J. C. Shorunkeh-Sawyerr; Dr H. C. Bankole-Bright; S. E. Beoku-Betts; Blackhurst, Agent, P.Z.; A. Goodwin, Agent A. and E.T.C.; J. Haysmore, Agent, Colonial Corporation; N. Nye c/o Canning and Nye; J. F. Boston, City Solicitor; G. A. Bishop; J. C. Newton, Agent, E.D. & Co., Alimamy Mohamed Jamburia, Alpha of Foulah Town; J. A. Songo-Davies; and C. May (Mayor).

65. *Ibid.*

66. CO267/615, Gov. to Sec. of State, 11 Feb. 1926.

67. CO267/615, Fiddian to Slater, 15 March 1926.

68. CO267/615, Slater to Amery, 20 Jan. 1926; *The African World* (July 1926), reporting Slater's speech.

69. CO267/615, Slater to Ellis, 16 Feb. 1926; Slater to Amery, 3 March 1926.

70. *Ibid.*

71. Members of the Strike Fund Committee were: E. S. Beoku-Betts, Dr Bankole-Bright, A. E. Tuboku-Metzger, J. C. Shorunkeh-Sawyer, J. F. Boston, G. A. Bush (President, African Chamber of Commerce), H. A. Morrison, W. P. Golley, R. Lumpkin (Alimamy Bunjie), B. W. Davies, T. G. Reffell, Alimamy Beelah (Foulah Town Headman), and A. A. Cole (Treasurer). On the first day £36 was collected. A Mende man gave 10s. 0d. The Sierra Leone Friendly Society in Lagos contributed £336 while Sierra Leoneans in Kumasi sent in £15. Liberia's colony of Sierra Leoneans contributed a sum of £10. By the end of March £500 had been collected and disbursed to the strikers. CO267/615 Slater to Amery, 11 Feb. 1926; *S.L.W.N.*, 6, 13 Feb. 1926; Conway, 'Labour protest', pp. 57–8.

72. Note 71 above. Quotes are from *S.L.W.N.* and Conway, 'Labour protest', pp. 49–63.

73. Note 72 above.

74. CO267/615 Slater to Ellis, 16 Feb. 1926.

75. Wyse, 'The 1926 Railway Strike', pp. 93–123.

76. CO267/615, Slater to Amery, 27 Feb. 1926 (tel.); Fiddian to Slater, 15 March 1926; Slater to Amery, 31 March 1926.

77. CO267/613/4084, Governor to Sec. of State, 20 April 1926.
78. *Ibid.*
79. *Ibid.*
80. *Ibid.*
81. A highly complimentary report was made on him by A. J. Dawe, the official responsible for Sierra Leone affairs in the Colonial Office, after his visit to Freetown in 1926. CO267/613/X4083, Slater to Amery, 19 April 1926, enclosing Confidential Reports on Staff by A. J. Dawe.
82. CO267/613/4084, Gov. to Sec. of State, 20 April 1926.
83. *Ibid.*
84. *Ibid.*
85. *Ibid*; CO267/596/51428, Slater to Churchill, 26 Sept. 1922; C.O. to Slater, 22 Nov. 1922. The levies were apportioned thus: Freetown – £36,635; Waterloo – £530; Mano – £6,110; Port Loko – £1,390; Makeni – £5,610; Kambia – £45, Bonthe – £500. Only Freetown was forced to pay the indemnity and Bonthe ('as the next in importance to Freetown, and one of the Chief Offenders') was at first pressed to pay, but Slater later transferred £500 from the balance of £4,530 of the House Tax Fund and credited it to the general revenue. In other words, Bonthe was not taxed after all. See CO267/595/8340, Maxwell to Churchill, 2 Feb. 1922; notes 92 and 99 below.
86. CO267/613/4074 Gov. to Sec. of State, 20 April 1926.
87. *Ibid.*
88. *Ibid.* See note 21 above.
89. *Ibid.* Slater had commented 'Strike action of Creoles [provided] good grounds for slowing Africanization and putting an end to demand [sic] for unofficial control of purse strings.'
90. Government Regulations, dated 16 April 1926, and signed by the Colonial Secretary, H. C. Luke. Printed in *S.L.W.N.*, 26 April 1926.
91. CO267/588/58875, Wilkinson to Milnor, 13 Nov. 1920; CO267/596/51428, Slater to Churchill, 26 Sept. 1922; CO267/597/53938, Slater to Churchill, 12 Oct. 1922; CO267/610/43609, Slater to Amery, 15 August 1925; CO267/616, Slater to Amery, 6 Nov. 1926.
92. CO267/616, Minutes by Fiddian, 27 March 1926. Correspondence on the City Council is in this volume.
93. *Ibid.*
94. *Ibid.*
95. *Ibid*; CO267/616, Slater to Amery, 6 Jan. 1926.
96. CO267/616, Sec. of State to Governor, 7 May 1926 (tel.). Correspondence on the O'Brien Commission is in CO267/617/FX6908.
97. Note 91 above.
98. *S.L.W.N.*, 5 Sept 1925; 19, 25 Sept. 1925 ff. The paper opened a discussion on Council Affairs through a series of articles under the heading 'Aims and Purposes of the Freetown Municipality'. Conceding that there had been lapses, it pointed out there had been good Mayors such as Samuel Lewis, J. H. Thomas, and E. H. Cummings, to name a few. The real problem was that the Council had no teeth. Originally the charter gave the Council jurisdiction over fire protection, public markets, slaughter houses, roads, sanitation, recreations, street lighting, etc. Later, for example, in 1912, these were reduced to fire protection, markets, street lighting, cemeteries, and water supply. Buell, p. 882.
99. CO267/595/8340, Maxwell to Churchill, 2 Feb. 1922.
100. Chapter 3, p. 45 above.
101. Note 98; CO267/616, Slater to Amery, 6 Jan. 1926; CO267/638/9850, Cookson to Fiddian, 15 June 1932; Wyse 'The 1926 Railway Strike', pp. 93–123. May served less

than one-third of his sentence; then he was released on health grounds. He died three years later. The file on May's trial is CO267/616 Xf 5148; *S.L.W.N.*, 26 Sept. 1925; 22 May; 12 June 1926.

102. See note 101; CO267/610/43609, Slater to Amery, 15 Sept. 1925, Minutes by the Colonial Office Staff.

103. CO267/617/Xf 6906, Slater to Amery, 8 Dec. 1926; *S.L.W.N.*, June–August 1926. Ironically when there was another Commission of Inquiry into the City Council in 1949, the Municipal President, a European government nominee, was absolved of all blame for the state of conditions in the Water Works Department of the Council. *West Africa*, 14 May 1949. Membership of the Municipality Board set up in 1927 (Freetown Municipality Ordinance, 1927) after an Interim Board of European Officials had been dissolved, was now made up of eleven members (as opposed to fifteen in the old Council), broken down thus: a European President (Mayor), plus five nominated members, including Europeans and five elected Africans. CO267/617/Xf 6906; FCBP (MSS. Brit. Emp. S.365 Box 82) Stevens to Hinden, 15 March 1949.

104. CO267/617 file Xf 6906, Affairs of the City Council Slater to Amery, 17 Dec. 1926 with enclosures.

105. CO267/612/44387, Bankole-Bright to Ormsby-Gore, 28 Sept. 1925, forwarding resume of their meeting.

106. CO267/617FX906, Affairs of the Freetown Municipality. See *Debates*, April, June, December 1926 for the full account of members' contributions, including a motion by Bright (which was lost) asking government to reconsider its decision on orders, dismissals and resignations to re-establish good economic conditions for the country.

107. *Ibid.*

108. *Ibid.*

109. *Ibid.*

110. CO267/617 fx F6906, enclosing papers on the City Council; for example, Slater to Amery, 17 Dec. 1926 forwarding accounts of the debates in the Freetown Legislature; Slater to Amery, 8 Dec. 1926, transmitting O'Brien's report.

111. Minutes on CO267/610/43609. The views of others are equally illuminating: 'The City Council has been a weak and leaky vessel ever since I can remember (H.L.)'; 'The Institution of these African Municipalities with their Mayors and (I suppose, Aldermen) is supposed to have a valuable (?) corrective influences, but I have never heard of one of them that was run cheaply and efficiently' (Strachey). Some of the initials in the minutes cannot be identified.

112. Minutes on CO267/616 (8 Feb. 1926; Buell, *Native Problems*, p. 890; Ormsby-Gore, *Report*, p. 188.

113. CO267/638/9850, Cookson to Fiddian, 15 June 1933. Sir George Purcell, the trial judge, later regretted going against the unanimous decision of the assessors who found May not guilty. Cookson reported that Purcell 'Wept bitter tears and said that he would never have convicted May if he had not thought this would be a popular move'; CO267/616/xf5148 (trial of May) Luke to Amery, 5 June 1926; *S.L.W.N.*, 12, 26 June 1926; Buell, pp. 882–3; CO553/132/33726/5, Col. Stanley's visit to West Africa (1943). Fiddian may be as prejudiced as his Colonial Office colleagues but he sometimes came up with some penetrating and discerning comments. For example, on the May trial he noted: 'All this is very deplorable, but this sort of thing is not unknown elsewhere. Indeed, I have heard of places inhabited almost if not wholly by white people where the only reason for the Mayor not being imprisoned was alleged to be that nobody thought it worthwhile to prosecute. All this proves nothing except that they have been unlucky in their Municipal Officials.' Ormsby-Gore jeered: 'They are a pack of rascals in Freetown.' CO267/616/xf 5148, file on May's trial.

114. CO267/625/X9115, Byrne to Amery, 5 June 1928; CO267/628/X9266, Young to Passfield, 13 September 1929; CO267/615, Slater to Amery, 11 Feb. 1926.
115. CO267/619/4244, Slater to Amery, 12 April 1927; CO267/621/4529, Luke to Amery, 9 August 1927; Ormsby-Gore, *Report*, 57, Conway 'Labour Protests', p. 58. Ernest Alfonso Richards, the President of the Union and Leader of the Strike, was put under police surveillance when he was invited by the Society from the Promotion of Cultural Relations between Russia and Foreign Countries to attend the tenth anniversary of the Russian revolution in Moscow in 1927. See CO267/622 f 4583.
116. For a conservative interpretation see Buell, *Native Problems*, pp. 887–90; cf. Conway, 'Labour protest'. Slater, for instance, told a London audience which included L. S. Amery, the Colonial Secretary, that the Strike was accompanied 'I say it with regret – by a Committee of Citizens of Freetown, who however laudable their motives, devoted their main energies to vilification of government ... just as power would have passed from Westminster to Eccleston Square if the recent strike in England had achieved any measure of success, so authority would have passed from Fort Thornton to Wilberforce Hall if that Committee had succeeded, even in a small degree in its policy, and any governor who had connived at such a transfer of authority would have been deservedly execrated for the wanton betrayal of his trust'! Reported in *S.L.W.N.*, 21 Aug. 1926 quoting *African World* of July 1926. And Professor Laski wrote in 1938, 'There is evidence of definite hostility in the service to the normal British ideas of Civil Liberty.' H. Laski, 'The Colonial Civil Service', *The Political Quarterly*, 9, 1–4 (1938), pp. 541–51.
117. Arif Hussain, 'The educated elite', pp. 485–97, discusses the contradictions of Nationalists and Empire loyalists; Bernard M. Magubane, *The Political Economy of Race and Class in South Africa* (New York, 1979), pp. 272–9.
118. CO267/615, Slater to Amery, 17 Feb. 1927.
119. CO267/615, Slater to Amery, 11 Feb. 1926.
120. *S.L.W.N.*, 7 Aug. 1926.
121. The correspondence on this incident is filed in CO267/616 X files 701–6000 (1926). Typically, Luke, the Acting Governor, in commenting on Bright's and Bett's absence interpreted it as a 'grossly disrespectful act towards H.M.'s Representative manifested during and after the Railway Strike'. On the other hand his comment on the absence of J. H. Philips, the European Mercantile Member, was mildly rebuking: 'I must regretfully admit that this gent has on more than one occasion established a lack of punctiliousness somewhat surprising in a man of his position.' See also Bankole-Bright to Secretary of State, 27 Sept. 1926.
122. CO267/616, Amery to Slater, 2 Nov. 1926.
123. Folios on this case are filed on CO267/633/9567 (1932).
124. *Ibid*; CO267/633/9567:31/1, Cookson to Passfield, 23 Jan. 1931 enclosing Petition from Bright to Lord Passfield (N.D.).
125. *Ibid*; Minutes by Colonial Office Staff.
126. Another case of the government letting off erring Africans was that which involved J. F. Boston and A. S. Hebron in 1922. They were both allegedly drunk in court, and the Attorney-General was so outraged that he wanted the two barristers suspended. Slater, just assuming office, was in a 'needless panic'. He did not want a 'riot in his hands' if they were suspended. He believed that this might give rise to popular resentment which might regard the action as vindictive. Happily, the two apologised for their misdemeanour, and the Colonial Office was relieved. It 'was a better way than to have to suspend them' CO267/595/16271, Slater to Churchill, 23 March 1922. However, this example was not quite the same as Bright's.
127. CO267/633, Colonial Office to Gov. of Sierra Leone, 14 March 1932; *Debates*, sessions 1929–30 and 1930–1. The records show that Bright was absent from the Legislative

Council sittings for 19, 26 May; 3, 12 Nov. 1930. He and Betts were both absent for the following sittings, 22 and 29 July 1931. Apparently the Colonial Office was referring to this session. But then if action had been taken against Bright it would have been unfair, because Betts too was guilty of an infringement.

128. *Debates*, 1929–30, for the listing of Members of Council. The Second Urban Member (E. S. Beoku-Betts) consistently appeared before the First Urban Member (Bright). At the Elections of 1929 Bright polled 962 votes while Betts secured 958 votes. A. E. Tuboku-Metzger (Rural Member) lost his seat to J. G. Hyde (182 votes vs. 252 votes). *S.L.W.N.*, 9 Nov. 1929.

129. CO267/645/22019, Acting Gov. (S.L.) to Cunliffe-Lister, 14 Nov. 1934.

130. *Ibid*; correspondence on the Wright renomination is in the above set of documents.

131. *Ibid*; cf. CO270/62, Executive Council Minutes, 22 Nov. 1926 at which the governor decided to influence the chiefs before a legislative measure was introduced in the Legislative Council.

132. Minutes by Fiddian on CO267/645/22019 15 Nov. 1934.

133. *Debates*, 4 Dec. 1924.

134. *Debates*, 25 June 1927.

135. CO267/658/32092, Moore to Ormsby-Gore, 26 April 1937.

5: IN THE LEGISLATIVE COUNCIL, 1924–1939: CONSTRUCTIVE OPPOSITION

1. Kessie, 'Bankole-Bright', *W.A.S.U.*, 2, 2 (April–June 1933), my emphasis.

2. CO267/600/21427, Slater to Devonshire, 16 April 1923.

3. See the argument for both sides in J. Alexander Gwyn, 'The failure of the jury system in Sierra Leone', *Supplement to The African World*, 26 March 1928; cf. E. S. Beoku-Betts's reply to the above in *The African World*, 31 Aug. for 1 Sept. 1928.

4. CO267/600/41163, Furley to Devonshire, 8 Aug. 1923; CO267/600/47931, Furley to Devonshire, 18 Sept. 1923, Colonial Office Minutes; Fyfe, *A History*, pp. 532–4.

5. See note 4 above.

6. *Debates*, 30 Aug. 1927.

7. CO267/600/21427, Slater to Devonshire, 16 April 1923. A police report, with the obvious intention of supplying evidence to show guilt, disclosed expenses undergone by I. O. Bright and his sister Mrs Marie Davies, alias Marie Deen, through purchases from England. CO267/600/24284, Furley to Devonshire, 1 May 1923; CO267/621/F4502, Minutes by Colonial Office Staff.

8. CO267/621/F4502 (file on Bankole-Bright), Bankole-Bright to Ormsby-Gore, 6 Aug. 1927. Minutes by Colonial Office Staff.

9. CO267/600/41163, Furley to Devonshire, 8 Aug. 1923 with enclosures.

10. *Ibid*.

11. CO267/600/21427, Slater to Devonshire, 16 April 1928. Colonial Office Minutes; CO267/600/41163, Furley to Devonshire, 8 Aug. 1923. Colonial Office Minutes and Colonial Office to Governor, 21 Sept. 1923.

12. CO267/603/19458, Slater to Thomas, 9 April 1924.

13. Minutes on CO267/600/21427, Slater to Devonshire, 16 April 1923; CO267/603/5246, Slater to Devonshire, 1924 (Memo).

14. See note above; CO554/46/61855, Wilkinson to Milner, 3 Dec. 1920 with enclosures.

15. *Ibid*; note 11 above.

16. CO267/603/19458, Slater to Thomas, 9 April 1924. A conference was called at the Colonial Office on 7 May 1924, chaired by Sir John Risley. Ellis, A. J. Harding and A. J. Dawe represented the Colonial Office. Governor Guggisberg attended the meeting on behalf of his colony, the Gold Coast. Sir J. Coombe, Chief Justice and Kingdom

(Attorney-General) represented Nigeria. McDonnell, the Attorney-General, watched the interests of Sierra Leone. In view of the strong views expressed at the meeting, especially from Nigeria, which was not keen on the W.A.C.A. proposal, it was agreed that the project be deferred. See also CO267/604/32034, Slater to Thomas, 18 June 1924, enclosing Draft Bill for the setting up of an Appeal Court in Sierra Leone; CO267/604/32053, Slater to Thomas, 25 June 1924. The Bill was read and then deferred on instructions from the Colonial Office 'until various questions of justice in the four West African Colonies (were) settled'. CO267/616/Xf5148, Luke to Amery, 22 June 1926.

17. CO267/600/41163, Furley to Devonshire, 8 Aug. 1923 with enclosures.

18. CO267/604/35249, Slater to Thomas, 24 July 1924; CO267/612/44387, Bankole-Bright to Ormsby-Gore, 28 Sept. 1925.

19. Ormsby-Gore, *Report*, 22, 57, pp. 158–9. Ormsby-Gore was accompanied by Hon. C. A. U. Rhys, J. E. W. Flood, and A. Bevir of the Colonial Office.

20. *Ibid*; *Debates*, 29 March 1926.

21. CO267/654/32137/1, Blood to Ormsby-Gore, 25 June 1936; H. C. Luke, *A Bibliography of Sierra Leone* (Oxford, 1952), pp. 14–18. Ormsby-Gore's view on the acculturation of the Blackman was this: 'This Englishman has naturally an instinctive dislike of "assimilation". We like to keep our life distinct from that of other races whether European or not. The more another people acquire our culture, our outlook, and our social habits, very often the wider becomes the gulf between us, we frequently get on better with people different from us, and we appreciate the differences more than the points we have in common.' Ormsby-Gore, *Report*, p. 23; cf. *S.L.W.N.*, 9 April 1924.

22. Ormsby-Gore, *Report*, pp. 159–60.

23. Cf. *Debates*, Governor's address, 26 Nov. 1923 and 30 Nov. 1926.

24. CO267/622 f4626, charges by Dr Bankole-Bright against Sir George Purcell and regarding the Assessors' Ordinance (1927). *S.L.W.N.* had hinted on 27 Aug. 1927 (quoting *West Africa* of 6 Aug. 1927) that Bankie was going to review Ormsby-Gore's *Report*. The pamphlet may have resulted from this review. See Minutes by Sir John Risley on this document cited here.

25. Minutes by McSweeny, Fiddian, Risley and Ormsby-Gore on CO267/622/4626 above.

26. *Ibid*; Colonial Office to Gov. of Sierra Leone, 6 Jan. 1928.

27. *Debates*, 29 March; 9 Dec. 1926; 30 Nov. 1927; Ormsby-Gore, *Report*, pp. 22, 57, 57, 158–9.

28. *Debates*, 9 Dec. 1926. Major Junner also found alluvial platinum in the Peninsula area (York) in May 1926, estimated to cover a region of 20 sq. miles, and likely to be of considerable importance. A nugget, 7·4 grams 4¾ dwts, was found and presented to the British Museum. CO267/620/f4416, Major Junner to Under Secretary of State, 12 July 1927; CO267/619/4235, Major Junner reporting his discovery of Iron Ore in Marampa in 1926; Sir George Beresford-Stooke, 'Sierra Leone Today', *African Affairs*, 53 (1954), pp. 56–65.

29. *Debates*, 9 Dec. 1926. In another debate two years later, the issues Bright raised in the Legco were such that the session could be called 'Protectorate Day'. *Debates*, 29 Nov. 1928.

30. *Debates*, 9 Dec. 1926. See a discussion of this in Wyse, 'On misunderstandings arising', pp. 409–15.

31. *Debates*, 9 Dec. 1926. Two years later Tuboku-Metzger and Bright were moved to thank Governor Byrne for his steadfastness in establishing the Mabang Agricultural Institute though the policy of previous governments had been one of discouragement because they felt Mabang would rival the government Institution at Njala. *Debates*, 29 Nov. 1928.

32. *Debates*, 9 Dec. 1926.

33. *Debates*, 24 Nov.; 30 Nov. 1927. Betts had given notice of the motion on 24 Nov. but the governor had asked him to hold it over and not bring it until the Supply Bill had been debated. Betts had insisted on bringing it in since the 'portions you wish deleted are essential portions of my motion'. His Excellency was unmoved; and he overruled Betts. The latter had to comply. The motion was read on 30 November.
34. *Debates*, 30 Nov. 1927.
35. *Debates*, 30 Nov. 1927; note 11 above.
36. *Debates*, 30 Nov. 1927. Songo-Davies had signed the petition of 1923. See CO267/600/41163, Furley to Devonshire, 8 Aug. 1923 with enclosures.
37. *Debates*, 30 Nov. 1927.
38. *Debates*, 30 Nov. 1927. Wright argued in defence of Purcell, that the good judge came in 1911 and since that time there had ben 96 cases with assessors. Purcell himself overruled over the unanimous decision of Assessors in only twelve cases i.e., $12\frac{1}{2}$ per cent as compared to Bright's figure of 95 per cent casualty under Purcell's hammer. I don't know where Wright got his figures from. Two documents were found covering the period 1901–27. The first one was in CO267/600 and it contained thirteen cases. Purcell presided over eight. All were found guilty by Purcell's court; while there was a split decision on one case, the others returned a verdict of not guilty. If this was the series of cases Bright was referring to then he was right in saying that there was as high a figure as 95 per cent casualty under Purcell. The second group of cases did not indicate the names of the judges, but it contained forty-nine cases. In all, sixty-two assessor cases were tried between 1901 and 1927 according to the above documents. See notes 4 and 6 above.
39. Indeed, Byrne wrote to the Colonial Office exulting that Bright was 'thoroughly shown up and received a hammering which, for the moment, even penetrated his thick skin...Wright, the African member and Songo-Davies spoke well for the government, particularly the former.' CO267/622f 4626, Byrne to Ormsby-Gore, 6 Dec. 1927.
40. *Debates*, 30 Nov. 1927; see also note 3.
41. *Ibid.* Interestingly enough the Colonial Office showed a rare sense of empathy for Bright when he visited Ormsby-Gore in London on 19 September. The minutes of the staff also indicated that they admitted the unfairness and injustice of the Ordinance: 'the state of the Law in the absence of a Criminal Appeal Court is hardly defensible' (H.B.?); 'I think we must use pressure over the Appeal Court and have another try' (Ormsby-Gore). CO267/621 f4502 (file on Bankole-Bright).
42. *Debates*, 30 Nov. 1927.
43. *Debates*, 29 Nov. 1928.
44. CO267/611/56923, Slater to Amery, 8 Dec. 1925 enclosing Report of the Select Committee on the Estimates for 1926; CO267/614, Report of the Select Committee on the Estimates for 1927; CO267/612/44387, Bankole-Bright to Ormsby-Gore, 28 Sept. 1925; *Debates*, 25 Nov. 1925.
45. CO267/612/44387, Bankole-Bright to Ormsby-Gore, 28 Sept. 1925; *Debates*, November and December 1925 and subsequent volumes.
46. Note 45 above.
47. CO267/604, Colonial Office to Governor, 11 July 1924. In 1924 Easmon petitioned for a review of his salary. He had been in government service for almost eleven years (yet to be completed on 8 July 1924) and six of those years he was on the maximum of his scale (£500 × 20 – £600). Supporting his application, Slater observed that were Easmon a European he would have gone from £650 – £1,000 × 50 – £1,150 after eleven years' service. Subsequently, Easmon was put on a £650 p.a. salary, effective from 1 Sept. 1925.
48. *Colonial Office List*, 1923 ff. Indeed, the Director of Education, Nicolson, did admit in 1938 that the designation of African Assistant Director of Education was a misnomer, because he 'does not do the job of an Asst. Director in any way'. This, of course, is

another example of the illusion of 'Krio power'. Designations did not correspond with the incumbent's 'power' or status! CO267/663/32041, A. B. Matthews to MacDonald, 3 June 1938.

49. CO270/64 (Legco Minutes, 1923–32), 24 March 1926; CO267/610/45464, Slater to Amery, 24 Sept. 1925; Colonial Office to Governor, 12 Dec. 1925.

50. CO267/603/5148, Slater to Devonshire, 20 Jan. 1924 forwarding financial reports covering the years 1903–23; CO267/603/17846 Slater to Thomas, 28 March 1924; Colonial Office to Governor, 5 June 1924 giving approval.

51. Petition by members of the Native Medical Service against the conditions of Service, signed by F. Campbell, W. O. Taylor and M. C. F. Easmon in 1919. They complained that there were no definite provisions for study leave, no definite regulations in the service compared to W.A.M.S.: appointments were made locally by the governor with no fixed number. Indeed, since the retirement of Dr Awunor-Renner the number had been reduced to three. The salary was unsatisfactory. See the Colonial Office response quoted (p. 100 above, note 62 in this chapter). CO267/581/33027, Wilkinson to Milner, 7 May 1919. The salary of African M.O.s was fixed at £500–£600; £600–£700 p.a.; CO267/596/ 30622 14 June 1922, Colonial Office Minutes: 'If Natives can be obtained who are capable of doing work, we want to obtain as many as possible of them, as the W.A.M.S. has become an expensive luxury, and where possible we want to limit our expenditure on it. But if we are to get trained Native M.O.s we must be prepared to face a little initial expenditure in fitting them for the job'; CO267/597/53938, Slater to Churchill, 12 Oct. 1922.

52. Slater admitted that Edwin's post would get up to £450 p.a. from 1 Jan. 1925. However, should he act as Post-Master-General he would be given a duty allowance of £96 p.a. CO267//605/2594, Slater to Amery, 27 Dec. 1924; Colonial Office to Governor, 3 Feb. 1925.

53. *Debates*, 25 Nov.; 3 Dec. 1925; CO267/612/44387 Bankole-Bright to Ormsby-Gore, 28 Sept. 1925.

54. CO267/600/36720, Furley to Devonshire, 10 July 1923.

55. CO267/53938, Slater to Churchill, 12 Oct. 1922; CO267/597/61062, Slater to Devonshire, 24 Nov. 1922; CO267/600/36720, Furley to Devonshire, 10 July 1923; CO267/604/32100, Slater to Thomas, 17 June 1924; *Colonial Office List*, 1922 ff. A double increment for outstanding performance by African Staff was proposed in 1923 by Slater – not more than two recipients every year. CO267/597/16273, Secretary of State to Governor, 4 May 1923.

56. In arguing the case for promoting Wright to the post, Slater explained that it would 'save £524–£784 (presumably because the two posts were now combined into one) – also advantageous in that it enables government to promote a deserving African Officer to a post hitherto reserved for Europeans'. Wright's predecessors, Noel Dawes and F. J. Fawcett, had been on salary scale £600 × 30 – £720 × 40 – £840. The governor proposed to place Wright on scale £400 × 20 – £500, but as we noticed above, the actual scale was £360 × 20 – £500. CO267/597/61062, Slater to Devonshire, 24 Nov. 1922; Devonshire to Slater, 8 Jan. 1923.

57. CO267/646/22090/1, Hodson to Fiddian, 9 May 1934; CO267/612/44387, Bankole-Bright to Ormsby-Gore, 28 Sept. 1925; CO267/614, Report of the Select Committee on the Estimates for 1927; CO267/633/9567:31/1, Cookson to Passfield 23 Jan. 1931; *Aurora*, 23 April 1921.

58. *Aurora*, 23 April 1921; *S.L.W.N.*, 26 Oct. 1918; *Debates*, 22 Nov. 1928; T. S. Gale, 'Official medical policy', p. 423; CO267/614/X6246, Luke to Amery, 26 July 1926: 'Portrait: The model mayor', *West Africa*, 10 Feb. 1951.

59. *Debates*, 3 and 4 Dec. 1925.

60. Deana Thomas's biography on 'Milton Margai', submitted for an M.A. degree to the University of Sierra Leone (1972) is the only full account on the career of Dr Margai in print. However, see John Cartwright, *Politics in Sierra Leone, 1947–1967* (Toronto, 1970) and *Political Leadership in Sierra Leone* (Toronto 1978).

61. CO270/64 (Legco Minutes, 1923–32), 16 May 1928; *Debates*, 16 and 19 May 1928 (my emphasis). Bankie's claim of encouraging Margai's parents to send Milton for medical training is in *Debates*, 29 July 1952. Margai did not deny this.

62. *Ibid*; CO267/581/33027, Wilkinson to Milner, 7 May 1919. Colonial Office Minutes.

63. CO267/646/22090/1 Hodson to Cunliffe-Lister, 15 May 1934. There was an interesting exchange in the Colonial Office that year when African doctors in Sierra Leone objected to the prefix African before their designation. The views of the officials put in bold relief the contradictions and the implicit racism in British Colonial Policy. First, the governor blamed Easmon, 'who ought to be grateful to government for allowing him earn such a comparatively large income (in private practice)', as the trouble-maker. And, while Fiddian admitted that 'it is simple humbug to say that there is no racial discrimination when a junior M.O. (even one still on probation) can be put in authority over a medical man, many years his senior', Archeson argued that an African was 'not suitable for senior or public Health post, not because he is an African, but simply because, even if intellectually capable, he doesn't possess the strength of character'. As for the petition, which was not supported by Hodson, the Secretary of State suggested that since the designation African Medical Officer was not used in Nigeria, it might be well to follow the example elsewhere. Thus the designation Medical Officer (Sierra Leone) was suggested. W.A.M.S. of course, ceased to exist in 1935, and was replaced by the Colonial Medical Service to which 'African Members were not eligible', but the government could deploy its staff as it saw fit. 'This of course would fit in with set down preconceptions.' It was a neat arrangement, rationalised thus: No you are not members of the new organisations; but since you are our employees we can deploy you as the need arises, based on our conception of what we think you are capable of doing! See Minutes on above, and Secretary of State to Governor 8 Dec. 1934; Moore to Cunliffe-Lister, 7 Feb. 1935; Macdonald to Moore, 19 Oct. 1935.

64. CO270/64 (Legco Minutes, 1923–32), 17 May 1928.

65. A good example of this attitude was demonstrated when Wilkinson told the Colonial Office, discussing the question of reorganising the Medical Service in Sierra Leone, that 'in the Protectorate no provision has been made for the needs of the population generally, nor is this necessary as the great majority prefer their native methods'. CO267/593/59778, Acting Governor Maxwell to Churchill, 10 Nov. 1921. But see also Gale, 'Official medical policy', 354 ff. for a favourable account of Wilkinson. It was not until 1928 that government made provisions to expand the Medical Services to the general population in the Protectorate. CO267/625/fx9088, Byrne to Amery, 12 April 1928; same to same, 2 Oct. 1928.

66. D. Thomas, 'Milton Margai', p. 41.

67. CO270/75 (Legco Minutes, 1939), 17 Nov. 1936; *Colonial Office List*, pp. 1923 ff.

68. Bright's sister, Lerina asserted that though her brother and Margai 'were political opponents, they were good friends'. Visiting her brother in a hotel in London she was surprised to find Margai with Bankie, drinking in the latter's room. Margai, then, as if by way of explanation, told her: 'Lerina, your brother is my brother, and a friend. I shall never forget him.' The late Thomas Decker confirmed that Margai and Bright never quarrelled outside politics. Interviews: LBT, 5 Aug. 1974; T. L. Decker, 12 Aug. 1975. Dr Fitzjohn, however, argued in his testimony that Bright supported Margai because Sierra Leone needed doctors, but would not want him to sit in the Legislative Council since he considered that this would take away his rights and privileges which was

220

unconstitutionally (*sic*) wrong! Others did not share that view, arguing that Bright was genuinely interested in getting Margai the job so that 'it will be an incentive for the others to go and pursue something'. His support for Margai earned him the resentment of the Reffells. The latter did not speak to him for years. Interviews: LBT, Fitzjohn, Lucan, Fergusson, Robinson on 5 Aug. 1974, 24 Oct. 1974, 21 Aug. 1974, 13 Oct. 1974 and 25 Aug. 1975 respectively.

69. *S.L.W.N.*, 3, 10, 17 Aug. 1935; CO267/655/32157. Enclosures in Blood to Ormsby-Gore, 8 Sept. 1936. But see CO267/635, Hodson to J. H. Thomas, 3 Sept. 1931 and Colonial Office to Governor, 24 Dec. 1931; *Legislation of the Colony of Sierra Leone* (1927), pp. 117–46.

70. *Debates*, 24 March 1926. Betts moved that the Bill be referred to a 'Select Committee to consider whether compensation should be paid to the owners of slaves, and in the meantime the opinion of the Chiefs should be obtained as provided under Section 6 of Cap. 170 of the laws'. Bai Kompa claimed: 'if the slaves want freedom they should redeem themselves or they should be redeemed so that we can put the money in the bank.'

71. *Debates*, 22 Sept. 1927; Sir Harry Luke, *Cities and Men: An Autobiography* (1956), 3, p. 11.

72. *Debates*, 24 March 1926; 22 Sept. 1927. However, see John Grace, *Domestic Slavery in West Africa with Particular Reference to the Sierra Leone Protectorate, 1896–1927* (London, 1975). He called the opposition of the Colony petulant. He believed that this damaged its reputation.

73. *S.L.W.N.*, 16 July 1938.

74. CO270/75 (Legco Minutes, 1933–9), 9 Nov. 1937.

75. *Debates*, 27 Nov. 1929. Bright was in fact a member of the Committee appointed to establish a scheme for training an Auxiliary Service of Medical Assistants in Sierra Leone. See CO267/628/fx9289 Byrne to Sidney Webb, 23 June 1929.

76. CO270/64 (Legco Minutes, 1923–32) 21 Nov. 1928; CO267/622fx 4629, Governor to Secretary of State, 9 Nov. 1927. While Dawe at the Colonial Office deplored the granting of a franchise to women, Ormsby-Gore waspishly commented: 'I really don't think it matters who votes in Freetown Municipality. The women are neither more nor less fitted than the men of that City.'

77. *S.L.W.N.*, 5, 12 Jan. 1929; CO270/75 (Legco Minutes, 1933–9), 9 Nov. 1937; *Debates*, 27 Nov. 1929.

78. Bright obviously felt strongly about this issue. He told the Legco that 'the environment and influence on young plastic minds must be wholesome and healthy'. *Debates*, 27 Nov. 1929.

79. *Daily Mail*, 15 Dec. 1958; *Sierra Leone Year Book* (1957).

80. Cobina Kessie, 'Dr. H. C. Bankole-Bright', *W.A.S.U.*, 2, 2 (April–June 1933); *W.A.S.U.*, 2, 'The Union at Home', 27 Sept. 1926.

81. P. O. Esedebe, 'W.A.S.U.'s Pan-African Role Reconsidered', *J.H.S.S.L.*, 2, 2 (July 1978), pp. 1–9.

82. Philip Garigue, 'The W.A.S.U.; a Study in Cultural Contact,' *Africa*, 23 (1953), pp. 55–69. The first Executive of the Union included W. Davidson Carrol (Gambia) – President; J. B. Danquah (Gold Coast) – Vice-President; Ladipo Solanke (Nigeria) – Secretary-General; J. Akanni Doherty (Gambia); Otto Oyekan During (Sierra Leone); F. O. Byass, (Nigeria) and R. S. Blay (Gold Coast) Members. See Esedebe, 'W.A.S.U.'s Pan-African role', pp. 1–9; G. O. Olunsanya, *The West African Students' Union and the Politics of Decolonization, 1925–1958* (Ibadan, 1982).

83. For instance, in September 1927, when he addressed *W.A.S.U.* on 'The maladministration of British justice in the Courts of Sierra Leone (The Assessors' Ordinance)'. CO267/622/F4626 with enclosures; *W.A.S.U.*, 5 (Sept. 1927). The phrase *Ogboni agba* means a senior elder in Yoruba.

84. CO270/75 (Legco Minutes, 1933–9) 9 Nov. 1937; CO270/74, Executive Council Minutes, 20 July 1937.
85. *S.L.W.N.*, 29 May, 5 June 1937.
86. Wyse, 'A. E. Tuboku-Metzger', in *Encyclopaedia Africana*, p. 156; *S.L.W.N.*, 20 March 1937. Mr J. C. Tuboku-Metzger died in 1982. His son, an engineer, now owns the business.
87: CO448/30. As usual, such awards were often given to offset something else. Slater had asked the Colonial Office to give preference to his recommendation of Sawyerr because he was anxious to see the unofficial community receive an honour 'after the recent generous recognition of officials'. Colonial Office Minutes. This series of documents (at the P.R.O., London) were closed for fifty years from 1925. When I consulted them in 1976 they had not yet been reopened. Bright gave one of the most beautiful funeral orations in the chamber of the Legislative Council on the death of Shorenkeh-Sawyerr. See *Debates*, 30 May 1929.
88. *Debates*, Governor's address, 30 Nov. 1926; correspondence on the V.D. Bill is in CO267/643/2156, Cookson to Cunliffe-Lister, 25 July 1933.
89. CO267/658/32092, Moore to Ormsby-Gore, 26 April 1937.
90. CO267/647/22130, Hodson to Cunliffe-Lister, 19 June 1934. The Colonial Office considered it a good move. 'A healthy spirit of loyalty to the Empire, and a desire to do their bit in time of emergency.' Minutes, Colonial Office to Governor, 31 July 1934 giving approval.
91. Incidentally, the decision to appoint an African to the Magistracy arose out of the Secretary of State's view (arrived at in 1936) that 'as so many Africans in West Africa take up the legal profession it is desirable when a worthy individual exists, to fill the post of Magistrate, or even more rarely a judgeship, to appoint him in order to show African lawyers that if and when they show credit in their profession they can rise to such posts rather than regard the legal profession as a base for politics, or the mere means of personal enrichment'. CO267/658/32092, Minutes by Lambert, Colonial Office, 27 Jan. 1937. The scale of the Sierra Leone Magistrate was the same as that of the African M.O.s (£500 × 24 – £600 × 30 – £720 p.a.), except that a magistrate would remain at the £500 point for three years. In Nigeria, African Police Magistrates earned £600 – £840 p.a.
92. CO267/658/32092 Moore to Ormsby-Gore 26 April 1937, enclosing the list of applicants and comments by his advisers; Colonial Office to Governor, 10 Feb. 1937.
93. Interview, J. C. O. Crowther, 9 Sept. 1974.
94. *S.L.W.N.*, 21 Aug., 1 Sept. 1937.
95. *S.L.W.N.*, 14 Aug. 1937.
96. *S.L.W.N.*, 8, 29 Feb.; 14 March 1936; 27 Feb. 10 April 1937; 23 Nov. 1940; 3 May 1941.
97. *S.L.W.N.* 23 Oct. 1943.

6: AT THE CROSSROADS: THE FLICKERING FLAMES OF CONGRESS AND THE CHALLENGE OF W.A.Y.L., 1936–1939

1. Penelope Hetherington, *British Paternalism and Africa, 1920–1940* (London, 1978).
2. CO267/635, Hodson to Thomas, 3 Sept. 1931; Colonial Office to Governor, 24 Dec. 1931; *Debates*, 4 May 1932.
3. CO267/655/32157, Blood to Ormsby-Gore, 8 Sept. 1936, with enclosures; F. A. N. Lisk, 'Industrial Relations in Sierra Leone', pp. 11–14. H. L. Van der Laan, *The Sierra Leone Diamonds: An Economic Study Covering the Years 1952–1961* (Oxford, 1965).
4. CO267/665, Jardine to Macdonald, 21 July 1938; CO267/665/32210, Jardine to MacDonald, 23 Nov. 1938; CO267/665/32199, Jardine to Macdonald, 23 Nov. 1938;

CO267/673/32254/8 (Nov. 1939); *S.L.W.N.*, 5 Feb. 1938, 'Happenings and occurences at Marampa Mines'; W. M. MacMillan, 'African development: (a) by external capital mining enterprise and the labour problem', in C. K. Meek et al., *Europe and West Africa: Some Problems and Adjustments* (London, 1940), pp. 42–72; F. J. Pedler, *Main Currents of West African History, 1940–1978* (London 1979), pp. 37–42.

5. Lisk, 'Industrial Relations'; M. H. Y. Koniki, 'Politics of protest in Colonial West Africa: The Sierra Leone experience', *The African Review*, 4, 3 (1974), pp. 423–58.

6. L. W. Wilson Papers (MSS. Afr. S.388) Box 1, Folio 5. Fenton joined the Sierra Leone Administration in 1915. He was appointed Secretary for Protectorate Affairs in 1940 and, when the post was abolished six years later, he became Chief Commissioner of the Protectorate. He retired in 1947. See Kilson, *Modernization*, ch. 8; C. Magbaily Fyle, *The History of Sierra Leone* (London, 1982), pp. 116–17; W. Barrows, *Grass Roots Politics in an African State: Integration and Development in Sierra Leone* (New York and London, 1976); Wraith, *Local Administration*, pp. 153 ff; Decker, *Our Paramount Chiefs*.

7. CO267/633/9569, 'Native disturbances in Kambia – the Haidara Kontorfilli episode', Cookson to Fiddian, 5 March 1931; David Moore-Sieray, 'Idara Kontorfili and the 1931 Insurrection in North Western Sierra Leone', B.A. Hons. History Dissertation, University of Sierra Leone, 1978: P. M. Jusu, 'The Haidara Rebellion of 1931', *S.L.S.* (N.S.), 3 (Dec. 1954); M. H. Y. Kaniki, 'The Idara rebellion of 1931: a reappraisal', *J.H.S.S.L.*, 1, 2 (June 1977), pp. 57–64.

8. See R. E. Turnbull's comment, 'the colony is extremely small, and indeed, relatively unimportant'. Minutes on CO267/665/32212, Jardine to MacDonald, 11 June 1938; CO267/658/32097, Jardine to Ormsby-Gore, 4 March 1938; cf CO267/641/2078, report by the Colonial Office Education Expert, Hans Vischer, on his visit to Sierra Leone in 1933 (22 June 1933).

9. CO267/654/32137/1, Blood to Ormsby-Gore, 25 Jan. 1936.

10. Minutes by A. Mayhew on CO267/659/32142, Colonial Office (1 June 1937). See also CO554/132/33721/5, notes on points arising in discussion with the Secretary of State on Wednesday 27 Oct. and Thursday 28 Oct. 1943.

11. CO270/74, Exco Minutes, 8 Oct. 1937.

12. L. W. Wilson Papers (MSS. Afri. S.388) Box 1, Encyclopaedia of Sierra Leone.

13. CO267/654/321377/1, Blood to Ormsby-Gore, 25 June 1936; CO270/74, Executive Council Meeting of 8 Oct. 1937; CO267/659/32142, Minutes by A. Mayhew (9 Nov. 1937). Blood was a compulsive writer, yet there is little of value in the correspondence on Sierra Leone which he left in his papers deposited at Rhodes House, Oxford. This is odd, considering the fact that next to Ceylon he had his longest service in Sierra Leone. See the Harry Blood Papers (MSS Brit. Emp. S.408 (4) Box 4); Micah Amolo, 'Trade Unionism and Colonial Authority: Sierra Leone, 1930–1945, *Trans. African Journal of History*, 8, 1 and 2 (1979), pp. 36–52.

14. 'For some reason which is rather hard to explain satisfactorily, Sierra Leone has for some years found it difficult to fill its higher posts by local appointments, despite the fact that it is the oldest seat of European education on the West Coast and it used to supply the rest of the Coast with Clerks.' CO267/678/32010, Minutes (29 July 1941). See also Minutes by A. J. Dawe on Blood to MacDonald, 27 Jan. 1939 (CO267/667) and CO267/665/32211, Jardine to MacDonald, 11 June 1938.

15. CO267/674/32036, Jardine to MacDonald, 11 Dec. 1939. Minutes by H. M. Grace.

16. CO267/654/32137/1, Blood to Ormsby-Gore, 25 June 1936. Memo by Colonial Office; and Colonial Office to Moore, 10 Nov. 1936. Apparently the Colonial Office was sufficiently concerned for it to instruct Governor Monckton-Moore on assuming his post, 'to give careful consideration to the possibility of developing its [i.e., the Colony's] economic and general welfare'. In fact a 1935 publication by one J. C. Meggit calling

Freetown a slum dwelling, and a further endorsement of this allegation by *West Africa* caused a mild uproar in the Colonial Office. See CO267/646/22078, Minutes by Fiddian, 5 May 1935. /Enclosures. See also CO554/132/33726/5 (1943).

17. CO267/655/32157, Blood to Ormsby-Gore, 8 Sept. 1936. Enclosures – Turbett gave lists of old and active members of N.C.B.W.A. and the names of secessionists. For instance, the late Archdeacon Cole, the late Mayor May, A. E. Tuboku-Metzger, J. F. Boston, Songo-Davies, Bright, Betts, T. J. Thompson, C. D. Hotobah-During (?), T. E. Nelson-Williams and F. A. Miller were active some years back; but the Shorunkeh-Sawyerrs (deceased in 1929), the Hebrons, C. E. Wright, E. H. Cummings and E. A. C. Noah (?) had shown little interest in Congress. In the 1930s the active congress participants were in addition to Bright (who had seceded for a short while, 1929–31), Betts, Tuboku-Metzger the father, O. J. V. Tuboku-Metzger the son, S. A. Hughes, T. J. Carew, A. Benka-Coker, J. M. Faulkner, W. Baanah-Davies, Dr I. E. C. Steady, T. S. French, Archdeacon T. S. Johnson, Wilfred S. Cole, F. A. Miller, Dr I. C. Pratt, Revd J. O. E. Taylor, Melville Wright, Dunstan Williams, Hadiru Deen (Secretary of Muslim Congress) etc. T. J. Thompson, E. A. C. Noah, S. J. Barlatt, Hotobah-During and Songo Davies were no more interested in Congress – 'Personal animosities have been responsible to a certain extent for the lack of interest taken by some of these gentlemen. The Sierra Leone branch is entirely in the hands of Beoku-Betts and Bankole-Bright', commented Turbett.

18. None of the major works on the political history of Sierra Leone has treated this episode in congress politics. See Kilson, *Political Change*; Langley, *Pan Africanism*; Spitzer, *The Creoles*. The *Weekly News* issues covering March to May, 1936 are perhaps the only published reference source for this episode.

19. Richard W. Hull, *Modern Africa*, p. 176.

20. *S.L.W.N.*, 14, 28 March; 4, 11, 18 April; 2, 9, 16 May; 6, 13 June 1936 contain full account of the conference. These references are comprehensive enough, and for brevity and space, cited references for this section will only be given when a point needs explaining. Documentary evidence on the financial position of Sierra Leone is in the following: CO267/635/9694:31/1 Hodson to Fiddian, 18 Sept. 1931; CO267/635/963:31/1 (1931); CO267/639/9898:32/1 (1932); CO267/637/9799:32/6 (1932); CO267/651/32103 (1935); CO267/654/32120 (1936–7). However, see A. J. G. Wyse, 'The Sierra Leone Branch', pp. 675–98.

21. For some reason that I was unable to find, an Executive Council decision in 1932 agreeing in principle to the appointment of travelling magistrates to take over the judicial work of the District Commissioners in the Protectorate was not implemented as projected in 1934 (Executive Council Minutes, 6–7 Sept. 1932. CO270/74/). N. A. C. Weir, an Administrative Officer in the Sierra Leone government service, 1936–43, wrote a memo on 'Future Political Development in Sierra Leone', 23 Jan. 1940. In it, among other suggestions, he recommended that D.C.s be relieved from petty magisterial work, supervising of the Sub-Treasury etc. so that they may spend more time in training Native Administrations to become fit to run their affairs with little intervention. (MSS. Afr. S.1151).

22. CO267/690/32411 Stevenson to Stanley, 16 March 1945; CO267/690/32415, 32419, 32410.

23. Revd Max Gorvie had an opportunity to publicise his views in the *Weekly News*, 18 July; 12 Sept. 1936. A more detailed discussion is contained in his book, *Old and New in Sierra Leone* (London, 1939); CO267/690/32435, Stevenson to Hall, 14 Jan 1946, ref. definition of 'Natives' and 'Non Natives'.

24. *S.L.W.N.*, 4 April 1936. Apparently a decision by the government in 1932 to allow private medical practitioners to treat government officials (a question Bankie had

consistently pursued) for a trial period of one year did not seem to have made much improvement on a basic grievance of medical practitioners, i.e., the refusal by government to accept medical certificates signed by the former for government employees. See CO270/74, Executive Council Minutes, 27 Sept. 1932.

25. Compare interpretations in works by Kilson and Langley cited in this book.
26. *S.L.W.N.*, 20 June 1936. Elizabeth Isichei gives another example of this 'national perspective' in her *History of West Africa Since 1800* (New York, 1977), p. 268: 'one notable exception to this general picture of disregard for the masses should be recorded. Several members of the Sierra Leone branch of the National Congress raised funds for striking Workers – a potential alliance which, significantly enough, caused the utmost alarm to the Colonial Government.'
27. *S.L.W.N.*, 20 June 1936.
28. George Padmore, 'Democratic advance in Sierra Leone', *Crisis*, 64, 3 (March 1957), pp. 149–52. An editorial note commented, 'this article explains why Sierra Leone politics have become a happy hunting ground for Scalawags'. Padmore, 'is one of the foremost experts on African problems'. But see Padmore's more complimentary views on Krio politicians in *How Britain Rules Africa*, ch. 9.
29. CO267/655/32158, Blood to Ormsby-Gore, 8 Sept. 1936. Enclosures and Minutes by Colonial Office Staff; *S.L.W.N.*, 13 June 1936; Blood Papers (MSS. Brit. Emp. S.408 (4)), Reminiscences.
30. Note 29 above; CO267/684/32010, Colonial Office Minutes on Stevenson to Stanley, 8 Dec. 1944. Draft letter of Secretary of State to Governor of Sierra Leone (undated); CO554/132/33726/5 (1943).
31. CO267/655/32157, Blood to Ormsby-Gore, 8 Sept. 1936; CO267/658/32092, Moore to Ormsby-Gore, 26 April 1937. Enclosures; *S.L.W.N.*, 20 March 1937, letter to the Editor by A. E. Tuboku-Metzger.
32. *S.L.W.N.*, 26 Dec. 1936.
33. *S.L.W.N.*, 16 July 1938. For instance, at a Congress Meeting of 1929, the organisation claimed credit for the establishment of W.A.C.A., the right granted to Protectorate inhabitants to appeal to the circuit court against a judgement by the District Commissioner, the stay over the closure of dispensaries in the villages and the scheme for the training of Medical Assistants to replace Dispensers in due course. See *S.L.W.N.*, 6 April; 4, 11 1929; CO267/655/32157, Blood to Ormsby-Gore, 8 Sept. 1936, enclosing Turbett's memo on Congress.
34. *S.L.W.N.*, 18, 25 May; 1, 8, 29 June; 6 July; 9 Nov. 1929.
35. *S.L.W.N.*, 7 May 1938.
36. CO267/667/32010, Jardine to MacDonald, 14 Dec. 1939. Nelson-Williams to Herbert Macauley, 10 May 1939 (Herbert Macauley Papers, Box 90, File 4).
37. *S.L.W.N.*, 25 Aug. 1935; *D.G.* 28 July 1938.
38. Note 17; *S.L.W.N.*, 8, 22, 29 Feb. 14, 28 March 1936. The defence counsel reflected the alignment of politics in Freetown. Betts and O. J. V. Tuboku-Metzger, the progressives, defended Bright; C. E. Wright, C. D. Hotobah-During, N. J. P. Metzger-Boston and H. J. Lightfoot-Boston, defended J. Fowell Boston.
39. *S.L.W.N.*, 6 July 1929. Ten years later O. G. R. Williams was dismayed over the fact that C. E. Wright had to be renominated for a third term in the Legislative Council. CO267/669/32010, Jardine to MacDonald, 14 Dec. 1939, Colonial Office Minutes.
40. Interview, T. L. Decker, 23 Sept. 1976.
41. FCBP (MSS. Brit. Emp. S.365) Box 86/2 Siaka Stevens to Rita Hinden, 15 March 1949; Amolo, 'Trade Unionism', p. 50. But see Deveneaux, *Power and Politics*, ch. 2 for his own interpretation.
42. Cf. article by Speedo (M. G. M. Cole), 'The Youth Movement, as I see it', enclosed in

225

CO267/666/32216, Activities of Wallace-Johnson and W.A.Y.L.; Deveneaux, *Power and Politics*, p. 17. He says the 'only real political activity' in pre-independence Sierra Leone was by I. T. A. Wallace-Johnson!

43. Much work has been done on Wallace-Johnson by Leo Spitzer and La Ray Denzer, among others. These two authors have written articles in the *International Journal of African Historical Studies*, 6, 3 (1973), pp. 413–52; pp. 565–601 in two parts, entitled, 'I. T. A. Wallace-Johnson and the West African Youth League'. Dr Denzer is finishing a biography on Wallace-Johnson. The short life history of W. J. presented here is therefore distilled from the writings of these people and other sources that would be cited; for example, CO267/665/32208, Jardine to MacDonald, 30 June 1938; and Jardine to O. G. R. Williams, 12 May 1938 enclosing reports on the life and activities of Wallace-Johnson; C. Forway, *Historical Dictionary*, pp. 225–7; Chin Sheng-Pao, *The Gold Coast Delegation to Britain in 1934: The Political Background* (National Chengchi University Studies in African Affairs; Republic of China, 1970). Pamphlet, 39 pp.; S. K. B. Asante, *Pan-African Protest: West Africa and the Italo-Ethiopian Crisis, 1934–1941* (London, 1971); M. H. Y. Kaniki, 'Politics of protest', pp. 423–58.

44. Wallace-Johnson claimed he was instrumental in uncovering the City Council scandal of 1926. Oddly enough, however, though he was in Freetown, for someone who was to identify himself with workers' causes, he did not seem to have taken part in the Railway Strike of 1926. See Spitzer and Denzer, 'I. T. A. Wallace-Johnson and the W.A.Y.L.', p. 417.

45. Yaw Twumasi, 'Press Freedom and nationalism under colonial rule in the Gold Coast (Ghana)', *J.H.S.N.*, 8, 3 (Dec. 1974), pp. 499–520; note 43 above.

46. S. K. B. Asante, 'I. T. A. Wallace-Johnson and the Italo-Ethiopian crisis', *J.H.S.N.*, 7, 4 (June 1975), pp. 631–46.

47. Interviews, T. A. L. Decker, 23 Sept. 1976; S. M. O. Boyle, 21 Dec. 1976.

48. A good example of this irreverence was his lampoon on Bright following the City Council elections in 1938. '(1) Death due to Political Diarrhoea and the collapse of the White House Demoniacal Maniac whilst diligently oscillating the Political pendulum of the Microscopic Cocus suspected in the Big Cigars and the Body Politic. (2) Funeral Ode: Dunstan could not stand,/Newton's an old man/Boisy's merely noisy/ so Bankie's heart is broke,/May they rest in Pieces.

   (3) *Ding Dung Bell!*
   Banky's in the well, who put him in?
   A little Youth in teen! Who'll pull him out?
   No! Never out. Oh what a jolly sight for Youth
   to see Big Banky in the well. Okay!!! Enclosed in CO267/671/32221, Blood to MacDonald, 14 Jan. 1939.

49. CO267/671/32208, Jardine & MacDonald, 30 June 1938; CO267/670/32210, Part 2 Jardine to MacDonald, 23 Sept. 1939; CO267/666/32216, Activities of Wallace-Johnson and the W.A.Y.L.; Kaniki, 'Politics of protest', pp. 423–58. For a hostile attitude to Johnson's populist approach, see *S.L.W.N.*s editorial of 13 May 1939.

50. Interviews, S. M. O. Boyle, former Secretary of W.A.Y.L., Freetown Branch, 21 Dec. 1976, Birmingham, England; T. A. L. Decker, 12 Aug. 1975; I. C. Hotobah-During, son of C. D., 1 Sept. 1974. Easmon, N. A. Cox-George, Ned John, and M. C. Marke were the 'backroom boys' of Boyle who edited *The African Standard*; *S.L.W.N.*, 21 May 1938.

51. Post, 'British policy and representative government', pp. 31–57; J. B. Webster, 'Political activity in British West Africa, 1900–1940,' in Ajayi and Crowder, *History of West Africa*, 2, pp. 568–95; John D. Hargreaves, *The End of Colonial Rule in West Africa* (The Historical Association, London, 1976). J. A. Sofola's *Dynamism in African Leadership: The American Influence* (Ibadan, 1981) is also relevant here to illustrate the new type of leadership.

52. E. T. Wilson, *Russia and Black Africa before World War II* (London, 1974); cf. Hargreaves, *Colonial Rule*, p. 16.
53. Historical background to Fabian Colonial Bureau Papers (MSS. Brit. Emp. S. 365).
54. CO267/673/32254/8 Delegation of League of Coloured Peoples meeting with Secretary of State for the Colonies, Malcolm MacDonald, on 21 Nov. 1939; CO267/676/32216, File on W.A.Y.L. Jardine to Dawe (private), 22 Feb. 1943; Asante, *Pan-African Protest*, pp. 190–8.
55. Interview, S. M. O. Boyle, 21 Dec. 1976; Bah, 'Bankole-Wright', pp. 132–3; M. Kilson, 'Nationalism and social classes in British West Africa', *Journal of Politics*, 20 (May 1958), pp. 368–86; Asante, *Pan-African Protest*, pp. 190–8.
56. *S.L.W.N.*, 5, 26 Feb. 1938.
57. *S.L.W.N.*14 Aug. 1937.
58. *S.L.W.N.*21 Aug. 1937.
59. Kaniki, 'Politics of protest', p. 432.
60. 'W.J. has raked up all the old complaints and he has discovered little that is new or original', CO267/665/32208, Jardine to MacDonald, 30 June 1938.
61. *S.L.W.N.*, 19 June 1937.
62. Kaniki, 'Politics of protest', pp. 435–40. There is a discrepancy in the dates here. Kaniki states that W.A.Y.L. was inaugurated at the meeting of 2 May 1938 (and this is confirmed by *S.L.W.N.* 14 May 1938). A police report by the Acting Commissioner, however, puts the date as 29 April 1938. The Executive, according to him, comprised A. Lisk-Carew, Photographer – President, Z. S. Faux, Treasurer, G. Tregson-Roberts and Mrs Edna Horton (nee Elliott), Joint Secretaries. The committee members included F. A. Miller, D. A. Yaskey and Mrs Elsie Commings-John. Another letter of 20 June 1938 gave a fuller list; C. Tregson-Roberts and Mrs Edna Elliot Horton were Joint Secretaries, and Wallace-Johnson, Organizing Secretary, F. A. Miller, chairman, M. S. Deen Alharazim, Elias Bamin, Vice Chairmen, President – A. Lisk-Carew, Vice-Presidents – M. S. Deen Alharazim and Agnes Macauley, Legal Adviser, C. D. Hotobah-During; Committee Members – A. Z. Deen Gabisi, A. B. Sillah, A. Benka-Coker, C. Cummings-John, H. E. S. Nylander, A. B. Ibrahim, Lottie Black, H. N. Thompson, D. P. H. George, M. Pinder Horton, E. D. B. Williams, S. M. O. Boyle, F. B. Hebron, A. C. Wilson, Victoria Jones, H. E. Faulkner, A. A. DeenGab, and A. S. Tejan-Sie. See CO267/665/32210, Jardine to MacDonald, 23 Nov. 1938; CO267/665/32208, Jardine to MacDonald, 30 June 1938, enclosing report from the Acting Police Commissioner.
63. *D.G.*, Xmas issue, Dec. 1939, 'Looking Backwards and Forward. A review of political events of 1939' by Thomas Decker; CO267/665/32210, Wages and conditions of labour for Africans (1938); CO267/665/32199, file on the Strike and S.L.D.C. 26 Dec. 1937 and 10 Jan. 1938; CO267/665/32208, Jardine to MacDonald, 30 June 1938 and CO267/666/32216, Activities of Wallace-Johnson and W.A.Y.L. See Kaniki, Lisk, Spitzer and Denzer for discussion in their cited works; Amolo,'Trade unionism', pp. 36–52.
64. Kaniki, 'Politics of protekst', p. 438; *S.L.W.N.*, 16 July 1938 claimed that 1,500 members, including representatives from the Protectorate were assembled at the meeting of 6 July 1938; *S.L.W.N.*, 18 June 1938.
65. Note 64 above.
66. Spitzer, *The Creoles*, pp. 180 ff.; Asante, *Pan-African Protest*, pp. 190–8.
67. See, for instance, J. M. Rose's column in *S.L.W.N.*, 19 March 1938; issues of 26 April and 28 June 1924 announcing the resuscitation of the Agricultural Society whose membership was open to Colony and Protectorate citizens.
68. Statistics supplied by Delco on the cost of living index, for example, had led Jardine to conclude that a labourer with family could subsist on 15s 0d. per month. CO267/665, Jardine to MacDonald, 27 July 1938. But, on further investigations, he was forced to admit the implications of the figures, which raised the cost of living to £1 10s. 2d., that

227

'it is clear that if the figures submitted are accepted, the standard wage [of 9d. per day] should be appreciably higher than it is at present'. As for commercial clerks they were on 'starvation wages' of 10s. 0d. to 30s. 0d. per month, and without any security. Though the governor deprecated the cynicism and exploitation by commercial firms, he argued that this resulted from 'the aversion of the educated Creoles to any form of occupation than sedentary employment', among other shortcomings. CO267/665/32199, Jardine to MacDonald, 23 Nov. 1938; CO267/665/32210, Jardine to MacDonald, 23 Nov. 1938.

69. Kaniki, 'Politics of protest', p. 440. According to S. M. O. Boyle, (21 Dec. 1976) Banja Tejan-Sie (Governor-General of Sierra Leone 1968–71) was Secretary of the Protectorate Branch of W.A.Y.L.; Amolo, 'Trade unionism', p. 48.

70. Interview, T. A. L. Decker, 12 Aug. 1975; S. M. O. Boyle, 21 Dec. 1976; cf I. C. Hotobah-During, 1 Sept. 1974.

71. Just two years previously Turbett had told the Colonial Office: 'This ancient and loyal colony may remain more conservative in its outlook for quite a time – more especially if Beoku-Betts and Bankole-Bright continue to be the people's representatives. There is no sign at the moment that the people in the colony are wavering in their allegiance', CO267/655/32157, Blood to Ormsby-Gore, 8 Sept. 1938 – enclosures.

72. Note 52 above. The Sierra Leone government was aware of W.J.'s socialist connections too. CO267/665/32208, Jardine to MacDonald, 30 June 1938.

73. CO267/670/32210/2 Part 1, Blood to MacDonald, 9 Feb. 1938.

74. *Ibid*; CO267/666/32216, Activities of W.J. and the W.A.Y.L.

75. *S.L.W.N.*11 June 1938; CO267/665/32210, Jardine to MacDonald, 21 July 1938 forwarding further data on the cost of living index covering government departments like Railway, Education and Agriculture; CO267/666/32216, Jardine complained to MacDonald on 28 Nov. 1938 'W.J. set my Commission at naught, and was contumacious, but has escaped punishment', CO270/74, Executive Council Minutes of 18 Jan. 1939; CO267/670/32210/2 Part 1, Blood to MacDonald, 9 Feb. 1938; CO267/671/32221, Blood to MacDonald, 14 Jan. 1939.

76. Note 75 above; *S.L.W.N.*, 14 Jan. 1939.
The breakdown is as follows:
Central Ward: C. A. Cummings-John 241 votes*
Central Ward: E. A. C. Davies 217 votes*
Central Ward: C. Dustan Williams 74 votes
              J. Newton Faulkner 63 votes
East Ward: O. J. V. Tuboku-Metzger* – Unopposed
West Ward: E. D. Morgan 110* votes
West Ward: J. E. Boisy Davies 100 votes
*Elected.

77. CO267/670/32210/2, Blood to MacDonald, 9 Feb. 1939, Colonial Office Minutes.

78. 'The Sierra Leone Youth League [the author preferred this name to W.A.Y.L.] as I see it, present and future', by Ade Sawyerr, *S.L.W.N.*, 16 July 1938.

79. Note 42 above.

80. *S.L.W.N.*, Jan.–April 1939; cf. April–Dec. 1938. These people, including Bankole-Bright, were 'collaborators of the British administration', states Asante, *Pan-African Protest*, p. 194.

81. *Debates*, May–June 1939; CO267/670/32210/2 Part 1 Jardine to Dawe (Private), 1 June 1939; CO270/74, Executive Council Minutes, 22 March; 5, 25 April; 5, 22 May 1939; Marcus-Jones, 'Protection of fundamental rights', pp. 88–103; Spitzer, *The Creoles*, pp. 205 ff.

82. Nelson-Williams was, of course, not a member of W.A.Y.L., and he did not approve of

the 'unbridled effusions' of the League. But he believed that the legislation struck at the very essence of the people's liberty. Hence his opposition. See his letter to Herbert Macauley, 10 May 1939 (Herbert Macauley Papers, Box 90, file 4). Various views can be gauged from *Debates*, May–June 1939. *D.G.* columnist, Thomas Decker, claimed that the purpose of the Bill 'was to put an end to the activities of the left wing in Sierra Leone today' (issues of 24, 25 May 1939).

83. CO267/670/32210/2 Part 1, Jardine to Dawe (Private) 1 June 1939; Jardine to Colonial Office (tel.), 18 May 1939.
84. CO267/667/32032, Jardine to MacDonald, 18 Jan. 1939. Enclosures; CO267/673/32267, Blood to Williams, 18 Sept. 1939.
85. CO267/670/32210/2 Part 1, Jardine to Dawe (Private) 1 June 1939; Jardine to Colonial Office (tel.), 18 May 1939. Public opinion as represented by the *Weekly News* seemed to have veered on to the side of law and order, if not in support of the government. While lamenting the need for the Three Bills, the general impression was that this legislation was occasioned by W.A.Y.L.'s excesses. Thus 'Speedo' denounced these so-called 'Saviours, anti-Christ and ridiculer of the Church. Let them go and leave the country in peace and quietness.' (27 May 1939 *S.L.W.N.*). C. E. Wright, S. J. S. Barlatt, Bankole-Bright and Blood all gave broadcast talks on the radio, making full use of the newly established Rediffusion Service, to explain why the laws were passed. Barlat believed that mutual distrust between the government and people had caused all this. He did not believe the people were intentionally subversive though their methods might have been ill advised and reprehensible. The *Weekly News* blamed mass demonstrations which did not help anyone. Apart from Bankie, the plea of the African spokesmen was to postpone these laws. See *S.L.W.N.*, 6, 13, 20, 27 May; 17, 24 June; 1, 15 July; 5 Aug. 1939; *D.G.* 17 June 1939.
86. Kilson, *Political Change*; Spitzer, *Creoles*; cf. Bah, 'Bankole-Bright', pp. 29–30; Kaniki, 'Politics of protest', pp. 449–50.
87. Interviews, T. A. I. Decker, 12 Aug. 1975; cf. E. J. Robinson, 20 Aug. 1975. This informant (aged 81 years when interviewed) claimed that he brought W.J. and Bankie together by stressing to the former that the latter, as a much older man, demanded respect from him.
88. *Debates*, 20 June 1939; interview, S. M. O. Boyle, 21 Dec. 1976; CO267/671/32221, Blood to MacDonald, 14 Jan. 1939; *S.L.W.N.*, 26 Nov.; 17 Dec. 1938; 3, 10 June 1939. E. F. Luke later defended Bankie in his case against Wallace-Johnson.
89. *S.L.W.N.* 17 Dec. 1938; 21, 28 Jan. 1939; interview, I. C. Hotobah-During, 1 Sept. 1974. Bright was represented by a European lawyer, C. J. Kempson, on the criminal summons case. He was granted bail on his own cognisance and, on 23 January, the judge discharged the accused.
90. *Debates*, 20 June 1939; CO267/673/32268, Bright to Jardine 27 June 1939. Enclosed in Jardine to MacDonald, 16 Sept. 1939.
91. CO267/669/32157, Blood to MacDonald, 21 Aug. 1939. Enclosing reply of Bankie (8 March 1939) to N.C.B.W.A.'s (Sierra Leone) letter of 17 March 1939.
92. *Debates*, 20 June 1939; CO267/673/32268, Bright to Jardine, 27 June 1939. Enclosed in Jardine to MacDonald, 16 Sept. 1939.
93. *Debates*, 20 June 1939.
94. *Debates*, 11, 23 May and 8 Sept. 1939; Kaniki, 'Politics of protest' pp. 450–2. His loyalty to Britain cannot have been more sincere than when he suggested at the time of financial stringency that the Legislative Council consider the advisability of voting a gift from the reserve Fund to the Imperial Defence of Britain to help her protect the dependency. Interestingly, this was turned down as the government had already spent £14,000 to reorganise the Sierra Leone Battalion of the R.W.A.F.F.

95. Interview: LBT, 4 Aug. 1974; *Debates*, 20 June 1939; CO267/665/32208, Jardine to MacDonald, 20 June 1938; CO267/666/32216, Jardine to MacDonald, 28 Nov. 12938.
96. *Debates*, 20 June 1939.
97. CO267/673/32268, Jardine to MacDonald, 16 Sept. 1939.
98. *S.L.W.N.* 17 Dec. 1938; CO267/671/32221, Blood to MacDonald, 14 Jan. 1939.
99. CO267/669/32157, Blood to MacDonald, 21 Aug. 1939.
100. *Ibid.*
101. M. Crowder, 'An African aristocracy'. *The Geographical Magazine*, 31, 4 (Aug. 1958), pp. 183–90; Blyden, 'Constitutional change' p. 335, note 9.
102. For instance, the late Thomas Decker once confessed that Bankie was 'one of the bravest persons I have come across'. Though he was not a great fan of Bright's he readily admitted that one knew where one stood with him. He could tell you what he thought of you and to hell with the consequences. Bankie was the first man to tell W.J. to his face 'you are a rabble rouser'. The ridiculousness of one pot calling another black apart, his forthrightness was not a virtue common among his contemporaries. Interviews; T. A. L. Decker, 12 Aug. 1975; LBT 7 Aug. 1974; Rogers Williams, 24 Aug. 1974.
103. *Debates*, address by Sir Douglas Jardine, 5 Dec. 1935; cf. CO267/667/32010, Jardine to MacDonald, 14 Dec. 1939.
104. CO267/670/32210/2 Part 1, Jardine to Dawe, 1 June 1939; *Debates*, May–June, 1939.
105. CO267/670/32210 Part 2, Jardine to MacDonald, 23 Sept. 1939; *S.L.W.N.*, 9, 6, 25 Sept. 1939 reported W.J.'s detention and conviction for the *African Standard* article of 11 Aug. 1939 'Who killed Fonnie?'.
106. CO267/670/32216, Jardine to MacDonald, 22 Feb. 1940. Colonial Office Minutes: *S.L.W.N.*, 21 Sept. 1940.
107. CO267/671/32245, notes on Sierra Leone made by Professor W. M. MacMillan in conversation with Mr A. J. Dawe, 20 Jan. 1939; CO267/270/32210/2 Part 1 Blood to MacDonald, 9 Feb. 1939; CO267/670/32210 Part 2, Dawe to Blood, 11 Feb. 1939; Blood to Dawe, 15 1939; J. D. Hargreaves, *Aberdeenshire to Africa: North East Scots and British Overseas Expansion* (Aberdeen, 1981), pp. 78–9.
108. See note above; CO267/671/32245, Conversation between A. J. Dawe and Sir Douglas Jardine, 17 Jan. 1939.
109. W. M. MacMillan, 'African development: (a) by external capital mining enterprise and the labour problem; (b) negative example of Sierra Leone', in C. K. Meek et al., *Europe and West Africa*, pp. 42–80.
110. *Ibid.*
111. CO267/670/32210/2 Part 1, Jardine to Dawe (private), 1 June 1939; CO267/670/32210 Part 2, Blood to Dawe, 15 March 1939; CO267/670/32210 Part 1, Blood to MacDonald, 9 Feb. 1939.
112. *Debates*, May–June 1939; CO267/670/32210 Part 2, Blood to Dawe, 15 March 1939; CO270/74; Executive Council Minutes 20 Oct. 1939.
113. Interviews, S. M. O. Boyle, 21 Dec. 1976; J. C. Lucan, 21 Aug. 1974; CO267/66/32216, Jardine to MacDonald, 28 Nov. 1938; *S.L.W.N.*, 16 Sept. 1939; 21 Sept. 1940.
114. *Ibid.*, CO267/678, Colonial Office Minutes, 1940/1.
115. *S.L.W.N.*, 2 Dec. 1939; CO267/667/302020, Jardine to MacDonald, 14 Dec. 1939. On the question of the disintegrative factor in colony political organisations, Marilla Van perhaps had good reasons to be smug when he recalled that the West End Benevolent Society had been going on apace since its inception on 25 Dec. 1917 (with a membership standing at eighteen); and this was no mean feat, he insisted 'in a place like Sierra Leone where jealousy and prejudice are so rife, and where these conditions are invariably a setback to the progress of organs of this kind, sometimes bringing them to wreck and ruin', *S.L.W.N.* 6 May 1939.

116. CO267/670/32210 Part 2, Blood to Dawe, 15 Marh 1939.
117. CO267/670/32210 Part 2, Jardine to MacDonald, 23 Sept. 1939.
118. Interview, S. M. O. Boyle, 21 Dec. 1976; Blyden, 'Constitutional change',pp. 176–7.

7: IN THE POLITICAL WILDERNESS: THE TURBULENT YEARS, 1939–1951

1. M. Crowder, 'The 1939–1945 war and West Africa', in Ajayi and Crowder, *History of West Africa*, 2, ch. 17.
2. See *S.L.W.N.*, *African Standard*, and *Daily Guardian* for 1939–45. One such demand for an enlarged Legislative Council pleaded for, and expressed the hope, that the Protectorate might come to enjoy the right of selecting its own representatives to sit in the Central Legislature. 'We cherish', said the *Weekly News* (24 Nov. 1945) 'the hope that such representatives will include, not only Chiefs, but other persons of ability and standing who may not be connected with a ruling house'.
3. CO267/677/32319, Jardine to Williams (private) 9 Oct. 1940.
4. *SLWN*, 2 Sept. 1939; 23 March 1946. Even the 'Leftist' *Daily Guardian* and the Krio culture Nationalist, Thomas Decker, supported the war. See issue of 11 Sept. 1939; cf. W. F. Gutteridge, 'Military and police forces in colonial Africa', in Duignan and Gann, *Colonialism in Africa, 1870–1960*, 2, pp. 286–319.
5. *African Standard*, 18 Aug. 1944.
6. *S.L.W.N.*, 15 Sept. 1945.
7. *African Standard*, 1 Sept. 1944.
8. *S.L.W.N.*, 28 Dec. 1940; 25 Jan. 1941.
9. Kilson, *Modernisation*, pp. 150–1; A. Creech Jones, 'The Colonies in the war', *The Political Quarterly*, 11, 1–4 (1940), pp. 384–95.
10. CO267/677/32319, Jardine to Williams (private), 9 Oct. 1940.
11. CO267/682/32303, Letter of the Secretary of the National Council for Civil Liberties in London, Elizabeth Ellen, 14 Dec. 1943; CO267/682/33726, Colonial Office Minutes, 27 and 28 Oct. 1943.
12. *African Standard*, 24 Nov. 1944.
13. *African Standard*, 24 Nov. and 1 Dec. 1944; Olajide Aluko, 'Politics of decolonization in British West Africa, 1945–1960', Ajayi and Crowder, *History of West Africa*, 2, ch. 18.
14. *S.L.W.N.*, 16 Sept. 1944.
15. Stevens to Hinden, 23 Nov. 1960 (MSS. Brit. Emp. S. 365) Fabian Colonial Bureau Papers (F.C.B.P.); Crowder, '1939–1945 war', p. 612–14. But see G. O. Olusanya, 'The role of ex-Service men in Nigerian politics', *J.M.A.S.*, 6, 2 (1968), pp. 221–32.
16. Aluko, 'Politics of decolonization', cf. Harold K. Jacobson, 'The U.N. and colonialism: a tentative appraisal', *International Organisation*, 16, 1 (1962), pp. 37–62.
17. *Ibid.*
18. C. R. Nordmann, 'The decision to admit unofficials to the Executive Council of British West Africa', *J.I.C.H.*, 4, 2 (Jan. 1976), pp. 194–205.
19. CO554/131/33702/64, Governor to Secretary of State, 25 March 1943.
20. C. Allen, *Constitutional Change*; Gershon Collier, *Experiment in Democracy*, p. 12.
21. Because 'we should refuse to be pushed into piece meal and hand-to-mouth expedients. If anything is to be done it should be on the basis of a well thought out policy which would cover West Africa as a whole…no need to rush into "gestures" of this kind for which there is no effective clamour at the moment and which are in conflict with long term principles of the policy propounded by Lord Hailey.' Minutes by A. J. Dawe on CO554/131/33702 (13 May 1942). See also O. G. R. Williams's view that 'on matter of expediency it would have to be conceded to obviate demands for it, since already conceded elsewhere', *ibid.*

22. CO554/131/33702 Minutes by A. C. Talbot, May 1942; cf. Nordmann, 'The decision to admit unofficials', pp. 194–5 who insists that Burns pushed through this scheme without pressure from African agitators.
23. CO554/131/33702, Letters from Burns to Moyne, 29 and 30 Jan. 1942; Stevenson to Burns, 2 Jan. 1942; Burns to Cranbourne, 8 July 1942. The governor of Sierra Leone was less than candid to say that there had been no agitation for expanding the Executive Council to admit African members. Williams recalled that the first Urban elected Member had asked in the Legislative Council on 12 May 1942 whether there were any changes contemplated for the reform of the Constitution of Sierra Leone, particularly for an increase of the number of people's representatives in the Legislative Council and a representative in the Executive Council. The Colonial Secretary had replied: 'no change is contemplated in present conditions, since any such proposal would require more exhaustive study than is now possible. The matter will be kept in view'. See also Bankole-Bright's reaction to Stevenson's statement about African representation. Press cuttings in Co554/131/33702; *Daily Guardian* 26 July 1939; *S.L.W.N.*, Sept. 1943. A letter from the West African Labour Federation signed by O. Wyndham urging reforms in the Legislature and in local government in the Colony was dismissed thus: 'Mr. Wyndham does not represent any organised body of labour opinion nor is the WALF registered as T.U., CO267/682/32354, Stevenson to Cranbourne 29 Aug. 1942. Minutes by A. C. Talbot and A. J. Dawe, August 1942.
24. Daily Guardian, article by J. M. Rose, 26 July 1939; article by Thomas Decker, 7 Jan. 1947; 'Sierra Leone Survey' by R. S. Easmon, in *S.L.W.N.*, 2 Oct. 1943.
25. CO554/131/33702, Stevenson to Colonial Office, 1 Nov. 1942 (tel.); and letters of 20 Aug, 27 Oct. 1942; CO554/131/33702/64, Gov. to Sec. of State, 25 March 1943 (tel.). Mins. by Dawe on CO554/131/33702/66 5 April 1943.
26. Governor's Reply to Address of Welcome by the Chief Justice, printed in *S.L.W.N.*, 23 Aug. 1941.
27. CO554/132/33726, Secret visit to West Africa by Colonel Stanley, Sec. of State to various governors, 30 June 1943.
28. CO267/683/32375, Discussion with Sir Hubert Stevenson, 12 Aug. 1943; CO554/132/33726/5, Col. Stanley's visit to West Africa (1943).
29. *S.L.W.N.*, 2 and 9 Oct. 1943. Michael Vane, *Black Magic White Medicine* (1957) has some interesting vignettes on Black and White relations and the medical needs of the country.
30. CO267/683/32375, Discussion with Sir Hubert Stevenson, 12 Aug. 1943; CO554/132/33726/5, Col. Stanley's visit to West Africa (1943).
31. *Ibid.*
32. CO267/684/32010, Minutes by O. G. R. Williams, 10 Nov. 1949.
33. CO554/132/33727, Constitutional development in West Africa C.O. Minutes (4 Sept. 1943).
34. *Ibid.* P. Hetherington, *British Paternalism and Africa*, p. 139; Ronald Robinson, 'Sir Andrew Cohen: Pro-consul of Africa Nationalism (109–1968)' in Gann and Duignan, *African Pro-Consuls*, pp. 353–64.
35. CO267/684/32010, Stevenson to Stanley, 8 Dec. 1944; CO554/132/33762/5 (1943); Blyden, 'Pattern of Constitutional development', p. 182; Hargreaves, *The End of Colonial Rule*.
36. CO267/684/32303/2, Minutes by O. G. R. Williams on his conversation with Wallace-Johnson on 23 Feb. 1945; *S.L.W.N.* 18 Nov. 1944.
37. N. 35. See Christopher Clapham, *Liberia and Sierra Leone*.
38. *Ibid.*
39. *Ibid.*

40. CO267/684/32303/2, Colonial Office Minutes (23 Feb. 1945). Draft letter of Colonial Office, March 1945.
41. *S.L.W.N.*, 18 Nov. 1944.
42. Logie Wilson Papers (MSS. Afr. S. 388), Box 1f3, Creole Background (Sierra Leone: New Constitution).
43. D. Bailey Papers (MSS. Afr. R. 47). Diary of July 1945 (?).
44. A few references will suffice to underscore this point; An editorial of *West Africa* on 7 July 1951 blamed the slow implementation and the forcible introduction of the 1947 Constitution on the opposition of the Krio politicians whose fear of being swamped by the Protectorate 'were groundless'. See also issues of September and October 1951. Dennis Austin in a five-part series on the 'People and Constitution in Sierra Leone' published in *West Africa*, 13, 20, 27 Sept. 4 and 11 Oct. 1952 was also critical of the Colony politicians. J. H. Price in *Political Institutions of West Africa* (1967) states that government had realised at the end of the war that it would take ten years before education in the Protectorate reached a level for admissible democracy, thus Stevenson had started Constitutional talks in 1947. But these ran into difficulties 'due to the intransigence of the Creole [sic] leaders and the absence of any obvious Protectorate leaders', p. 155; G. Padmore, 'Democratic advance in Sierra Leone' *The Crisis*, 64, 3 March 1957, pp. 149–52; cf. Blyden, 'Constitutional change', p. 225.
45. C. Allen *Change*; Aluko, 'Politics of decolonization'; Webster et al., *West Africa since 1800* (new edition, 1980), part 5 ff.; Crawford Young, 'Decolonization in Africa', in Duignan and Gann, *Colonialism*, pp. 450–502. But see W. M. MacMillan, *The Road to Self Rule: a study in Colonial Evolution* (London, 1959).
46. Henry S. Wilson, *The Imperial Experience* (Minneapolis, 1977), 8, p. 303; J. D. Hargreaves, 'Assumptions, expectations and plans: approaches to decolonization in Sierra Leone', Paper presented to Anglo-French Colloquium on Independence and dependence: the relation of Britain and France with their former territories, Paris, 6–8 May 1976.
47. Clapham, *Liberia and Sierra Leone*, p. 39, states: 'The Creoles, despite their high educational and managerial attainments, were prevented from establishing any appreciable linkages with the hinterland either administratively, since the key posts were until very shortly before independence in the hands of the British officials, or economically since they were prohibited from owning lands in the Protectorate and their early trading networks were ousted by alien competition'; interviews: J. C. O. Crowther, 9 Sept. 1974; T. A. L. Decker, 12 Aug. 1975; *S.L.W.N.*, 20 May 1916; 17 March 1917; 15 July 1922.
48. Interview: T. A. L. Decker, 12 Aug. 1975. See also R. S. Easmon's column, *S.L.W.N.* 2 Oct 1943. He wrote, 'The plain truth is that the white man in the colonies has no need for the truly educated African; and any African who has the true education to stand up for what he knows is right (and it is amazing how wrong our government often is), is automatically labelled anti-British.' This point is underscored by the complaint of an outraged European doctor, W. C. E. Bowen, who considered that because he had been insulted by a Krio Pastor who told him he should knock before entering his house, the Medical Department and the government had been disrespected! See note 81, p. 202 above, and Hargreaves, *End of Colonial Rule*, 52 ff.
49. *Daily Guardian*, 1 Aug. 1946; Collier, *Experiment in Democracy*, p. 13.
50. CO267/684/32069, Ramage to Stanley, 16 June 1945; M. Kilson, 'Grass roots politics in Africa: local government in Sierra Leone', *Political Studies* 12, 1964, pp. 47–66.
51. *Debates*, 21 Nov. 1947; Logie Wilson Papers (MSS. Afr. S. 338). Box 1f3, Creole background.
52. N. 50 above.
53. For instance, an advert put out by the Education Department for application for

scholarship awards for teacher training in Njala (Agricultural) Training College, specified that 'Candidates must be of Protectorate origins'. The *Daily Guardian* of 24 Aug. 1946 condemned it as breeding disunity. The government also objected to Sarif Easmon soliciting funds for Fourah Bay College from the Chiefs. It claimed that the fund drive was a private arrangement. *Debates*, 21 Nov. 1947; 27 May 1948 ref. speech by Akintola Wright, a nominated Colony member.

54. *S.L.W.N.* 22 Jan. 1944; *Daily Guardian*, 2 and 10 Aug. 1946; 1 and 6 Aug. and 28 Nov. 1946.

55. *Daily Guardian*, 7, 14, 31 Dec. 1946; 19 Nov. 1946.

56. *S.L.W.N.*, 7 April 1945; 22 Dec. 1945; *Daily Guardian*, 23 Sept. 1946; 15 July 1946.

57. *D.G.* 23 Sept. 1946; D. Bailey Papers (MSS. Afr. R. 47) diary 1930–47. The entry for July (1945?), fols. 27–8, reads: 'First District Chiefs' Conference and a real livewire assembly...collecting subscription to send a boy to be a doctor'. Bailey was District Commissioner for Port Loko District.

58. *Standing Instructions, Secretariat No. 10* of 1910 from the Hon. Colonial Secretary to District Commissioners giving them wide powers over the chiefs. Logie Wilson Papers (MSS. Afr. S. 390) fol. 4; *D.G.* 10 Aug. 1946; 12 Aug. and 11 Sept. 1947; Thomas Decker, *Our Paramount Chiefs of the Sierra Leone Protectorate*. Pamphlet published by the *Daily Guardian* (n.d., *circa* 1948), 15pp; and *Counter-Proposals for a New Constitution for Sierra Leone*. Dedicated to P.C. Alimami Sorie of Binle, Kambia District (n.d.), 16pp.; *Debates*, Dec. 1947 and April 1948.

59. *D.G.* 2, 3, 6, 10 Aug. 1946; Logie WIlson Papers (MSS. Afr. S. 388) Box 1f3, Creole Background (SL: New Constitution).

60. Allegations of mistreatment of Paramount chiefs were made by P.C. A. G. Caulker in the Legislative Council in 1942. Colonial Office reaction was that the dates were mixed up and the allegations were vague and had not been proved. CO267/683/32367, Stevenson to Stanley, 31 March 1943; Fabian Colonial Bureau Papers (MSS. Bri. Emp. S. 365 Box 86/1B), article by Kon Sengo, 'Another taxation without representation'. He makes the point that in the Protectorate Assembly the chiefs were a tool of government and that they were not given much respect. R. B. Kowa, writing to Kenneth Little, the sociologist, on 17 Jan. 1948, dismissed the Protectorate Assembly as a place full of illiterate chiefs where even the 'literate ones could not fully understand the proceedings of Council'; Kilson, *Modernization*, pp. 147–8.

61. *D.G.*, 10 Aug. 1946.

62. F.C.B.P. (MSS. Brit. Emp. S. 365 Box 86/2), Stevens to Hinden, 17 Jan. 1949.

63. F.C.B.P. (MSS. Brit. Emp. S. 365 Box 86/2f 47) Paramount Chief R. B. S. Koker to F.C.B. 17 Dec. 1946. Enclosing speech on Protectorate Jubilee Celebrations Day, 2 Dec. 1946. For development analysis in Sierra Leone, see J. Barry Riddell, *The Spatial Dynamics of Modernization in Sierra Leone* (Evanston, 1970).

64. On this, see D. L. Sumner, *Education in Sierra Leone* (Sa. Leone, 1963), especially ch. 4; Riddell, *Spatial Dynamics*, 61–70. The Protectorate figure of 16,000 included 1,700 Native Administration School Children. A Colonial Office Advisory Committee on education meeting in 1943 noted that 11,000 of the 20,000 children of school-going age in the Colony peninsula went to school while only 10,000 or 3% of a population of 340,800 children attended school in the Protectorate. Papers in file on educational development plans for Sierra Leone, CO267/678/32036/2 (1943).

65. CO270/87, Sierra Leone Sessional Papers, no. 3, 1954. The following were medical students on government scholarship: A. O. Stuart, J. C. Mends, I. B. Amara, W. Priddy, A. A. Hardy, Miss J. Spain, Miss E. Ryan-Coker, E. V. J. King, L. E. Taylor, D. M. Yilla, S. A. T. Horton, Miss B. A. C. Coker, Miss B. E. O. Williams, I. B. Taqi, S. B. Banya, Miss B. O. D. Fraser, Miss R. J. B. Cole and Miss R. H. Eleady-Cole. The dental

students were: J. T. O. Vincent, D. E. Felix, R. N. Cummings, R. E. Metzger, S. G. Caulker, and A. E. Dove. Private medical students included: H. M. Conteh, Miss Walter-Nicol, Miss Davies, S. J. Benjamin, B. Renner, T. Boardman and E. Luke. Three years later, in answer to a question by Bankole-Bright, the government revealed that it had offered (1951–6) thirty-nine scholarships to Protectorate students and ninety-seven to Colony aspirants. See *Debates*, 27 Sept. 1956.

66. Cf. G. Collier, *Experiment in Democracy*, p. 158.
67. R. B. Kowa to K. Little, 17 Jan. 1948 (MSS. Brit. Emp. S. 365, Box 86/1B); Kilson *Political Change*, pp. 154–60; cf. Cartwright, *Leadership*, pp. 92–3.
68. *D.G.* 4 and 11 July 1946. *West Africa* of 7 July 1951 and Austen's article in *West Africa* of 27 Sept. 1952 hold that the SOS was originally set up to encourage co-operative agriculture, 'but became a political organisation under Margai to fight for Protectorate rights under the New Constitution'. The founding members were: J. Karefa Smart, . J. Manley, Siaka Stevens, Doyle Sumner, T. M. Williams and F. S. Anthony. Paramount Chief Julius Gulama was made Honorary President.
69. See J. Cartwright's views in his *Politics in Sierra Leone*, p. 51.
70. *West Africa*, 6 Sept. 1952; Cartwright, *Politics in Sierra Leone*, p. 56; cf. David Thomas, 'E. N. Jones, 1884–1954', *Encyclopaedia Africana*, pp. 83–5; Blyden, 'Constitutional change', pp. 192–3. The *Sierra Leone Observer* (10 April 1954) favoured Sankoh, when he died in March 1954, with a short and anodyne tribute 'to a great Sierra Leonean' who believed in unity.
71. For instance, Professor Eldred Jones recalls that his Sierra Leone Socialist Party aimed at enlisting 'as many people from the Protectorate' as possible, 'but we discovered that most of the interested and articulate ones were Civil Servants who were willing to co-operate with us behind the scenes but could not openly join a political party. We had very solid support from people like the late Mr. A. J. Momoh, and Mr. S. B. Daramy...They came to our meetings at which we developed plans for the development of various aspects of the country, but were unable to participate publicly in our activities.' Personal communication, 1 Nov. 1978. Cartwright also offers this interesting view on Colony/Protectorate relations: 'where it became clear at an early stage that Britain was going to devolve some power willy-nilly to one or other indigenous group, mutual suspicions and fears that the other side might gain a permanent advantage quickly swamped such prospects of co-operation'. *Leadership*, pp. 40–1. See his other submission on pp. 92–3 of the same reference.
72. CO267/679/32118/39, Minutes on resolutions by Sierra Leone Civil Servants in 1935, 1942, and 1943; Cartwright, *Politics*, p. 38. Bright claimed that he voted for Momoh in the City Council Election of 1948. See *Debates*, 29 July 1952.
73. *D.G.*, 23 Sept. 1946. Except for the obvious non-Krio names in this list, other Western surnames may not necessarily be Krio.
74. *D.G.* 19 Nov. 1966. Professor A. Williams has also recalled that during his childhood Protectorate leaders like Bai Koblo, Alimamy Dura of Binkolo, Chief Gulama (Krio Chief, as he was fondly known), were regular visitors at the Williams' homes in Bo and Freetown. The Williams children were brought up to call the members of Margai's first cabinet uncle, but politics spoiled all these good relations after 1950. Interview, Prof. A. Williams, 21 Aug. 1975. As for Milton Margai's relationship with the Krio family of A. E. Tuboku-Metzger it is difficult to clarify this in the absence of documents.
75. W. H. Fitzjohn, *Ambassador of Christ and Caesar*, p. 22.
76. *S.L.W.N.*, 22 Sept. 1945.
77. *D.G.* 26 April 1927; cf. issues for 6 Sept. 1945, 15 Jan. and 9 July 1945.
78. *D.G.* 7, 14, 31 Dec. 1946.
79. *S.L.W.N.*, 8 Dec. 1945. E. B. Williams was President of the Bo Football League, while A. Bakarr, his Bo African Club colleague, was Captain of the Protectorate XI.

80. *S.L.W.N.*, 18 March 1944; *Fourah Bay College Fund*, pamphlet (n.d.) 33pp.
81. Goldsworthy, *Colonial Issues in British Politics.*
82. *Ibid*; n. 34 above; CO554/132/33727, memo on constitutional development in West Africa, 4 Sept. 1943.
83. CO554/131/33702, Minutes by O. G. R. Williams 28 Oct 1942. CO554/132/33727, Minutes by O. G. R. Williams, 4 Sept. 1943.
84. *Proposals for the Reconstitution of the Legislative Council in Sierra Leone* (Sessional Paper No. 2 of 1948): *D.G.* 27 May 1948; Allen, *Change*; Marcus Jones, 'Fundamental rights', pp. 40–5.
85. Kilson, *Political Change*, p. 169.
86. N. 86 above; *Debates*, 27, 31 May; 4 June 1948.
87. *D.G.* 19 Feb. 1946.
88. F.C.B.P. (MSS. Brit. Emp. S. 365 Box 86/1B): R. B. Kowa (to K. Little, 17 Jan. 1948) wanted a free franchise in the Protectorate; and he denounced the officials who were bent on 'dictating their policies to Africans, even intelligent ones'. Albert Margai told Miss H. Nicolson (8 March 1948) that the Stevenson proposals were 'cowardly excluding the intelligentsia of the Protectorate from the Constitution'.
89. Kilson, *Political Change* pp. 163–9; Cartwright, *Leadership*, pp. 92–3; articles by Austin in *West Africa*, 13, 20, 27 Sept.; 4, 11 Oct. 1952. Fitzjohn, for instance, claimed that he was drawn into politics to combat the pretentious arrogance of people like Bright, Zizer, and Otto During. Interview: Dr W. H. Fitzjohn, 2 Oct. 1974.
90. Interview, Prof. A. Williams, 21 Aug. 1975. Koblo, for instance, was one of the most extreme anti-Colony members from the Protectorate. When he spoke he addressed himself to his 'indigenous countrymen', as opposed to the 'strangers' from across the sea. However, with his tongue in his cheek, he conceded that 'for the past twenty-five years our Colony representatives have sought the interests of the Protectorate all the time'. *Debates*, 17 May 1948; 19 Dec. 1950. It may have a direct bearing on this question though we may not find another supporting evidence, but Kilson's claim (*Political Change* p. 250), that a European firm helped Milton Margia to launch the Sierra Leone Observer in 1949 (not 1950) raises an interesting question of how many Europeans may have helped the Protectorate people to challenge the people in the Colony in the contest for the leadership in Sierra Leone.
91. Kilson, *Political Change*, p. 163.
92. *D.G.* 28 April 1948; 1, 14, 16 June 1948; *Reconstruction of the Legislative Council in Sierra Leone* (Sessional Paper No. 8 of 1948); *Debates*, 21 Nov. 1947; 4 June 1948. Indeed the First urban member, Otto During, made a special point of emphasising that the Colony had conceded majority to the Protectorate as long ago as 1943 when it was suggested that the Protectorate be divided into thirteen electoral districts with a seat each. However, the contention was over the issues of qualification, literacy and the position of the chiefs. See also Stevens's letter confirming Otto During's position in F.C.B.P. *loc. cit.*, Stevens to Hinden, 4 July 1950.
93. *D.G.*, 25, 26 May 1948.
94. *West Africa*, 10 Sept. 1949.
95. *West Africa*, 10 Sept. 1949.
96. Letter to the Editor by Margot Parish, *West Africa*, 26 April 1952.
97. J. C. Zizer, 'An eclipse of the Sierra Leone Creoles and a threat to autonomy', 'The new constitution within the people's gallery', 'The climax', written in June and October 1948, and revised 3 Aug. 1950. These were published by the *Daily Mail*. However, the material used here was extracted from a collection of papers owned by Mrs Alice Wilson of Freetown, a keen amateur historian. Papers in this collection will be referred to hereafter as the Mrs Wilson Collection. For a discussion and analysis of this dualism in Sierra Leone, see Blyden, 'Constitutional Change', p. 211 ff.

98. Editorial comment on a letter by W. B. Wright blaming the dualism of British policies for the feud between the Colony and the Protectorate, *West Africa*, 26 Jan. 1952; 1, 22 March, 12 April, 3 May, 7 June 1952 ref. to the Frank Inkumsah/Bankole-Bright paper war. But see, for instance, governor Beresford-Stooke's views on this matter in his letter to W. L. Gorell Barnes of the Colonial Office, 3 May 1952: CO554/699.
99. 'Political prospects in Sierra Leone' article by J.D.H. [agreaves], *World Today* 9 (1953), pp. 208–217.
100. Interview: S. M. O. Boyle, 21 Dec. 1976, Birmingham, England
101. Interview: Pa E. J. Robinson, 25 Aug. 1975; J. C. O. Crowther, 9 Sept. 1974.
102. *S.L.W.N.* 1943; A. J. G. Wyse, 'F. A. Miller', *Encyclopaedia Africana*, p. 117.
103. One informant said of Sankoh that he was not a Christian, while Wallace-Johnson could not be trusted. Interview, Pa J. C. Lucan, 21 Aug. 1974. I think this resentment against Sankoh was derived from his decision to establish his own evangelistic church that promised to bring new dimensions to Christianity. See his latter to Rita Hinden asking for a typewriter and duplicating machine to publish his tracts: F.C.B.P. (MSS. Brit. Emp. S. 365, Box 82). See Blyden, 'Constitutional change', pp. 192–3, for his views on the rift in the Krio leadership.
104. Cf. Kilson, *Modernization*, p. 169.
105. A. Cohen, 'The politics of ritual secrecy', *Man*, 6 (1971), pp. 427–48.
106. CO554/131/33702, Press cuttings of article by Bankie published in the *Daily Mail* of 18 Nov. 1942.
107. *S.L.W.N.*, 16 Sept. 1944; 26 Feb. and 18 March 1944. My attention was drawn to an article 'Local government reform in Sierra Leone, 1943–48' by Gilbert A. Segkoma, while I was revising these drafts. It is published in *Africana Research Bulletin*, 12, 3 (June 1983). It argues the case that local pressure forced the government to modify its policy on the Municipality Ordinance passed in 1945. Segkoma could have gone further to state that government's acquiescence in 1948 was designed to forestall further demands from the Colony for legislative reforms and to 'appease' them for the institutional changes in the Protectorate.
108. *S.L.W.N.* 4 Sept. 1943; 30 Oct. 1943; Bah, 'Bankole-Bright', pp. 31–72.
109. *S.L.W.N.*, 4 Sept. 1943.
110. *S.L.W.N.*, 30 Oct.; 27 Nov. 1943. Polling was disappointing.
111. *S.L.W.N.*, 9, 23 Oct. 1943.
112. *S.L.W.N.*, 8 Jan., 6 May, 10 June 1944. E. F. Luke, who may have been on a retainer from Bright, since he featured in most of his court cases, represented the petitioner. C. E. Wright and O. I. E. During appeared for Reffell. The legal spit reflected the political division in the leadership; Bah, 'Bankole-Bright', p. 32.
113. In one he had a fight with his wife, Maude Bankole-Bright, over property. He won the suit. *S.L.W.N.*, 23 Nov.1940. In another he was issued a criminal summons for perjury. Bankie was defended by E. F. Luke and Melville C. Marke. The Police Magistrate, F. S. Protheroe, ruled that there was 'not sufficient evidence for committing case for trial, and the accused was discharged', *S.L.W.N.*, 3 May 1941.
114. *S.L.W.N.*, 29 Jan. 1944.
115. *S.L.W.N.* 18 Feb. 1944.
116. *S.L.W.N.*12 Feb. 1944.
117. *S.L.W.N.*11 March 1944.
118. *Supplement to the African World*, 7 April 1917.
119. *West Africa*, 24 Dec. 1949.
120. For instance, Simpson says, 'The Creole formed a political party to protect their favoured position in the colonial administration. And the protectorate peoples formed their own political party to wrest power from the Creoles.' Simpson, 'Ethnic conflict in Sierra Leone', pp. 153–88; Irving Kaplan et al., *Area Handbook for Sierra Leone*

(Washington, 1976), *passim*, has some curiously interesting views on the Krio position in the Colonial Establishment. However, see M. Crowder, 'An African Aristocracy', pp. 183–90; note 98 above.

121. This statement was made during the briefing of Colonel Stanley, prior to his visit to West Africa in 1943: 'As regards Sierra Leone, the Secretary of State said that he felt the position in the Colony peninsula was quite hopeless, and that all that could be done was to try and hold the present position until there had been sufficient development to provide Protectorate representatives who could really hold their own with the Creoles of the Colony.' CO554/132/33726/5, notes on points arising in discussions with the Secretary of State on Wednesday 27 OCt. and Thursday 28 Oct. 1943.

122. M. Crowder, 'The 1939–1945 War', p. 16.

123. CO367/678/32020/8, Memo on subjects of discussion by the elected and nominated members of the Legislative Council of the Colony of Sierra Leone presented to the Rt Hon. the Secretary of State for the Colonies, 3 Oct. 1943; Allen, *Change*; *S.L.W.N.*, 4 Sept. 1943; *Debates*, 21 Nov. 1947; 27, 31 May 1948.

124. For instance, *S.L.W.N.*, 18 Nov.; 24 Oct. 1944.

125. *S.L.W.N.*, 9 Dec. 1944.

126. *S.L.W.N.*, 2 Feb. 1945.

127. *S.L.W.N.*, 9 Dec. 1944; *African Standard*, 9 Feb. 1945.

128. See note 98 above. The interpretations of lawyers can be read in: Collier, *Experiment in Democracy*, p. 36; Marcus Jones, 'Fundamental rights', pp. 47–72; *The Colonial Territories Progress Reports – Cmd.* 7715, 1948–1949 (H.M.S.O.,1949); F. Inkumsah to Bankole-Bright, letter published in *West Africa*, 7 June 1952. In answer to a question raised in 1923 by A. J. Shorunkeh Sawyerr, the Attorney-General explained that swearing an oath of allegiance did not make the 'Protectorate Native' a British Subject, nor 'is he a British Subject'; though the Protectorate Natives were aliens, in view of the fact that 'alien' was sometimes used in a derogatory way the word was avoided. In any case, he went on, it was not proposed to limit the right of the Protectorate members in any way. When the Nominated members moved a motion asking that the Protectorate be declared a British Colony, the Attorney-General countered that Shorunkeh-Sawyerr was asking for annexation, and since the Protectorate was outside H.M.'s Dominions, annexation might cause international complications. Besides, as the Colony had been legislating for the Protectorate, why should not inhabitants of this area come in as natives not as British subjects? he asked. The point was immaterial. Slater, on the other hand, believed that if there should be a petition for annexation, that should come from Protectorate Natives themselves. *Debates*, 28 Dec. 1922; 26 Nov. 1923. I am still at a loss to understand the logic of the above. However, see Blyden, 'Constitutional change', pp. 111–32.

129. H. C. Hollins, a District Commissioner in Sierra Leone, explained in a paper that a 'Creole, born in Freetown, Bonthe, Waterloo and other parts of the Colony is a "non native"'. 'If a child is born to a Creole mother and father he is non native, but if a Creole married a native woman (country fashion) or keeps her as a friend, and she bears him a child that child is a native' (Fitzjohn, *Ambassador*, p. 22). Similarly 'all children born in the colony are non natives, whatever their parents are, but such children do not always claim this, as it would mean losing their right as natives...easy way to determine a non + native if he has paid settlers fees (£1.0s. 0d), and non-natives cannot own land in the Protectorate' (MISS. Afr. S. 672): Marcus Jones, 'Fundamental rights', pp. 46 ff; R. Lewis, *Sierra Leone*, pp. 36–9. In fact, Thomas Decker suggested in 1947 that elected Colony members of Legislative Council be made ex-officio members of the Protectorate Assembly; for instance; a General Purpose Committee could be a Permanent Secretariat in which Protectorate and Colony members could exchange views throughout the year. This would facilitate communication and liaison. See *Daily Guardian*, 11 Sept. 1947.

130. CO267/688/32348, Reconstruction of City Council, Part 2; CO267/690/32397/1, for relevant documents. Minutes by O. G. R. Williams, 17 March 1945 and memo by Mayhew, 5 June 1945 etc. With reference to the demand for a reconstituted Legislative Council, one Colonial Office functionary observed: 'To grant a majority at the present time would plainly be impossible as it would be exclusive of the Protectorate in actual practice – being that local government is a suitable field for training in the responsible administration of public business and that [the] Freetown Ordinance which confers powers similar to those enjoyed by local authorities in U.K. provides full scope for this – constitutional reform is bound up with the success or reverse of the new Protectorate Assembly', minutes by unidentified Colonial Office official (13 March 1946) on CO267/688/3248. The Freetown Municipality Ordinance Bill was passed on 4 May 1948, after certain amendments had been made. Otto During supported the Bill. *Debates*, 4 May 1948.

131. *Ibid.* According to Sekgoma's article, substantial changes were conceded by the government on clauses 16, 43 and 53. See note 107 above; Wraith, *Local Administration*, pp. 20–1.

132. Pp. 208, 212, and 216 above.

133. Apart from standard works already referred to, such an interpretation is contained in publications like Mary Louise Clifford, *The Land and People of Sierra Leone* (New York 1974); J. H. Price, *Political Institutions*, Aluko, 'Politics of decolonization,' pp. 622–63. The phraseology used here is implicit in the works cited. But see its actual use in C. Allen, *Change*, p. 10; Collier, *Experiment in Democracy*, p. 27; and *West Africa*, 1949–51. Bereford-Stooke, for instance, told Goreell Barnes that even with all the legislative goodwill possible, unification could not be achieved 'until the Creoles become less intransigent', CO554/699, Beresford-Stooke to Gorell Barnes, 3 May 1952. In debates on these issues in the Legislative Council the chiefs found themselves in a dilemma. While some welcomed this literacy test, there were others who were resentful because of the pressure put on them by the Colony. *Debates*, 1947–50.

134. J. B. Wester, 'Political activity in British West Africa', p. 593.

135. Cecil Magbaily Fyle, *A History of Sierra Leone*, pp. 116–119. Dr Fitzjohn in his *Ambassador of Christ and Caesar*, p. 15, recollected that the premium placed on an educated leader amongst his people was so great that he was elected for Moyamba District Council in his absence! *Progress Report on the Development Programme for 1951* (Sessional Paper No. 2 of 1951); Kilson, 'Grass Roots Politics', pp. 47–99.

136. The members were the Hon. Attorney-General, Ragnes Hyne – Chairman, Acting-Secretary for Protectorate Affairs, H. Childs; J. C. O. Crowther; Otto I. E. During, P.C. Y. B. Sandy, R. B. Marke, S. Patterson, P.C. Morekpa Forewai, J. Akinola Wright, M. Z. Pappas, P.C. Bockarie Samba, P.C. Mana Luseni, P.C A. Demby and P.C. Bai Farima Tass II, Dr R. S. Easmon, A. H. L. Barlatt, and N. A. W. Cox-George – Extraordinary members. Report of the Select Committee appointed by the Acting Governor on Monday, 31 May 1948 to consider *Proposals for a Reconstitutional Legislative Council in Sierra Leone* (Sessional Paper No. 7 of 1948); *Debates*, 31 May, 4 June 1948.

137. *Ibid.*

138. Even Zizer disapproved of the walkout. See his article, 'The Climax' (Mrs Wilson Collection). Other criticisms can be found in the Thomas Decker column in *D.G.*, 14, 16 June 1948.

139. S. A. Akintoye, *Emergent African States* (Hongkong, 1976), p. 147.

140. *D.G.*, 4, 5 May 1948.

141. N. A. Cox-George, 'Writing from the heights of Mount Aureol', in *The West African Review*, August 1949, pp. 877–80 and 891; *D.G.*, 14, 16 June 1948.

142. Dennis Austin, 'The Years of Negotiation', *West Africa*, 20 Sept. 1952, p. 873.

143. Aluko, 'Politics of decolonization', p. 646. Siaka Stevens also told Rita Hinden about a strike at Marampa Mines in September 1950, and civil unrest in about five Chiefdoms in the Protectorate. He attributed these to 'a reflection of the age of awareness and self consciousness [a] result of [the] return of ex-soldiers and the common man's forward look.' F.C.B.P. (MSS. Brit. Emp. S. 365 Box 82), Stevens to Hinden, 23 Nov. 1950.

144. F.C.B.P. ref. above. Stevens to Hinden, 17 Jan. 1949. Even Bai Koblo and Bai Farima Tass II were opposed to illiterate chiefs being given membership of the Legislative Council. Bai Farima Tass II quipped that this would make *the chiefs send their children to school. Reconstitution of the Legislative Council in Sierra Leone* (Sessional Paper, No. 8, 1948). (My emphasis.)

145. F.C.B.P. *loc. cit.*, Stevens to Hinden, 15 March 1949.

146. *Ibid.* Stevens to Hinden, 3 Dec. 1949.

147. *Ibid.* Stevens to Hinden, 4 July 1950. (My emphasis.)

148. For instance, *West Africa* for 1947–1952. Specific examples have been quoted above.

149. *Ibid*; Austin, 'Years of negotiation' in *West Africa*, 20 Sept. 1952, p. 873.

150. Padmore, *How Britain Rules Africa*, p. 351; compare his cited article in *The Crisis* 64, 3 (March 1957), pp. 149–50. See his diatribe in *The African Vanguard*, 17 and 19 Jan. 1957.

151. Quoted in D. Austin, 'The roots of disunity', *West Africa*, 13 Sept. 1952, p. 846.

152. *Debates*, 9 Dec. 1926.

153. Dennis Austin, 'The S.L.P.P. comes to power', *West Africa*, 4 Oct. 1952, p. 917. The other parties forming this solidarity group included Otto During's Positive Action Group, The Sierra Leone Democratic Party, The West African Civil Liberties and National Defence League incorporating the West African Youth League (S.L. Section), The Sierra Leone Socialist Party. The Sierra Leone Political Party, The Rural Areas Council, The Fourah Bay and Foulah Town Communities, The African Unofficial Colony Members of the Executive and Legislative Councils, etc. It succeeded a previous All-Colony organisation – the Combined Committee. See its resolution, dissolving itself and establishing the N.C.S.L. on 11 Aug. 1950. *African Standard*, 25 Aug. 1950.

154. Interview: Pa Rogers Williams, 23 Aug. 1974.

155. N. 153 above.

156. *West Africa*, 1, 22 March; 12, 26 April; 3 May; 7 June; 1952.

157. Ahmed Alhadi, *The Re-emancipation of the Colony of Sierra Leone* (Freetown, 1956).

158. Interview, Pa J. C. Lucan, 21 Aug. 1974. A copy of an S.D.U. hand-bill is printed in Blyden, 'Constitutional change', p. 317–19, n. 112.

159. Blyden, 'Constitutional change', pp. 417–20.

160. *West Africa*, 8 Sept. 1951; *Sierra Leone Observer*, 28 Jan., 10 June 1950; *S.L.W.N.*, 3, 10, 17, 24 Nov. 1951.

161. *Reconstitution of the Legislative Council of Sierra Leone* (Sessional paper No. 2 of 1950); Austin, 'Three years of negotiation', *West Africa*, 20 Sept. 1952.

162. As more than one researcher has suggested, Sir George was pro-Protectorate. And he exerted a great deal of effort to reconcile the traditional and educated elites in the Protectorate. See C. Allen, *Change.*; Marcus Jones, 'Fundamental rights', p. 562; Bankole Timothys' tribute in *West Africa*, 2 May 1983, p. 1096.

163. *West Africa*, 4 Aug. 1951.

164. Dr Fitzjohn, however, insisted that the S.L.P.P. fought the elections 'as a party, but not in all the constituencies'. Interview, Dr W. H. Fitzjohn, 2 Oct. 1974. Dr J. R. Scott's coverage of the elections in 'The Sierra Leone Election, May, 1957', in W. J. M. MacKenzie and K. E. Robinson (eds.) *Five Elections in Africa* (Oxford, 1960), pp. 168–268, reported that the S.L.P.P. nominated candidates for six of the seven Colony seats and won one, i.e., Mustapha's, while that for Sherbro declared for the S.L.P.P. after the election. The N.C.S.L. therefore won five seats (in the Colony); and in the

Protectorate S.L.P.P. candidates stood individually. *S.L.W.N.*, 17 and 24 Nov. 1951, gave the following results: C. M. A. Thompson (N.C.S.L.); Bankole-Bright (N.C.S.L.); M. S. Mustapha (People's Party); Rogers-Williams (N.C.S.L.); J. C. O. Crowther (Waterloo and British Koya Political Party).

165. Austin, 'The danger of easy success', *West Africa*, 11 Oct. 1952, pp. 941–2.
166. *West Africa*, Dec. 1951. L. Sankoh claimed four for N.C.S.L., two for S.L.P.P. and one for the Waterloo and British Koya Political Party. 'On the face of it, one would conclude that the N.C. had won the election.' Quoted in C. Fyfe, *Sierra Leone Inheritance* (1964), p. 330.
167. Cf. Aluko, 'Politics of decolonization', p. 647 who stated that 'it was the S.L.P.P. that won the general election under the 1951 Constitution'. Elizabeth Isichei, *History of West Africa Since 1800* (New York, 1977), p. 288; J. B. Webster et al. *The Revolutionary Years: West Africa Since 1800* (new edn, London, 1980), pp. 361–62, gave the S.L.P.P. six Seats against five for the National Council!
168. Webster, *The Revolutionary Years*, p. 365; cf. Akintoye, *Emergent Africa*, p. 153, Thomas S. Cox, *Civil Military Relations in Sierra Leone*, p. 123; cf. Collier, *Experiment in Democracy*, pp. 64–5.
169. Webster, p. 365; Akintoye, *Emergent Africa*, pp. 147–8; Cox, *Civil Military Relations*, p. 123; Collier, pp. 64–5.
170. Interviews; LBT 5 Aug. 1974; J. C. O. Crowther, 9 Sept. 1974; Pa Rogers-Williams, 23 Aug. 1974. The latter went so far as to assert that the governor had asked Bright and Wallace-Johnson to see him the next day to 'receive a mandate to form a government'. Scott, 'Sierra Leone election', p.191. In point of fact, it is difficult to get at the truth because of the conflicting claims put by the disputants during debates in the Legislative Council in 1951–3. From the evidence of Wallace-Johnson, Thompson and Bright, there is a strong suggestion that the governor had indeed intimated to Bright that he would be in the Executive Council. Bright also made some attempts to consult with Milton Margai to work out an arrangement, but the latter was uncooperative. He rejected overtures from Bright. This was why N.C.S.L. kept on insisting that the governor's decision to call for a head count so that he could appoint an Executive Council was a betrayal, and his action unconstitutional. However, see *Debates*, 31 Jan. 1952; 14 and 15 Dec. 1953 for speeches by Wallace-Johnson, Margai, Columbus Thompson, Bright and Paul Dunbar. On the other hand, Lamina Sankoh puts the blame for this rupture squarely on the shoulders of Bright and his party. While the S.L.P.P. were accommodating, the N.C.S.L. was obdurate; then he rather illogically argued that by an agreement on 27 November 1951 the Protectorate members had pledged themselves to support the S.L.P.P., and that Bright's belief in the assurance by the governor that he would be included in the Executive Council was based on 'Dame Rumour'. In other words, when the Legislative Council opened on 28 November 1951 the house was greeted with a *fait accompli* symbolised by this prior agreement among the Protectorate members. The postures enacted in the Chamber therefore were really an exercise at melodrama. The dice had already been loaded against Bright's party. See extracts of L. Sankoh's 'The two Ps or Politics for the People' (n.d.), in C. Fyfe, *Sierra Leone Inheritance*, pp. 329–35.
171. Interview, Dr. W. H. Fitzjohn, 2 Oct. 1974. Siaka Stevens' *What Life Has Taught Me* (1984) and a personal communication from Alpha Lavalie who interviewed him a month before the ex-president's death make it clear that the Protectorate members had no intention of accepting Bright as a leader or as a member of the Executive Council.
172. Roy Lewis, *Sierra Leone*, pp. 230–3; Scott, 'Sierra Leone election', p. 191 hint at some prior consultation between the Colony leaders and the governor, and that they may have been led to expect inclusion in the government 'being the majority party in the limited field of declared party contest', but the next day they were amazed to find that the

governor had changed his mind. Scott suggests that this change may have been due to instructions form London or because the governor had ascertained the attitude of Margai.

173. Interview; Pa Rogers-Williams, 23 Aug. 1974.

174. *Debates*, 28 Nov. 1951; *Speech and Address by Governor Beresford-Stooke on the Opening of the first session of the Legislative Council* (Sessional Paper No. 3 of 1951).

175. Interview; LBT, 5 Aug. 1974. Her exact words were: 'Your Excellency, we are like two hills that can never meet, but if, by your magnetic influence, you can bring us together'. Many versions are given. Wallace-Johnson's own version was 'by your magnetic force to bring these two mountains together' came nearest to Lerina's. Bright claimed that he had been maligned and quoted out of context. He had said: 'there were two hills apart, but I went further and told the governor that after they had made the blunder it was for them to bring the two hills together again'. Columbus Thompson explained that his leader had said 'Your Excellency we are like two hills that cannot meet, but by your magnetic force you can bring us together', then Margai exclaimed in anger, 'No, Y.E. we have had four years of this, and it would serve no purpose.' S.L.P.P. members were, however, convinced that Bright had specifically said that the Protectorate and the Colony were like two hills that would never meet, without modifying the statement. But they were consistently silent over Milton Margai's own outburst. They refused to place it in context with Bright's statement. See *Debates*, 31 Jan. 1952, 29 July 1952; 14 and 15 Dec. 1953.

176. Interview; Dr W. H. Fitzjohn, 2 Oct. 1974. He maintained that Bright did not qualify his speech. Deana Thomas, 'Margai', p. 151, pointed out, however, that S.L.P.P. accounts alleged that Bright made his speech before Margai's outburst.

177. Interview, J. C. O. Crowther, 9 Sept. 1974.

178. Interviews: Pa Rogers-Williams, J. C. O. Crowther, 23 Aug. and 9 Sept. 1974, respectively.

179. Interviews; Dr W. H. Fitzjohn, 2 Oct. 1974; Hannah Neale, 2 Aug. 1974 and 26 April 1983; Pa A. M. Fergusson, 13 Oct. 1974; T. L. Decker, 12 Aug. 1975. the nephew of Bright, Dr O. Bright-Taylor, once confided in a conversation with me, 28 January 1976, that he could trace relations of the Brights in Kambia and various places in the Provinces.

180. Interview, Pat Maddy, 22 April 1983. Calabar, Cross River State, Nigeria. See also Bah, 'Bankole-Bright', p. 63 quoting *West Africa*, 4 May 1957 which reported a statement by Bright: 'We want independence only when we have men of intelligence to make it work.'

181. Conversation with Prof. Canon H. A. E. Sawyerr, Barbados, January 1980, and Freetown, 29 April 1983.

182. Interview; Hannah Neale, 2 Aug. 1974.

183. Interviews; W. H. Fitzjohn, 2 Oct. 1974; J. C. O. Crowther, 9 Sept. 1974. However, I find Dr Fitzjohn's statement that had Bankie 'not made that statement I strongly feel that the governor would have insisted that one person from the other side should be included in the government', difficult to reconcile with his earlier submission that the Protectorate had decided to use its numbers not to vote for any of the six Colony members, i.e. (N.C.S.L. (5) plus Edmundson, government nominee, if any of these names were put up. Fitzjohn, *Ambassador*, p. 24; Scott, *Sierra Leone election'*, p. 191.

184. Lewis, *Sierra Leone*, p. 230.

185. Interview, J. C. O. Crowther, 9 Sept. 1974, *Debates*, 14 Dec. 1953.

186. Fitzjohn, *Ambassador*, p. 23, exaggerates when he said 'S.L.P.P. won the 1951 November Elections under the stevenson Constitution.' But he qualifies this: 'It should rightly be said that it was after the election that several members who stood as independents eventually declared party affiliation. This move gave the S.L.P.P. its overwhelming victory over the National Council in Freetown – victory that was constitutionally decided in the first meeting of LegCo, December 1951.'

242

187. Austin, 'The danger of easy success', Part 5 of 'People and Constitution in Sierra Leone', *West Africa*, 11 Oct. 1952.
188. *Debates*, pp. 1951–7; Fitzjohn, *Ambassador*, pp. 25–7.

8: SECOND INNINGS IN PARLIAMENT: THE TWILIGHT YEARS, 1951–1957

1. CO270/87, Sessional Paper, no. 5 of 1954; *West Africa*, 22 June 1957; *Debates*, Dec. 1953. Addresses of Welcome by M. A. S. Margai, the Minister of Health, Agriculture and Forests, Bankole-Bright and the Governor, Sir George Beresford-Stooke.
2. Interview; LBT, 5 Aug. 1974; *West Africa*, 21 Sept. 1957; *Command paper No.* 451, 1957–1958 (H.M.S.O., 1958).
3. Interviews; W. H. Fitzjohn, 2 Oct. 1974; Pa Fergusson, 13 Oct. 1974; cf. LBT, 11 Oct. 1974; M. C. F. Easmon, 'Sierra Leone doctors', pp. 8–96. Paul Dunbar, minister without portfolio, told Bright that he was suffering today because of himself. He acknowledged the good work Bright had done in the twenties and suggested that Bright 'would have been a member of this party today but he denied it', *Debates*, 14 Dec. 1953.
4. *West Africa*, 6 Sept. 1952; cf. *Sierra Leone Observer*, 4 Dec. 1954. 'Sherbro Boy' remembered Bright's stout defence 'of the people of the Protectorate on the emancipation controversy', but wondered why he had changed.
5. Blyden, 'Constitutional change', p. 97.
6. See, for instance, *African Standard*, 3, 10, 17 and 24 June 1 July 1955. Other contemporary papers carried stories of financial irregularities; Pedler, *Main Currents of West African History*.
7. Interview; LBT, 5 Aug. 1974. The background to this section can be read in *West Africa*, Jan.–June 1952; *Debates*, 1951–3; Collier, *Experiment in Democracy*, pp. 18–20; Roy Lewis, *Sierra Leone*, 228–33. For the governor's reasons against accommodation, see his letter to Barnes in CO554/699, 3 May 1952 in response to a letter from the Colonial Office dated 19 April 1952 marked 'Secret and Personal' (ibid.).
8. Interview; LBT, 5 Aug. 1974.
9. Scott, 'Sierra Leone election', p. 187; cf. Lewis, pp. 232–233. W.J.'s letter to the Editor of *West Africa*, 26 April 1952 insisted on two points of disagreement: the franchise which made elections direct in one area and indirect in another; and the continuing overwhelming influence of the governor in the affairs of the country. These, among other things, made the Constitution undemocratic. Yet, when Bankie moved a motion of impeachment against the government on 29 July 1952, embracing these very issues, Wallace-Johnson found it convenient to be sick, and so he was absent during the debate. See *Debates*, 29 July 1952. Bankie's running fight with *West Africa* is in the following issues: 1, 22 March; 12 April; 3 May; 7 June 1952.
10. Letter of Inkumsah, *West Africa*, 7 June 1952.
11. Letter of Bankole-Bright, *West Africa*, 3 May 1952; see issue of 22 March 1952.
12. Lewis, *Sierra Leone* and 'Creoledom revisited', *The Geographical Magazine*, 37, 1 (May, 1964), pp. 9–19; M. Crowder, 'An African aristocracy', pp. 183–90; cf. J. D. H. [argreaves], 'Political prospects in Sierra Leone', *World Today*, 19 (1953), pp. 208–17; Deveneaux, *Power and Politics* ch. 2. I do not think anything illustrates Bright's belief in Britain better than this statement made in 1954: 'I feel that ultimately British justice will triumph and right will substitute for might'! *D.M.*, 24 July 1954. Magubane, *Political Economy of Race*, pp. 274–6, argues that this same belief in British 'fair play' was inherent in the philosophy of early black African activists in South Africa.
13. But, according to Goldsworthy, *Colonial Issues in British Politics*, pp. 9–20, since Sierra Leone was 'not included in the strategically important territories to Britain', the Colony inhabitants did not merit the consideration shown to British Settlers in these territories.

However, see Blyden, 'Pattern of constitutional development', pp. 116–22; MacMillan, *Self Rule*, pp. 220–2.

14. Marcus Jones, 'Fundamantal rights', pp. 61–71.
15. Letters in Mrs Wilson's collection (37 Waterloo Street, Freetown).
16. Marcus Jones, 'Fundamental rights', pp. 61–71. Public interest in this question had already died down by this time. The *Daily Mail*, hard pressed for space to publish tributes and condolences on the death of Sir Milton Margai in May, and congratulations and pledges of loyalty to Albert Margai on his elevation to the Prime Ministership, could spare only one publication. On 8 May it flashed in banner lines that the S.D.U. case was hopeless, its suit against the British Attorney-General was 'without legal foundation'. The learned judge, Wilberforce, sympathised with the Settlers' concerns but he was really powerless to give a decision on the matter since the merger of the two units (challenged by the S.D.U.) was proclaimed by the Sierra Leone Independence Act passed by an independent country in 1961, and not by an Order-in-Council. This could not be challenged.
17. Blyden, 'Constitutional change', pp. 193–5.
18. *West Africa*, 17 May 1952; letter to the Editor by W. B. Wright, *West Africa*, 26 Jan. 1952; also letter by Davidson Nicol in *African Affairs*, 53 (1954), p. 157, suggesting that the teaching of Mende and Temne in Colony schools might help Colony Krios to understand their Protectorate compatriots better; *Daily Mail*, 21 and 27 May 1957; *African Standard*, 1950 calling for unity and co-operation.
19. For Bankie's denunciations, see *D.M.*, 22 June 1956; cf. *African Vanguard*, 18 May 1956; *Evening Dispatch*, 25 June 1956.
20. *African Vanguard*, 20 April 1957; 24 Sept. 1957; *D.M.*, 20, 23 and 24 July 1954 for Smart's articles, and issues of 25 and 27 Aug. for John Nelson-Williams' rejoinder to Smart.
21. Kilson, *Political Change*, p. 228.
22. He polled 541 votes, beating his opponent, Metcalfe-Cole, by 255 votes. *West Africa*, 1 Dec. 1951. In all his speeches in the Legislative Council Mustapha never once referred to himself as Krio, though he usually implied that he was a Liberated African descendant.
23. Conversation with Professor Canon H. A. E. Sawyerr at Barbados, 20 Jan. 1980; M. C. F. Easmon, 'P.C. Bai Kur, M.B.E., M.L.C., a biographical sketch of one of Sierra Leone's oldest Chiefs', *S.L.S.* (N.S.), 2 (June 1956), pp. 193–9; Sir George Beresford-Stooke, 'Sierra Leone today', *African Affairs*, 53 (1954), pp. 56–65. Bright himself acknowledged P.C. Bai Kur in the Legislative Chamber as a schoolmate whom he had not seen for fifty years. *Debates*, 29 July 1952.
24. Scott, 'Sierra Leone election', pp. 180 ff; Marcus Jones, 'Fundamental right', p. 161; cf. Collier, *Experiment in Democracy*, p. 34.
25. Scott, 'Sierra Leone election', pp. 188–90.
26. Scott, pp. 190–1; Foray, *Dictionary of Sierra Leone*, pp. 196–7.
27. *Colonial Territories Progress Reports. Cmd 8553, 1951–1952* (H.M.S.O., 1952).
28. *Assumption of Ministerial Portfolios (Sessional Paper No. 1, of 1953)*; *Sessional Paper No. 3 of 1953; Cmd 8856, 1952–1953* (H.M.S.O., 1953); *CO270/87, Sessional Paper No. 2 of 1954. The Duties and Functions of the Provincial Administration Under the Ministerial System* (1954).
29. Kilson, *Political Change*, p. 175.
30. J. D. Hargreaves, 'Western democracy and African society', *International Affairs*, 31, 3 (1955), pp. 327–34.
31. *Debates*, 1951–7.
32. Quoted in Marcus Jones, 'Fundamental right', p. 39; Blyden, 'Constitutional change', pp. 218–19. However, see Hargreaves' analysis of the limitations of a government

between the transitional stage of a 'representative majority' and 'responsible government' in *Problems of Constitutional Development in West Africa: an outline for group discussion* (Dept of Extra-Mural Studies, F.B.C., 1953) 60 pp.

33. *Debates*, 29 Nov. 1951; 31 Jan. 1952; 25 July 1952; 29 July 1952 and 3 Dec. 1953, etc.
34. *Debates*, 29 July 1953.
35. Blyden, 'Constitutional change', p. 211.
36. *D.M.*, 7 Oct. 1955; *Debates*, 1951–7.
37. *Debates*, 31 Jan. 1952; 3 Dec. 1953; 4 Dec. 1953.
38. *D.M.*, 13 July 1957.
39. *Sierra Leone Observer*, 18 Nov. 1950; *D.M.* for 1950–7.
40. *Debates*, 25 July 1952; *D.M.*, 16 Aug. 1954.
41. See contemporary papers for this period, e.g., the *Daily Mail* of 19 March 1957 reported the seizure of 491 uncut diamonds at Lungi Airport.
42. *Debates*, 22 March 1954; 17, 20 Dec. 1954.
43. *D.M.*, 20, 29 Sept.; 1, 4 and 5 Oct. 1955; *Debates*, 29 Sept. 1955. See Van der Laan, *Sierra Leone Diamonds*, ch. 1, for discussion.
44. *D.M.*, 8 Oct. 1955.
45. *D.M.*, 8 Oct. 1955; *Sierra Leone Observer* (30 Jan. 1954) expressed the hope that no discriminatory legislation would be passed against the Syrians and Lebanese 'Of all the aliens in Sierra Leone these people have contributed to the economic and social development more than any other. According to the laws of the country nobody is forced to part with his property, and if the Creoles were foolish enough to part with the best business area in the Colony to Lebanese and Syrians they have themselves to blame and should suffer the consequences.'
46. *Debates*, 20, 21 Dec. 1954; *D.M.*, 21 Dec. 1954.
47. *Ibid.*
48. *Debates*, 25 July 1955.
49. *D.M.*, 12 and 17 Sept. 1955.
50. Interview, J. C. O. Crowther, 9 Sept. 1974.
51. Bankie took ill in February and was hospitalised. When he was discharged in April the *African Vanguard* (4 April 1957) reported the governor's observation on Bright that 'his is a hard and sometimes discouraging position but he is to be congratulated on the way in which he was [*sic*] maintained the high parliamentary traditions of the opposition.' *D.M.*, 15 April 1957.
52. For the internal problems of the S.L.P.P., see *West Africa*, 29 Nov.; 27 Dec. 1952. The splits and factions in the party as well as other parties, N.C.S.L. and U.P.P., were reported in *African Vanguard*, 13 July 1957 (the resignation of Ahmed Alhadi from N.C.S.L. because of 'Strife and discrimination within the party'); 6 Dec. 1957; *D.M.*, 10 and 11 April 1957, etc.: Cartwright, *Politics in Sierra Leone*; Beresford-Stooke, 'Sierra Leone today', pp. 56–65.
53. C. M. Fyle, *The History of Sierra Leone*, pp. 130–6; C. P. Foray, *Historical Dictionary*, 113.
54. Fyle, p. 128; Kilson, *Modernization*, pp. 189–90. Contemporary papers freely reported these incidents in the 50s.
55. *Report of the Commission of Inquiry into the Strike and Riots in Freetown, Sierra Leone, during February 1955* (Sierra Leone Govt 1955); Lisk, 'Industrial relations', pp. 223 ff.; *Daily Mail*, 1955; *African Standard*, 1955, etc; *The Times* (London), 14, 18, 26 Feb.; 6 June 1955.
56. Fyle, pp. 128–9.
57. A few Protectorate names could be found on the platform of the Party, for example I. B. Turay, who was to speak with Gershon Collier, J. M. Rose, and C. M. Thompson at

a public meeting of 27 Nov. 1957. Copy of the Advertisement of the meeting in Mrs Wilson's Collection.

58. Interview: LBT, 7 Aug. 1979. *The African Vanguard* (27 April 1957) gave a different interpretation. It claimed that some members of the N.C.S.L. party did not want Lerina to stand because they did not want to make it a family affair. And when she went to file her papers she fumbled with them until closing time. She failed to register, because of her own fault! But see Scott, 'Sierra Leone election', pp. 234–5. He supports Lerina's claims.

59. These were advertised with gusto by the indestructible Wallace-Johnson in his handouts called *Think*; interview: LBT, 5 Aug. 1974.

60. *Report of the Commission of Inquiry into the Strike.* For a critique of the Shaw Commission, which it called a 'white-wash job on the Stooke-Child Party (i.e., S.L.P.P.)', see *African Standard*, 3 June–1 July 1955.

61. For example, Albert Margai's letter of 8 March 1948 to Miss Nicolson of the Fabian Colonial Bureau (MSS. Brit. Emp. S. 365 Box 86/1B); *Debates*, 25 July 1955.

62. A. R. Dumbuya, 'National integration in Guinea and Sierra Leone: a comparative analysis of the integrative capacities of single- and dominant-party regimes', pp. 121–6; Scott, 'Sierra Leone election'; *D.M.*, 14 July; 28 Dec. 1954.

63. Scott, 'Sierra Leone election', p. 181; Keith Lucas, 'Electoral reform in Sierra Leone', *Political Studies*, 3, 1955, pp. 97–108.

64. *Collected Statements of Constitutional Proposals, Sept. 1955* (Sierra Leone Govt Printer, 1955).

65. *Ibid.*

66. *Ibid.* These proposals, suspiciously, look like those submitted by Juma M. Sei and George S. Panda (students at Fourah Bay College). One individual, Farid A. Assib, suggested that electoral districts be created in the Protectorate and the artificial boundary between the Colony and the Protectorate be entirely abolished 'if the government has any intention of unifying the people and bridging the existing gap'; *D.M.*, 12 Sept. 1955; Keith Lucas, 'Electoral reform', pp. 97–108.

67. N. 66 above, *D.M.*, 12 Sept. and 17 1955.

68. Scott, 'Sierra Leone election' pp. 177 ff.; C. Allen, *Change.*

69. Scott, 'Sierra Leone election'.

70. See Deanna Thomas, 'Milton Margai', p. 165. Pre-elections paper warfare between R. Sarif Easmon in defence of the Krio, and Berthan Macauley, H. E. B. John, S. T. Navo and W. H. Fitzjohn, for the S.L.P.P., can be followed in the *Daily Mail*, 22, 26, 27, 29 Nov. and 3 Dec. 1956. See also J. M. Rose's column and Chief Sam Ekoti-Eboh, the Nigerian minister's appeal to Sierra Leoneans to 'forget tribalism', in *Daily Mail*, 1 and 30 Nov. 1956 respectively; issue of 15 Nov. (editorial); *African Vanguard*, 17, 19 Jan.; Feb.–March, 4 and 27 April 1957.

71. N. 58 above. In their pre-election speeches, Bright claimed that there was 'no dismal horizon for us'. Milton Margai asked the electorate to 'Remember our past achievements', *D.M.*, 2, 3 May; 29 August 1957.

72. Scott, 'Sierra Leone election'; *D.M.*, 10, 11 and 15 April 1957.

73. A. R. Dumbuya, 'Charts on political organisation in Sierra Leone' (pamphlet at F.B.C. Library, Mt Aureol); Scott, 'Sierra Leone election', pp. 257 ff. for an analysis of the election.

74. After his resignation in July, there was a power vacuum and a tussle among his lieutenants for the number one position. Eventually, C. M. Thompson emerged as the leader of N.C.S.L., assisted by Lerina Bright-Taylor and J. M. Rose. *African Vanguard*, 6 Dec. 1957. Bankie told his party after the election, that 'if you have anything to be proud of, it is the result of the election. We lost our seats because of honesty and non-corruption': *ibid.*, 29 Aug. 1957. Wallace-Johnson was expelled from the U.P.P. in June.

He called the leader, C. B. Rogers-Wright, a fascist dictator. *Ibid.*, 13 June 1957; *West Africa*, 7 Sept. 1957.

9: BANKOLE-BRIGHT AND COLONIAL POLITICS: AN ASSESSMENT

1. Introduction, p. 1 above. The degree and the form of help given by Margai was recounted differently by those interviewed. For instance, his sister, Lerina, explained that Sir Milton gave him the honour of 'lying in State', because he considered that he had worked for Parliament and Sierra Leone. A coffin was also supplied. (5 Aug. 1974). Professor Sawyerr revealed (29 April 1983) that when Bankie died the Prime Minister specifically asked him to officiate in the funeral ceremonies. Margai was responsible for his funeral. Many more claims have been made by sundry people, which we cannot list here.
2. *Daily Mail*, 24 Dec. 1958.
3. *Daily Mail*, 15 Dec. 1958.
4. *West Africa*, 27 Dec. 1958.
5. Tribute by I. T. A. Wallace-Johnson, *Daily Mail*, 24 Dec. 1958. (My emphasis.)
6. Conversation with Prof. Canon Sawyerr, Cordrington College, Barbados, 20 Jan. 1980 and Freetown, 29 April 1983.
7. Interview, T. A. L. Decker, 12 Aug. 1975.
8. C. Foray, *Historical Dictionary*, 4.
9. Fitzjohn, *Ambassador*, p. 28.
10. *Daily Mail*, 17–20 Dec. 1958.
11. Conversation with Pat Yulisa Maddy, Calabar, Cross River State, Nigeria, 22 April 1983.
12. For an analysis of a colonial governor's position in his dependency see L. H. Gann and Peter Duignan, *The Rulers of British Africa, 1870–1914* (London, 1978) ch. 5.
13. See ch. 5 of this work.
14. Interview, Dr Bright-Taylor, 1 Jan. 1976.
15. The Committee included Bankole-Bright, C. E. Wright, J. A. Gallagher, A. J. Momoh, the Honourable Director of Education, the Director of P.W.D. and the General Manager of the Sierra Leone Railway. *S.L.W.N.*, 28 Oct. 1939. I was unable to find out whether the work of the Committee was resumed with its composition unchanged; CO270/87, *Sessional Paper No. 3 of 1954, T. C. Luke Report on Medical Salaries and Private Practice (1954)*.
16. Kup, *Sierra Leone*, p. 201.
17. In this regard we may quote Hilary Blood's opinion on Margai 'must be the mildest and most unexpected leader Africa has yet produced. He has little of the dynamism that is common to other African politicians who are thrusting their countries towards independence... His qualities lean rather towards the diplomatic. But his shrewdness is what Sierra Leone most needs – and it is doubtful if a more virulent leader could have brought his country to the brink of independence so soon'. Hilary Blood Papers (MSS. Brit. Emp. S. 408 (4) 'Man in the News', Box 4. For an example of official displeasure against Easmon see CO261/646/22090/1, Hodson to Cunliffe-Lister, 15 May 1934.
18. W. H. Crocker Papers (MSS Afr. S. 323), Notes on the Gold Coast and Sierra Leone 1913–58.
19. Cited in Marcus Jones, 'Fundamental rights', p. 39.
20. Bright was a member of the Royal Colonial Society (the present Royal Commonwealth Society), 1927–32. E. S. Beoku-Betts became a member, 1931–56 (source: Royal Commonwealth Society Library, Northumberland Avenue, London).
21. D. Simpson, 'Ethnic conflict', pp. 154–5; Cecilia Jayne Adams, 'Constitutional

247

development in Sierra Leone, 1955 to 1962', M.A. thesis, Howard University, 1962, p. 9.

22. Simpson, 'Ethnic conflict', p. 153.
23. Irving Kaplan, Margarita Dobert, James L. McLaughtan, Barbara J. Marvin and Donald P. Whitaker, *Area Handbook for Sierra Leone* (Washington, D.C. 1976), p. 2.
24. The same view is implied in this extract from E. A. Boateng, *A Political Geography of Africa* (Cambridge, 1978), p. 119: 'Not until proper safeguards for the people of the protectorate could be agreed upon did the British hand over power to the people of Sierra Leone'.
25. Kaplan et al. *Area Handbook*, p. 3.
26. *Ibid.* p. 10; Deveneaux, *Power and Politics*, ch. 2.
27. These have been indicated in the text. But see Gann and Duignan, *The Rulers of British Africa* (London, 1978), ch. 7, 'The African assistant'; R. S. Jordan, 'The Creoles and the Civil Service'. Seminar paper cited. He contends that 'although in the decades prior to the end of the colonial period they (the Krios) were not as influential as they had been earlier in the higher Civil Service of the colonial bureaucracy...they still held at the time of granting of independence...a dominant influence in the Christian churches, the judiciary, the Civil Service, the Medical profession and education. There was no doubt that in terms of the bureaucratic "infrastructure" of the new State, the Creoles were the most important group'; cf. Gaffney, 'Administration and the administrative service in Sierra Leone', pp. 19–20. See also Note 21 and above, and Pauline Baker, *Urbanization*, *inter alia*, for parallels in Nigeria, for example.
28. Filomena Chioma Steady 'Protestant women's associations in Freetown, Sierra Leone', in Nancy J. Hafkin and Edna G. Bay, *Women in Africa: Studies in Social Change and Economic Change* (Stanford, 1976), pp. 213–37.
29. CO267/663/32041 Jardine to MacDonald, 14 June 1938.
30. *Debates*, 29 Nov. 1928. By the turn of the century, Africans 'began to fill only routine jobs as opportunities were closed for promotion and special service'. There were few liberal concessions, but generally 'the rank and file of African Civil Servants were paid at a lower rate than the whites and could not rise into senior positions'. Gann and Duignan, *Rulers of British Africa*, p. 258.
31. CO267/663/32041 Jardine to MacDonald, 14 June 1938.
32. Quoted in Jordan, 'The Creoles and the Civil Service', p. 5.
33. See n. 27 above.
34. *Debates*, 9 Nov. 1937.
35. *S.L.W.N.*, 16 Sept. 1922; G. A. Gollock, *Lives of Eminent Africans* (New York, 1928; rpt. 1969), pp. 138–41; C. Fyfe, *Sierra Leone*, p. 290.
36. But see Barbara E. Harrell-Bond, Allen M. Howard, and David E. Skinner, *Community Leadership and the Transformation of Freetown, 1801–1976* (The Hague, 1978), pp. 168–9. However, the above pages have adequately advertised the contributions of Bright and his sister, Lerina, to education in the country.
37. Possibly this prompted C. D. Hotobah-During to complain bitterly against government's proposal to establish a secondary school with money from taxation when 'the greater majority of the people in the Protectorate were neglected without Schools or hospitals'. *S.L.W.N.*, 4 Jan. 1919. See also Mohamed Sidi Bah, 'A history of the Prince of Wales School, 1925–1982' B.A. Hons. History dissertation, Fourah Bay College, USL, 1982; *D.G.*, 2, 24 July 1945.
38. CO267/596, Address of welcome presented by a Committee of Educated Africans in the Northern Province of the Protectorate of Sierra Leone, 1922; CO267/678/32036/1, Ramage to Stanley, 19 July 1943; Colonial Office to Treasury, 17 Sept. 1943; Treasury to Colonial Office, 14 Oct. 1943 approving a scholarship scheme for higher education 'to

enable young men and women of Sierra Leone to obtain higher education so that they may qualify themselves to take an increasing and more enlightened part in administration of their own country'. A proposal of ten scholarships was put forward. The first beneficiary under this scheme was Davidson Nicol. See *D.M.*, 22 Dec. 1958 and *Debates*, 3 Dec. 1953 for Koker's outburst. Dr Davidson Nicol (personal communication, August 1988) has, however, informed me that before his time Solomon Cole, Edward Davies, and John Bassir were all sent to Yaba to study for the London inter B.Sc. in 1938 and 1939. E. F. Brandon went on a departmental scholarship to study printing in London.

39. For instance, *S.L.W.N.*, 4 Jan. 1919; 27 Oct. 1923; Bah, 'The Prince of Wales school', p. 32.

40. The total value for palm produce in 1925, for example, was £1,246, 599. But it did not sustain an upward trend. See Buell, p. 868. For complaints about the financial situation in Sierra Leone, the following are useful: CO267/596/2830, Maxwell to Churchill, 30 May 1922; CO267/581/32920, Wilkinson to Milner, 15 May 1919; CO267/597/53938, Slater to Churchill, 12 Oct. 1922; cf. CO267/603/5148, Slater to Devonshire, 20 Jan. 1924; Byrne to Passfield, 30 Nov. 1929, CO267/634/9575:31/1, Financial Position of Sierra Leone. Minutes in the Colonial Office, 12 May 1931, etc.

41. For instance, according to Roy Lewis' estimates, Africans held 116 out of 535 senior posts in the Sierra Leone Civil Service in 1952 (*Sierra Leone*, pp. 217–20); cf. Legislative Council figures for 1951 of 591 Senior Posts: 162 held by Africans, 369 occupied by Europeans and 60 vacant; Gaffney, 'Administration', ch. 3. A. M. M. Heogvelt and A. Tinker, 'The role of Colonial and post Colonial States in imperialism: a case study of the Sierra Leone Development Company', *J.M.A.S.*, 16. 1 (March 1978), pp. 67–79, state that between 1930 and 1976 the total economic benefits from the Ore Mines operated by Delco yielded only 17·25 per cent revenue to Sierra Leone while 82·75 per cent found its way back into the coffers of British capitalism. The mind boggles in attempting to imagine what little was left to develop the Protectorate, not to talk of using it to educate Colony children!

42. *Debates*, April–August 1927.

43. *Civil Service List*, 1930 (Govt Printer: Freetown 1930).

44. O. Adewoye, 'Sierra Leonean immigrants in the field of law in Southern Nigeria, 1862–1934', *S.L.S.*, (O.S.), 26 Jan. 1920, pp. 11–28; J. B. Webster et al., *History of West Africa*, p. 118, state that as late as 1925, 44 of Nigeria's 56 barristers were of 'Creole descent'. See also G. S. Coleman, *Nigeria – Background to Nationalism* (1965), pp. 157–8, for figures of home remittances forwarded by Sierra Leoneans and Gold Coasters to their countries.

45. Marcus Jones, 'Fundamental rights', pp. 562–3.

46. Scott, 'Sierra Leone election', p. 169; P.C. Lloyd, *The New Elites of Tropical Africa* (Oxford, 1966), p. 16. But see A. J. G. Wyse, 'The Krio diaspora: an investigation into negative reports on Krio impact on the interior of Sierra Leone', paper presented at UNESCO Conference on the Cultural Contribution of the Blacks of the Diaspora to Africa, Cotonou (Benin), 21–5 March, 1983, 18 pp.

47. A former civil servant recalled in his memoir that his parents had lived in the interior for years. He too saw some service in the Provincial Administration, and he married a granddaughter of Momodu Wakka, an Arabic tutor at Fourah Bay College. See S. A. D. Peters, *A Memoir* (Govt Printing Dept, *N.D.*); Professor Canon Sawyerr also remembered that there was a Krio 'Colony' in Bauya (20 Jan. 1980).

48. Georges Ballandier, 'Social changes and social problems in Negro Africa', in Collin W. Stillman (ed.), *Africa and The Modern World* (Chicago, 1955; rpt. 1967), pp. 55–69; Marcus Jones, 'Fundamental rights', p. 39.

49. Foreword by Eldred Jones to Peters, *Memoir*, ch. 5 and p. 49.

50. Collier, *Experiment in Democracy*, p. 27.
51. Lewis, *Modern Portrait*, pp. 20–34.
52. Ahmed Alhadi, *The Re-emancipation of the Colony of Sierra Leone* (1951).
53. Kilson, *Modernization*, p. 169.
54. Collier, *Experiment in Democracy*, pp. 64–5.
55. See for example, *West Africa*, 17 May 1982.

Bibliography

A. UNPUBLISHED SOURCES IN VARIOUS ARCHIVES

1. Public Record Office, London
The documents in this Archive form the bulk of my material from official sources. The following were useful and relevant:

(i) CO267/ Series (Sierra Leone)
1898–1946 (the volumes were consulted serially and chronologically).
(ii) CO270 Executive Council Minutes
/44 1910–1913
/48 1917–1919
/62 1924–1931
/74 1932–1940
(iii) CO270/64 Legislative Council Minutes, 1923–32
/75 Legislative Council Minutes, 1933–9
(iv) CO554 West Africa
/15 1913
/46–51 1920–1 (Correspondence on the N.C.B.W.A. Mission to London, 1920–1921.)
CO554/131 (Appointment of African Members to the Executive Council, 1942.)
CO554/132 (Constitutional Developments in West Africa 1943.)
(v) CO448 Honours Correspondence
(vi) CO728 Honours Register
(vii) CO879 Confidential Prints

2. C.M.S. Archives, 157 Waterloo Road, London, S.W.1
The documents in this collection, as well as those in the Methodist Archives, contain very useful information on Church/State relations. It is also clear from the ones consulted that the Church was not free from the prejudices of the period. However, only a tiny part of the material collected was used in this book:
CA1/0178(n) MSS Revd James Quaker, 1851–1880 (letters, reports and circulars). Native Pastor: Grammar School, 1851–80. Secretary, Sierra Leone Auxiliary Church Missionary Association, 1872–3.
G.3A1/C Letters of Revd James Denton, Local Secretary of the C.M.S., and Principal of Fourah Bay College, to the C.M.S. London (illuminating on Church politics and black/white relations).

3. The Methodist Missionary Society Archives, 25 Marylebone Road, London, N.W.1
The comment in 2. also applies here. The papers are arranged in boxes under 'Correspondence':

Bibliography

Sierra Leone and the Gambia
File 1918–19
Box 1924–7 (Sierra Leone)
WMMS 4th Report, 1929 (printed in 1930).

4. Rhodes House Library, Oxford
The yield in this collection was disappointing, but those private papers that were consulted offered valuable insights into the colonial mentality of the white administrator. The Fabian Colonial Bureau Papers (F.C.B.P.) contained interesting information from Sierra Leoneans who confided in the Secretary of the Bureau, Dr Rita Hinden. Those used in this group of documents were:
MSS. Afr. R. 44 D. Bailey Papers, Diary, 1930–47.
MSS. Afr. S. 323 W. H. Crocker, Notes on the Gold Coast and Sierra Leone, 1913–58.
MSS. Afr. S. 388–390 L. W. Wilson Papers Box 1 Encyclopaedia of Sierra Leone: boxes 2 and 3 Chronological Diary of Events.
MSS. Afr. S. 399 Maj-General A. J. H. Dove, C.B. MSS. Sapper Officer, Sierra Leone, Director of Sierra Leone Survey. Letters to his parents, 1925–9.
MSS. Afr. S. 672 N. C. Hollins, MSS. Sierra Leone, 1921–36.
MSS. Afr. S. 1151 N. A. C. Weir, D.C. Administrative Services, Sierra Leone, Personal Diary, 1936–43.
MSS. Brit. Emp. S. 280 Peter White, Topographical Surveyor, Sierra Leone, 1927–30. Letters to his family.
MSS. Brit. Emp. S. 296 Alfred Claud Hollis MSS. Autobiography.
MSS. Brit. Emp. S. 365 Fabian Colonial Bureau Papers (F.C.B.P.): historical background to F.C.B.P., boxes 81, 82/2, 86/1A, 86/1B.
MSS. Brit. Emp. S. 408 (4) Hilary H. Blood Papers. Box 1.
NATHAN MSS. 248/249 Governor of Sierra Leone, 1898–9. Correspondence, 1898–1913 (including letters from F. A. Miller and Sir Samuel Lewis).

5. Royal College of Surgeons Archive, Edinburgh
Records of Bankole-Bright's medical studentship are deposited in the R.C.S., Edinburgh. Ms D. U. Wardle, the librarian, was most helpful in directing me to those documents that were relevant to the study. Details of Bright's academic record are arranged by year. There are no call numbers.

6. The Sierra Leone National Archive (on the campus of Fourah Bay College, University of Sierra Leone), Freetown, Sierra Leone
The documents consulted in this collection are few and scattered. Materials in the archive are being catalogued. However, references from the Archive have been cited in the footnotes.

7. Ibadan University Library, Ibadan, Oyo State, Nigeria
The Herbert Macauley Papers.

8. Miscellaneous
M.B.H.S. School Register (by courtesy of the then Vice-Principal, Mr Willie Pratt).

9. Private papers
C. D. Hotobah-During MSS. These consist mainly of uncompleted drafts of his autobiography (by courtesy of his son, I. C. Hotabah-During, Freetown, Sierra Leone).

Mrs A. Wilson Collection. Documents and letters (including one of gratitude from Bankole-Bright) on political questions of the day, for instance, the S.D.U. case, and pamphlets by J. C. Zizer. (By courtesy of Mrs A. Wilson, 37 Waterloo Street, Freetown, Sierra Leone.)

The T. A. L. Decker collection of newspapers has been indicated in the references.

10. List of interviewees in alphabetical order
S. M. O. Boyle, W.A.Y.L. member and associate of Wallace-Johnson, activist/journalist.

Mrs Lerina Bright-Taylor, sister of Bankole-Bright, a keen educationalist, female activist and Asst Secretary-General of N.C.S.L. She died in 1976.

Dr Onodi Bright-Taylor, Medical Practitioner (in Norway), nephew of Bright.

Hon. J. C. O. Crowther, a contemporary of Bright. Rural Area Representative in the Legislative Council, 1939–57.

T. A. L. Decker, amateur historian and able journalist. Chief Information Officer, Sierra Leone Government (retired), now deceased.

Pa A. H. Fergusson, contemporary and friend of Bright's. Retired Customs Officer. Deceased.

Rev. Dr W. H. Fitzjohn, Protectorate member of Moyamba District in the Legislative Council, 1951–7; cleric and diplomat.

I. C. Hotobah-During, son of C. D. Hotobah-During.

Pa J. C. Lucan, President/Founder of S.D.U. Maternal uncle of E. S. Beoku-Betts. Deceased.

Pat Yulisa Maddy, well-known Sierra Leonean playwright and novelist.

Rev. Isaac Ndanema, Senior Assistant Librarian, Fourah Bay College, U.S.L.

Mrs Hannah Neale, mass communicator, niece of Bright.

Pa T. J. Robinson, friend of Bankole-Bright, active citizen. Deceased.

Pa J. Rogers-Williams, N.C.S.L. member of the Legislative Council, 1951–7. Bright's associate. Deceased.

Professor Canon Harry A. E. Sawyerr, Former Principal of Fourah Bay College and Acting Vice-Chancellor, University of Sierra Leone, 1968–73. Professor Emeritus, Department of Theology, F.B.C. Deceased.

Prof. A. D. Williams, Professor of Mathematics, Fourah Bay College, University of Sierra Leone.

B. PUBLISHED PRIMARY SOURCES

1. Official publications
Collected Statements of Constitutional Proposals, Sept. 1955 (S.L. Govt. Printer, 1955).

Colonial Office List (H.M.S.O., 1923–61).

Parliamentary Command Papers: 7715 (1948–9); 7958 (1949–50) 8243 (1950–1); 8553 (1951–2); 8856 (1952–3); 451 (1957–8).

Report of the Commission of Inquiry into the Strike and Riots in Freetown, Sierra Leone, During February 1955 (Sierra Leone Govt., 1955).

Bibliography

Sessional Papers (Sierra Leone): nos. 2, 7, 8, 17 (1948); 4 (1949); 2 (1950); 2, 3 (1951) and 1, 3 (1953).
Sierra Leone Blue Books, 1919–1927 (Sierra Leone National Archive, Mt Aureol).
Sierra Leone Legislative Council Debates, Sessions 1923/4–1957.
The African Bureau No. 3, Sierra Leone and The Gambia (April 1958, London).

2. Newspapers and magazines

Some newspapers were consulted at Colindale Newspaper Library, London, and at S.O.A.S., London University. There were large gaps in the issues. For instance, the *Weekly News* collection at S.O.A.S. Library was much fuller (though in delicate condition) than that in Colindale. There were no copies of Wallace-Johnson's *African Standard* in the Newspaper Library, while the holding for Bright's *Aurora* covered 16 April–31 Dec. 1921, excluding May 28. When I visited the library in 1977, newspapers from 1940 onwards were being filmed, and I had no opportunity to consult any covering this period. The list below indicates those consulted in various places in London and Freetown and the period covered. Issues of *West Africa* were of course much easier to consult. The *Weekly News* was the most useful and informative of all the papers investigated. Copies of other Sierra Leone newspapers were fragmentary. The late Mr T. A. L. Decker kindly let me look at his private copies of *African Standard* and *Daily Guardian*. I found them useful for the 1940s.

African Standard (1941–5)
African Vanguard (1956–7)
African World (1926)
Aurora The People's Organ (April–Dec. 1921)
Colonial and Provincial Reporter (C.P.R.) (1918–19)
Daily Guardian (*D.G.*) (1938–49)
Daily Mail (*D.M.*) (1954–64)
Evening Dispatch (1956)
Methodist Herald (1887)
Sierra Leone Guardian and Foreign Mail (*S.L.G.F.M.*) (1910–19)
Sierra Leone Observer (1950–4)
Sierra Leone Weekly News (1892–1951)
The Student (1904–10, Edinburgh Univ. Library, Scotland)
The Times (1955)
W.A.S.U. (1926–37)
West Africa (1949–58)

C. UNPUBLISHED THESES AND DISSERTATIONS

Adams, Cecilia Jayne, 'Constitutional development in Sierra Leone, 1955–1962, M. A. Howard, 1962.
Bah, Mohamed Alpha, 'Dr Herbert C. Bankole-Bright and his impact on the growth of constitutional government and the development of political parties in Sierra Leone, 1924–1957', M. A. Howard, 1977.
Bah, Mohamed Sidi, 'A History of the Prince of Wales School, 1925–1982', B.A. Hons. History, (F.B.C.) Sierra Leone, 1982.
Blyden, E. W., III, 'Sierra Leone: pattern of constitutional change, 1924–1951', Ph.D., Harvard, 1959.
Dumbuya, A. R. 'National integration in Guinea and Sierra Leone: a comparative analysis of the integrative capacities of single – and dominant – party regimes', Ph.D., Washington, 1974.

Gaffney, Henry H. Jun., 'Administration and the administrative service in Sierra Leone', Ph.D. Columbia, 1967.

Gale, T. S. 'Official medical policy in British West Africa, 1870–1930', Ph.D., London, 1972.

Jones, W. S. Marcus, 'The protection of fundamental rights and freedoms of the individual in Sierra Leone', LL.D. Yale, N.D.

Lisk, F. A. N., 'Industrial relations in Sierra Leone', M.Sc. (Econs.), Queen's, Belfast, 1970.

Moore-Sieray, David, 'Idara Kontorfili and the 1931 Insurrection in North Western Sierra Leone', B.A. Hons. Hist. (F.B.C.), Sierra Leone, 1978.

Stephen, D. A. Vonque, 'A history of the settlement of liberated Africans in the Colony of Sierra Leone during the first half of the 19th Century', M. A. Durham, 1962.

D. RESEARCH AND CONFERENCE PAPERS

Hargreaves, John D., *Problems of Constitutional Development in West Africa: An Outline for Group Discussion* (Dept. of Extra Mural Studies, F.B.C., 1953) 60 pages.

Hargreaves, John D., 'Assumptions, expectations and plans: approaches to decolonization in Sierra Leone', Paper presented at the Anglo-French Colloquium on Independence and Dependence: the relation of Britain and France with their former territories, Paris, 6–8 May 1976.

Jordan, R. S., 'The Creoles and the Civil Service in Sierra Leone, 1957–1969', Paper presented at the Sierra Leone Symposium, University of Ontario, 7–9 May 1971 (Institute of Commonwealth Studies Library, London) 28 pp.

Leighton, N. O. 'The Lebanese Community in Sierra Leone: the role of an alien trading minority in political development', paper presented at the fifteen annual meeting of the African Studies Association, Philadelphia, Pennsylvania, 8–11 Nov. 1972 (Institute of Commonwealth Studies Library, London).

Wyse, A. J. G., 'Politics in Colonial Sierra Leone: the example of the Sierra Leone Branch of the National Congress of British West Africa, 1918–1940', Public Lecture, 25 Oct. 1978.

Wyse, A. J. G., 'The Krio diaspora: an investigation into negative reports on Krio impact on the interior of Sierra Leone', Paper presented at UNESCO Conference on the Cultural Contribution of the Blacks of the Diaspora to Africa, Contonou (Benin), 21–5 March 1983, 18 pp.

E. PUBLISHED SECONDARY SOURCES (SELECTED LIST)

Ajayi, J. F. A., *Christian Missions in Nigeria, 1841–1891: the Making of a New Elite* (North Western University Press: Evanston, 1965).

Akintoye, S. A., *Emergent African States* (Hong Kong 1976).

Asante, S. K. B., *Pan-African Protest: West Africa and the Italo-Ethiopian Crisis, 1934–1941* (Longman: London, 1977).

Ayandele, E. A., *The Missionary Impact on Modern Nigeria, 1842–1914* (Longman: London, 1966).

The Educated Elite in the Nigerian Society (Ibadan: University Press, 1974).

Bibliography

Baker, Pauline H., *Urbonization and Political Change: The Politics of Lagos, 1947–1967* (Berkeley, 1974).

Best, R. J., *A History of Sierra Leone Railway, 1899–1949* (Govt Printers: Sierra Leone, 1949).

Buell, R., *The Native Problem in Africa* 1 (London, 1928).

Cartwright, John R., *Politics in Sierra Leone, 1947–1967,* (University of Toronto Press, 1970).

Political Leadership in Sierra Leone (University of Toronto Press, 1978).

Clapham, C., *Liberia and Sierra Leone: An Essay in Comparative Politics* (Cambridge University Press, 1976).

Collier, Gershon, *Sierra Leone: Experiment in Democracy in an African Nation* (New York University Press, 1970).

Cox, Thomas S., *Civil–Military Relations in Sierra Leone: A Case Study of African Soldiers in Politics* (Harvard University Press: Cambridge, Mass., 1976).

Crowder, M., *West Africa Under Colonial Rule* (Hutchinson: London, 1968).

Deveneaux, Gustav H. K., *Power and Politics in Sierra Leone* (African Universities Press: Ibadan, 1982).

Fitzjohn, W. H., *Ambassador of Christ and Caesar* (Day Star Press: Ibadan, 1975).

Foray, Cyril P., *Historical Dictionary of Sierra Leone* (Scarecrow Press: London, 1977).

Fyfe, Christopher, *A History of Sierra Leone* (Oxford University Press, 1962).

Sierra Leone Inheritance (Oxford University Press, 1964).

Africanus Horton: West African Scientist and Patriot, 1835–1883 (Oxford University Press, 1972).

and Jones, E. (eds.), *Freetown: A Symposium* (University of Sierra Leone: Freetown, 1968).

Fyle, C. Magbaily, *The History of Sierra Leone* (Evans Brothers: London, 1981).

Grace, John, *Domestic Slavery in West Africa With Particular Reference to the Sierra Leone Protectorate, 1896–1927.* (Frederick Muller: London, 1975).

Hailey, Lord William, *African Survey* (Oxford University Press, 1957). First published in 1938, revised in 1956.

Hancock, W. K., *Survey of British Commonwealth Affairs: Problems of Nationality, 1918–1936* (Oxford University Press, 1937).

July, R. W., *The Origins of Modern African Thought: Its Development in West Africa During the 19th and 20th Centuries* (Fred A. Praeger: New York, 1967).

Kaplan, Irving et al., *Area Handbook for Sierra Leone* (The American University: Washington, 1976).

Kilson, M., *Political Change in a West African State: A Study of Modernization Process in Sierra Leone* (Harvard University Press, 1966).

Kimble, P., *A Political History of Ghana: The Rise of Gold Coast Nationalism, 1850–1924* (Oxford University Press, 1963).

Kohn, Hans and Sokolsky, Wallace, *African Nationalism in the Twentieth Century* (London, 1965).

Kopytoff, J. H., *Preface to Modern Nigeria: the Sierra Leoneans in Yoruba, 1830–1890* (University of Wisconsin Press: Madison, 1965).

Kup, A. P., *Sierra Leone: A Concise History* (David & Charles: Newton Abbot, 1975).

Langley, J. Ayodele, *Pan-Africanism and Nationalism in West Africa, 1900–1945* (Clarendon Press: Oxford, 1973).

Lewis, W. Arthur et al., *Attitudes to Africa* (Penguin Books: Harmondsworth, 1951).

Lewis, Roy, *Sierra Leone: a Modern Portrait* (H.M.S.O.: London, 1954).

Lloyd, P. C., *The New Elites of Tropical Africa* (Oxford University Press, 1966).

Luke, Sir Harry, *A Bibliography of Sierra Leone* (Oxford University Press, 1925).
    Cities and Men: An Autobiography 3 vols. (Geoffrey Bles: London, 1953–6).

MacMillan, W. M., *The Road to Self-Rule: A Study in Colonial Evolution* (Faber and Faber: London, 1959)..

Magubane, Bernard M., *The Political Economy of Race and Class in South Africa* (Monthly Review Press: New York and London, 1979).

Olusanya, G. O., *The West African Students' Union and the Politics of Decolonization, 1925–1958* (Daystar Press: Ibadan, 1982).

Ormsby-Gore, W., *Report of his Visit to West Africa During the Year 1926* (H.M.S.O.: London, 1926).

Padmore, George, *How Britain Rules Africa* (Wischart Books: London, 1936).

Pedler, Frederick, *Main Currents of West African History, 1940–1978* (Macmillan: London, 1954).

Peters, S. A. D., *A Memoir* (Govt Printing Dept: Freetown, n.d.).

Peterson, J. E., *The Province of Freedom: A History of Sierra Leone, 1787–1870* (Northwestern University Press: Evanston, 1969).

Porter, Arthur, *Creoledom* (Oxford University Press, 1963).

Price, J. H., *Political Institution of West Africa* (London, 1967).

Spitzer, L., *The Creoles of Sierra Leone: Responses to Colonialism, 1870–1945* (University of Wisconsin Press: Madison, 1974).

Stevens, Siaka, *What Life Has Taught Me* (The Kensal Press: Bourne End, Bucks., 1984).

Sumner, D. L., *Education in Sierra Leone* (Govt Printer: Freetown, 1963).

Tamuno, T. N., *The Evolution of the Nigerian State: The Southern Phase, 1898–1914* (Humanities Press: New York, 1972).

Van der Laan, H. L., *The Sierra Leone Diamonds: An Economic Study Covering The Years 1952–1961* (Oxford University Press, 1966).

Walker, J. W. St George, *The Black Loyalists: The Search For A Promised Land in Nova Scotia and Sierra Leone, 1783–1870* (Longman and Dalhousie University Press: London and Dalhousie, 1976).

Webster, J. B., Boahen, A. A. and Tidy, M. *West Africa Since 1800: The Revolutionary Years* (Longman: London, 1980) (new edition).

West, Richard, *Back to Africa: A History of Sierra Leone and Liberia* (Holt, Rinehart and Winston Inc.: New York, 1970).

Wight, M., *The Development of the Legislative Council, 1600–1945* (Faber and Faber: London, 1946).

Wilson, Ellen Gibson, *The Loyal Blacks* (G. P. Putnam's Sons: New York, 1976).

Wraith, Ronald, *Local Administration in West Africa* (Allen and Unwin: London, 1972) (second edition).

Bibliography

Pamphlets and Articles

A Booklet of the Entrance Register of the C.M.S. Grammar School (1935).

Adewoye, O., 'Sierra Leonean immigrants in the field of law in Southern Nigeria, 1862–1934', *SLS* (N.S), 26 Jan. 1970, pp. 11–28.

Alhadi, Ahmed, *The Re-Emancipation of the Colony of Sierra Leone* (Sierra Leone Collection, F.B.C. Library), 1956, 23 pp.

Allan, C., *Constitutional Change, 1863–1967* (Sierra Leone Collection, F.B.C. Library), 1967, 12 pp.

Aluko, Olajide, 'Politics of Decolonization in British West Africa, 1945–1960', in Ajayi, J. F. A. and Crowder, M. (editors), *History of West Africa* (Longman: London, 1974), 2, chapt. 18, pp. 622–63.

Amolo, Milcar, 'Trade Unionism and Colonial authority: Sierra Leone, 1930–1945', *Trans African Journal of History*, 7, 1 and 2 (1979), pp. 36–52.

Asante, S. K. B., 'I. T. A. Wallace-Johnson and the Italo-Ethiopian Crisis', *J.H.S.N.*, 7, 4 (June 1975), pp. 631–46.

Beoku-Betts, E. S., 'The failure of the jury system in Sierra Leone', *Supplement to the African World*, Aug.–Sept. 1928.

Beresford-Stooke, Sir George, 'Sierra Leone today', *African Affairs*, 53 (1954), pp. 56–65.

Buxton, T. F. V., 'The Creole in West Africa', *Journal of African Society*, 12 (1912–13), pp. 385–94.

Cohen, Abner, 'The politics of ritual secrecy', *Man*, 6 (1971), pp. 427–48.

Conway, H. E., 'Labour protest activity in Sierra Leone during the early part of the twentieth century', *Labour History*, 15 Nov. 1968, pp. 49–63.

Crowder, M., 'An African aristocracy', *The Geographical Magazine*, 31, 4 (Aug. 1958), pp. 183–90.

'West Africa and the 1914–1918 War', *Bulletin D'Ifan*, Series B, 30, 1 (1968), pp. 227–47.

'The 1939–1945 war and West Africa', in Ajayi and Crowder, *History of West Africa*, 2, chapt. 17, pp. 596–621.

Decker, Thomas, *Our Paramount Chiefs of the Sierra Leone Protectorate* (Freetown, c. 1948) pamphlet, 15 pp.

Counter Proposals for a New Constitution for Sierra Leone (1948), 16 pp.

Eluwa, Gabriel I. C., 'The National Congress of British West Africa: a pioneer nationalist movement', *Genève Afrique*, 11, 1, 1972, pp. 33–51.

Esedebe, P. O., 'The independence movement in Sierra Leone', *Tarikh*, 4, 1 (1971), pp. 15–20.

'WASU's Pan-African role reconsidered', *Journal of the Historical Society of Sierra Leone*, 2, 2 (July 1978), pp. 1–9.

Fourah Bay College Fund Committee. Pamphlet (n.d., c. 1948), 32 pp.

Fyfe, Christopher, 'The life and times of John Ezzidio', *S.L.S.* (N.S.) 4 (1955), pp. 213–23.

'The Sierra Leone press in the nineteenth century', *S.L.S.* (N.S.) 8 (June 1957), p. 234.

Gale, T. S. 'The disbarment of African medical officers by the West African medical staff: a study in prejudice', *J.H.S.L.*, 4, 1 and 2 (Dec. 1980), pp. 33–44.

Garrigue, Philip, 'The WASU: a Study in Culture Contact', *Africa*, 32 (1953), pp. 55–69.

Gwyn, J. Alexander, 'The failure of the jury system in Sierra Leone', *Supplement to the African World*, 26 March 1928.

Hair, P. E. H., 'Africanism: Freetown's contribution', *Journal of Modern African Studies*, 5, 4 (1967), pp. 521–39.

Hanna, Marwan, 'The Lebanese in West Africa: how and why they came', *West Africa*, 19 and 26 April 1958.

Hargreaves, J. D., 'Sir Samuel Lewis and the Legislative Council', *S.L.S.* (N.S.), 1 (1953), pp. 40–52.

'Colonial Office opinion on the constitution of 1863', *S.L.S.*, (N.S.) 5 (1955), pp. 2–10.

'Western Democracy and African Society', *International Affairs*, 31, 3 (1955), pp. 327–34.

'The establishment of the Sierra Leone Protectorate and the insurrection of 1898', *Cambridge Historical Journal*, 12 (1956), pp. 56–80.

Hoogvelt, Ankie M. M. and Tinker, Anthony, 'The role of Colonial and post Colonial States in imperialism: a case study of the Sierra Leone Development Company', *J.N.A.S.*, 16, 1 (March 1978), pp. 67–97.

Hussain, Arif, 'The educated elites: collaborators, assailants, nationalists: a note on African nationalists and nationalism', *J.H.S.N.*, 7, 3 (Dec. 1974), pp. 485–97.

Ijagbemi, A., 'The Freetown Colony and the development of 'legitimate' commerce in the adjoining territories', *J.H.S.N.*, 5, 2 (June 1970), pp. 234–65.

Jones-Quartey, K. A. B., 'Sierra Leone's role in the development of Ghana, 1820–1930', *S.L.S.* (N.S.) 10, (June 1958), pp. 73–83.

'Sierra Leone and Ghana: nineteenth century pioneers in West African journalism', *S.L.S.* (N.S.) 12 (Dec. 1959), pp. 230–244.

Kaniki, M. H. Y., 'Attitudes and reaction towards the Lebanese in Sierra Leone during the colonial period', *Canadian Journal of African Studies*, 7, 1 (1973), pp. 97–113.

'Politics of protest in Colonial West Africa: the Sierra Leone experience', *The African Review*, 4, 3 (1974), pp. 423–58.

'The Idara rebellion of 1931: a reappraisal', *J.H.S.S.L.*, 1, 2 (June 1977), pp. 57–64.

Killingray, D., 'Repercussions of World War I in the Gold Coast', *J.A.H.*, 19, 1 (1978), pp. 39–59.

Kilson, Martin, 'Nationalism and social classes in British West Africa', *Journal of Politics*, 20 (May 1958), pp. 368–87.

'Grass roots politics in Africa: local government in Sierra Leone', *Political Studies*, 12 (1964), pp. 47–66.

'The National Congress of British West Africa, 1918–1936', in R. I. Rotberg and Ali Mazrui (editors), *Protest and Power in Black Africa* (Oxford University Press, 1970), pp. 571–88.

'Social forces in West African political development, in P. J. M. McEwan (ed.), *Twentieth Century Africa* (Oxford University Press, 1970), pp. 1–16.

Kirk-Greene, A. H. M., 'On governorship and governors in British Africa' in Gann and Duignan, *African Pro-Consuls*, 209–64.

Langley, J. Ayodele, 'The Gambia Section of the National Congress of British West Africa', *Africa*, 50, 4 (Oct. 1969), pp. 382–95.

Laski, Harold, 'The Colonial Civil Service', *Political Quarterly*, 9, 1–4 (1938), pp. 541–51.

Lewis, Roy, 'Creoledom revisited', *The Geographical Magazine*, 37, 1 (May 1964), pp. 9–19.

Little, Kenneth L., 'The significance of West African Creole for Africanist and Afro-American Studies', *African Affairs*, 49 (1950), pp. 308–19.

Lucas, Keith B., 'Electoral reform in Sierra Leone', *Political Studies*, 3 (1955), pp. 97–108.

Luke, T. C., 'Some notes on the Creoles and their land', *S.L.S.* (O.S.) 21 (1939), pp. 53–66.

Lynch, Hollis R., 'The native pastorate controversy and cultural ethno-centrism in Sierra Leone, 1871–1874', *J.A.H.*, 5, 3 (1964), pp. 395–413.

MacMillan, W. M., 'African development: (a) by external capital mining enterprise and the labour problem', (b) 'Negative example of Sierra Leone', in C. K. Meek et al., *Europe and West Africa: Some Problems and Adjustments* (Oxford University Press, 1940), pp. 42–80.

Memorial of the Celebration of the Jubilee of Her Majesty's Reign and of the Centenary of Sierra Leone, 1887 (W. B. Whittington & Co.: London, 1887).

Nordman, Curtis R., 'The decision to admit unofficials to the Executive Councils of British West Africa', *Journal of Imperial and Commonwealth History*, 4, 2 (January 1976), pp. 194–205.

Omu, Fred I. A., 'The "new era" and the abortive press law of 1857', *S.L.S.* (N.S.), (July 1968), pp. 2–14.

'The dilemma of press freedom in Colonial Africa: the West African example', *J.A.H.*, 9, 2 (1968), pp. 279–98.

Orr, Charles A., 'Trade Unionism in Colonial Africa', *The Journal of Modern African Studies*, 4 (1966), pp. 65–81.

Post, K. W. J., 'British policy and representative government in West Africa', in P. Duignan and L. H. Gann, *Colonialism in Africa, 1870–1962* (Cambridge University Press, 1970), pp. 31–57.

Probyn, L., 'Sierra Leone and the natives of West Africa', *Journal of the African Society*, 23 (April 1907), pp. 250–8.

Scott, D. J. R., 'The Sierra Leone election, May 1957', in W. J. M. Mackenzie and Kenneth E. Robinson (eds), *Five Elections in Africa* (Clarendon Press: Oxford, 1960), pp. 168–268.

Simpson, Dick, 'Ethnic conflict in Sierra Leone', in Victor A. Olarunsola (editor), *The Politics of Cultural Sub-Nationalism in Africa: Africa and the Problem of 'One State, Many Nationalisms'* (Doubleday & Co.: Garden City, N.Y., 1972), pp. 153–88.

Spitzer, Leo and Denzer, La Ray, 'I. T. A. Wallace-Johnson and the West African Youth League', *Intenational Journal of African Historical Studies*, 6, 3 (1973), pp. 413–52, 561–601, parts 1 and 2.

Steady, Florence Chioma, 'Protestant Women's Associations in Freetown, Sierra

Leone', in Nancy J. Hafkin and Edna G. Bay, *Women in Africa: Studies in Social Change and Economic Change* (Stanford University Press: Stanford, 1976), pp. 213–37.

Tamuno, Tekena N., 'Some aspects of Nigerian reaction to the imposition of British Rule', *J.H.S.N.*, 3, 2 (Dec. 1965), pp. 271–94.

'Governor Clifford and representative government', *J.H.S.N.*, 4, 1 (1967), pp. 117–24.

'The role of the Legislative Council in the administration of Lagos, 1886–1913', *J.H.S.N.*, 4, 4 (June 1967), pp. 555–70.

Thomas, David, 'E. N. Jones, 1884–1954', in *Encyclopaedia Africana: The Dictionary of African Biography: Sierra Leone and Zaire* (Reference Publications Inc.: Michigan, 1979), pp. 83–5.

Webster, J. B., 'Political activity in British West Africa, 1900–1940', in Ajayi and Crowder, *West Africa*, 2, pp. 568–95.

Wyse, Akintola J. G., 'Research notes on Dr Bankole-Bright: his life, 1883–1939', *A.R.B.*, 5, 1 (1974), pp. 3–27.

'Some thoughts on themes in Sierra Leone history', *J.H.S.S.L.*, 2, 1 (Jan. 1978), pp. 228–39.

'The Sierra Leone Creoles, their history and historians', *Journal of African Studies*, 4, 2 (Summer 1978), pp. 65–73.

'On misunderstandings arising from the use of the term "Creole" in the literature on Sierra Leone: a rejoinder', *Africa*, 49, 4 (1979), pp. 405–15.

'The 1919 strike and anti-Syrian riots: a Krio plot?', *J.H.S.S.L.*, 2, 1 and 2 (Dec. 1979), pp. 1–14.

'The 1926 Railway Strike and Anglo-Krio Relations: An Interpretation', *The International Journal of African Historical Studies*, 14, 1 (1981), pp. 93–123.

Searchlight on the Krios of Sierra Leone: an ethnographical Study of a West African People (Institute of African Studies Occasional Paper No. 3: Fourah Bay College, 1980).

'A. J. Abayomi-Cole', p. 35; 'H. C. Bankole-Bright', p. 40; 'S. J. S. Barlatt', p. 42; 'Alimamy Bunjie', p. 50; 'A. O. Johnson', p. 82; 'F. A. Miller', p. 117; 'J. C. Shorunkeh-Sawyerr', p. 146; 'S. B. Thomas', p. 154; 'A. E. Tuboku-Metzger', p. 156, in *Encyclopaedia Africana: Sierra Leonéaire*, Reference Publications, Inc.: Algonac, Mich., 1979.

Young, Crawford, 'Decolonization in Africa' in Duignan and Gann (eds.), *Colonialism in Africa*, pp. 450–502.

Index

Abayomi-Cole, Dr J. 22, 23, 24, 30, 35, 43;
  see also Professor Abayomi-Cole
Aborigines 51, 52
Aborigines' Protection Society, London 89
Aborigines' Society 22, 51–3; see Sierra
  Leone Aborigines' Society (S.L.A.S.)
Abuke-Thomas see Thomas, S.B.
Accra 90
Administrative Officers 28
Advisory Council 19
African Agriculturists 115
African Civil Servants' Association 143
African doctors 27, 100
African graduates
  salaries 98
African lawyers 27, 45
African personnel
  conditions of service 97
African Progressive Union 22, 103
African traditional government 40
Afro-West Indian Association 10
Agricultural Banks 113, 115
Agricultural Society 22
Akibo-Betts, D. T. 23
Akintoye 155
Akiumi 47
Albert Academy 104
Alderman 76, 153
Alhadi, Ahmed 158
Alharazim, S. Deen 131
Aliens' (Expulsion) Ordinance
  amendment 171
All People's Congress Party 178
Alluvial diamond miners 108
Amery, Col. Sect L.C 82
Amolo 110
Anglican Bishop of Sierra Leone 69
Anglo-Krio relations 25, 65, 70, 185
Anti-Slavery Society 38
Anti-Syrian riots, 1919 29, 37, 68

Appeal Court 89
Appeal in Criminal Cases 95
A.P.U. 38
Arbitrational Tribunal 130
Aristos 7, 12
Arkeboh-Betts see Akibo-Betts
Asante 45
Assembly of Chiefs 50, 102
Assessors' Ordinance 20, 45, 61, 63, 87, 89,
  90–6, 102, 112, 124, 127, 181, 183
Assistant Colonial Secretary
  African 98, 99
Assistant Controller of Customs 98
Assistant Director of Education
  African 98
Assistant District Commissioner 27, 104
Assistant Postmaster-General 98, 116
Assistant Treasurer
  African 98
Asquith 38
Atlantic Charter, 1941 134
Attorney-General 20, 43, 106, 111
Awunor-Renner, Dr W. 9, 27, 150
Awunor-Renner, family name 30
Aymer 113
Azikiwe 104, 119

Ballandier, Prof. G. 189
Bangura, Bobboh 49
Bankie see Bankole-Bright
Bankole-Bright, Dr Herbert Christian 3, 5,
  7–10, 12–13, 15, 16, 24, 25, 28, 41–3,
  46, 47, 56, 57, 59–66, 68, 71, 74, 78, 81,
  83, 87, 88, 90–2, 95–107, 111, 116, 118,
  119, 120, 124, 125–7, 130–2, 148, 149,
  157–62, 164, 165, 168, 170, 171, 172,
  176, 177, 180, 182, 184
  anti-protectorate 10
  Civil suit 82
  death 179

Index

fight against officialdom 183
libel suit 125
Masonic Lodge 14
Opposition Leader 163
physician 11
political affairs 14
political awareness 10
political enemies 116
politics 36
public speaker 181
record of achievements 182
Sierra Leone history 180
Bap, Kohn 151
Bar Association 22, 123
Barber, E. 65
Barlatt, R. C. P. 35, 43
Barlatt, S. J. S. 17, 27, 35, 57, 74, 81
Barnes, W. L. Gorell 165
Barton, P. F. 72
Bata Shoe Company 113
Benka-Coker, A. 125
Beoku-Betts, Ernest Samuel 19, 23, 27, 35,
    42, 45, 56, 57, 59–61, 74, 81–3, 88, 96,
    97, 102, 105, 106, 112, 121, 126, 128,
    131, 150, 164, 173, 175, 176, 182
    Police Magistrate 116
Beoku-Betts, Ronald 169, 172
Beresford-Stooke, Gov. 151, 158, 160, 163,
    165
Betts see Beoku-Betts
Bishop, Addah Maude 12
Bishop of Sierra Leone 71, 79
Bishop, Theophilus Colenso 12
Bills 129, 130
Black Englishmen 17, 31
Black Returnees 31
Blake, T. A. 51
Blood, Hilary Randolph R. 91, 110, 114,
    115, 122, 123, 132
Blyden, Edward 23, 168, 169, 170, 177
Bo
    Krio Community 143
Bo African Club 143
Bo School 29
Bolsheviks 126
Bonthe District 65
Boston, J. Fowel 74, 77, 80, 82, 88, 89, 90,
    97, 116, 132, 134
Bourdillon, Sir Bernard 135
Boyle, S. M. O. 119, 129, 131, 147
Boyle-Hebron, Janet Syble 59
Bridgeman, R. 119

Bright and Betts 60, 61, 74, 81–3, 88, 101, 106
Bright, I. O. 96
Bright, Jacob (Galba), father 3, 5, 11, 60
Bright, Jacob Galba Iwuchuka, son 11, 60
Bright, John 3–6, 11
Bright, John St Hawley Ekundayo 11
Bright, Letitia 5
Bright, Mary Ann 6
Bright-Taylor, Lerina 113
Britain
    imperial defence 112
    imperial power 32
    political development 39
    West African Colonies 33
    West African subjects 38
British administration 13, 55
    cadre of literate Africans 5
British Citizenship 152
British Commonwealth 177
British culture 40
British Crown Colony 19
British Empire 10, 128
British Government 28, 38, 165
British Imperial War Fund 133
British Institutions 28
British justice 112
British Law 28
British mentality 17
British Nationality Act 1948 152
British Parliament 19
British philanthropists 3
British raj 117, 186
British rule
    rebellion 29
British subjects 28
British West Africa
    press development 46
British West African Court of Appeal 37
Brown, James 51
Brown, M. S. 35
Bruce, Dr Nanka 47
Bryne, Governor J. A. 94, 96, 100
Bunce Island 24
Bungie, Alimamy 116; see William Rainy
    Lumpkin
bureaucracy 50
Bureh, Kandeh 175
    legion service 133
Burns Sir Alan 135
Burton, Richard F. 18
bus service 80
Buxton, Lord 108

Camerouns 32
Campbell, F. 100
Campbell, Major J. M. 120
Cardew, Governor Frederic 18, 48, 110
Carew, Samuel Edward 169; *see also*
  P. C. Bai Kurr
Carew, Walter 93
Carpenters' Defensive Union 22
Carriers' Corps 118
Case, S. H. A. 22, 24
Casely-Hayford, family name 30
Casely-Hayford, J. E. 33, 38, 46, 47, 96, 111,
  128
Caulker, P. C. Albert G. 133–5, 150
Caulker, W. Caramba M. 49
Chalmer's Report 189
Chamber of Commerce 6, 12, 22
Chief Clerk 98
Chief Commissioner 40
Chief Executive Officer 48
Chiefs' Conference 139
Children's Festival 40
Childs, Hubert 160
Chinsman, J. B. 24
Churchill, Winston 38, 40, 68, 134
City Council *see* Freetown City Council
Civil Servants 98
Civil Servants' Association 22
Civil Service 48
  Africanisation 133, 172
  discrimination 37
  senior posts 187
civilisation 3, 28
Clifford, Sir Hugh 39, 41, 47
C.M.S. Grammar School 6, 8, 30
'Cocoa' Nicol 6
codes and regulations 28
Coker, S. J. 35
Coker, Ulric 125
Cole, Gumner Emmanuel G. 122, 124,
  134
Cole, M. G. M. 124
Colenso-Bishops, family name 6
Colenso-Bishop, T. 20
Coleridge-Taylor G. 168
Collegiate (W.A.M.) School 118
Collier, Gershon 190
Colonial administration 39
  policy 42
Colonial Charter 124
Colonial Civil Service 99, 104
Colonial Development Act 1929 108

Colonial Development Fund 111
  1924 47, 55, 56, 73
  1947 144, 152
  1951 176
  1957 177
Colonial Office 82, 95, 97, 100, 101, 110,
  114, 115, 123, 127, 135, 137
Colonial Office Advisory Committee on
  Education 111
Colonial Secretary 47, 63, 98, 110, 128
Colony
  annual football match 143
  educational development 187
  establishment 28
  inhabitants 28, 29
  political co-operation 143
  political mobilisation 121
  protectorate 24, 42, 52, 132, 142, 185, 189
  rift 30
  Urban and Rural representatives 56, 57
  West Africa 40
Colony born 114
colony for freed slaves 18
Colony politicians 50, 52, 53, 101, 102, 108,
  110, 121, 145, 147, 152, 179
  constitutional reforms 137
Colony/Protectorate relations 29, 48–50, 55,
  56, 112, 114, 147, 160
colour bar 27
Comintern 119
Comintern Conference, Moscow 118
Commercial Enterprise 46
Commercial Pool 120
Commission of Inquiry (Riot) 175
Committee of Citizens 125, 127, 149
Committee of Educated Aborigines 23, 48,
  49–52
Commonwealth leaders 33
Community of merchants 4
conditions of service 97
Congress 23, 33, 37–9, 43, 44, 47, 51,
  114–16, 121, 127, 128; *see also*
  N.C.B.W.A.
  financial affairs 46
  Protectorate representation 36
Congress Day 46
Congress Movement 41
Congress politicians 41
Congress Secretary 113
Connaught Hospital 46
Coomber, Chief Bai 94, 102
co-operative group 113

Index

Co-operative Institution 113
Constitution, 1863 20
Constitution, 1924 47, 55, 56, 73
constitutional changes 1947 16
constitutional changes 1951 179
constitutional development 54
constitutional history 19
constitutional reforms 45, 139
constitutional rights 111
cosmopolitanism 152
cost of living index 123
Cotay, A. B. 146
Councillors 109
Court of Appeal 45, 90, 93, 96, 112, 115
Cox-George 147, 149, 154, 155
Creoles *see* Krios
Cricket League 59
Crown Colony 50
Crown Colony government 19
Crown Office 91
Crowther, J. C. O. 18, 124, 147, 162, 163, 173
cultural movements 22
Cummings, E. H. 20, 35, 65, 74
Cummings-John, Constance 103, 123
Curtis, N. E. Ansumana 51
Customs Department 118
'Cutlass' Metzger 6

Danquah, J. B. 103, 104
Daphne's Nursing Home 13
Dauphin, E. J. 8
Davies, Broughton 5
Davies, E. A. C. 35
Davies, Prof. J. S. T. 116
Davies, W. J. 113; *see also* Faduma, Prof.
    Orishatukeh
Dawe, A. J. 76, 80, 111, 135
Decker, Thomas 52, 143, 146, 148, 149, 180
Deen, H. 35
Defence Force Scheme 106
Defence Regulations Act 129
Delco Mines 102, 129, 130
    liberal mining concessions 108
    workers 109, 120
Deportation Bill 124, 127
Deportation of Undesirable British Subjects
    124
Diamond Agreement 1955 172
    diamond smuggling 171
    diamonds 108
    discrimination 37
District Commissioners 50, 112, 115, 140

District Councils 139, 142, 152, 154
District Officer 27
Dorman, Sir Maurice 166, 167
Dove, A. J. H. 69
Dove, family name 30
Dove, Frederick William 33, 36–8, 128
Dove-Cut Private School 8
Downing Street 20
Dress Reform Society 22
Du Bois, W. E. B. 13, 33
Duncan 46
During, mutineer 124
During, Ben T. 27
During, Otto I. E. Oyekan 118, 125–6, 137,
    158

early settlers 16
Easmon, A. E. 13
Easmon, family name, 30
Easmon, M. E. F. 32, 99, 100, 150, 169
Easmon, R. Sariff 118, 147
E.B.I. Movement 168
Economic and Industrial Conditions 130
Educated Protectorate Africans 139
Education Officers
    African 98
Educational policy 113
Edward VIII, King 63
Edwardian dandy 13
Edwin, V. K. 98, 99
Elected Municipality 26
Elected representation 25, 26
Election petition 149
Elections
    1924 57
    1934 83
    1957 177
Elective legislature 26
Electoral system 176
Elliot Commission on Higher Education 144
Ellis, W. D. 28, 54
Eluwa 33
Emergency Fund Committee 22, 52
European
    doctors 97, 100, 101
    Supervisor 98
European civilisation 28
European District Commissioner 65
Evans, T. J. 46
Executive Council 72, 110, 136
Ezzidio, John 20, 21
Ezzidios, family name 4, 19

Index

Fabian Colonial Bureau 117, 144
Faduma, Prof. Orishatukeh 23, 35, 46, 47;
    see also W. J. Davies
Faremi Works 104
Farmers Association 22
Faux, T. A. 8
Felix, Abigail Harris 82, 107
Fenton, J. S. 100, 140
Fiddian, A. 76, 88
Finance Minister 170
Fishing industry 113
Fitzjohn, J. A. 24, 34, 35
Fitzjohn, Dr W. H. 159, 160, 172, 180
Flood, J. E. W. 40
Fofana, Alimami 42
Forestry and Agriculture Departments
    110
Fort Thornton 26
Fourah Bay College 8, 46, 98, 143
    Fund 144
    protectorate graduate 100
Frazer, A. K. 105
Free Settlers 158
Freemasonry 148
Freetown 90
    Chamber of Commerce 52
    constitutional legitimacy 16
    economic survival 28
    health conditions 26
    Madingo tribal headman 42
    naval base 122
    political awareness 16
    political stupor 116
Freetown City Council 6, 21, 23, 24, 26,
    37, 45, 63, 64, 70, 76, 111, 118, 154,
    188
    dissolution 76, 78, 110
    finances 77
    local elections 123
    Medical Officer 13
    O'Brien Commission 74
    reconstitution 133, 152, 153
    women 103
Freetown Municipality *see* Freetown City
    Council
Freetown newspapers 24
Freetown Press 25, 140
    literary output 24
Freetown Rifle Club 105
French 113
French Expansion 78
Fyfe 20, 21, 188

Galaba Bright *see* Galba Bright
Gambia 41, 45, 47
Garratt-type engine 80
Garvey, Marcus 33, 41
Gaumont, Lt. 65
General Elections 159
General strike 1955 174
George, Lloyd 138
George VI, King
    coronation 106
Ghana 27, 30, 32, 36, 39, 41, 45–7, 115, 118,
    119, 135, 137, 162
Gibraltar Methodist Church 6
Goddard, T. N. 83, 85
Gold Coast *see* Ghana
Gold Coast Leader 33
Gold Coast Union 103
Goldie, Sir George Taubman 3, 6
Golly, W. P. 35
Gorvie, Rev. Max 36, 112, 115
Government Bo School 43
Government House 90
    At Homes 26
    official functions 82
Government publications
    Royal Gazette 23, 65
Government survey
    medical students 141
Governor's Council 19
Grace, Rev. H. M. 111
Graduates
    African 98
Grant, Marcus Chamberlain 169, 174, 175
Grant, William 'Independent' 20, 21, 23, 30
Grants, family name, 19
Great War 32
Greywood, Prof. E. J. 11
Guggisberg, Sir Frederick 39, 41
Gulama, P. C. Julius 142

Haddon-Smith, G. B. 26
Haidara Kontor Filli Rebellion 1931 109
Hailey, Lord 135, 136, 138, 186
Hardie, Keir 10
Hargreaves, Prof. John D. 170
Hayford, Casely *see* Casely-Hayford
'Head Head' Thomas *see* Thomas,
    Malamah
Hebron, A. S. 20, 34, 35, 59
Heddle, Charles 19
Hein, H. Van *see* Van Hein, H.
Heisler, Rev. F. B. 46

267

Index

Hill Station
  white residents 26
Hinden, Rita 108, 117, 156
Hinterland affairs 21
H.M.S. *Caenarvon* 32
Horton, Africanus Beale 5, 23
Horton, Edna Elliot 119
Hotobah-During, C. B. 16, 105, 118, 131
House of Assembly 155
House of Commons 68
House of Representatives 155, 177
House rents 109
Hut Tax War 18, 21, 29, 178
Hyde, J. G. 68, 105, 116

Immigration and Labour 105
Imperial Institute 30
  parliament 20
  power 31, 47
  Status Law Adoption Ordinance 105
  War Effort 133
Independents (Party Politics) 159
Indian Association 10
Inkumsa, Frank 166
Inness, Dr W. D. 72
Institution for the Destitute 120
International Negro Workers 119
International Trade Union Committee of
  Negro Workers 119
Intertribal Association 22, 52
Interstate Estates 15, 68
'Iron Pot' Coker 6
Isichei, Elizabeth 18

Jardine, Governor Douglas 122, 125, 127,
  128, 131, 134, 135
  report 110
Jarret, C. V. 125
Jarret, M. L. 13
Jenkins-Johnston, J. 35
John, Uel 63, 99
Johnson, Caleb 92
Johnson, Dr Obadiah 40
Johnson, Revd F. H. 35
Jones, A. N. 74
Jones, Arthur Creech 144
Jones, Eldred 147, 190
Jones, Revd E. N. *see* Sankoh, Lamina
Jones, H. M. 38
Jones, Marcus 189
Jones, S. B. 153
Jones, S. T. 35

Joseph, George 10
Judicial Reforms 45
Jurors and Assessor's Ordinance 95
Justice of Peace 12
Justice Wilberforce decision 168

Kabia-Williams, H. T. 49, 51, 52
Kai-Kai, Hon. P. C. Jai 171
Kamara, A. B. Magba 175
Kamara, Alpha 49
Kamara, Bassi 49
Kamara, E. Kareba 49
Kamara, J. R. 49
Kamara, S. E. Carew 49
Kamara, Sembu 49
Kaniki, Martin 120, 122
Kanne, D. Labour 49
Kaplan 185
Karefa-Smart, Dr John 49, 110, 112, 113,
  122
Keith Lucas Commission 176
Kenya
  black majority rule 166
Kenyatta, Jomo 118
Kilson, Martin 22, 23, 33, 52, 190
Kimble, D. 53
King, C. D. B. 64
King Tom Cemetery 62
King's Own Creole Boys, The 32
Knox, J. F. 35
Koblo, P.C. Bai 146
Koker, P. C. R.B.S. 141, 171, 187
Kompa, P. C. Bai 56, 96, 102, 105
Kono District
  diamonds 108
Kono Progressive Movement 169, 174
Kontorfilli, Haidara 109
Koroma-Hollowell, D. B. 49
Koromah, A. R. 49
Koromah, Vamba 49
Kpaka, Chief John Mana 125
Krio regiment 32
Krios 3, 11, 16, 18, 27–9, 34, 44, 48, 49, 55,
  70, 73, 76, 91, 122, 130, 138, 139, 157,
  162, 185, 188
  affluence 19
  British mentality 17
  court cases 166
  education 17
  elites 26, 37, 104
  enlisting 133
  exiles 188

government posts 111, 190
leadership 117, 148, 149
lores, rituals and customs 7
political and social recognition 18
political influence 19
political power 188
politicians 50, 53–4, 70, 110, 116, 132, 145, 154
post-independent Sierra Leone
power 189, 190
social ambitions 17
Kurr, P.C. Bai *see* Carew, Samuel Edward
Kutvu University 118

Labor, J. S. 24, 35
Labour 105
  Bureaux 113
  conditions 123
  Union 118
  unrest 69, 108
Labour Party 10, 117
Labour Secretary 130
Ladepon, W. S. 131
Lagos 90
Land-tenure system 108
Lands, Mines and Labour Minister 172
Langley, Ayodele 33, 43
Lauriston Gardens, Edinburgh 9
Law 5
  reforms 105
League Against Imperialism 119
League of Coloured Peoples 134
League of Nations Union 38
Lebanese 29, 30, 61, 68
  representation 37
Legal Department 27
Legislative Council 6, 19–22, 26, 29, 32, 37, 41, 48–50, 53–5, 59, 61, 63, 64, 66, 67, 81, 83, 84, 87, 93, 97, 102, 104, 112, 114, 116, 118, 122, 124–8, 145, 148, 150, 152, 153, 170, 177, 181, 189
  constitution 75
  elections 1939 131
  expansion 133
  nominated members 85, 105, 111
  Paramount Chiefs 93
  reconstituted 154, 160
  representatives 21
  Urban members 105
Legislative Council Chamber 97, 100, 102
Legislative Ordinance
  Article 22 83

Lewis, Sir Samuel 4, 20, 21, 23, 28, 30, 50
  knighted 21
Lewis, William 4
Lewises, family name, 19
Liberated Africans 3, 4, 17
  first generation 5
Liberia 46, 64
Lightfoot-Boston, Henry J. 86, 106
Limited Creole Society 22
Lisk-Carew 121
Local Congress
  conference 111
London Committee 41
London delegation 38, 46
London Hospital 9
London Mission 39
Lower House of representatives 154
Lucan, J. C. 158
Lugard, F. 108
Luke, E. F. 150
Luke, H. C. 67, 73, 102
Luke, J. B. 35
Lumpkin, William Rainy *see* Bungie, Alimamy

Mabang Agricultural Institute 94
Mabella Coaling Depot 121
MaCarthy, L. E. V. 27, 35, 36, 128
Macauley, C. A. E. 46
Macauley, Herbert 116
Macauley, John 24
Macleod, Ian 166
MacMillan, Prof. W. M. 108, 129
MacMillan report 129
Madingo tribal headman 42
Margai, Albert 154, 163, 179
Margai, Dr Milton A. S. 1, 99–101, 122, 142, 148, 157, 161, 162, 164, 172, 173, 179, 184, 190
  Chief Minister 163, 170
  government 165
  knighted 178
  Premier 170
  Prime Minister 178, 183
Magazines
  African World 38
  Hansard 161
  Student 10
  West Africa 38, 138, 147, 159, 164, 168, 179
Magistrate Courts' Ordinance 1905 104
Magubane, B. 81

Index

Malamah-Thomas, J. H. 20, 24, 35
Malamah-Thomases, family name 6, 19, 128
Mammah, J. L. 51
Marampa
  Delco Mines 102
  iron ore 108
  Mines 121
Maroons 17
Martyn, Adam 7
Masanke Plantation 102
Masonic Lodge 14
Massaly, J. C. 101
Master and Registrar 98
Master of the Supreme Court 7
Maternity Hospital 111
May, Mayor Cornelius 14, 20, 35, 46, 92, 116
May, Revd J. Claudius 8, 23, 24
May family 24
Mayhew, A. 110
Mayor of Freetown 12, 35, 65, 76
Mbriwa, Tamba S. 169, 174
Mcdonell, F. J. 14, 42, 68, 73
Mechanics' Alliance 22
Medical Officers 98
  of Health 99
  practitioners 13
  Reforms 46
Mendes 29
Mercantile Association 20, 21
Mereweather, E. M. 26
Methodist Boys High School 8, 30
Metzger, Dr G. N. 13, 35
Metzger, Sam 172, 173
Metzger-Boston, N. J. P. 105, 119
Miller, F. A. 51, 52, 118, 132, 148
Mills, Kitson 47
Mills, T. Hutton 38, 47
Milner, Lord 40
Mineral Ordinance 1927 101
Mining Ordinance 1927 108
Ministers 170
Momoh, A. J. 143
Monkton-Moore, Governor 104, 106, 111
Morel, E. D. 40
Morgan, E. D. 68, 125, 164
Morrison, C. R. 99
Moscow Comintern Conference 118
Mountain railway
  closed 80
Moyamba Chiefs Conference
  scholarships 140

M'Paki, Ansumana 151
Municipal Board 78
Municipal Burial Fees 62
Municipal Corporation 19
Municipal Council see Freetown City
  Council
Municipality 110
mutiny 122, 124
  of the Gunners 121

National Congress of British West Africa 13, 22, 31–3, 37, 53
  Executive Committee 51
  London Committee 38
National Council of Sierra Leone 157–60, 165, 166, 169, 172, 173, 176, 177
National Defence League 121
Native Administration (Indirect Rule) 1937 109
Native Authorities 110, 139
Native Authority Administration 139
  chiefs 28
Native Defence Force 22
Native industries 27
Naval base 122
Nelson-Williams, John 178, 180
Nelson-Williams, T. E. 25, 45, 105, 106, 116, 125
Newspapers 29
  The African Standard 129, 146, 151
  The Artisan 22, 24
  Aurora 14, 15, 24, 25, 41
  Colonial and Provincial Reporter 14, 24
  The Creole Boy 14, 24
  Daily Guardian 134, 140, 142, 143, 146
  Daily Mail 168, 179, 180
  The Negro and the Sierra Leone Weekly
    Advertiser 23
  The Sierra Leone Observer and
    Commercial Advocate 24, 146, 172
  The Sierra Leone Ram 24
  The Sierra Leone Times 24
  The Sierra Leone Weekly News 12, 14, 24, 34–6, 41, 44, 47, 52, 53, 55, 66, 77, 78, 117, 119, 120, 124, 136, 138, 140, 146, 150, 151
  The West African Mail and Trade Gazette 24
  West African Reporter 23
New Year honours 1934 106
Nicol, W. G. 8
Niger 6

Nigeria 3, 11, 27, 32, 39, 41, 45, 54, 115, 119, 135, 162
Labour Union 118
Nigeria Progressive Union 103
Njala
Forestry and Agriculture Departments 110
Njala Agricultural College 93
Njala Agricultural Scheme 91
Njala Training College 44
Nkrumah, K. 104, 119
Noah, E. A. C. 36
Non-Associated Societies' Hall 10
Northern Province
educated citizens 23
Norton, Lt. Col. 72
Nova Scotians 4, 16, 17

Oakbrook 34
O'Brien, C. 75, 76, 78
O'Brien Commission 74, 78
O'Brien report 79, 80
Ogboni Society *see* National Council of Sierra Leone
oi Polloi 119, 127, 128, 161
Oldfield, Revd F. S. 46
Olusanya, Prof. G. O. 33, 104
Omoniyi, Bandele 11
Omu, Fred I. 23
Order-in-Council 19
Ordinance, 1905 89
Ormsby-Gore, W. G. 40, 63, 75, 76, 78, 90, 91, 93, 95, 129, 186
Ormsby-Gore's report 92, 94, 96

Padmore, George 114, 157
palace coup 178
Palmer, Balogun 168
Palmer, E. R. 125
Pan-Africanism 103
Africanist movements 35
West African Movement 31, 34
Paramount Chiefs 52, 54, 56, 75, 104, 109, 124, 139, 174
party politics 159
Parker, D. C. 35
Parrodi, Chief Justice 65
Parry, Edgar 110
Peninsula Road 111
People's Party 142
Perjury Ordinance 94, 95, 112
Peters, S. A. D. 190
Phillips, J. H. 91

Police Clerk 104
Police Magistrate 65, 106, 116
Political movement 48
parties 21, 157, 159
upheavals 108
Port Loko
mineral deposits 93, 108
Positive Action Group of the Council 158
Postal Workers' Union 121
Pratt, I. B. 19, 20
Pratt, Isaac 4
Pratt, Ishmael Charles 10, 13
Pratt, S. A. J. 168
Prempeh of Asante 48
Press Development 46
Prime Minister 99, 178
Prince of Wales 63
Prince of Wales affairs 105
Prince of Wales School 98
principal 113
Printing Office 62
Privy Council 82
Probyn, Gov. Leslie 26, 27, 30
Proclamation of the Protectorate
golden jubilee 140, 143
Professor Woermann 32
Protectorate 151, 163, 184
Assembly 137–41, 152, 156, 159
born 14
educated elite 14
education 138, 186
krio influence 28
legal reforms 105
majority 154
Medical Assistants 102
medical graduate 101
minerals 108
party 158
people 151–2
political and social development 114
politicians 146
proclamation 28
pro-protectorate policy 110, 111
reform 112
representation 36
representatives 97
Senior District Officer 109
slavery 101
under development 91
unofficial majority 145
voting 159
W.A.Y.L. 121, 122

271

Index

Protectorate Courts' Jurisdiction Ordinance 105
Protectorate Courts' Jurisdiction Ordinance 1903 28
Protectorate Educated Progressive Union 140
scholarships 140
Protectorate Native Laws Ordinance 1905 28, 50
Protectorate Ordinance 94, 95, 112
Protectorate Organisation Society 142
Protectorate Schools
vernacular 102
Provincial administration 125
Public Works Department 70
Puisne Judge 164
Purcell, G. K. T. 88, 90, 92
Pyne-Bailey, S. C. C. 125

Quaker, Revd James 4
Queen's Advocate 35

Rabbit, Inspector 65, 68
Raffan, P. W. 68
Railway Staff Committee 80
Railway Strike 66, 69, 80, 121
political dimensions 70
Railway Workers' Union 70, 80
Rainy, William 23, 24
Rambler 34, 115, 121, 133
Randle, A. G. 163, 171
Randle, Dr J. K. 32
Rate Payers' Association 22, 23
Reffell, Dr G. C. E. 99, 101, 105, 148
Reffell, T. J. 35
Registered Medical Practitioner 100
Renner, Dr E. A. 150
Renner-Dove, Dr A. F. 112
Representative government 97, 162
Richards, J. T. 35
Right of Appeal 89
Riot Damages Act 74
Risley, J. 92
Robert, Revd J. T. 8
Rochester, H. M. S. 125
Rogers-Wright, C. B. 169, 174, 178
Rogers-Wright, J. 98
Rose, J. M. 135, 168
Royal College of Surgeons, Edinburgh 9
Royal Infirmary, Edinburgh 9
Rowe, Governor Samuel 48
Rural Area Member 104, 125
Rule Making Committee 105

Salary of Government Employees
differentials 99
revision 183
Sanitary and Medical Reforms 37
Sankoh, Lamina 81, 107, 142, 149, 183
saros 3, 5
Savage, Dr Akiwande 10, 33
Sawpit 6
Sawyerr, Ade 115, 123
Sawyerr, A. J. 20; see Shorunkeh-Sawyerr, A. J.
Sawyerr, Prof. Can. Harry 147, 162, 169, 180
Sawyerr, T. J. 20, 23
Sawyerrs, family name 19
Seamen's Union 121
Secretary-General 115
Secretary of State 54, 97, 123, 131
Sedition Bill 124
Select Committee 64, 67, 145, 154
self-governing black community 19
self-government 39, 111
self rule see self government
Senate 155
Senior Medical Officer of Health 99
Senior Officers
African 98
Settlers' Descendants' Union 158, 166, 167, 168
Sharp, Granville 19
Shepherd, Hannah Selina 7
Sherbro Judicial Council 154
Sherbro Urban District 159
Short, Alfred A. 150
Shorunkeh-Sawyerr, A. J. 30, 32, 35, 50, 55, 59, 105, 116, 121
Shorunkeh-Sawyerr, family name 6, 11
Shorunkeh-Sawyerr, J. C. 24, 35, 64, 71, 74, 81, 116
Shyngle, Egerton 38
Sierra Leone 41
Anglican Bishop 69
Bishop 71, 79
British Administration 114
British Crown Colony 19
constitutional development 54
constitutional history 19
cost of living index 123
development 91
development of politics 24
diamond smuggling 171
imperial defence 127

independence 168, 173, 178
labour conditions 123
overhauling of legal system 112
politics 25, 29, 59, 118
post independent 190
Prime Minister 99
Queen's Advocate 35
Trade Unionism 110
Sierra Leone Aborigines' Society see
 Aborigines' Society
Sierra Leone Agricultural Society see
 Agricultural Society
Sierra Leone Bar see Bar Association
Sierra Leone Bomber Fund 133
Sierra Leone Chamber of Commerce see
 Chamber of Commerce
Sierra Leone Citizenship 155
Sierra Leone Colony 3
Sierra Leone Committee 41
Sierra Leone Courts
 British justice 92
Sierra Leone Cricket League see Cricket
 League
Sierra Leone Development Company see
 Delco
Sierra Leone Farmers' Association see
 Farmers' Association
Sierra Leone Friendship Society 188
Sierra Leone Government 98
 Railway Department 69
Sierra Leone Independence Movement 169,
 177
Sierra Leone Infantry 133
Sierra Leone Intertribal Association see
 Intertribal Association
Sierra Leone Labour Party 119
Sierra Leone Native Defence Force see
 Native Defence Force
Sierra Leone Organisation Society 142
Sierra Leone People's Party 142, 159, 160,
 168, 176, 177, 191
 anti-Krio feeling 175
 leadership 183
 legislators 172
Sierra Leone Police Force 68
Sierra Leone Progressive Independent
 Movement 169
Sierra Leone Protectorate
 Registered Medical Practitioner 100
Sierra Leone Railway 109
Sierra Leone Selection Trust 129, 172
 liberal mining concessions 108

Sierra Leone Workmen's Union 62
Singer Betts, C. W. 59
Singer Betts, family name 6
Slater, Ransford 47–50, 54–8, 62–4, 67, 68,
 70–2, 75, 76, 79, 90, 92, 99, 105
Slave trade see slavery
slavery 18, 24, 101
 abolition 5
Slavery Bill 102
Small, E. F. 38, 118
Smart, J. H. Cheetham 98, 99
Smart, N. D. J. 168
Smith, C. Wallis 125
Smythe, Flt. Lt. John H. 133
Social and labour unrest 108
socialism 118
Socialist Trade Unionist 117
Solanke, Ladipo 103
Solomon, H. C. 35
Sorenson, A. 119
Soviet Union 119, 122
Spain, J. H. 88
Spitzer, Leo 43
Strike 1926 69
Strike Fund 71, 81
Strikes 123
Staff Superintendents 98
Standing Finance Committee 135
Stanley, Col. Oliver 135, 136, 138
Stanley, W. B. 65
Starvation wages 109
Statutes' book 90, 91
Steady, Revd E. I. C. 112
Steady, H. M. 35
Steady, Philomena C. 186
Stevens, Siaka 110, 117, 122, 154, 156, 163,
 168, 170, 172, 178
Stevenson, Gov. Hubert 134–7, 144
Stevenson Constitution 1947 144, 153, 158,
 159, 165
Stocks-Baber affair 66
Stocks, E. H. 65
Sumner, Revd A. T. 36, 62, 99
Sumner, Doyle 35
Supervisor of Customs 98
Supply Bill 94
Supreme Court 98, 112
 embarrassment of judges 90
Supreme Court Ordinance 105
Supreme Courts of West Africa 115
Syrian immigration 105
Syrians see Lebanese

Index

'Tabacca' George, family name 6
Taka Wuroh *see* Macauley, John
Tamuno, Prof. T. N. 21
Tass, P. C. Bai Farma 163
Taylor, Revd W. Ojumiri 100, 131
Taylor-Cummings, E. H. 65, 99, 105, 147, 150
Taylor-Kamara, I. B. 175
Temnes 29
Territorial Army 133
Tew, M. L. 82
Thomas, Revd B. L. 43
Thomas, Deanna 101
Thomas, E. A. 133
Thomas, George C. 125, 129, 131, 147
Thomas, J. J. 20
Thomas, Malamah *see* Malamah-Thomas
Thomas, S. B. (Abuke) 30, 94
Thompson, Columbus, M. A. 160, 163, 173
Thompson, T. J. 24
Town Clerk
  Fraud 77
Trade Union Congress 121
Trade Unionism 110, 118, 129
  legislation 121
Trade Union Ordinance 130
Trade Unions 22, 113, 121
  leadership 117
Treasury Clerk 104
Tregson-Roberts, C. 121
Trial by Assessors 87, 89, 95
  by jury 89
Tuboku-Metzger, A. E. 8, 23, 24, 27, 50, 51, 57, 63, 74, 79, 93, 94, 97, 104, 116, 121
Tuboku-Metzger, D. J. V. 113, 123, 127, 132, 150
Turbett, I. J. F. 111, 116
Turner, S. D. 35

U.A.C.
  Masanke Plantation 102
Under-Secretary of State 92
Under-Secretaries 43
Undesirable Literature Bill 124
Unemployment 108, 115
Unemployment bureaux 113
Union for Students of African Descent 103
United National Front 178
United Nations of the Empire 33
United Progressive Party 169, 177
Upper House of Representatives 154
Urban Members 105

Van Hein, H. 38, 47
Venereal disease 112
Vergette, Dudley E. A. 15, 65, 68
Vice-Principal
  Prince of Wales School 98
Voting irregularities 177

W.A.S.U. Hostel
  funding 104
W.A.Y.L.
  Krio membership 122
  protectorate 121, 122
Wallace, O. 46
Wallace-Johnson, I. T. A. 8, 15, 25, 110, 115, 117–34, 138, 147, 158, 162, 163, 165, 169, 170, 172, 173, 179, 182, 183
  communism 122
  independence 15
  libel 129
Wellesley-Cole, Dr R. B. 143
war 1938–9 122
War Bonus gratuities 70
War Department Amalgamated Workers' Union 121
War Office, London 5
war years 1939–45 133
Wellington Village 3, 4
Wesleyan Methodist Boys High School
  Juvenile Missionary Association 9
West Africa
  political leaders 102
West African Civil Liberties 121
West African Colonies
  Executive Councils 134
West African Colonies and Protectorate 40
West African Congress 34
West African Court of Appeal 45, 90, 93, 112, 115
  establishment 97
West African Medical Service 9, 46
West African Medical Staff 27
West African Press Union 37, 46
West African Regiments 133
West African Students' Union 38, 87, 102–4
West African University 37, 46
West African Youth League 119–28, 130–2, 147
West End Benevolent Society (1917) 22
West End Limba and Limited Creole Society 22
Western concepts 28
Western culture and imperialism 29

Index

West Indies 54
White Administration 26, 68
Whitehall 20, 40, 77, 83, 90, 135
Whitehall officials 63
Wilberforce, Justice 168
Wilberforce, Memorial Hall 41, 56, 71, 81
Wilhelmine Germany 32
Williams, Dunstan 112
Williams, E. B. 143
Williams, Dr J. A. 46
Williams, O. G. R. 60, 111, 132, 137, 138
Williams, R. B. 5
Williams, Rogers 157, 163, 173
Williams, T. Maila 49
Wilson, D. O. 14
Wilson, Logie 110, 139, 146
Wilson, Ven. Arch. 35
Wilson, Woodrow 33
Women
  Assembly Membership 102
  City Council 103

right to vote 102
right to work 113
women's franchise 102
Wood, S. R. 47
Workers' Compensation 130
Wright, C. E. 20, 74, 79, 84, 86, 94–6, 105,
  116, 132, 133, 147
Wright, E. J. 27, 50
Wright, Frances 150
Wright, J. R. 99
Wright, P. W. H. 177
Wright, Rt. Revd George W. 69

Yaskey, Alex D. 120
Young People's Progressive Union 22
Yumkella, P. C. 174

Zimbabwe
  black majority rule 166
Zizer, J. C. 147
Zizer, James R. 171

275

AFRICAN STUDIES SERIES

37 Amilcar Cabral: Revolutionary Leadership and People's War
    Patrick Chabal
38 Essays on the Political Economy of Rural Africa
    Robert H. Bates
39 Ijeshas and Nigerians: The Incorporation of a Yoruba Kingdom, 1890s–1970s
    J. D. Y. Peel
40 Black People and the South African War 1899–1902
    Peter Warwick
41 A History of Niger 1850–1960
    Finn Fuglestad
42 Industrialisation and Trade Union Organisation in South Africa 1924–55
    Jon Lewis
43 The Rising of the Red Shawls: A Revolt in Madagascar 1895–1899
    Stephen Ellis
44 Slavery in Dutch South Africa
    Nigel Worden
45 Law, Custom and Social Order: The Colonial Experience in Malawi and Zambia
    Martin Chanock
46 Salt of the Desert Sun: A History of Salt Production and Trade in the Central Sudan
    Paul E. Lovejoy
47 Marrying Well: Marriage, Status and Social Change among the Educated Elite in
    Colonial Lagos
    Kirstin Mann
48 Language and Colonial Power: The Appropriation of Swahili in the Former Belgian
    Congo, 1880–1938
    Johannes Fabian
49 The Shell Money of the Slave Trade
    Jan Hogendorn and Marion Johnson
50 Political Domination in Africa: Reflections on the Limits of Power
    edited by Patrick Chabal
51 The Southern Marches of Imperial Ethiopia: Essays in History and Social
    Anthropology
    edited by Donald Donham and Wendy James
52 Islam and Urban Labor in Northern Nigeria: The Making of a Muslim Working Class
    Paul M. Lubeck
53 Horn and Crescent: Cultural Change and Traditional Islam on the East African Coast,
    500–1900
    Randall L. Pouwels
54 Capital and Labour on the Kimberley Diamond Fields 1871–1890
    Robert Vicat Turrell
55 National and Class Conflict in the Horn of Africa
    John Markakis
56 Democracy and Prebendal Politics in Nigeria: The Rise and Fall of the Second
    Republic
    Richard A. Joseph
57 Entrepreneurs and Parasites: The Struggle for Indigenous Capitalism in Zaire
    Janet MacGaffey
58 The African Poor: A History
    John Iliffe
59 Palm Oil and Protest: An Economic History of the Ngwa Region, South-eastern
    Nigeria, 1800–1980
    Susan M. Martin
60 France and Islam in West Africa, 1860–1960
    Christopher Harrison

61 Transformation and Continuity in Revolutionary Ethiopia
Christopher Clapham
62 Prelude to the Mahdiyya: Peasants and Traders in the Shendi Region, 1821–1885
Anders Bjorkelo
63 Wa and the Wala: Islam and Polity in Northwestern Ghana
Ivor Wilks

278